LIVING LIBERATION IN HINDU THOUGHT

LIVING LIBERATION IN HINDU THOUGHT

EDITED BY

Andrew O. Fort
and
Patricia Y. Mumme

State University of New York Press

Published by
State University of New York Press, Albany

Printed in the United States of America

For information, address State University of New York Press,
State University Plaza, Albany, N.Y., 12246

Production by Diane Ganeles
Marketing by Nancy Farrell

Library of Congress Cataloging-in-Publication Data

Living liberation in Hindu thought / edited by Andrew O. Fort and
Patricia Y. Mumme.
p. cm.
Includes index.
ISBN 0-7914-2705-6 (cloth). — ISBN 0-7914-2706-4 (pbk.)
1. Mokṣa. 2. Perfection—Religious aspects—Hinduism.
3. Hinduism—Doctrines. I. Fort, Andrew O. II. Mumme, Patricia Y.
BL1213.58.L58 1996
294.5′22—dc20 95-3018
CIP

10 9 8 7 6 5 4 3 2 1

Contents

Part II: Yoga and Renunciation in Living Liberation

Figures

Preface

The genesis for this book was Andrew Fort's interest in tracing the development of the concept of *jīvanmukti* in Advaita Vedānta, and his concomitant desire to understand better how other thinkers and schools of thought looked at living liberation. He organized a panel on living liberation in Hindu thought for the American Academy of Religion (AAR) meetings in 1989, where Christopher Chapple, Paul Muller-Ortega, Lance Nelson, Kim Skoog, and he presented earlier versions of their essays, to which Patricia Mumme responded. The chapters from Mackenzie Brown, Daniel Sheridan, and Chacko Valiaveetil resulted from discussions with Fort and Mumme at those and other AAR meetings. Both Fort and Mumme have read the evolving drafts of all the chapters and deeply appreciate all the work and reworking our authors put into their essays, even if the editing sometimes seemed like "textual harassment." Both editors have learned a great deal in this process. We would like to thank Mackenzie Brown and Lance Nelson for reading and commenting on drafts of some of these chapters. Fort would also like to thank both the Religion department at Texas Christian University and his family for supportive environments at work and at home. He, like many contributors, remains in awe of Trish Mumme's editorial efforts and prowess.

We have used standard transliteration for Sanskrit and Tamil. Translations of original texts are those of each author, unless otherwise indicated.

Introduction:
Living Liberation in Hindu Thought

Andrew O. Fort

Questions concerning the attainment of human perfection, or liberation, have animated religious thinkers across many cultures, past and present. All religious traditions address the urge to realize one's true nature, to gain identity or communion with the highest reality, and simultaneously to end finitude and become free from sin and evil, ignorance and desire. Hindu thinkers have made significant contributions to this conversation.

In the Hindu tradition,[1] liberation (*mokṣa, mukti*) from the cycle of suffering and rebirth (*saṃsāra*) is the supreme goal of human existence, and much has been written about the path to and nature of release. A question that regularly arises in this context is whether liberation is possible while living—that is, embodied. Unlike religious thinkers in many other cultures, who generally focus on salvation after death, Hindu authors and schools of thought frequently claim that embodied liberation, often called *jīvanmukti,* is possible, though there is no consensus about exactly what one is liberated from or to. Other thinkers hold that one is inevitably still bound while embodied, and that no ultimate state is achievable while living. In addition to disputes about the possibility of embodied liberation, there are differing views on the types, degrees, or stages of liberation, some attainable in the body and some not.

Despite the range and vigor of these disputes, no existing book approaches recording the full variety of questions asked, much less the myriad answers given, about the nature of living liberation in Hindu thought. Individual authors such as A. G. Krishna Warrier,[2] A. K. Lad,[3] L. K. L.

Srivastava,[4] and Chacko Valiaveetil[5] have produced studies describing the views of several Hindu schools on living liberation. However, no one to date has published a collection like this one, in which each chapter is authored by a scholar specializing in the thinker, philosophical school, or texts the chapter addresses.

Let us further clarify what this book does and does not cover: the essays collected here look at living liberation according to major thinkers living during the era of classical Indian civilization or texts written during that period. Each chapter, based on close readings of selected texts, will show how one or more specific schools or thinkers define liberation and, where applicable, characterize one liberated while living. In addition, each of the authors shows how one teaching on *jīvanmukti* is distinguished from the views of other schools or thinkers, and what problems appear (and possibly remain unresolved) within that teaching. The editors have striven to ensure that each chapter is both philosophically accurate, as well as accessible to those who are not familiar with the broad sweep of Hindu thought.

While the chapters include some literary, historical, and exegetical analysis, they focus on philosophical and/or theological issues. Such issues reflect our focus on classical texts and the schools or traditions that follow them, rather than on popular images of living liberation. However, it is certainly the case (as some of our chapters suggest) that the *jīvanmukti* ideal has had broad appeal beyond Sanskrit texts or formal philosophical schools. One might well expect this when the option to gain release in this very body, not only after the cessation of life, is claimed to be possible. The plausibility of living liberation to many Hindus can be seen in the long tradition of sages, saints, and *siddhas* worshipped throughout the subcontinent, from ancient times to the present. These figures and their followers deserve study, but would require methods and expertises beyond the scope of this book.

Readers will also note that we have not included modern Indian interpretations of living liberation in this volume. Indian thinkers from the era of British influence have been affected by a wide diversity of new ideas, often quite foreign to classical Indian thought. To do justice to the views of *jīvanmukti* seen in the writings of figures like Swami Vivekananda, Sarvepalli Radhakrishnan, Sri Aurobindo, or Ramana Maharshi would and should demand a separate volume.[6]

Our focus on classical Hindu thought allows us to begin with certain shared assumptions. All thinkers discussed here accept the pervasiveness of suffering and ignorance experienced by embodied beings within the cycle of birth and death (*saṃsāra*). All further agree that embodied beings possess some form of self or soul apart from the body and mind. Finally, all accept that life's goal is to end desire-filled action (*karma*) that leads to bondage and rebirth. This is accomplished through liberating insight into the true Self and/or devotion to a personal Lord. Despite these commonalities, one finds no consensus in Hindu thought about the nature of either living *or* final liberation. Given the enormous variety of religious and philosophical traditions which make up "Hinduism," this diversity is hardly surprising. The following chapters reveal final liberation conceived in various ways: as the cessation of ignorance about the non-dual nature of Self (*ātman*) and ultimate reality (Brahman) which brings serenity and bliss; as release from suffering brought on by compulsive mental activity into perfect solitude (*kaivalya*); or as a soul's joyous communion with a personal loving Lord. These conceptions will shape the respective school's visions of living liberation.

While the diversity of traditions considered by our contributors militates against any uniform treatment of living liberation, the reader will notice certain questions and problems arise repeatedly in these chapters. While these questions are not exhaustive, they certainly indicate the range of issues which relate to living liberation. Some frequently addressed groups of questions include:

- What is the relation of liberation to embodiment? Does embodiment inevitably mean suffering and ignorance of nonduality or separation from God? Is living liberation even possible, and if so, is it truly equal to bodiless liberation?

- How do forms of bondage such as *karma* (or, in Śaivism, the *malas*) limit or prevent liberation? What kind of *karma* is removed, when, and by what, on the path to liberation?

  How are *karma* and ignorance related? Does one cause the other? Is liberation prompted by knowledge alone, or is something more needed? Does any remnant of ignorance remain for an embodied being after liberation has been won? How does this remnant limit this being?

- How does one overcome the obstacles to liberation? By knowledge, devotion, yogic practice, renunciation, and/or performing Vedic ritual duties? Is one of these key? Do they work together?

  Of what or whom must one gain knowledge? Is devotion to a form of God necessary or helpful, and if so, which one? How is this devotion expressed? How does the Lord respond? What relationship does the Lord have with those who have won liberation, both before and after death?

  How are processes of purification and Yogic enstasis (*sa-*

mādhi) related to liberation? Does Yogic practice merely open the way to and/or safeguard liberation, or does Yogic realization bring liberation itself? Can one "backslide"?

- If one can be liberated while living, how does such a person act in the world? Do one's actions change after obtaining the highest embodied state? How and by whom is liberation recognizable? If renunciation is required, what is renounced? Must the living liberated being conform to *dharmic* norms?

Chapter Summaries

The essays fall loosely into three groups. The first three chapters consider the idea of *jīvanmukti* according to key thinkers of three different schools of Vedānta: Śaṅkara's Advaita, Rāmānuja's Viśiṣṭādvaita, and Madhva's Dvaita. Next are three chapters on texts that focus on yogic disciplines and renunciation in living liberation; they examine ideas of liberation while embodied in the classical Sāṃkhya and Yoga schools, the "Yogic Advaita" of Vidyāraṇya's *Jīvanmuktiviveka*, and the perfect renunciation (and devotion) of the epic and Purāṇic figure Śuka. Finally we look at two very different models of living liberation in Śaivism: those of the tantric Kāśmīrī Śaivism of Abhinavagupta and of the Tamil Śaiva Siddhānta of Meykaṇṭār and his followers. The conclusion identifies and explores common themes and crucial disputed points within and among the various teachings on living liberation.

In our first chapter, Lance Nelson surveys the development of the *jīvanmukti* doctrine according to the Advaita (non-dual) Vedānta tradition of Śaṅkara (fl CE 700). Nelson shows that while Advaitins generally hold that living liberation is possible and the highest goal of life, they find that justifying this idea within Advaitin metaphysics is problematic. The central problem is this: if the body (and mind) are bound by *karma*, and thus are part of ignorance, and ignorance completely ceases with liberating knowledge, how can one be embodied (ignorant) *and* liberated? Nelson looks at texts from the *Upaniṣads* and the *Bhagavad Gītā*, as well as Śaṅkara's commentaries. For Advaitins, these texts indicate that when one realizes the body is not the Self and then acts with utter detachment, one can be said to be liberated while living. In this view, bodilessness is not a physical condition, but a state of realization.

A few Advaitins find the notion of liberation while living fundamentally flawed, claiming that liberation must entail the end of all *karma* and immediate disembodiment. However, most Advaitins hold that the body continues after liberation due to the persistence of a special form of *karma: prārabdha*, or currently manifesting, *karma*. Like a potter's wheel that continues to spin even after the potter departs, the body remains for a time due to *prārabdha-karma* even after realization. The idea that *prārabdha-karma* must be exhausted before physical disembodiment is the linchpin for later Advaitin philosophical arguments for the possibility of liberation while living. Nelson shows that, from the Upaniṣads to Śaṅkara and later Advaitins, there is much wrestling with, and no unanimity about, the nature and role of *prārabdha-karma*. He points out that, in order to "save" *prārabdha-karma* as the substratum of bodily continuity from powerful critiques that objected to this notion's logical inconsistencies, later Advaitins describe increasingly subtle (or baroque?) manifestations of ignorance, such as a remnant (*leśa*) or impression (*saṃskāra*) of ignorance that takes form as *prārabdha-karma*. Some claim a *leśa* remains after knowledge, just as a slight trembling continues even after one recognizes that a snake is merely a rope. Others, including Śaṅkara, suggest (though often only in passing) that full liberating insight may be present only when one is in meditative enstasy (*samādhi*). Thus, Nelson makes clear that Advaitins never settle on a definitive, unproblematic position about how living (embodied) liberation is possible.

In a final section, Nelson also takes an interesting and original look at how Advaitins might use Īśvara, the Lord, as a model for understanding the *jīvanmukta*. While doing this, he illustrates the Advaitins' ambivalence in endorsing the notion that liberation is complete while one is still embodied, since they say that participation in empirical existence, even by the Lord, is inevitably limited. According to Nelson, the problem of achieving liberating knowledge while acting in mundane existence is resolved by seeing Īśvara, who is active yet (almost) free from ignorance, as exemplar for the living liberated being. One example is Kṛṣṇa in the *Bhagavad Gītā*. Still, both Īśvara and the *jīvanmukta*, Nelson points out, are limited, and even constituted, by ignorance and its adjuncts conditioned by *karma*. Perhaps, he suggests, we might look at Īśvara as "a kind of eternal *jīvanmukta* of cosmic dimensions. Is the Lord not, like the *jīvanmukta*, liberated but somehow not yet fully liberated?" As this question implies, the Advaitin ideal is ultimately not *jīvanmukti* but bodiless *kaivalya* (absolute isolation) beyond the false "magic show" of empirical existence.

Kim Skoog offers the first of two essays on theistic Vedāntins who reject Advaitin *jīvanmukti* and the non-dualist perspective in general, and instead insist that Brahman is ultimately a personal Lord, Viṣṇu-Nārāyaṇa. Using formal philosophical analysis, Skoog critically analyzes how the eleventh-century Viśiṣṭādvaitin, Rāmānuja, in his commentary on the *Brahma*

Sūtra 1.1.4, attempts to refute Śaṅkara's claims about the nature of liberation, particularly that liberation is truly possible while living.

According to Skoog, Rāmānuja distorts Śaṅkara's view, finding him a "subjective idealist." If, as Rāmānuja claims, Śaṅkara argues that the world (including the body) is an illusion, then it would follow that realization of the world's illusoriness should cause the cessation of all appearance (including the body). One could not, therefore, be both realized and embodied. However, Skoog points out that Śaṅkara is actually a "qualified realist"; that is, he does not simply say "the world is unreal," but asserts the world has provisional reality, though its existence is inexplicable (*anirvacanīya*). Thus, Skoog argues, Rāmānuja's critique fails.

Skoog goes on to explain that Rāmānuja holds that the empirical world and individual self are real and different from the Lord, and that the limited, *saṃsāra*-bound self acts and inevitably suffers while embodied. Thus, true liberation necessarily means the cessation of embodiment. In Rāmānuja's view, one must perform ritual and devotional acts to remove bondage and gain the grace of the Lord, which then frees the soul. The liberated soul then reaches the highest end, communion with the Lord in his heavenly abode, but only after death. Advaitins reject all the above, and, as Skoog points out, argue only that the cessation of *awareness* of embodiment *as real* is necessary for liberation. For Śaṅkara, the self is a pure, immutable witness (*sākṣin*) that is never really bound and not part of the world. Thus, while purifying action might be a useful preliminary, no finite activity can ultimately free the unlimited Self: only knowing Brahman liberates, and this happens while embodied.

Daniel Sheridan's essay shows that while Madhva, the thirteenth-century dualist Vedāntin and anti-Advaitin polemicist, also rejected the Advaitin concept of *jīvanmukti*, he did accept the possibility of "direct and immediate knowledge of God" or *aparokṣa-jñāna* while living. Sheridan claims that embodied existence after Dvaitin *aparokṣa-jñāna* is substantively different but functionally similar to Advaitin *jīvanmukti*. For Madhva, liberation is the personal, eternal, and blissful enjoyment (*bhoga*) of Lord Viṣṇu, not knowing the non-dual Brahman of Advaita. Madhva, like Rāmānuja, also contends that liberation from *saṃsāra* must occur after death, though enjoyment of God can begin, even if not fully manifesting, while living.

Sheridan shows that for Madhva the means (*sādhana*) to attain liberating knowledge of God include the Advaitin components of renunciation (*vairāgya*), textual study (*śravaṇa*), reflection (*manana*) and meditation (*dhyāna* or *nididhyāsana*). However, Madhva adds the crucial element of devotion (*bhakti*) absent in Advaita. All knowledge (*jñāna*), he claims, is really part of *bhakti*, for the highest knowledge dispels the ignorance of the self's independence and fosters love of and devotion to Viṣṇu. Sheridan makes clear that Madhva adamantly holds, contra Advaita, that everything, including ignorance, is derived from and dependent (*paratantra*) on the self-existent (*svatantra*) personal God/Brahman. We are bound by the ignorance that blocks knowing our dependence on God, and one of the most pernicious kinds of ignorance is the Advaitin notion of non-dualism of self and ultimate reality. Why the Lord creates ignorance is a mystery (but no more mysterious than how ignorance and knowledge can coexist—via *prārabdha-karma*—in Advaita). Yet, like Advaita, Madhva holds that one can have the highest knowledge—here *aparokṣa-jñāna*—while living and still remain embodied for a time due to *prārabdha-karma*. We therefore see Sheridan's point about the functional equivalence of *aparokṣa-jñāna* and *jīvanmukti*, an equivalence eventually made explicit by Vyāsatīrtha, Madhva's 16th century commentator.

In our next section, we examine living liberation in texts emphasizing renunciation and yogic practice, sometimes in addition to or as opposed to a supreme knowledge. Christopher Chapple focuses on conceptions of living liberation in the classical texts of Sāṃkhya and Patañjali's Yoga (though one finds relatively little abstract theorizing about the liberated state in either school). While Sāṃkhya and Yoga share the same basic metaphysics, their techniques to gain liberation are quite different. Chapple shows that Sāṃkhya's emphasis is "on the cultivation of knowledge and non-attachment for liberation," while Yoga stresses "several practices designed to reverse the influence of afflicted tendencies [*saṃskāra*], replacing them with purified modes of behavior."

According to Chapple, the *Sāṃkhya Kārikā* describe living liberation as utter detachment and freedom from compulsive thought and action while still embodied. When one realizes "I am not," one ceases to act, withdraws from *prakṛti*, the realm of manifestation, while the *puruṣa* or detached witness attains perfect solitude (*kaivalya*). Although past impressions (*saṃskāra, vāsanā*) creating the notion of an "I" force one to remain alive for a time, no attachment remains.

Chapple continues that Patañjali's *Yoga Sūtra* emphasizes techniques for liberation that bring about the cessation of all afflicted action (*kleśa-karma*) through extensive meditation, the development of detachment, and rigorous mental purification. This purification process, culminating in meditative enstasy (*samādhi*), minimizes attachments to the world and ego by "subtilization" (*pratiprasava*), the most familiar version of which is the eight-limbed yogic path. No explicit term for living liberation appears here, yet one sees that despite the Yogin's process of purification that "burns" all impressions, some "sterile" impressions still remain, thus allowing for liberation while embodied. According to Vyāsa, the process of eradicating afflicted action continues until the moment of death. Chapple (like Nelson with the Advaitin *jīvanmukta*) finds the liberated being in Yoga to be like Īśvara, free from afflicted action. In fact, Chapple shows that later Sāṃkhya and Yoga writers are increasingly influenced by Advaitin thought, even incorporating the term "*jīvanmukti.*" This might be called "returning the favor," for Śaṅkara and the Advaitin tradition have made ample use of the potter's wheel analogy found in *Sāṃkhya Kārikā* 67–8.

Chapple closes by arguing that Yoga's emphasis on purification could have been influenced by the Jaina model of liberation through a progression of purificatory stages called "*guṇasthānas.*" Sāṃkhya and Yoga, he suggests, might be read as sequential *sādhanas*: first, Sāṃkhya leads the individual to a state of discerning knowledge equivalent to the right insight (*samyag-darśana*) of Jainism's fourth *guṇasthāna*. Yoga then takes the individual through an elaborate course of meditative discipline to actual living liberation, equivalent to the Jaina thirteenth or *sayoga-kevalin-guṇasthāna*, when the liberated being remains due to a little leftover *karma* governing bare bodily existence.

Like the *Yoga Sūtra*, Vidyāraṇya's *Jīvanmuktiviveka*, a syncretic fourteenth-century Advaita text, also holds that yogic discipline is not only an essential part of the path to liberating knowledge, but a practice that must be continued thereafter to eradicate any residual karmic impressions. In his essay on the *Jīvanmuktiviveka*, Andrew Fort writes that Vidyāraṇya, unlike Śaṅkara, "claims that Yoga and ascetic renunciation (*saṃnyāsa*) together both lead to *and* express the liberating knowledge (*jñāna, vidyā*) of Brahman." While Vidyāraṇya is Advaitin in holding that knowledge of non-duality is the fundamental cause of liberation while living and that *yoga* alone is insufficient for liberation, his emphasis on the necessity of yogic practice both to gain release by Brahman-knowledge and to safeguard this knowledge by removing leftover *karma* is quite un-Advaitin. He also differs from Śaṅkara in arguing that repeated yogic practice can even overcome the necessity of experiencing *prārabdha-karma*. Thus, Fort argues that Vidyāraṇya's thought diverges from Śaṅkara's "mainstream" Advaita toward a "Yogic Advaita," greatly influenced by Patañjali's Yoga, the *Laghu Yogavāsiṣṭha*, and the *Bhagavad Gītā*.

Fort claims that "Yogic Advaita" is also apparent in Vidyāraṇya's closely connecting renunciation (*saṃnyāsa*) and *jīvanmukti*. Vidyāraṇya holds that renunciation (including non-attachment and isolation), like yogic practice, both leads to and follows knowledge. The supreme renunciate, called both *jīvanmukta* and *paramahaṃsa yogin*, is described as both a knower of Brahman and a master of yoga. And since the highest knowledge is ultimately greater than yogic *samādhi,* so the knower passes beyond practicing conventional *saṃnyāsa,* for mental detachment through knowing the Self is more basic to liberation than performing duties or bodily renunciation (although a liberated being doesn't actually violate the norms of *dharma*).

Finally, Fort points out that Vidyāraṇya seems to concur with many mainstream Advaitins that, while liberation is certainly possible in life, embodied liberation is not quite equal to liberation without a body (*videhamukti*). Fort goes on to show, however, that Vidyāraṇya puts a new twist on this issue by arguing that one can have bodiless liberation *while embodied,* if bodiless liberation is considered freedom from future, not present, embodiment.

Issues of renunciation and conformity to *dharma* are also central to C. Mackenzie Brown's essay. Both Fort's and Brown's chapters further reveal that discussion of *jīvanmukti* is not limited to systematic philosophical thinkers; living liberation is considered in popular and enormously influential Hindu literature such as the epics and Purāṇas. Brown raises the important question of how one can recognize a *jīvanmukta* as he considers the figure of Śuka in the *Mahābhārata,* the *Bhāgavata Purāṇa,* and the *Devī-Bhāgavata Purāṇa*. In all, Śuka is considered a perfected being and an ideal renunciate, but the forms of perfection and renunciation vary with each text, particularly concerning the issue of whether householding allows for renunciation and if it is compatible with living liberation.

In the *Mahābhārata,* the wise king Janaka teaches Śuka that liberated existence is marked by utter indifference that is unmoved by temptation. Learning that he need not be a householder, but must simply realize the Self of all, Śuka does so and becomes liberated. And although he does not seem to recognize his own liberation clearly, the text indicates Śuka's perfected non-attachment to be so great than even modest maidens unselfconsciously bathe nude in his presence (implicitly recognizing his status by ignoring him). On the other hand, in the *Bhāgavata Purāṇa* Śuka becomes what Brown calls an "enlightened idiot of dazzle and dirt." Śuka is here a truly radical renunciate whose worldly attachments have been burned out by his devotion to Kṛṣṇa, and who is thus wary of householding and the entire *varṇāśrama-dharma*. Due to his extreme detachment and his cognizance of the divine in all, feces and gold are alike to him. In this text, Śuka's wisdom and beauty are hidden in imbecility, bodily neglect, and grime. While certainly noticed, Śuka is recognized as liberated only by those so detached and pure as to be beyond opposites like purity and pollution.

Finally, Brown describes Śuka in the Śākta-influenced *Devī-Bhāgavata Purāṇa*. In this text, Śuka learns that householding and perfect renunciation are compatible. As in the *Mahābhārata*, Śuka is taught by Janaka (who is interestingly, as Brown points out, of "Videha" or "the bodiless"), a liberated householder who even teaches renunciates. Janaka instructs Śuka to go through the discipline provided by the life-stages (*āśrama*) and to follow the rules of *dharma* to aid the world's welfare. Janaka claims that inner indifference is true renunciation; while Śuka is attached to being non-attached, Janaka, a king, is free from all attachment even while ruling. Unlike the *Bhāgavata*'s Śuka, who wanders naked, Śuka in the *Devī-Bhāgavata* returns home and becomes a householder-renunciate ("married, with children"). In this text, the liberated Śuka is hard to recognize precisely because he is so ordinary. Brown points out that while both texts teach the importance of intense, loving devotion to God, the form of love is different: in the *Bhāgavata*, norm-breaking passionate love is primary; in the *Devī-Bhāgavata*, society-supporting mother love is most fundamental. Still, as Brown concludes, in neither case is Śuka's living liberation easy to recognize.

The essays by Paul Muller-Ortega and Chacko Valiaveetil, dealing respectively with the Kāśmīrī Śaivism of the influential thinker Abhinavagupta and the Tamil Śaiva Siddhānta of Meykaṇṭār and his followers, offer two very different models of living liberation in Śaiva thought. While sharing many concepts and terminology when describing the world, the soul, its bondage, and the path to liberation, their ontologies are as far apart as their geographical locations: Kāśmīrī non-dualism might well be considered more radical than that of Advaita, while the southern school's dependent pluralism is reminiscent of Madhva's Dvaita Vedānta.

Muller-Ortega consider *jīvanmukti* according to the Kāśmīrī Śaiva or Trika-Kaula branch of Hindu Tantra. He begins by discussing the problem of defining Kāśmīrī Śaivism, a term that has had various meanings. The tantric Śaivas of Abhinavagupta's lineage (which Muller-Ortega deals with here) hold one can gain liberation even while embodied if granted a sufficient "descent of energy" (*śaktipāta*). According to Muller-Ortega, Abhinavagupta (eleventh century) emphasizes the importance of one's identity with Śiva by means of direct and conscious yogic realization ("entering the domain of the Heart"), rather than by mere intellectual comprehension. In the *Parātriṃśikā-vivaraṇa*, Abhinava holds that "the *jīvanmukta* becomes co-equal with Śiva as the possessor and wielder of the cosmic powers" called *śaktis*, and obtains "unitive perception of the omnipresence of Śiva." The tantric *jīvanmukta*, when liberation is accomplished (*siddha*), thus passes beyond the *varnāśrama-dharma*, renunciation, and all polarities. He becomes free like Śiva, and may perform transgressive rituals which demonstrate transcendence of *dharma* and brahminical purity.

Muller-Ortega shows that the Kāśmīrī Śaivas claim that both bondage and the path to liberation derive from Śiva. Śiva freely wills His self-concealment and limitation, and also wills liberation through *śaktipāta*. Śiva "constructs a zone of contraction of limitation, through which he then forces himself to traverse, and the result is the finite, transmigrating self." As with the Śaiva Siddhāntins, the "contractive zone" is constituted by impurities (*malas*), and from this impure, limited condition one ascends back to identity with Śiva through thirty-six *tattvas* (adapted from Sāṃkhya and seven states called *pramātṛs* or "experiencers." In the highest state, when one realizes "I am Śiva," all 'objectivity' is assimilated into blissful, unified consciousness, which is Śiva, and one is liberated while living.

Chacko Valiaveetil describes *jīvanmukti* in Śaiva Siddhānta, focusing on Meykaṇṭār's *Śivajñāna Bodham* (thirteenth century) and its commentators. Valiaveetil explains that the saints of this school wrote hymns praising "the gracious Lord who saved them from the fetters of *saṃsāra* and calling on men to take refuge under his Sacred Feet." Śaiva Siddhāntins claim that neither Śaṅkara's Advaitin *jñāna* nor ritual action can, by itself, bring release; only selfless *bhakti* allows humans to obtain the liberating grace of the Lord. According to its adherents, Śaiva Siddhānta is "the true Advaita which upholds the absolute supremacy of God and at the same time unhesitatingly accepts the reality of the world and souls." The path to liberation is dominated by the progressive surrender of the self to the love and grace of the Lord. *Jīvanmukti* is both realization while living of union with the Lord and the simultaneous freeing from bonds or *malas* that impede, and can cause relapse from, liberation. The *mala*-circumscribed love of self is gradually replaced by loving (comm)union: "the soul becomes one with the Lord without losing its individuality, so that they are neither one nor two." Valiaveetil adds that Siddhāntins must safeguard this liberated state by repeated meditation on and worship of the Lord (as Vidyāraṇya holds one must safeguard *mukti* by yogic practice).

Valiaveetil also addresses aspects of the "*karma* problem" discussed in other chapters, including the question of why a liberated being still has *karma* and remains in a body always prone to suffering. Part of the answer lies in the Siddhāntin view that embodied liberation exists to provide the opportunity to experience communion with Śiva in this very world and then to express the Lord's love and grace to others. In addition, and again like Vidyāraṇya, the liberated being transcends conventional morality, here due to his utter detachment and single-minded devotion to Śiva. However, this being still sets an example for others and protects himself from relapse by associating with other Śaiva *bhaktas*, using sacred emblems (ashes, beads, and so forth), and worshipping temple images.

Patricia Mumme's concluding essay seeks to identify common ground, recurring themes, and fundamental tensions among the views of *jīvanmukti* presented in the earlier chapters. She identifies three general positions on *jīvanmukti* in the various schools and authors represented here: strong, which includes those who clearly define living liberation as a discrete state; medium, which describes those who accept the concept, but without defining it so clearly or discretely; and weak, which includes those who reject the notion of full liberation while living. According to this model, Advaita and Sāṃkhya positions are strong, Madhva's and Rāmānuja's positions are weak, and the remaining authors or schools hold views in the medium range. Mumme explores whether and to what extent the strength of a school's position on living liberation correlates with its stance on some related doctrinal issues: its overall metaphysics, its doctrine of God or Īśvara, and its claims about the kinds of *karma* and conscious experience characterizing the individual in the highest attainable living state.

She also considers the need many schools felt to assert the existence of liberated teachers, and the varying claims thinkers made about the behavior of *jīvanmuktas*, including their degree of conformity to dharmic norms. Mumme suggests that the preponderance of Vaiṣṇava schools in the weak position can be explained by noting that, unlike other schools discussed here, they do not need to validate the authority of their founding teachers and *gurus* by called them *jīvanmuktas*. In the Vaiṣṇava tradition, teachers and *gurus* are usually seen as descents (*avatāra*) of either Viṣṇu or his associates. She concludes with some suggestions for future research, such as investigating living liberation in Buddhism and in neo-Vedānta.

Notes

1. Defining "Hinduism" is, of course, a controversial and unresolved issue and one that is not central to our book. For our purposes, "Hindu" authors and schools of thought refer to those who take the Veda and *Itihāsa-purāṇa* as authoritative, and/or worship some form of Viṣṇu or Śiva. We add the latter phrase because much of devotional (particularly Śaiva) Hinduism is Vedic in only the most tangential sense.

2. *The Concept of Mukti in Advaita Vedānta* (Madras: Univ. of Madras, 1961). Krishna Warrier describes various Indian conceptions of liberation on the way to positing the superiority of the Advaita Vedāntin view.

3. *A Comparative Study of the Concept of Liberation in Indian Philosophy* (Burhanpur: Gindharlal Keshavdas, 1967). Lad's writing is heavily influenced by Western philosophical concepts, and he gives a neo-Vedāntin reading of liberation in Indian thought.

4. *Advaitic Concept of Jīvanmukti* (Delhi: Bharatiya Vidya Prakashan, 1990). Srivastava's book, also largely neo-Vedāntin, gives a cursory examination of non-Advaitin views of living liberation.

5. *Liberated Life* (Madurai: Dialogue Series, 1980). Valiaveetil (a contributor here) has also looked at living liberation according to a variety of schools, focusing ultimately on Śaiva Siddhānta.

6. Some of these modern Indian thinkers have argued that the Hindu notion that one gains liberation in this very life—as opposed to a salvation only after death—is evidence of the superiority of Hindu religious ideas over those of the West. They say the *jīvanmukti* ideal indicates that Hindu thought offers a highly positive view of the possibilities of human existence, what might be called a truly extraordinary "human potential movement." I plan to document some of these ideas in future publications.

PART 1

Living Liberation in Vedānta Traditions

CHAPTER 1

Living Liberation in Śaṅkara and Classical Advaita: Sharing the Holy Waiting of God

Lance E. Nelson

Introduction

> I experience the non-dual [Reality as clearly] as a *bilva* fruit on the palm of my hand; I see my body as the cast-off skin of a snake. Though I appear as if living, my attainment of the supreme goal is incontestable.[1]

In this passage, the eleventh-century Advaitin, Sarvajñātman, describes his experience of living liberation, or *jīvanmukti*. Although not all Hindus agree, most followers of Advaita (non-dualist) Vedānta accept this state as a real possibility and hold its attainment to be a primary goal of spiritual practice. The idea of living liberation suggests that an embodied human being[2] can live in a state somehow beyond ordinary phenomenal limitations. We shall see that the creators of the classical Advaita tradition[3] were equivocal on the question of whether living liberation is total liberation. Still, there can be no doubt that this idea is among the most important and most distinctive contributions India has made to world spirituality. Adumbrated in the Upaniṣads, it found its first formal articulation in the Buddhist concept of Nirvāṇa "with residual conditions" (*saupādisesa-nibbāna*), the state enjoyed by the liberated "worthy one" (*arhat*) prior to death. In recent times modern, Western-educated Vedāntins have cited living liberation as an important argument for the superiority of the Hindu non-dualist vision over Western religion. Radhakrishnan, for example, argues that *jīvanmukti* offers the fulfillment of religious aspiration as "an experience of the present, not a prophecy of the future."[4] The notion suggests a bold alternative to the idea of salvation as a goal to be attained beyond death. It holds out the prospect—intriguing to modern minds—that we need not abandon life to live its final truth.

The Hindu ideal of *jīvanmukti* is important both anthropologically and theologically. It speaks, of course, of the potential of the human, but it may also reveal something of the nature of the divine. Here, I take inspiration from one of Mircea Eliade's many discerning remarks about Indian thought. The liberated saint establishes, he tells us, "a new and paradoxical mode of being—*consciousness of freedom*, . . . which exists [otherwise] only in the Supreme Being, Īśvara."[5] The parallel drawn here between the liberated sage and the divine is important, though the Advaita tradition itself does not make much of it. I wish, in this chapter, to underline the importance of this parallel. Further, I want to suggest how a hermeneutic of living liberation based on the Advaitic understanding of God can illumine, reciprocally, both concepts: *jīvanmukti* and Īśvara.

A good portion of this chapter will be devoted to conceptual groundwork. I will describe in some detail Advaita's concept of liberation (*mukti, mokṣa*) and the assumptions that give it its particular form. I will also outline key moments in the history of the development of the non-dualist idea of living liberation. Without denying the profound significance of Advaita's thought on this subject, I will nevertheless show that, because of its deep-rooted bias against the phenomenal world, the tradition's acceptance of *jīvanmukti* is not entirely wholehearted. In particular, I will demonstrate that in Advaita neither the sage who lives liberation nor perhaps even Īśvara himself, who "lives" liberation on a cosmic scale, are as fully free as modern interpreters have held.

Since I confine my attention here to classical Advaita, my primary source will be Śaṅkara (eighth century), the founding teacher (*ācārya*) and foremost authority of the tradition.[6] But I will also draw upon the work of other early Advaitins and certain later followers of Śaṅkara. Many of the latter found the concept of *jīvanmukti* problematic; some rejected it outright. The difficulties they had justifying the idea will lead us into a consideration of the relation between the saint "liberated while living" (*jīvanmukta*) and God.

About the moral dimensions of living liberation, Śaṅkara says very little. He does suggest that the *jīvanmukta* has compassion and concern for others, that he is childlike, unostentatious, retiring, and detached, and that he works for the well-being of the wider community.[7] Otherwise, Śaṅkara simply assumes that conventional brahminical ethical standards apply here as elsewhere. Space being limited, therefore, I will ignore the ethics of *jīvanmukti* and focus on its metaphysical foundations.

Liberation in Śaṅkara's Thought

Śaṅkara defines liberation in the abstract terms of ontology. It is, he says, "absolute, unchangingly eternal, all-pervading like space, devoid of all modifications, ever content, partless, self-luminous by nature, a state in which exist neither good, evil, nor their effects, neither past, present, nor future." As such, it is no different from the supreme Reality, Brahman.[8] Indeed, Śaṅkara tells us that liberation simply *is* Brahman.[9] He links this abstract truth, however, with an existential counterpart, the well-known Upaniṣadic experience of Brahman as the true Self (Ātman) within each person. Liberation—identical with ultimate Being—is also the interior reality that transcends and yet supports the phenomenal individual. In Śaṅkara's words, "*mokṣa* is the true nature of the Self, like heat of fire."[10]

It follows from this that liberation is not something that can be brought into existence, as if it were a product of action (*sādhya*). Nor is it something that can be acquired (*anāpya*). Rather the opposite is true: it has no beginning (*anārabhya*), and it is eternal (*nitya*). Being our very Self, it is eternally accomplished (*nitya-siddha*), eternally attained (*nityāpta*).[11] Ontologically speaking, we are always liberated.

Gauḍapāda expresses this idea hyperbolically. From the standpoint of the highest Truth, he proclaims, there is no bondage, no seeker of liberation, and no one who is liberated.[12] His point is that we should not think of liberation as a process or as an attainment newly accomplished in time. Although it may appear otherwise, *mukti* is in truth an atemporal state that has always been ours. Vācaspati Miśra uses milder but still somewhat paradoxical language to drive the same point home: "On the removal of that [ignorance], the blissful nature, though attained [eternally], becomes attained, as if it were not attained [already]. Grief, misery, etc., though abandoned [eternally], become abandoned, as if they were not abandoned [already]."[13]

To speak of attaining liberation is, therefore, figurative—accurate only from the epistemological point of view. The human experience of bondage—our sense of not being liberated—is a problem of our not being aware of what we already have. Advaita traces this unawareness to spiritual ignorance (*avidyā*), under which the individual self (*jīva*) has been laboring for an eternity of past time. The *jīva* may, however, gain awareness of its true nature as Brahman at any moment through scripturally mediated knowledge (*jñāna*). Because ignorance is the source of our bondage, knowledge—not works, faith, or moral improvement—is the means of awakening to liberation. We are told: "Only through knowledge of Truth can liberation be realized."[14] The valorization of *gnosis* is, when Śaṅkara follows his highest vision, radical: Brahman-knowledge is the necessary and sufficient condition of *mukti*, which depends on no other factor.

From this perspective, the rise of knowledge, the destruction of ignorance, and the realization of liberation occur simultaneously. There is not the slightest delay between the cause and its final effect. He writes: "The scriptures, teaching that liberation occurs immediately upon knowledge of Brahman, deny any interval in which action is to be performed."[15] Glossing *Bhagavad Gītā* (*BhG*) 13.30, Śaṅkara says, "When—at which time—he sees the separate state of beings abiding in the one Self, . . . then—at that very time—he attains Brahman, he becomes Brahman."[16] One who realizes the Ātman, we are told, "is liberated, even without wishing for it."[17]

Śaṅkara insists in more than one passage that Brahman-knowledge, once attained, is completely—and permanently—effective in removing ignorance and granting liberation. He tells us that neither liberation nor the knowledge that leads to it admit any degrees or gradations:

> There cannot be in knowledge any distinction characterized by superiority as opposed to inferiority, because that which is inferior is not knowledge at all, and only that which is superior is knowledge. Therefore, in knowledge there can be only the distinction of having arisen earlier as opposed to later. But in liberation itself no distinction whatever is possible.[18]

From this point of view liberation is an absolute state, realized either completely and permanently or not at all. There should be no need for it to be deepened, stabilized, or preserved through meditation or other yogic disciplines.[19] Says Śaṅkara: "Refinement is not possible by adding anything to it, for liberation is of the nature of Brahman, whose pre-eminence cannot be added to. Nor can it be improved by removing some defect, for liberation is of the nature of Brahman, which is eternally pure."[20]

Living Liberation

It is a fundamental premise of Advaita that the entire universe, including the body and mind associated with the *jīva*, is a phenomenal reality having its source in ignorance (*avidyā*). The question, then, arises: In what sense can ordinary experience persist after *avidyā* has been removed by knowledge? Is not the Advaitin compelled to hold that the empirical world—and the body–mind of the liberated individual as well—must vanish simultaneously with the destruction of its cause? If so, liberation would seem to entail literal and immediate disembodiment.

Śaṅkara in many instances speaks as if this were the case. "Knowledge," he tells us, "arises of itself and cancels ignorance, and on account of that, this entire world of names and forms together with its inhabitants, which had been superimposed by ignorance, vanishes away like the world of a dream."[21] Again: "In the supreme state (*paramārthāvasthā*), all empirical experience is absent (*sarva-vyavahārābhāva*)."[22] Śaṅkara's disciple Sureśvara tells us that the awakened one sees nothing but the Self: *guru*, scriptures, and individual existence have vanished (*NS* 4.37).

Nevertheless, there is a strong tradition—originating in scripture and elaborated by the teachers of Advaita—that liberation is a state that can be lived in this human body. To be sure, the ancient scriptures do not use the technical term *jīvanmukti*, popular in the later tradition. Śaṅkara himself uses it once only, in the past participle form (*jīvanmukta*). He comments on *BhG* 6.27: "Having become Brahman, he is liberated while living."[23] In Śaṅkara's mind, therefore, *jīvanmukti* has not yet become a technical term. Nevertheless the concept, if not the term itself, is present in Śaṅkara and his scriptural sources—in their discussion of liberation and especially in their insistence on the radical sufficiency of knowledge to grant access to that state.[24]

Bṛhadāraṇyaka Upaniṣad (*BU*) 4.4.14, for example, declares: "Verily, even here (*ihaiva*) we may know this."[25] At 3.8.10, the same text states that the one who leaves this world without knowing Brahman is pitiable. Truth is attained by those who know Brahman in this world (*iha*), according to *Kena Upaniṣad* 2.5, but "great loss" accrues to those who do not so know. "He attains *Brahman* here (*atra brahma samaśnute*)," says *Kaṭha Upaniṣad* (*Kaṭha*) 2.3.14. *Aitareya Upaniṣad* 2.1.5–6 reports that Vāmadeva realized the Self while still in his mother's womb, and the tradition knows him as having subsequently lived a productive life as the seer of the fourth book of the *Ṛg Veda*.[26]

Bhagavad Gītā 5.28 tells us that the ascetic who has controlled his senses and attained identity with Brahman is eternally liberated (*sadā mukta eva*). This is possible, we read at 5.23, "prior to release from the body (*prāk śarīra-vimokṣaṇāt*)." The text advocates the realization of Self as non-doer—a state tantamount to liberation—as a prerequisite for its ideal of detached participation in the world. The essential teaching of the *Gītā*, in fact, turns on the premise that the enlightened Self will remain free no matter how vigorously the body engages in works. Śaṅkara, in his commentary (*BhGŚ*), stresses that the sage must renounce action because of its incompatibility with *jñāna*. Nevertheless, he accepts the *Gītā's* message that such renunciation is not merely or even necessarily physical: "[The Brahman-knower] does nothing whatever, though engaged in action, because he has realized the Self, which is actionless."[27] This realization is equivalent to *mukti*:

> The ascetic who, . . . before undertaking action, has realized his self as Brahman, the actionless, inner Self that dwells in all, . . . acting only for the maintenance of the body, abiding in knowledge, is liberated (*mucyate*). . . . Because all his actions are burnt in the fire of knowledge, he is liberated without any obstacle (*apratibandhena mucyate eva*).[28]

The teacher of the *Gītā* insists that work for the welfare of the world is compatible with Self-knowledge. Śaṅkara agrees (*BhGŚ* 3.25, 4.20).

The *Brahma Sūtra* (*BS*) at 3.4.51 teaches the possibility of attaining knowledge in this life (*aihikam*). At 4.1.13 it declares, in the spirit of the *Gītā*, that action does not cling to the realized sage. Śaṅkara indicates that this is because the knower (*jñānin*) has realized that the Self is not the agent of action. *BS* 3.3.32 teaches that certain realized saints may do more than merely remain alive. If God has given them a special office or mission (*adhikāra*), they may retain their individuality after death and even return to earth to do good works by taking on additional bodies. In his commentary (*BSŚ*), Śaṅkara explains: "We see from the epics and Purāṇas that some, though knowing Brahman, attained new bodies."[29]

Śaṅkara many times repeats this idea—that liberation is possible here, in this life. The great Vedāntic saying "That thou art," he tells us, refers to a condition of identity with Brahman that already exists. We should not interpret it to mean, "That thou wilt become after death."[30] *Muṇḍaka Upaniṣad* (*MuU*) 3.2.9 proclaims, "He who knows Brahman becomes Brahman."[31] Śaṅkara comments that this occurs "in this world . . . even while alive (*loke . . . jīvann eva*)." Elsewhere he teaches: "Being Brahman, they attain the bliss of Brahman—i.e., liberation—here, even while living (*iha jīvann eva*)."[32]

Under *BS* 1.1.4, Śaṅkara speaks of *mokṣa* as "unembodiedness" (*aśarīratva*),[33] drawing on the Upaniṣadic notion that the Self is eternally unembodied (*aśarīra*).[34] He explains that our identification with the body and its correlates is an adventitious superimposition that ceases upon Brahman-realization. But he by no means wants to suggest liberation requires literal disembodiment. While embodiedness is caused by false knowledge (*mithyājñāna*), the unembodiedness—and, by definition, the liberation—of the Self is an eternal reality (*aśarīratvaṃ nityam*). "Therefore," he concludes, "since embodiedness is a result of a false perception, the knower (*vidvān*) is unembodied, even while living (*jīvato 'pi*)."[35]

To support this thesis, Śaṅkara quotes *BU* 4.4.7. This is perhaps the most important proof text for the idea of living liberation. The verse declares: "He attains Brahman even here (*atra brahma samaśnute*)." In his commentary on the Upaniṣad (*BUŚ*), Śaṅkara glosses this sentence: "He attains Brahman, identity with Brahman, i.e., liberation, living in this very body. Hence liberation does not require such things as going to another place."[36] The Upaniṣad continues: "As the cast-off skin of a snake lies on an anthill, dead, abandoned, even so lies this body. Then one is disembodied (*aśarīra*), immortal."[37] In juxtaposition with the first part of the passage, Śaṅkara takes this as showing the attitude of complete detachment a liberated sage (*vidvān muktaḥ*) has toward his body. When the snake casts off its old skin, it no longer regards the skin as part of itself. Similarly, the consciousness of the liberated saint is no longer identified with its former physical instrument. The body, says Śaṅkara, lies "*as if* dead (*mṛtam iva*)." The Self realizes it is not, has never been, and never will be associated with any corporeal frame. It thus becomes effectively disembodied, hence liberated, even though the physical organism may continue to function.[38] Elsewhere Śaṅkara declares: "The embodiedness of the Self is simply a matter of non-discrimination; its disembodiedness, of discrimination." In support, he quotes *Kaṭha* 1.2.22, "bodiless, though in bodies," and *BhG* 13.31, "Although dwelling in a body, [the Self] neither acts nor becomes contaminated."[39]

From its inception, then, the Śaṅkara tradition is able to assert that the presence or absence of embodiment is not the defining feature of liberation. On this argument, the critical factor is not literal freedom from the body—that would make *jīvanmukti* impossible. What is required is rather a figurative disembodiedness, the transcendence of bodily consciousness, the destruction of the unenlightened identification with the psycho-physical organism. This the *mukta* may achieve while living.

Vācaspati Miśra (tenth century) states this understanding succinctly: "If being embodied were real, it could not cease during life; it is, however, caused by illusory knowledge, and that can be removed by the rise of true knowledge even during life (*jīvatāpi*)." Unembodiedness, he reminds us, is the Self's very nature. So it is a condition impossible for the Self ever to have lost.[40]

Bhāratītīrtha-Vidyāraṇya (fourteenth century)[41] recognizes the ultimate irrelevance to liberation of the presence or absence of the body at *Pañcadaśī* (*PD*) 2.103–104. He urges us there not to take *BhG* 2.72 too literally when it suggests that one attains to Brahman "at the last moment (*anta-kāle*)." Interpreting the phrase from a radical Advaitic perspective, he proclaims that the last moment is not the time of death but the point at which one realizes the truth of non-duality. For the realized saint, actual death then becomes insignificant: "Let him give up his life while healthy and seated, or diseased and rolling on the ground, or even unconscious. He is not affected by illusion in any way."[42] What the *mukta* has realized, and has become, remains unchanged.

Later Advaita distinguishes between living liberation and disembodied liberation (*videhamukti*), which the liberated sage is said to attain at death. Śaṅkara does use the term "isolation" (*kaivalya*) to designate the situation that obtains after the *mukta's* body has ceased to function. I will say more about this idea further on. But Śaṅkara does not, so far as I can determine, use the term *videhamukti*.[43] To the extent that one accepts the characterization of *mokṣa* given above, it is hard to see how there can be any real change after death in the essential nature of the liberation already attained during life. Any suggestion that *videhamukti* is a soteriological advance over *jīvanmukti* would weaken Advaita's professed non-dualism, implying a more realistic conception of embodiment than the strict Advaita *gnosis*-orientation allows.[44] For one who is already liberated, Śaṅkara declares, "there is no further liberation to be accomplished."[45] We have just seen how, from this point of view, even the embodied knower of Brahman has realized the unembodiedness of the Self. Death itself then ought to be negligible, bringing no greater freedom. Śaṅkara can wax emphatic on this idea: "For the knower who dies there is no change of condition—no state different from that experienced while living. There is just no further embodiment."[46] Whatever change it may entail in the realm of appearance, death cannot, as long as *jñāna* has the potency Śaṅkara here ascribes to it, bring any higher degree of liberation.

Jīvanmukti: Difficult to Justify but Necessary for Salvation

Advaitins have found, however, that it is one thing to extol *jīvanmukti* but another to work out a theoretical justification for it. The difficulty, of course, is that the body, mind, and activity of the *jīvanmukta* are held to be products of *avidyā*. But *avidyā* is supposed to be destroyed by the knowledge that allows the sage to realize liberation. Living liberation is therefore a paradoxical—and, according to some, contradictory—notion. It implies the co-existence of two incompatible principles—namely, knowledge and ignorance, with the former held sufficient to completely abolish the latter.

Seeing no way out of this dilemma, some Advaitins have felt obliged to concede that *jīvanmukti* is indeed an impossibility. This is especially true of the proponents of the "one-soul theory" (*eka-jīva-vāda*). These radical non-dualists teach a kind of solipsistic idealism of only one *jīva*. Therefore, they reject the idea of *jīvanmukti* outright as pointless. Since there is only one experiencer, what would be the purpose, after it is liberated, of the continuation of body or world? The whole business vanishes instantly. This is one form of the doctrine of "immediate liberation" (*sadyomukti*), to be discussed below. Prakāśānanda (early sixteenth century), the most well-known exponent of this way of thinking, argues extensively against the mainstream Advaitic conception of living liberation. He asserts that Vedic texts teaching *jīvanmukti* are only commendatory (*artha-vāda*). Their purpose is to inspire the aspirant to study Vedānta. He argues that the liberated preceptors of Advaita, however useful for the seeker, are in actuality false appearances. Given the absence of proof, he declares, the universal acceptance of living liberation is but blind tradition.[47]

The *ekajīvavādins*' suggestion that the teachers of Vedānta are mere fabrications of ignorance is a necessary corollary of their doctrine that there is only one *jīva*. This teaching is, however, a clear attempt to avoid the demands of a well-established Advaitic tradition, one that is embarrassing to both the *ekajīvavādins*' solipsistic position and their teaching that only immediate, disembodied liberation is possible. Brahman knowledge, mainstream Advaitins have always agreed, can be acquired only with the aid of a teacher who has himself realized Brahman.

MuU 1.2.12 states that one desirous of knowledge should approach a teacher who is learned in the scriptures and established in Brahman (*brahma-niṣṭha*). *Kaṭha* 1.2.8 reads, following Śaṅkara: "When taught by an inferior, it cannot be truly understood. . . . Unless taught by one who has attained identity, there is no way to it."[48] *Chāndogya Upaniṣad* (*ChU*) 6.14.2 declares, "a person having a teacher knows (*ācāryavān puruṣo veda*)." Śaṅkara suggests that, if the body falls immediately at the time of the rise of knowledge, there can be no qualified teacher, and this dictum of *śruti* would be meaningless (*ChUŚ* 6.14.2). According to *BhG* 4.34, knowledge is to be imparted by "knowers who have realized the Truth (*jñāninas tattva-darśinaḥ*)." Śaṅkara comments: "Only knowledge taught by those who have true knowledge is effective, no other."[49] We must, says the *PD*, receive instruction from teachers who know the Truth (*ācāryāt tattva-darśināt*). Sages such as Yājñavalkya, this text reminds us, were well known for their teaching. Without the notion of *jīvanmukti*, we could not explain such actions (*PD* 1.32, 7.184). The continuity of the Advaita tradition thus depends on the existence of a lineage of realized teachers. "If the body of one who has seen the truth (*dṛṣṭa-tattva*) falls immediately," argues Vimuktātman (tenth century), "there will be no liberation, for there will be no preceptor and, consequently, no acquisition of knowledge."[50]

Śaṅkara's Justifications of Living Liberation

As a Vedāntin, Śaṅkara is first and foremost an exegete of the Vedic revelation. His most important justification of living liberation consists, therefore, in appeals to the authority of scripture. In the Upaniṣads he finds ample support for his concept of a radical *gnosis* that, once attained, is capable of granting liberation irrespective of empirical conditions. He pulls concepts and images from the texts and holds them before us as truths garnered from revelation. We have seen many examples of this strategy already, perhaps the most striking being the paradoxical metaphor of "embodied unembodiment" derived from the *BU* and the *Kaṭha*.

Śaṅkara also appeals to the evidence of post-Vedic scripture (*smṛti*). He refers especially to the *Gītā's* teaching on the sage of steady wisdom (*sthita-prajña*), whom he regards as an example of one liberated in the body.[51] But at least in one passage he seems to think the truth of embodied Brahman-knowledge is more a matter of direct apprehension than a question open to theoretical proof or disproof. In an unusual appeal to the authority of experience he declares: "It is not a subject for debate whether the knower of Brahman remains embodied for some time or not. For how can one's knowing Brahman—felt profoundly in one's own heart—and [simultaneous] bearing of a body be contested by another?"[52] Here, the Advaita tradition believes, the commentator alludes to his own realization of the Absolute and his consequent state of living liberation.[53]

Śaṅkara is most exciting intellectually when his job as an exegete allows him to follow his ontological bent. In this mode, drawing support from select Upaniṣadic passages, he speaks from the point of view of Advaitic *jñāna*. He portrays *mokṣa* as a realization that happens in time only by appearance. Brushing aside empirical limitations as irrelevant, he appears as a champion of a thoroughgoing non-dualism.

At *BS* 4.1.15, however, Śaṅkara encounters a rather different approach to the question of embodied Brahman-knowledge. The *sūtra* speaks in the more popular categories of religious morality and yogic psychology, and Śaṅkara allows it to lead him into a different kind of argument for living liberation. Instead of looking at it ontologically as an eternally accomplished reality, he now attempts to justify it from the point of view of its expression within the domain of space and time. Following the *sūtra* and associated scriptural passages, he offers an explanation in terms of the theory of *karma*. He thus entertains certain questions that, however irrelevant to the strict non-dualist *gnosis*-orientation, are important in the domain of popular religious teaching. The discussion, we shall see, leads to a more commonsense notion of embodiment than Śaṅkara otherwise allows.

The *sūtra* in question addresses a problem stemming from the teaching, found in both the Upaniṣads and the *Bhagavad Gītā*, that knowledge of the Self destroys all karmic residues. Thus *MuU* 2.2.8 declares of the knower, "His *karmas* are destroyed." *BhG* 4.37 proclaims, "The fire of knowledge reduces all *karmas* to ashes."[54] The question naturally arises, How can the physical body of the knower continue if his *karma* is no more? The assumption, universal in South Asian religion by Śaṅkara's time, is of course that physical embodiment is a karmically conditioned state. Without *karma* there can be no body. The *sūtra's* answer to this objection is simple: ". . . only the past [merit and demerit] that has not begun to produce effects [is destroyed]."[55] The idea, as Śaṅkara explains it, is that knowledge does not destroy all *karma*. It eradicates only the *karma* that is "stored up" (*saṃcita*) as a result of actions in a past life, or in this life before the rise of knowledge. Such *karma* is as yet inactive, not having begun to bear its fruits in experience. But the situation is different for *karma* that is "commenced" (*prārabdha*), that is, *karma* that has begun to yield its results in the present life. Already active, it is not subject to the power of knowledge, and it is therefore not destroyed.[56]

Despite the apparent mutual exclusivity of knowledge and *karma*, Śaṅkara concedes that there is, in one respect, a certain dependence of the former on the latter: "The rise of knowledge cannot occur without dependence on an accumulation of *karma* of which the effects have already commenced."[57] That is to say, were it not for the *karma* that led to one's present life—one's meeting the preceptor, one's study of Vedānta, and so on—one would not have attained knowledge. But once *karma* has become productive, nothing can stop it. No doubt the *mukta* may have reclaimed, through knowledge, his ontological independence of *karma*. Even so, he must continue to experience the results of the portion of his karmic store that has become active, until it is exhausted. As an arrow, once released, can only be allowed to fly until it spends its initial impetus, *prārabdha* must be permitted to run its course.[58] Another analogy given is the potter's wheel, which continues to spin even after the potter ceases pushing it, until its momentum dissipates.[59] Thus, the body of the knower of Brahman must continue to exist until activity and experience exhaust all remaining *prārabdha-karma*, at which time physical death ensues.

Is *Jīvanmukti* Complete Liberation?

In explaining the *prārabdha-karma* theory, Śaṅkara makes a significant concession. Once we admit the continuation of *karma*, we must also accept, in some sense, a continuation of the force of *avidyā*: "Even though annulled, wrong knowledge persists for a time, . . . because of its residual impression (*saṃskāra*)."[60] The intention seems to be to create a basis for the persistence of *karma*, on the assumption that, without some lingering force of ignorance, the *prārabdha* would have no support (*avaṣṭambha*,

BSŚ 4.1.19). It would have to dissolve like the false appearance it truly is. But this doctrine is problematic, because it is not clear how it fits with Śaṅkara's teaching that knowledge destroys all ignorance, that knowledge and ignorance cannot coexist in the same individual, and that even knowledge itself as a mental state cannot persist after having accomplished its result.[61] Śaṅkara attempts to circumvent this problem by speaking of the persistence of an *impression* of ignorance rather than ignorance itself. Nevertheless, it remains difficult to square this idea with Advaitic doctrine of the radical sufficiency of knowledge for uprooting ignorance without remainder.[62] As long as the impression of ignorance and the continued activity of *karma* persist, there would seem to be the prospect of the sage's liberation being somehow limited. Elsewhere, we have seen, Śaṅkara emphatically denies the possibility of partial liberation. Is he now saying that the presence of *karma* (read: a physical body) does, after all, constitute an obstruction to the knower's freedom?

One would not expect to find the great Advaitin slighting *jñāna* in favor of *karma*. But at least in the case of *prārabdha-karma* he does. In his commentary on *BU* 1.4.7, to give the most remarkable example, he speaks of the "weakness of the operation of knowledge (*jñāna-pravṛtti-daurbalya*)," in comparison with that of *prārabdha*: "Because the fruition of the *karma* that has produced the body is inevitable, activity of speech, mind, and body will be necessary, even after the attainment of right knowledge. As the flight of the arrow that has been released [is stronger than any effort to arrest it], the *karma* that has already become active is stronger (*balīyas*) [than right knowledge]." In the face of this admission, Śaṅkara finds it necessary to add an uncharacteristic reference to yogic praxis. The Brahman-knower, in some cases, may need to employ methods of disciplined concentration to overcome the power of *prārabdha-karma*: "Therefore one must maintain a continuous stream of recollection of Self-knowledge by having recourse to the strength of disciplines (*sādhana*) such as renunciation and detachment."[63]

In several of the passages in which he discuses *prārabdha*, Śaṅkara suggests something very much like the later Advaitins' concept of *videhamukti*. That is, he introduces the idea of a literally disembodied, post-mortem liberation that he appears to think of as a soteriological advance over the state enjoyed by the living Brahman-knower. Commenting on *BS* 3.3.32, 4.1.15, and 4.1.19, for example, Śaṅkara indicates that the knower does not achieve his final goal until after his *prārabdha* is exhausted. Only with the "fall of the body" (*śarīra-pāta*) that comes with the dissipation of karmic momentum, he says, does the knower achieve perfect "isolation" (*kaivalya*) or "rest" (*kṣema*), terms connoting complete transcendence of all empirical awareness. And only when this occurs does the knower truly "attain Brahman (*brahma sampadyate*)."[64]

The scriptural source of this line of thinking is *ChU* 6.14.2: "For him the delay is only so long as he is not released, then he attains."[65] Śaṅkara cites this text frequently in support of the *prārabdha-karma* theory. On the passage itself, he comments: "[The delay is] in attaining the essence of the Self which is Being. . . . Until the fall of the body (*deha-pāta*) caused by the exhaustion of the *karma* by which the body is commenced, this is the meaning. At that very time, he attains Being."[66] From one who speaks of liberation as an absolute state, without gradations, such talk of further "attainment" is perplexing. For Śaṅkara to suggest *prārabdha-karma* as an explanation of the *mukta's* continued embodiment is by itself not problematic. But it does raise questions when he suggests that *prārabdha* somehow limits the *mukta's* attainment. After all, this is the master who teaches his students to proclaim boldly: "I *am* the eternally accomplished *mokṣa*."[67] If continued embodiedness itself is no hindrance to full liberation, why should the principles invoked to explain it be such? Or is embodiedness somehow a lingering imperfection after all? In this connection, compare Śaṅkara's comments on *ChU* 6.14.2, just cited, with his remarks on *BU* 4.4.6: "This knower is Brahman in this very life, though he appears to have a body, as it were. . . . Because he has no desires that obstruct his being Brahman, therefore, 'being but *Brahman* he is merged in Brahman' in this very life, not after the fall of the body (*śarīra-pāta*)."[68] Here, Śaṅkara holds to the more radical non-dualist vision we have been considering all along. The liberated sage is Brahman while living; he does not have to attain Brahman after death. How do we explain the striking contradiction between these two positions?

One possibility is that the *prārabdha-karma* doctrine and its implication that final attainment must be postponed until the death of the body represent an exegetical compromise. Śaṅkara is interpreting texts considered ancient even in his time. Though he regards them as impersonal expressions of eternal truth, they do not necessarily reflect his post-Buddhist, non-dualist metaphysics.[69] Thus, it may have been unavoidable for Śaṅkara to make some kind of concession (or adaption) to the more realistic worldview of these texts. The language of post-liberation "attainment" (*sampatti*), in fact, occurs only in connection with *ChU* 6.14.2, from which it is derived.[70]

Another possibility is that these notions, especially the idea of delay, are all articulated only from the viewpoint of empirical appearance (*vyavahāra*). From the time of Gauḍapāda, the characteristic method of Advaitic teaching has been to postulate a preliminary view and then cancel it in favor of a higher one (*adhyāropa-apavāda*). As Karl Potter reminds us, the subtleties of Advaita's "paradoxical double-level" view of reality can be applied to the *jīvanmukta* as easily as to other problems.[71] Indeed, this way of approaching the question of living liberation became important in certain texts produced by the late Śaṅkara tradition. The *Vivekacūḍāmaṇi* (*ViCū*) and the *Aparokṣānubhūti*, for example, explicitly deny that *prārabdha-karma* has any hold on the knower who is identified with the Self. They argue that the scriptures that speak of the total destruction of ignorance by knowledge should be taken seriously. It is only to satisfy the ignorant, they assert, that *prārabdha* has been postulated as an "exoteric doctrine" (*bāhya-dṛṣṭi*).[72] Modern Hindu interpreters seem to favor such a strategy. Thus R. Balasubramanian writes: "Though the knower of Brahman . . . is not bound by the aggregate of mind-sense-body and is, therefore, disembodied from his own perspective, yet from the *vyāvahārika* perspective the body which has been sublated as false continues for some time till the exhaustion of *prārabdha-karma* through experience."[73] Is then the notion of the sage living out of a set of limitations imposed by his *prārabdha* a preliminary view, intended to speak to the concerns of unenlightened outside observers? It is, at least, legitimate to ask.

Although Deutsch may be overstating the case to speak of *karma* in Advaita as a "convenient fiction," he is certainly correct when he says, "There is nothing within the state of being designated by 'Brahman' or 'Ātman' that admits of being subject to *karma*."[74] Śaṅkara himself declares, "With the sole exception of liberation, everything else comes within the realm of ignorance."[75] When he relativizes even scripture itself as something to be transcended in liberation,[76] how much more must he do the same for all *karma*, including *prārabdha*?

Passages can be found in Śaṅkara from which such a denial of the ultimacy of the *prārabdha-karma* doctrine would logically follow. At *BSŚ* 1.1.4, for example, he presents as the view of his opponents the idea that embodiedness is caused by merit and demerit and that, consequently, disembodiedness can come only when the body falls. Against this position, he argues that the embodiedness of the Self is merely apparent: it is caused by wrong knowledge only. Because the Self has no real relationship to the body, it cannot acquire merit and demerit. The idea that merit and demerit can cause the embodiment of the Self, he concludes, must therefore be false. In his commentary on *BhG* 18.48, Śaṅkara comes even closer to undercutting the *prārabdha-karma* doctrine. He declares that for the knower, "there can be no question of any remainder (*śeṣa*) of what was superimposed by ignorance."[77]

But it is still true that Śaṅkara never explicitly negates or relativizes the notion of *prārabdha-karma*. Indeed the suggestion at *BUŚ* 1.4.7, discussed above, that the *jīvanmukta* may have to engage in spiritual discipline to avoid being unduly influenced by *prārabdha*, would seem to preclude the notion that Śaṅkara speaks of it only from the empirical (*vyāvahārika*) point of view. If the *jīvanmukta* himself has to take cognizance of *prārabdha*, and perhaps even struggle to overcome it, it cannot be merely a device to satisfy the mind of the ignorant onlooker. So we must remain open to another interpretation: that Śaṅkara understands *prārabdha* as a significant limitation, one that the knower can by no means dismiss completely. The ideas expressed in his commentaries on *ChU* 6.14.2 and *BS* 4.1.15 imply that *jīvanmukti* is a state in which one is liberated and yet somehow must still undergo a further liberation, a further attainment, at death. As J. G. Arapura suggests, Śaṅkara describes a "waiting for *mukti*" that, because it is under the sway of knowledge, can itself be considered *mukti*, yet without making the waiting pointless.[78] One thinks in this connection of *Kaṭha* 2.2.1: "Being liberated [already], he is liberated."[79] What could this second liberation involve? What would make waiting for it meaningful for one who is already liberated? Surely it is not the promise of some change in the essential nature of the liberated state. Śaṅkara has ruled this out. The total falling away of empirical experience is the only possibility. At *BSŚ* 4.4.16, Śaṅkara suggests that *kaivalya* is characterized by an "absence of specific cognition" (*viśeṣa-saṃjñābhāva*). In this respect, he says, some have compared it with the state of deep sleep. This helps us understand what he means when, at *BSŚ* 3.3.32, he speaks of the *mukta's* ultimate state as complete "cessation in isolation" (*kaivalya-nivṛtti*).

Whatever Śaṅkara's final view might have been, and I think we have to say that we cannot be sure, it is significant that the classical Advaita tradition has clung tenaciously to the *prārabdha-karma* theory and the associated idea of a continuing force of ignorance. These notions, along with *ChU* 6.14.2 and its idea of delay, are invariably introduced in post-Śaṅkara discussions of *jīvanmukti*. Most important, these ideas are not relativized by shifts in ontological perspective—phenomenal "truth" to absolute Truth, *vyāvahārika* to *pāramārthika*—except in late, popular texts such as those already mentioned. Rather, they are taken quite seriously, as we shall now see.

Justifications of *Jīvanmukti* in Post-Śaṅkara Advaita

The majority of post-Śaṅkara Advaitins believe in the possibility of *jīvanmukti*. All but Maṇḍana Miśra (actually a contemporary of Śaṅkara) accept the theory of *prārabdha-karma* as well. They give the *prārabdha* concept little elaboration, however; most present essentially the same argument by analogy used by the great preceptor. They devote greater effort to further articulating the notion of the effect or remnant of ignorance that remains to support the operation of *prārabdha*. In general, we can observe a concern to minimize the impact on the *jīvanmukta* of any residual element of bondage. Nevertheless, none of the classical Advaitins are willing to discount its power altogether. Indeed, we shall see that all of them understand the continuance of *prārabdha* and its support as to some degree, greater or lesser, a limitation on the fullness of *mokṣa*.

Maṇḍana Miśra in his *Brahmasiddhi* (*BSdh*) is perhaps the first of the classical Advaitins to use *jīvanmukti* as a technical term.[80] Maṇḍana is exceptional, however, and his approach differs from that of Śaṅkara and other Advaitins, in that he denies that *prārabdha-karma* can be operative in *jīvanmukti*. Going against Śaṅkara's analogy, Maṇḍana claims that the flying arrow of commenced *karma* can be stopped. Knowledge does indeed destroy all *karma*. Maṇḍana's divergence from the mainstream here seems, however, to be of little consequence. The body still continues in liberation—not from *prārabdha* itself, to be sure, but from the impressions (*saṃskāra*) of both *avidyā* and *prārabdha*. So the analogy of the continued movement of the potter's wheel serves Maṇḍana just as well as Śaṅkara. Maṇḍana refers in addition to the trembling that persists—due to the *saṃskāra* of the fear—even after one knows an apparent snake to be nothing but a rope. For Maṇḍana, the ripening of *karma* that supports *jīvanmukti* is an appearance (*vipākābhāsa*), a mere semblance (*ābhāsa-mātra*) that does not bind the liberated individual.[81]

Sureśvara (eighth century), in his commentary on Śaṅkara's *BUŚ*, explains the appearance of desires and other imperfections in the knower as having their origin in the body, which continues because of commenced *karma* (*BUBhV* 1.4.1529). In his *Naiṣkarmyasiddhi* (*NS*), he makes no mention at all of *prārabdha*. He does speak, however, of the effects of ignorance (*moha-kārya*). These may continue even though ignorance itself has been completely destroyed (*vidhvastākhila-moho 'pi*). He echoes the illustration of the trembling that may persist even after the snake has vanished (*NS* 4.60).

Vimuktātman (tenth century) denies that *ChU* 6.14.2 teaches that the sage has to wait until death to realize Brahman. Indeed, he says, realization is possible only for the embodied. After death it is impossible. While thus emphatically accepting the doctrine of *jīvanmukti*, he has a quarrel with the belief of Śaṅkara and others that an impression (*saṃskāra*) of ignorance can exist in the absence of ignorance itself. What will support it? He therefore insists that not an impression but an actual remnant or residuum (*leśa*, *śeṣa*) of ignorance remains (*IS* 1.9). While this move from impression to remnant would seem to threaten a more serious limitation on the *mukta's* freedom, Vimuktātman is, among the classical post-Śaṅkara Advaitins, the most unequivocal supporter of the *jīvanmukti* doctrine. He takes great pains to minimize the effect of the *avidyā-leśa* on the *mukta*. The remnant of ignorance, he declares, "skillfully brings about a mere appearance of the remainder of *prārabdha* enjoyment."[82] The sage's knowledge is not obstructed thereby:

> There is no conflict between knowledge and the experience of *prārabdha-karma*. So the body of the knower remains until the experience of *prārabdha* is completed. Here, just as knowledge does not contradict experience [of *prārabdha*], so experience does not contradict knowledge.[83]

Sarvajñātman (eleventh century) uses a variety of terms to designate the aftereffect of *avidyā* that supports *prārabdha*, including scent (*gandha*), shadow (*chāyā*), remnant (*leśa*), and impression (*saṃskāra*). The process of exhausting the *prārabdha-karma* that leads to the *mukta's* final freedom (*kaivalya*) at death, he says, is sustained by a "scent of darkness" (*dhvānta-gandha*). This lingering influence of ignorance accounts for the remnant or shadow of duality (*dvaita-leśa*, *dvaita-cchāyā*) experienced by the *jīvanmukta* (*SŚ* 4.40–46). However problematic the idea of *jīvanmukti* may be, we must admit it "because it is a matter of direct awareness (*pratīteḥ*)." "In this case," he believes, "one's own experience (*svānubhūti*) must be the authority."[84]

Citsukha (thirteenth century) identifies *prārabdha-karma* as the cause, in *jīvanmukti*, of a remnant (*leśa*) of *avidyā* or *māyā*. He defines this residue as a "special form (*ākāra*) of ignorance." Anticipating the later distinction between the "projecting" and "concealing" powers of *māyā*, discussed below, Citsukha explains that ignorance, though one, has at least three forms. The first creates the illusion that the universe is real. The second causes us to take the various constituents of the empirical world seriously as having practical utility. The third is responsible only for the bare appearance (*pratibhāsa*) of the forms of objects in immediate perception. With the arising of knowledge, the first and second modes—which give rise to the sense of duality—are dissolved. But the third is not. It remains to support the empirical experience of the *mukta*. According to this author, no one should deny the possibility of *jīvanmukti* out of mere prejudice, for its truth is proclaimed in all the scriptures (*śruti-smṛti-purāṇādiṣu*).[85]

Bhāratītīrtha-Vidyāraṇya (fourteenth century) also argues for the continuance of the body on the basis of residual impressions. He uses the analogies of the momentum of the potter's wheel and the fear that lingers as an aftereffect of an illusory snake. He refers as well to the scent of flowers that remains in the vase after the flowers are removed. (Other authors mention the persistence of the odor of garlic.)[86] While knowledge destroys ignorance immediately and completely, the residual impression (*saṃskāra*) of ignorance and its products—the body and the universe—may continue for some time longer. The effects are not opposed to knowledge directly, as is their cause, ignorance. For those who have difficulty with the idea of the *saṃskāra* persisting without *avidyā*, its material cause, Bhāratītīrtha is flexible. He is also willing to accept the presence in *jīvanmukti* of a remnant (*leśa*) of ignorance (*VPS* 1.165–166; *PD* 7.244). In the *PD*, however, he seems to think the idea of remnant unnecessary. This text argues for the possibility of an interval elapsing between the destruction of the material cause, *avidyā*, and the disappearance of its effects by reference to a doctrine from the Nyāya system. The color of an object may persist for a moment, the Naiyāyikas admit, even after the object itself has been removed from sight. But if the effect can exist without its cause for one moment, the Advaitin argues, why not for many moments?[87] The length of the interval between the destruction of ignorance and the disappearance of its effects—the *mukta's* empirical experience—is determined by the *prārabdha-karma*.

Madhusūdana Sarasvatī (sixteenth century) repeats these arguments, for both *saṃskāra* and *leśa*, complete with the analogy of the flower's scent. He also develops the view found in Citsukha that ignorance has various forms (*ākāra*). For Madhusūdana *avidyā* has two fundamental powers (*śakti*): the projective (*vikṣepa*) and the concealing (*āvaraṇa*). The former is responsible for manifesting all the forms and phenomena in creation. The latter performs the function of obscuring the unchanging Reality that underlies the whole. Knowledge, says Madhusūdana, destroys only the concealing power of *avidyā*. It leaves the creative potency of the *vikṣepa-śakti* intact to maintain the bodily activity of the *mukta*. Following Citsukha, he asserts that this projective aspect of *avidyā* itself has three aspects. Each creates a different perception of the world of duality: the first as real (*dvaita-satyatva*), the second as merely provisional (*vyāvahārika*), and the third as illusory (*prātibhāsika*). This third, most attenuated, power of ignorance constitutes an innocuous residuum (*leśa*). It does not detract from the realization of the knower, nor does it tie him to the results of his activity. Nevertheless, it remains capable of supporting the outworking of *prārabdha* until the latter is exhausted.[88]

Reservations about *Jīvanmukti* in Post-Śaṅkara Advaita

Post-Śaṅkara Advaitins are thus, on the whole, anxious to find support for the idea of *jīvanmukti*. Nevertheless, most have misgivings. The radical "one-soul" theorists such as Prakāśānanda, we have seen, flatly deny the notion of living liberation. While mainstream Advaitins disagree emphatically with this idea, their support for *jīvanmukti* is not without a measure of ambiguity.

Several among those who accept *jīvanmukti* seem to do so as one possible theory rather than as a final position. That is, they are not willing to rule out the prospect that the rise of knowledge may entail total, instantaneous transcendence of empirical form. Arguments for this possibility, which they know as "immediate liberation" (*sadyomukti*), cannot, they believe, be completely dismissed.

Maṇḍana, for example, cites *MuU* 2.2.8. This verse, we have seen, suggests that knowledge destroys all *karmas* (note the plural) without remainder. Maṇḍana sees that this passage is difficult to reconcile with the concept of *prārabdha-karma* and that it compels consideration of the *sadyomukti* position. Some might rightly object, Maṇḍana notes, that the notion of immediate liberation negates the traditional ideal of the sage of "steady wisdom" (*sthita-prajña*), extolled at *BhG* 2.54–71. And indeed, Maṇḍana himself is willing to tolerate this outcome. He concedes that such an individual might not be a fully liberated sage (*siddha*) after all, but only an advanced aspirant (*sādhaka*).[89]

Sureśvara in his *Naiṣkarmyasiddhi* presents a similar treatment of the *sadyomukti-jīvanmukti* question. He begins by teaching that right knowledge once and for all destroys all ignorance and all becoming (*akhilaṃ bhavam*) without remainder (*NS* 4.57). On this view, there is "no ignorance left unconsumed."[90] He then goes on to admit what he calls "another traditional teaching" (*aparas sāmpradāyikaḥ*, *NS* 4.60). This, as explained above, is the possibility of a lingering "effect of ignorance." Jñānottama (twelfth century), in his comments on this passage, explains the first view as the "immediate liberation" position (*sadyomukti-pakṣa*) and the second as the doctrine of living liberation (*jīvanmukti-pakṣa*).

Sarvajñātman repeats this pattern. Prior to his discussion of *jīvanmukti*, he presents as a valid alternative the view that the rise of knowledge brings all empirical existence to an immediate end. In support, he marshals an array of arguments for *sadyomukti* that were later more fully developed by Prakāśānanda (*SŚ* 4.38–39). The rise of knowledge instantly destroys the entirety of ignorance and all its products. Passages of scripture describing *jīvanmuktas* are therefore merely for inspiration. Fully enlightened teachers cannot exist; they must be fabricated by ignorance (*avidyā-parikalpita*, *SŚ* 2.225, 227, 233).

Unlike the above three teachers, Prakāśātman (tenth century) is firm on the possibility of *jīvanmukti*. It must be accepted, he tells us, because there are numerous scriptural references to paradigmatic sages such as Vyāsa. Nevertheless, his treatment shows us just how limited the post-Śaṅkara Advaitin's conception of *jīvanmukti* can become. Despite his unmistakable affirmation of the state, Prakāśātman willingly describes certain ways in which living liberation is flawed. Most striking is his account of the unsteadiness of the *mukta's* experience. One cannot, he believes, be aware of the world and one's identity with Brahman at the same time. Only when one is in meditative enstasis (*samādhi*) can one enjoy oneness with the Self. At other times, however, the knower slips into dualistic awareness (*dvaita-darśana*) because of the continued activity of his bodily *karma*, which remains as a defect (*doṣa*) to cloud his vision.[91]

Both Citsukha and Bhāratītīrtha continue this theme. For Citsukha, *prārabdha* is to be taken seriously as a "potent" (*prabala*) force that functions as an obstruction (*pratibandha*) to the power of knowledge. The remnant of *avidyā* that it forces upon the *mukta* is transcended only through meditative enstasis or death:

> In the case of the *jīvanmukta*, a remnant of *māyā* is not destroyed. Though it disappears in the state of *samādhi*, at other times it remains as the cause of the appearance (*ābhāsa*) of the world and the body. When the enjoyment of the fruits of the *prārabdha-karma* comes to an end, it ceases.[92]

Bhāratītīrtha describes the continuance of the residual impression of ignorance as a defect (*doṣa*) and *prārabdha-karma* as an obstacle (*pratibandhaka*). The final *mokṣa* is not attained until the *prārabdha* is exhausted and the body falls (*VPS* 1.165–166). Meanwhile, by the force of this *karma*, the Brahman-knower is subject to desires and may even sometimes lapse into doubts (*PD* 6.263, 7.245–246). This is not surprising, for Bhāratītīrtha, like his predecessors just mentioned, believes that awareness of unity and the perception of multiplicity cannot coexist:

> One should not think it possible for the *jīvanmukta* to have the experience of the oneness of the Self (*ātmaikyānubhava*) and the cognition of duality (*dvaita-darśana*), which are mutually contradictory, at the same time. For we do not assert their simultaneity, but rather that they arise and are overpowered in succession.[93]

The experience of non-duality thus being unstable, any activity on the *jīvanmukta's* part is interpreted as a sign that he has fallen into dualistic awareness. Even the minimal daily round permitted a *saṃnyāsin* is suspect: "The activity of going about for alms," we are told, "is caused by the defect of *prārabdha*."[94] This understanding leads Bhāratītīrtha to conceive an unusual argument in support of the standard Advaitic view that the renouncer ought not participate in Vedic rites. Such rituals must conform to fixed schedules, he reminds us. Once begun they must be brought to their proper conclusion. But the functioning of the karmic obstruction that would allow the *mukta* to participate in activity is unpredictable. Even when it manifests itself, it is unsteady: "For the knower of Reality, the emergence (*udbhāva*) of the defect caused by commenced *karma* is not fixed as to place and time, and it is not possible for it to continue long enough for him to complete any [ritual] performance that he has undertaken."[95]

Underlying such discussions is the implication that the *jīvanmukta* is better off—somehow more fully liberated—when in *samādhi* than when aware of body and world. This is confirmed by Madhusūdana Sarasvatī, who describes with approval a scheme from the *Yogavāsiṣṭha* that admits three degrees in the attainment of *jīvanmukti*. At the highest level, the *mukta* enters a state of *samādhi* so deeply absorbing that he can neither rouse himself nor be roused by others. He has no cognition of difference whatever (*sarvathā bheda-darśanābhāva*). Rather, he is constantly and completely identified with the Self (*sarvadā tanmaya*). Others, then, must take care of his bodily needs. Having attained total disengagement from the world, he abides always in a state of unalloyed supreme bliss. He then merits the title "most excellent knower of Brahman."[96]

Given such praise of world-oblivion, it is not too surprising to find Madhusūdana devaluing *jīvanmukti* as "mere liberation" (*mukti-mātra*), in comparison to the "supreme liberation" (*parama-mukti*) attained when one breathes one's last breath. As desirable as *jīvanmukti* may be, it is not the same as the final state. There is, Madhusūdana claims, a greater manifestation of bliss in the final mental mode (*vṛtti*) that leads to *parama-mukti* than in that which grants *jīvanmukti*. This is because the latter is contaminated by the projective power of ignorance maintained by *prārabdha*, while the former is not.[97]

Commenting on Madhusūdana, Brahmānanda Sarasvatī (early eighteenth century) is perhaps as doubtful as one can be about living liberation without denying it altogether. He argues that the persistence of ignorance in the form of a *saṃskāra* in *jīvanmukti* makes any talk of the cessation of ignorance in that state only figurative. True liberation (*mukhyo mokṣaḥ*) can only be disembodied, post-mortem liberation, because ignorance truly ceases only at the time of death.[98]

What are we to make of the reservations expressed by these writers? Although they disagree on details, all concur that any continued embodiment is somehow, whether through impression or remnant, a product of ignorance. They agree, furthermore, that this ignorance constitutes in some sense a limitation of the liberated state. Indeed, they harbor strong doubts that perfect knowledge can coexist with any form of empirical awareness. Some scholars, we have seen, argue that Advaita offers a sophisticated "two-level" approach to this problem, inclusive of both *pāramārthika* and *vyāvahārika* perspectives. However, orthodox post-Śaṅkara Advaitins do not use this strategy. Maṇḍana wonders whether any embodied person can be more than an advanced *sādhaka*. Prakāśātman and Bhāratītīrtha hold that one cannot have non-dual awareness and empirical consciousness at the same time. Even Śaṅkara suggests that yogic praxis might be necessary to counter the effects of *prārabdha*. So it is not a question of, as modern interpreters would have it, both complete *mukti* from the liberated sage's *pāramārthika* perspective and karmically limited *mukti* from that of the ignorant observer. On the contrary, for these writers, the dominant figures of post-Śaṅkara Advaita, it must be either one or the other.[99]

In short, despite the generally vociferous defense of the possibility, and indeed the necessity, of *jīvanmukti* offered by the post-Śaṅkara Advaitins, the idea remains problematic for them. Although eminently desirable, living liberation is finally a limited state. The classical Advaita tradition stays wedded to the theory of karmic obstruction derived from *ChU* 6.14.2 and *BS* 4.1.15. The *jīvanmukta* must wait, looking forward to a final *kaivalya* or, in the later tradition, *videhamukti*. Advaita never finds a way of fully appropriating for the liberated sage the vision of a seemingly embodied yet fully liberated Brahman-knowledge that Śaṅkara articulates when he is in his ontological mode. The master's scholastic followers allow themselves to fall into what could easily be described as an excessively realistic interpretation of *avidyā*, *karma*, and embodiedness. Despite protestations to the contrary, Advaita winds up with a vision of *jīvanmukti* that is not all that different from the Sāṃkhya position, that is, a waiting for the passing away of the world with a view to eternal, absolute "isolation" in spirit.[100] The tradition thus loses sight of and even seems to qualify its most central doctrine: that knowledge has the radical power to neutralize ignorance and bondage irrespective of embodiedness or the lack thereof. Śaṅkara himself was, for the most part, much bolder than his followers on this point. Nevertheless, he himself introduces the weaker trend of thought in his discussion of *prārabdha*. He is thus to some extent responsible for the history of compromise that surrounds Advaita's thinking on living liberation and karmic limitation.

Īśvara as Paradigm for Living Liberation

It is both curious and revealing that the proponents of Advaita have never explored to any significant extent one avenue of thought that might have helped them toward a more adequate conceptualization of living liberation. At the very heart of their tradition lies a paradigm that affirms dramatically the combination of knowledge, liberation, and continued empirical consciousness that the ideal of *jīvanmukti* seems to entail. As Eliade has suggested, it is the idea of Īśvara.

The Lord creates, maintains, and destroys the entire cosmic display. He serves as the underlying and directing cause of the infinite number of karmic forces—*prārabdha* and otherwise—that are playing themselves out in his vast universe (*BSŚ* 2.1.34). He causes beings to be bound in *saṃsāra*, directs them to act in accord with their *karma*, and effects their release by his grace (*BSŚ* 2.3.41–42). Yet all the while the Lord remains unaffected by the suffering and the defects of the individual souls (*BSŚ* 2.3.46). He is, in Śaṅkara's words, "eternally free of ignorance" (*nitya-nivṛttāvidya, BSŚ* 3.2.9). In the midst of his ceaseless cosmic activity he is "eternally pure, enlightened, and liberated" (*nitya-śuddha-buddha-mukta, BhGŚ* 1.1). Far from being the victim of *avidyā*, Īśvara is its wielder, the controller of *māyā* (*māyāvin, māyā-niyantṛ*),[101] projecting the world in mere play.

There is thus one paradigmatic instance of the coexistence of perfect knowledge and perfect liberation with awareness of, and activity in, the world. But recall Eliade's suggestion that the *jīvanmukta* attains a similar divine and paradoxical mode of being. Does the logic of Advaita not, in fact, move the liberated sage toward a posture of freedom identical to Īśvara's? Sarvajñātman tells us that the Lord is different from the transmigrating *jīva* in at least three respects: He is free of ignorance, free of ego-sense (*ahaṃkṛti*), and ever liberated (*SŚ* 2.175–188). But are not these qualities—freedom from ignorance, ego, and bondage—precisely the characteristics of the *mukta*, as defined by Śaṅkara? To be sure, the liberated sage may have realized his freedom only lately, in time. In that sense, the liberation of the *jīva* is not eternal. Once attained, however, *mokṣa* is beyond time. This Śaṅkara emphasizes repeatedly.

Leaving aside for the moment limitations the liberated sage may suffer due to his *prārabdha-karma* and any associated trace of ignorance, it is not difficult to find in Śaṅkara suggestions of the ultimate identity of *jīva* and Īśvara. "To assume the otherness of *jīva* and Īśvara is not proper," he says. "*Jīva* is not other than Īśvara, but its knowledge and lordship are obscured by its conjunction with the body."[102] Again: "The distinction between *jīva* and the Supreme Lord is based on wrong knowledge alone, not on reality itself."[103] Elsewhere, Śaṅkara speaks of "the false idea of difference between Īśvara and the transmigrating self, caused by non-discrimination, which results in the latter's connection with limiting adjuncts such as the body."[104] Twice in the *Upadeśasāhasrī* Śaṅkara declares, "I am Īśvara."[105]

Despite these and other suggestive passages, post-Śaṅkara Advaita never seriously explores the idea of the identity of the liberated sage and Īśvara. The theme of the sage's oneness with God is developed only in the thought of Appayya Dīkṣita (sixteenth century), an Advaitin who was deeply influenced by Śaivism. Appayya writes that the attainment of liberation, even in its literally disembodied form, involves, not the realization of oneness with the transcendent Brahman, but rather identity with Īśvara. This is a consequence of his preferred theory of relation of *jīva* and Īśvara. For Appayya, the Lord is Brahman itself, but appearing as the original (*bimba*) of which the *jīva* is a reflection (*pratibimba*). *Mukti* is the merger of the reflection (*jīva*) in its original, which in this view is Īśvara, not the pure Absolute. Appayya therefore understands liberation as the attainment of Lordship (*īśvaratva*), i.e., conscious identity with the personal God. It is not, or not yet, the realization of complete identity with the transpersonal Brahman. As long as other reflections—other *jīvas*—continue to exist, the Lord also must continue to exist as their *bimba*, and there can be no final merger in the Absolute for the souls that have attained identity with him.[106]

Advaitins have not generally accepted Appayya's theory.[107] Nevertheless, Advaita does recognize that the localized psycho-physical individuality of each *jīva* is always at the same time a part of the cosmic adjunct (*upādhi*) of Īśvara.[108] It must follow, then, that the *jīvanmukta* enjoys this connection with the Lord also, at least as long as his individuality endures. The difference is that the *mukta's* connection is manifest, unobscured by ego. The logic of Advaita requires that, with the attainment of liberation, the sage's false identification with the mind-body complex must vanish. Having realized his nature as *Ātman*, the *mukta* should have completely withdrawn from connection with empirical limitations, like—says the Chāndogya Upaniṣad—the snake who has shed its skin. What appears to be his own activity ought now to be completely surrendered to, and governed by, Īśvara.[109] Thus, Madhusūdana proclaims that the *jīvanmukta's* "life and breath are directed by the Supreme Lord."[110] Strictly speaking, of course, the analogy of the snake and its skin would be inaccurate here. There should properly be no more snake at all, because the liberated Brahman-knower ought to have ceased to exist as an individual ego-center. Nothing should remain but the primordial reality: on one hand, the unbounded pure consciousness of Brahman, abiding timelessly as the Self of all; on the other, Īśvara's cosmic activity. And there is no reason why the latter should not continue to include the *jīvanmukta's* former individuality, together with its karmic momentum, its actions, and perhaps even its desires and doubts.

Such, at any rate, is the vision of liberation that enables the *Bhagavad Gītā*—and the Advaita tradition itself when it follows its deepest insight—to show God as exemplar for the liberated sage. Again, I follow Eliade:

> It could be said that the essence of the doctrine revealed by Kṛṣṇa is contained in the formula: "Understand Me and imitate Me!" For everything that he reveals regarding his own Being and his "behavior" in the cosmos and in history is to serve as model and example for Arjuna.[111]

Consider the way in which the third chapter of the *Gītā* draws together our understanding of God and the *mukta*. In verses 20–26, Kṛṣṇa invites us to reflect on the parallels between his mode of action as God and that of the liberated sage. He holds up his cosmic activity as paradigmatic: "I have, O Pārtha, in the three worlds nothing whatever I must do, nothing unattained that must be attained. Yet I continue in action."[112] Kṛṣṇa advises knowers (*vidvān*) to remain involved in the world in the same manner he does: to follow his divine example.

In his comments on *BhG* 3.25, Śaṅkara makes the equation of the Lord's mode of activity and that of the sage even more explicit. Glossing the text, Śaṅkara assumes the voice of Kṛṣṇa. We hear God, eternally liberated, speaking to those who have become liberated in time. The Lord speaks to them fraternally, as if they were almost his equals, teaching them how to live their new mode of existence in the way he always has: "Like Me (*aham iva*), if you or others are knowers of the Self and are [thus] conscious of having attained all that is to be attained, you must continue to work for the benefit of others, even though there is no necessity for you to do so." Introducing verse 26, he continues: "For Me or any other knower of the Self desirous of effecting the welfare of the world, there is no action to be done but that which is for the welfare of the world."[113] Here a few small words—"Like Me," "For Me or any other knower"—are invested with profound implications. Śaṅkara's Kṛṣṇa brings the *jīvanmukta* and Īśvara very close indeed.

This homology between the activity of God and that of the knower emerges most clearly in Śaṅkara's comments on *BhG* 2.11. There he writes that we cannot understand the activity of the knower of Brahman in any ordinary way. Only the divine paradigm is adequate. "The action of the knower, being similarly free from ego and the desire for results, is like the action that Lord Vāsudeva [Kṛṣṇa] performed in fulfillment of his duties as a warrior."[114]

The reference in this passage to the earthly activity of Kṛṣṇa reminds us of the concept of *avatāra*, or divine incarnation. Śaṅkara uses it here to throw light on the activity of the *mukta*. If the Lord and his cosmic activity are paradigmatic in a general way, then the concept of his particular embodiment as *avatāra* may be a singularly instructive special case. Again we turn to Śaṅkara:

> The Blessed Lord . . . controlling his own *māyā*, . . . appears (*lakṣyate*), to work the welfare of the world, as if possessed of a body (*dehavān iva*), as if born (*jāta iva*), though in reality he is unborn, imperishable, the Lord of all beings, in nature eternally pure, free, and liberated.[115]

The Lord, again, is eternally liberated (*nitya-mukta*) and completely in control of *māyā*. Even when he—embodied as the *avatāra*—seems to be in *māyā's* grip, it is only "as if" (*iva*). In reality he is above the appearance. But if the *jīvanmukta* has realized a state homologous with Īśvara, his embodiment ought to be qualified with a similar "as if." Śaṅkara bears this out: "The knower is Brahman in this very life, though he appears as if possessed of a body (*dehavān iva lakṣyate*)."[116] Note carefully the language used in both passages—one describing the *avatāra's* mode of being, the other that of the *jīvanmukta*. It is identical. The passage from Sarvajñātman at the beginning of this chapter further confirms that, like the embodiment of the *avatāra*, the *mukta's* is deceptive: "I appear as if living (*jīvann iva*)." When Śaṅkara holds up the activity of Kṛṣṇa as a model for the life of the *jīvanmukta*, then, it is not merely for inspiration. With the exception, of course, of the Lord's power to control the universal *māyā*,[117] the liberated sage is called to—and has a real potential for—an authentic realization of the divine mode of being.

Even Īśvara Suffers Limitation

But what about *prārabdha-karma* and the trace of ignorance that is invoked to support it? Do not these elements of living liberation—which have no claim on the Lord's experience—cause the homology between the *jīvanmukta* and Īśvara to break down? Perhaps. But before the parallel is abandoned, let us see if we can extend it a bit further. Perhaps it will help us to gain insight into the limitations of living liberation as well.

Again using Īśvara as the paradigm, consider Śaṅkara's view that "the Supreme Lord neither identifies with a body nor imagines pain to be his own." It is this lack of false identification, we are told, that allows Īśvara to be free from the sufferings and other defects of the individual souls (*BSŚ* 2.3.46). But, if such lack of empirical identification is the condition of the Lord's freedom, it is—the tradition asserts—a qualification possessed by the *mukta* as well. The latter, then, should enjoy a similar benefit. Why must the liberated sage be limited by the karmic momentum that governs his psycho-physical apparatus? No doubt, *prārabdha-karma* determines the activities and potentials of his empirical adjuncts. But no Advaitin would suggest that this could impinge on his transcendent identity as Self. The *mukta* has homologized himself to the divine by shifting his identity to the transcendent. He ought no longer to be limited in his true being by anything that conditions his empirical personhood.

Suppose, on the other hand, we admit what many Advaitins seem to fear: that *prārabdha-karma* does somehow limit the *jīvanmukta's* freedom. Even so, it need not necessarily upset the homology between the liberated sage and God. On the contrary, it could further confirm its heuristic power. Reversing the paradigm, we can look at Īśvara in light of the *jīvanmukti* doctrine. This move, though unconventional, is perhaps even more illuminating. It forces us to remember something typically forgotten: Īśvara himself is not without constraint. Indeed, it may be that he suffers from limitations similar to those faced by the *jīvanmukta*.

Śaṅkara, for example, is clear that the possibilities of the Lord's activity are limited by *karma*, in this case by the *karma* of his creatures. The Lord must, when acting to direct the destinies of *jīvas*, take their karmic limitations into consideration. Otherwise, he would be accused of injustice (*BSŚ* 2.1.34). Do such considerations bind him? If not, why should the *mukta* who has realized his identity with the infinite be bound by having to take the *prārabdha-karma* of his particular psycho-physical being into account when expressing himself empirically?

Again, if the *jīvanmukta* is limited by a remnant of ignorance, we must remember that there is a sense in which Īśvara too is limited—even constituted—by ignorance. On this Śaṅkara writes:

> Like space conforming to adjuncts such as pots and jars, the Lord conforms to adjuncts of name and form created by ignorance. . . . The Lord's being a Lord, his omniscience and his omnipotence, all depend on limitations caused by adjuncts which are products of ignorance.[118]

Īśvara is thus by definition Brahman limited by *avidyā*.[119] His existence as the Lord consists in his interaction with ignorance in the form of a cosmic *upādhi*, shot through and through with the endless *karmas* of countless beings. For this reason, Madhusūdana Sarasvatī is willing to suggest that the Lord is conditioned in a way that the soul that has attained complete liberation is not. Both Īśvara and the *mukta* are, he tells us, free of "unknowing" (*ajñātva*). They are thus fully aware of their nature as Brahman. But the Lord, unlike the *mukta*, remains defined by the ignorance that is the cause of the world (*jagan-nidānam ajñānam*).[120]

We move, therefore, toward understanding Īśvara as a kind of eternal *jīvanmukta* of cosmic dimensions. Is the Lord not, like the *jīvanmukta*, liberated but somehow not yet fully liberated? The Brahman-knowing sage waits for the final *kaivalya* that consists in absolute release from the body and mind that occasion his limited "soulhood" (*jīvatva*). Is Īśvara likewise waiting, so to say, for his own *kaivalya*? Is he waiting, as in Appayya's model, for all *jīvas* to be liberated so he can have his final rest, his cosmic *kṣema*? Is he anticipating his own *parama-mukti* or *videhamukti*, his own final liberation from the karmically conditioned adjuncts that constitute his "Godhood" (*īśvaratva*) and thus limit his true nature as Brahman? If so, his waiting will be endless, because the universe is, by definition, endless. So in this sense, at least, his limitation will be all that much greater than that of the *jīvanmukta*.[121]

Conclusion

The doctrine of *jīvanmukti* has emerged as a cornerstone of modern Advaitic faith. One reason, of course, is the intrinsic interest of the concept itself: it has a power and an attraction that is undeniable. Who would not be fascinated by the notion of living the infinite within the boundaries of the finite? But the *jīvanmukti* ideal is also significant for historical reasons, namely, that it has an important place in the Hindu counterattack against the nineteenth century Western critique of Hinduism. In the face of accusations that Hinduism is a backward and idolatrous faith (frequently based on misinformation, missionary bias, or even willful distortion), modern Advaitins have naturally retaliated, marshalling arguments for the superiority of their own religious vision. To this purpose, they have often, as in the remark by Radhakrishnan quoted at the beginning of this chapter, invoked the idea of living liberation. Contrasting their ideals with conventional religious understandings that promise true freedom only after death, modern Advaitins celebrate the possibility of complete spiritual emancipation while still living.

I recognize and am quick to honor this valorization of *jīvanmukti* as a legitimate expression of modern Hindu faith and experience. Nevertheless, my research leads me to the conviction that the living liberation offered by the classical Advaita tradition[122] is rather more limited than modern advocates would like to admit. No doubt Śaṅkara and other Advaitins present strong arguments for *jīvanmukti* when writing in their strictly ontological mode. These arguments have been presented above, and I hope I have succeeded in conveying their full force. They are taken, with ample justification, as the authentic Advaitin position by contemporary interpreters. Still, careful study shows that the classical writers fail to commit themselves fully to their own highest vision of living liberation. This fact has been obscured by the tendency of neo-Vedāntins to ignore the compromises the classical tradition makes on the question of *prārabdha-karma*.

Advaita, it should be remembered, was formulated by and for a narrow spiritual elite of male Brahmins, primarily *saṃnyāsins*, who alone were believed qualified to fully appropriate its import. Its authors and propagators saw themselves as standing at the pinnacle of a long transmigratory climb, ready at last to abandon *saṃsāra* without looking back.[123] It was never intended to be a philosophy for the general public, let alone an answer to the concerns of historically-oriented Western moralists. Despite their differences, all the major authors of the tradition were world-renouncers, and all share the assumption that *any* experience of the world is somehow, whether through impression (*saṃskāra*) or actual remnant (*leśa*), based on ignorance. If awareness of the world continues, we are told, it is caused by a defect (*doṣa*), occasioned by an obstruction (*pratibandhaka*). The implication is that the ideal state is one in which there is no empirical experience, of the world or anything else. As long as *prārabdha-karma* continues, of course, this is not possible. In *kaivalya*, however, the liberated consciousness attains complete disjunction from the world: mind, body, and nature. This, and not *jīvanmukti*, is the ultimate aim of classical Advaita. As in Sāṃkhya, from which Śaṅkara borrows the term *kaivalya*, the Advaitin *saṃnyāsin* thinks of his final goal under the metaphor of absolute isolation. He yearns for freedom in disembodiment (*videhatā*). The intense detachment generated by Brahman-knowledge allows for a figurative disembodiment in life, even while the body lingers under the influence of its karmic momentum. This is, unmistakably, a state of immense religious significance, as I have tried to show. But the fact that the *jīvanmukta's* continued bodily awareness must be supported by a lingering trace of ignorance points to a still higher goal. As Bhāratītīrtha tells us, the liberated sage whose *karma* causes him to undergo further empirical experience suffers like one undergoing forced labor (*viṣṭi-gṛhīta-vat*).[124] Literal disembodiment at death—*kaivalya* or *videhamukti*—is the preferred state.

We should be under no illusions that classical Advaita celebrates the state of living liberation as one in which the *mukta* has "non-dual perception" of the world *as* Brahman.[125] I have already shown that Prakāśātman, Bhāratītīrtha, and others believe that the *jīvanmukta* only truly overcomes duality when in the introversion of *samādhi*. Śaṅkara himself, where he does speak of the *mukta's* continued empirical experience, uses the analogy of a person with an eye defect. Persons with double vision, he suggests, may continue to see two moons even though they know better. Knowledge of the true situation does not cause the second moon to disappear. The false appearance remains, but is known to be a malignant intrusion.[126] Vācaspati uses a similar disease model to explain the experience of the *jīvanmukta*. Although knowers of Brahman may continue to engage in empirical activity, they do not perceive the world as identical with the Absolute: "For example, even though knowing for certain that sugar is sweet, persons afflicted by a disorder of the bile continue to experience a bitter taste. [We know this] because having tasted [sugar], they spit it out, and then discard it."[127] In both examples, the Advaitin compares the *mukta's* empirical experience to a perception known to be false, but introduced regrettably by an illness.

Sarvajñātman, to be sure, speaks of seeing duality in liberation as if it were a "wondrous painting" (*citram iva, SŚ* 4.54). And Bhāratītīrtha likens the *jīvanmukta's* experience of the world to witnessing a "magic show" (*indra jāla, PD* 7.180), possibly here intending a positive connotation. But most metaphors in the texts of classical Advaita speak clearly of the sage's distaste for continued empirical awareness. Maṇḍana speaks of the *jīvanmukta* as one who experiences his body as a mere shadow (*chāyā-mātra, BSdh* 3). Sarvajñātman goes on to declare, "I see the universe as if it were a burnt rope . . . and my body as the cast-off skin of a snake."[128] Other Advaitins say the world appears to them like a burnt cloth. Though it may retain its shape, it is ineffectual (*SLS* 4). Bhāratītīrtha himself declares that phenomenality, if it remains in liberation, is like a dead rat, a corpse, a knife rendered blunt (*PD* 7.279–282). Empirical existence for the *jīvanmukta* is, then, a magical phantasm at best. But it is one that is ontologically hollow, exhausted, a mere husk or shadow. It is experienced as a remote, inexplicable other trespassing in the self-luminous fullness of the Self. The *jīvanmukta* waits for its disappearance.

Given our homology between the liberated sage and Īśvara, we are pushed inexorably toward the question of how God himself experiences the world. The question is intriguing. It is also, no doubt, presumptuous. Whether for this reason or not, Hindu scripture gives hardly a hint as to its resolution, and Advaita itself is silent.[129] But perhaps some suggestion of an answer can be drawn from our homology, proceeding now from the *jīvanmukta's* end. If the sage in living liberation has, as the tradition claims, shifted his identification to the transcendent, we can strictly no longer talk of his experience at all, since his individuality has evaporated. We must speak rather of the experience of Īśvara through the particular medium that used to constitute the *mukta's* body-mind. That is to say, descriptions of the experience of the *jīvanmukta* should be read as descriptions of the experience of God through a particular psycho-physical apparatus.

One might imagine that God's experience of his cosmos would be a glorious vision of non-duality, shining with the radiance of the Absolute. But if we take the experience of the *jīvanmukta* as our guide—as we must, since there is no other evidence—we can only be disappointed. We have no grounds for assuming anything more interesting than the sage's perception of the world as a shadowland of *mis*perception. But perhaps it is precisely here that our homology is most revealing. Put simply, it serves to remind us of and highlight Advaita's deep metaphysical bias against the world. Why do we find in the orthodox Śaṅkara tradition no vibrant celebration of non-dual experience of, and unity with, the cosmos—at least on Īśvara's part, if not the *jīvanmukta's*? Why do we have to look elsewhere for this spirit of final world reclamation, to Tantric non-dualism, as in Ramakrishna or Kashmir Śaivism, or to Mahāyāna Buddhism? Because in the end the Advaita tradition fails to present a true non-dualism of world and Absolute—as many would like to understand the term today.[130] It is rather an acosmic monism. It achieves its non-duality not inclusively but exclusively. Empirical reality is admitted in a provisional way, but in the end it is cast out of the Absolute, out of existence. From the highest (*pāramārthika*) perspective, the world is simply not there. This being the case, how can Īśvara's participation in the world *not* limit him, and in ways that closely parallel the *jīvanmukta's* experience?

Both the *jīvanmukta* and Īśvara abide in a state that is intermediate between bondage and final Advaitic liberation. For both there is a "consciousness of freedom," as Eliade puts it, and a direct apprehension of immortality. But for both this awareness is combined with a persistent element of bondage. Both God and the *jīvanmukta* remain, once again, liberated yet in a critical sense waiting to be liberated. Still, the value of this waiting ought not be gainsaid. Because it is already free in great measure, it is holy. That Īśvara's waiting is paradoxically both timeless and eternal invests it with a profundity that is incalculable. The *jīvanmukta* is privileged to share a portion of this holy waiting of God, before attaining the final freedom that lies utterly beyond phenomenality.

Abbreviations

AS — *Advaitasiddhi of Madhusūdana Sarasvatī*. Edited by N. S. Ananta Krishna Sastri. Parimal Sanskrit Series, no. 7. Delhi: Parimal Publications, 1982.

Bhā — *The Bhāmatī of Vācaspati on Śaṅkara's Brahmasūtrabhāṣya*. Edited and translated by S. S. Suryanarayana Sastri and C. Kunhan Raja. Madras: Theosophical Publishing House, 1933. (All translations cited are my own.)

BhG	*Bhagavad Gītā*. See *BhGŚ*.
BhGŚ	*Śrīmadbhagavadgītā with the Commentaries Śrīmat-Śānkarabhāṣya with Ānandagiri, Nīlakaṇṭhī, Bhāṣyotkarṣadīpikā of Dhanapati, Śridharī, Gītārthasaṃgraha of Abhinavaguptācārya, and Gūḍhārthadīpikā of Madhusūdana*. Edited by Wasudev Laxman Sāstrī Panśīkar. 2d ed. Delhi: Munshiram Manoharlal Publishers, 1978.
BSdh	*Brahmasiddhi by Acharya Maṇḍanamiśra*. Edited by S. Kuppuswami Sastri. Sri Garib Das Oriental Series, no. 16. Delhi: Sri Satguru Publications, 1984; reprint, Madras Government Oriental Series, no. 4. Madras: Government Oriental Manuscripts Library, 1937.
BS	Bādarāyaṇa. *Brahma Sūtra*. See *BSŚ*.
BSŚ	*Brahmasūtra with Śāṅkarabhāṣya*. *Works of Śaṅkara in Original Sanskrit*, vol. 3. Delhi: Motilal Banarsidass, 1985.
BU	*Bṛhadāraṇyaka Upaniṣad*. See *BUŚ*.
BUŚ	*Bṛhadāraṇyakopaniṣad with Śāṅkarabhāṣya*. Edited by Kāśīnātha Śāstrī Āgāśe. Ānandāśrama Sanskrit Series, no. 15. Poona: Ānandāśrama, 1953.
BUBhV	*Shri Sureshvarāchārya's Bṛhadāraṇyakopaniṣadbhāṣyavārtikam*. Edited by Shri S. Subrahmanya Shastri. Advaita Ratna Manjusha, nos. 23 and 30. Mt. Abu: Mahesh Research Institute, 1982, 1990.
ChU	*Chāndogya Upaniṣad*. See *TPUŚ*.
ChUŚ	*Chāndogya Upaniṣad* with Śaṅkara's *Bhāṣya*. See *TPUŚ*.
IS	*Iṣṭasiddhi of Vimuktātman*. Edited by P. K. Sundaram. Madras: Swadharma Swaarajya Sangha, 1980.
Kaṭha	*Kaṭha Upaniṣad*. See *TPUŚ*.
MāU	*Māṇḍūkya Upaniṣad*. See *TPUŚ*.
MāK	Gauḍapāda. *Māṇḍūkya Kārikā*. See *TPUŚ*.
MāUKŚ	*Māṇḍūkya Upaniṣad* with Gauḍapāda's *Kārikā* and Śaṅkara's *Bhāṣya*. See *TPUŚ*.
MuU	*Muṇḍaka Upaniṣad*. See *TPUŚ*.
MuUŚ	*Muṇḍaka Upaniṣad* with Śaṅkara's *Bhāṣya*. See *TPUŚ*.
NS	*The Naishkarmya-Siddhi [Naiṣkarmyasiddhi] of Sureśvarāchārya with the Chandrikā of Jnānottama*. Edited by G. A. Jacob. 2d ed. Bombay: Government Central Book Depot, 1906.
PD	*Pañcadaśī of Śrī Vidyāraṇya Swāmī*. Edited and translated by Swami Swahananda. Madras: Sri Ramakrishna Math, 1975. (All translations cited are my own.)

PPV	*The Pañcapādikā of Śrī Padmapādācārya with the Pañcapādikāvivaraṇa of Śrī Prakāśātman*. Edited by S. Śrīrāma Śāstrī and S. R. Krishnamurthi Śāstrī. Madras Government Oriental Series, no. 155. Madras: Government Oriental Manuscripts Library, 1958.
SLS	*Siddhāntaleśasaṃgraha of Appayya Dīkṣita*. Edited by S. S. Suryanarayana Sastri. Vol. 2. Madras: University of Madras, 1937.
SŚ	*Saṃkṣepaśārīrika of Sarvajñātman*. Edited and translated by N. Veezhinathan. Madras: University of Madras, 1985. (All translations cited are my own.)
SŚSS	*Saṅkṣepaśārīrika by Sarvajñātma-muni with a Gloss Called Sarasaṅgraha [by Madhusūdana Sarasvatī]*. Edited by Bhau Sastri Vajhe. Kashi Sanskrit Series, no. 18. Varanasi: The Chowkhamba Sanskrit Series Office, 1924.
TP	*Tattvapradīpikā of Citsukha*. Edited by Kāshinath Shāstrī. Bombay: Nirnayasāgar Press, 1915.
TPUŚ	*Ten Principal Upanishads with Śāṅkarabhāṣya. Works of Śaṅkara in the Original Sanskrit*, vol. 1. Delhi: Motilal Banarsidass, 1964.
UpSā	*Upadeshsāhasrī [Upadeśasāhasrī] of Srī Samkarāchārya: A Thousand Teachings*. Edited and translated by Swami Jagadananda. Madras: Sri Ramakrishna Math, 1961. (All translations cited are my own.)
ViCū	*Vivekacūḍāmaṇi of* [?] *Śrī Śaṅkarācārya*. Edited and translated by Swāmī Mādhavānanda. Calcutta: Advaita Ashrama, 1982. (All translations cited are my own.)
VPBh	*Vedāntaparibhāṣā of Dharmarāja Adhvarin*. Edited and translated by S. S. Suryanarayana Sastri. Adyar, Madras: The Adyar Library, 1942.
VPS	*The Vivaraṇaprameyasaṅgraha of Bhāratītīrtha*. Edited by S. S. Suryanarayana Sastri and Saileswar Sen. Andhra University Series, no. 25. Waltair: Āndhraviśvakalāpariṣad, 1941.
VS	*Vedāntasāra of Sadānanda*. Edited and translated by Swami Nikhilananda. Calcutta: Advaita Ashrama, 1978.

Notes

1. advaitam apy anubhavāmi kara-stha-bilva-tulyaṃ śarīram ahi-nirvlayanīva vīkṣe / evaṃ ca jīvanam iva pratibhāsamānaṃ niḥśreyasādhigamanaṃ ca mama prasiddham (*SŚ* 4.55). On the identification of the body with the skin of a snake, see the discussion of *BU* 4.4.7, below.

2. I must point out that only Śaṅkara taught that liberation could, with rare exceptions, be attained only by world-renouncing monks (*saṃnyāsins*). For him and other conservative Advaitins, moreover, monkhood was open only to male Brahmins. The obvious result is that the orthodox Advaita tradition was accessible only to a narrow male elite. (See Lance Nelson, "Theism for the Masses, Non-Dualism for the Monastic Elite: A Fresh Look at Śaṅkara's Trans-Theistic Spirituality," in *The Struggle Over the Past: Fundamentalism in the Modern World*, ed. William Shea [Latham, MD: University Press of America, 1993].) I strive to use non-sexist language in this chapter as much as possible. However, it would be a misrepresentation in this context to use such gender inclusive pronominal constructions as "he or she" when referring to the liberated sage, who must here be a *saṃnyāsin*.

3. By "classical" or "orthodox" Advaita, I mean that represented in works of Śaṅkara, his disciples Sureśvara and Padmapāda, and the elite, conservative, scholastic *saṃnyāsin* tradition that follows them. This chapter focuses almost entirely on this tradition, from Śaṅkara through Madhusūdana Sarasvatī and his disciples. I therefore exclude from detailed consideration—in addition to the views of modern "neo-Vedāntins"—such texts as the *Yogavāsiṣṭha* and the *Aṣṭāvakragītā*, which teach an *advaita* more idealistic than Śaṅkara's, and popular Advaitic manuals that have been influenced by them. I also exclude the many so-called minor works of Śaṅkara. Almost all of these are late, of doubtful authorship, and strongly influenced by the *Yogavāsiṣṭha*, yogic teachings, Tantrism, or combinations thereof. (See Note 6, below.) This means that I do not intend to deal here with the concept of *jīvanmukti* as it appears in the *Yogavāsiṣṭha*, or with works such as the *Jīvanmuktiviveka*, which are heavily dependent on the *Yogavāsiṣṭha*. It is worth noting, however, that the notion of *jīvanmukti* as a particularized ideal may well have originated outside of the orthodox Advaita tradition in the popular ascetic traditions that produced these texts. See J. G. Arapura, "The Question as to the Jīvan-Mukti 'Ideal,'" in *Hermeneutical Essays on Vedāntic Topics* (Delhi: Motilal Banarsidass, 1986), 124–134.

4. S. Radhakrishnan, *The Principal Upaniṣads* (London: George Allen & Unwin, 1953), 118.

5. Mircea Eliade, *Yoga, Immortality and Freedom*, 2d ed., Bollingen Series LVI (Princeton: Princeton University Press, 1969), 100.

6. Following the majority of modern scholars, I define Śaṅkara as the author of the major commentaries bearing his name (on the *BS*, the *BhG*, the major *Upaniṣads*, and the *MāK*) and the one original work that can safely be attributed to

him, the *UpSā*. I do not take into account the many other works (such as the popular *ViCū*) that are reverently—but we now think mistakenly—ascribed to Śaṅkara. See Karl H. Potter, ed., *Encyclopedia of Indian Philosophies*, Vol. III: *Advaita Vedānta up to Śaṅkara and His Pupils* (Princeton: Princeton University Press, 1981), 115–116, 294–295, 320; also Sengaku Mayeda, *A Thousand Teachings: The Upadeśasāhasrī of Śaṅkara* (Tokyo: University of Tokyo Press, 1979), 6. On Śaṅkara's dates, see Potter, 14–15, 116; Mayeda, 3.

7. parānugraha, loka-saṃgraha (*BhGŚ* 3.25, 4.20). See also *UpSā* (metrical portion) 2.1.6; *BSŚ* 3.4.50. For more on the ethical implications of *jīvanmukti*, see Andrew O. Fort, "Knowing Brahman While Embodied: Śaṅkara on Jīvanmukti," *Journal of Indian Philosophy* 19 (December 1991): 371–373, 380, and 387–388, n. 44.

8. idam tu pāramārthikaṃ, kūṭastha-nityaṃ, vyomavat sarva-vyāpi sarva-vikriyā-rahitaṃ nitya-tṛptaṃ niravayaṃ svayaṃ-jyotiḥ-svabhāvam / yatra dharmādharmau saha kāryeṇa kāla-trayaṃ ca nopāvartete / tad etad aśarīratvaṃ mokṣākhyam / . . . atas tad brahma yasyeyaṃ jijñāsā prastutā (*BSŚ* 1.1.4, p. 14). Compare *BSŚ* 2.1.14: "Liberation is unchangingly eternal (kūṭastha-nityatvān mokṣasya)."

9. brahma-bhāvaś ca mokṣaḥ (*BSŚ* 1.1.4, p. 17).

10. nityaś ca mokṣaḥ . . . agny-uṣṇa-vad ātmanaḥ svabhāvaḥ (*BUŚ* 4.4.6).

11. *BSŚ* 1.1.4, pp. 14, 16; 3.4.52; *BUŚ* 4.4.6.

12. na baddho na ca sādhakaḥ / na mumukṣur na vai mukta ity eṣā paramarthatā (*MāK* 2.32).

13. tan-nivṛttau prāptam apy ānanda-rūpam aprāptam iva prāptam bhavati; tyaktam api śoka-duḥkhādy atyaktam iva tyaktam bhavati (*Bhā* on 1.1.4, p. 156).

14. kevalād eva tattva-jñānān mokṣa-prāptiḥ (*BhGŚ* 2.20).

15. śrutayo brahma-vidyānantaraṃ mokṣaṃ darśayantyo madhye kāryāntaraṃ vārayanti (*BSŚ* 1.1.4, p. 15). Compare:

> In everyday life a form is revealed as soon as the light reaches the observer's eye. Similarly, ignorance of the Self disappears the very moment knowledge arises."
>
> yathā loke draṣṭuś cakṣuṣa ālokena saṃyogo yat kālas tat kāla eva rūpābhivyaktiḥ / evam ātma-viṣayaṃ vijñānaṃ yat kālaṃ tat kāla eva tad-viṣayājñāna-tirobhāvaḥ syāt (*BUŚ* 1.4.10).
>
> Precisely at the time right knowledge arises, its result—being the Self of all—is realized.

samyag-darśana-kālam eva tat-phalaṃ sarvātmatvaṃ darśayati (*BSŚ* 3.3.32).

16. yadā yasmin kāle bhūta-pṛthag-bhāvaṃ . . . ekasmin ātmani sthitam ekastham anupaśyati . . . brahma saṃpadyate brahmaiva bhavati tadā (*BhGŚ* 13.30). Ānandagiri, Śaṅkara's earliest commentator, glosses:

> Liberation is exactly simultaneous with the rise of knowledge.
>
> jñāna-samāna-kālaiva muktiḥ (*Ānandagirivyākhyā* on *BhGŚ* 13.30).

17. jñānaṃ . . . ātmany eva bhaved yasya sa necchann api mucyate (*UpSā* [metrical portion] 2.4.5).

18. na ca tasyām apy utkarṣa-nikarṣātmako 'tiśaya upapadyate nikṛṣṭāyā vidyātvābhāvād utkṛṣṭaiva hi vidyā bhavati / tasmāt tasyām cirācirotpatti-rūpo 'tiśayo bhavan bhavet / na tu muktau kaścid atiśaya-saṃbhavo 'sti (*BSŚ* 3.4.52).

19. I will show below that Śaṅkara and his followers retreat from this bold *gnosis*-orientation. Andrew Fort will describe in some detail in Chapter Five how Vidyāraṇya diverges from it.

20. saṃskāraḥ . . . na tāvad guṇādhānena saṃbhavati, anādheyātiśaya-brahma-svarūpatvān mokṣasya / nāpi doṣāpanayanena, nitya-śuddha-brahma-svarūpatvān mokṣasya (*BSŚ* 1.1.4, p. 17).

21. vidyā svayam evotpadyate tayā cāvidyā bādhyate / tataś cāvidyādhyastaḥ saloko 'yaṃ nāma-rūpa-prapañcaḥ svapna-prapañca-vat pravilīyate (*BSŚ* 3.2.21).

22. *BSŚ* 2.1.14. Compare the following:

> When the [five] elements, manifested with the form of effects, causes, and objects, being the cause of the Self's becoming an individual self, are dissolved by the knowledge of Brahman that arises from the instructions imparted by the teacher and the scriptures, they disappear. Immediately upon their disappearance, this individual selfhood also dissolves, like the foam and bubbles created by waves. For example, when their causes such as water or red-colored lac are removed, the reflections of the sun and moon [in the water, and the red color reflected in] crystal, etc., disappear. Only the [sun,] moon, etc., themselves remain, as they are in reality. In the same way, [when the world disappears with the rise of knowledge,] pure Intelligence—infinite, unbounded, pellucid—[alone] remains.
>
> tāni yadā kārya-karaṇa-viṣayākāra-pariṇatāni bhūtāni ātmano viśeṣātma-khilya-hetu-bhūtāni śāstrācāryopadeśena brahma-vidyayā nadī-samudra-vat pravilāpitāni vinaśyanti / salila-phema-budbudādi-vat teṣu vinaśyatsv anv evaiṣa viśeṣātma-khilya-bhāvo vinaśyati / yathodakālaktakādi-hetv-

apanaye sūrya-candra-sphaṭikādi-pratibimbo vinaśyati candrādi svarūpam eva paramārthato vyavathiṣṭhate / tadvat prajñānam anantam apāraṃ svacchaṃ vyavatiṣṭhate (*BUŚ* 2.4.12).

23. brahma-bhūtaṃ jīvanmuktam (*BhGŚ* 6.27).

24. Arapura 1986: 125–131. See Note 3.

25. ihaiva santo 'tha vidmas tad vayam.

26. See also *BU* 4.4.7; *MuU* 2.1.10. On Vāmadeva, see *BSŚ* 3.4.51, *SŚ* 3.349–350, *PD* 9.35.

27. karmaṇy abhipravṛto 'pi niṣkriyātma-darśana-sampannatvān naiva kiṃcit karoti saḥ (*BhGŚ* 4.20).

28. yaḥ . . . prāg eva karmārambhād brahmaṇi sarvāntare pratyag-ātmani niṣkriye saṃjātāma-darśanaḥ saḥ . . . śarīra-yātrā-mātra-ceṣṭo yatir jñāna-niṣṭho mucyate . . . jñānāgni-dagdha-sarva-karmatvād apratibandhena mucyate eva (*BhGŚ* 4.21).

29. brahma-vidām api keṣāṃcid itihāsa-purāṇayor dehāntarotpatti-darśanāt (*BSŚ* 3.3.32).

30. na hi 'tat tvam asi' ity asya vākyasyārthas tat tvam mṛto bhaviṣyasīty evaṃ pariṇetuṃ śakyaḥ (*BSŚ* 3.3.32).

31. brahma veda brahmaiva bhavati.

32. brahmaṇi nirvṛtiṃ mokṣam iha jīvann eva brahma-bhūtaḥ san adhigacchati prāpnoti (*BhGŚ* 5.24). See also Śaṅkara's remarks on *Kaṭha* 2.2.1.

33. mokṣākhyam aśarīratvaṃ nityaṃ iti siddham (*BSŚ* 1.1.1, p. 14).

34. *Maitrī Upaniṣad* 4.6, for example, speaks of "the supreme, the immortal, the bodiless (*aśarīra*) Brahman" (brahmaṇaḥ . . . parasyāmṛtasyāśarīrasya). I will refer to *Kaṭha* 1.2.22 and *BhG* 13.31 in the text of this chapter below.

35. tasmān mithyā-pratyaya-nimittavāt saśarīratvasya siddhaṃ jīvato 'pi viduṣo 'śarīratvam (*BSŚ* 1.1.4, p. 22).

36. atrāsminn eva śarīre vartamāno brahma samaśnute brahma-bhāvaṃ mokṣaṃ pratipadyat ity arthaḥ / ato mokṣo na deśāntara-gamanādy apekṣate (*BUŚ* 4.4.7).

37. tad yathāhi-nirlvayanī valmīke mṛtā pratyastā śayīta, evam evedaṃ śarīraṃ śete, athāyam aśarīro 'mṛtaḥ.

38. *BUŚ* 4.4.7. Compare *ViCū* 547–550.

39. tathā vivekāviveka-mātreṇaivātmano 'śarīratvaṃ saśarīratvaṃ ca, mantra-varṇāt "aśarīraṃ śarīreṣu" [*Kaṭha* 1.2.22] iti, "śarīra-stho 'pi kaunteya na karoti na lipyate" [*BhG* 13.31] iti (*BSŚ* 1.3.19).

40. yadi vāstavaṃ saśarīratvam bhavet, na jīvatas tan nivarteta; mithyā-jñāna-nimittaṃ tu tat; tac cotpanna-tattva-jñānena jīvatāpi śakyaṃ nivartayitum / yat punar aśarīratvaṃ tad asya svabhāva iti na śakyaṃ nivartayitum, svabhāva-hānena bhāva-vināśa-prasaṅgād ity āha—nityam aśarīratvam iti (*Bhā* on 1.1.4, p. 233).

41. A number of influential works, including the *Vivaraṇaprameyasaṃgraha* (*VPS*), the *Pañcadaśī* (*PD*), and the *Jīvanmuktiviveka*, are traditionally attributed to a writer named Vidyāraṇya. But the identity of this Vidyāraṇya—and indeed whether or not he was a single individual—has been a matter of scholarly dispute. Of the various discussions of this issue, Mahadevan's remains the most satisfactory. While I believe that more research is necessary before a final verdict can be rendered, I am willing for purposes of this discussion to accept Mahadevan's conclusion that the *VPS* and the *PD* were written by the same author. This important post-Śaṅkara Advaitin was known sometimes as Bhāratītīrtha, sometimes by the additional appellation Vidyāraṇya ("Forest of Wisdom"), and sometimes by both names together. Mādhava-Vidyāraṇya, the author of the *Jīvanmuktiviveka* and other works, appears to be a different individual. In order to avoid confusion, I will speak of the author of the *VPS* and the *PD* as Bhāratītīrtha. See T. M. P. Mahadevan, *The Philosophy of Advaita* (Madras: Ganesh & Co., 1969), 1–8, and the same author's *The Pañcadaśī of Bhāratītīrtha-Vidyāraṇya: An Interpretive Exposition*, Madras University Philosophical Series, no. 13 (Madras: University of Madras, 1969), xiv–xv.

42. nīroga upaviṣṭo vā rugṇo vā viluṭhan bhuvi / mūrchito vā tyajatv eṣa prāṇān bhrāntir na sarvathā (*PD* 2.106). Compare *ViCū* 556.

43. It is not listed in T. M. P. Mahadevan, ed., *Word Index to the Brahmasūtra-bhāṣya of Śaṅkara*, 2 pts. (Madras: University of Madras, 1973). Nor is it to be found in Francis X. D'Sa, ed., *Word-Index to Śaṅkara's Gītābhāṣya* (Pune: Institute for the Study of Religion, 1985). My sense is that the term *videhamukti* becomes prominent in Advaita only under the influence of the *Yogavāsiṣṭha*.

44. See S. S. Suryanarayana Sastri's comments in *VPBh*, p. 217, and his article "Jīvanmukti," in *Collected Papers of Professor S. S. Suryanarayana Sastri*, ed. T. M. P. Mahadevan (Madras: University of Madras, 1961), 246; see also Debabrata Sinha, "On Immortality and Death—Notes in a Vedāntic Perspective" in *Perspectives on Vedānta: Essays in Honor of Professor P. T. Raju*, ed. S. S. Rama Rao Pappu (Leiden: E. J. Brill, 1988), 176.

Similar reservations must be expressed, for similar reasons, regarding the post-Śaṅkara Advaitins' distinction between living liberation and immediate liberation (*sadyomukti*). For Śaṅkara *sadyomukti* does not mean, as it often does in later Advaita, instant and literal disembodiment. He uses it in contrast with the term *kramamukti*, which describes the gradual "liberation by stages" attained by worshipers of the conditioned (*saguṇa*) Brahman. See *BhGŚ* 5.23–28, 8.23–27; *BSŚ* 1.1.11, 1.3.13, 4.3–4.

45. na tasya mokṣo 'nyaḥ kartavyo 'sti (*BhGŚ* 5.28).

46. na hi viduṣo mṛtasya bhāvāntarāpatir jīvato 'nyo bhāvo dehāntara-pratisaṃdhānābhāva-mātreṇaiva (*BUŚ* 4.4.6). Compare the teaching of the modern sage, Ramana Maharshi: "There are no stages in Realization or *Mukti*. There are no degrees of Liberation. So there cannot be one stage of Liberation with the body and another when the body has been shed. The Realized Man knows . . . that nothing, neither his body nor anything else, exists but for the Self. To such a one what difference could the presence or absence of a body make?" (Arthur Osborne, ed., *The Teachings of Bhagavan Sri Ramana Maharshi in His Own Words* [New York: Samuel Weiser, 1978], 193).

47. *Vedāntasiddhāntamuktāvalī* 26 (*Vedāntasiddhāntamuktāvalī of Prakāśānanda*, edited and translated by Arthur Venis, Gokuldas Sanskrit Series, no. 4 [Varanasi: Chaukhambha Orientalia, 1975], 137–143).

48. na nareṇāvareṇa prokta eṣa suvijñeyaḥ . . . ananya-prokte gatir atra nāsti.

49. ye samyag-darśinas tair upadiṣṭaṃ jñānaṃ kārya-kṣemaṃ bhavati netarat (*BhGŚ* 4.34). See also *UpSā* (metrical portion) 2.1.3, 6; 2.2.45.

50. dṛṣṭa-tattvasya cet tadaiva śarīram patet, tadā ācāryābhāvād vidyālābhān mokṣābhāvaḥ (*IS* 1.9).

51. *BSŚ* 4.1.15. See *BhG* 2.54–71.

52. api ca naivātra vivaditavyaṃ brahma-vidā kaṃcit-kālaṃ śarīraṃ dhriyate na vā dhriyate iti / kathaṃ hy ekasya sva-hṛdaya-pratyayaṃ brahma-vedanaṃ deha-dhāraṇaṃ cāpareṇa pratikṣeptuṃ śakyeta (*BSŚ* 4.1.15).

53. M. Hiriyanna, *Outlines of Indian Philosophy* (Bombay: George Allen & Unwin, 1973), p. 381, n. 2.

54. kṣīyante cāsya karmāṇi (*MuU* 2.2.8); jñānāgniḥ sarva-karmāṇi bhasmasāt kurute (*BhG* 4.37).

55. anārabdha-kārye eva tu purve (*BS* 4.1.15).

56. See *BSŚ* 4.1.15 and *ChUŚ* 6.14.2. The later Advaita tradition teaches the formula of three kinds of *karma*: (1) *saṃcita*, "accumulated" *karma* that has not yet begun to bear fruit, (2) *prārabdha*, "commenced" *karma*, or that portion of the *saṃcita* that has been activated and has begun to produce effects, leading to one's present birth and playing itself out in the experiences of this life, and (3) *āgāmin*, "coming" *karma* being earned in this life to yield, unless cut short by knowledge, results in the future. The latter is also called *saṃcīyamāna* (being accumulated) and *kriyamāna* (being performed). It, like *saṃcita*, is destroyed by Brahman-knowledge, after which the knower accumulates no more *karma*, even though he acts under the influence of *prārabdha*.

57. na tāvad anāśrityārabdha-kāryaṃ karmāśayaṃ jñānotpattir upapadyate (*BSŚ* 4.1.15).

58. *BSŚ* 3.3.32, *ChUŚ* 6.14.2, *BUŚ* 1.4.10, *BhGŚ* 13.23.

59. *BSŚ* 4.1.15. Compare *Sāṃkhya Kārikā* 67.

60. bādhitam api tu mithyājñānaṃ . . . saṃskāra-vaśāt kaṃcit-kālam anuvartata eva (*BSŚ* 4.1.15).

61. *BUŚ* 3.5.1; *MāUKŚ* on *MāU* 7.

62. It has more than once been pointed out that the flying arrow and the spinning potter's wheel are unstoppable because they are (on the level of discourse intended in the example) real entities with real momentum. But *prārabdha karma* and the body it supports are (according to Advaita) unreal fabrications, products of ignorance. In making such comparisons, Śaṅkara is giving *prārabdha* a reality that, according to his own ontology, it does not deserve. See Fort 1991: 377–378. (See Note 7).

63. yadyapy evaṁśarīrārabdhakasya karmaṇo niyata-phalatvāt samyag-jñānaprāptav api avaśyam bhāvinī pravṛttir vāṅ-manaḥ-kāyānām / labdha-vṛtteḥ karmaṇo balīyastvāt / mukteṣvādi-pravṛtti-vat / tena pakṣe prāptaṃ jñāna-pravṛtti-daurbalyam / tasmāt tyāga-vairāgyādi-sādhana-balāvalambena ātma-vijñāna- smṛti-santatir niyantavyā bhavati (*BUŚ* 1.4.7).

64. *BS* 3.3.32; 4.1.15; 4.1.19. I am grateful to Professor Fort for alerting me to the significance of the language in these passages.

65. tasya tāvad eva ciraṃ yāvan na vimokṣye 'tha sampatsya iti.

66. sad-ātma-svarūpa-sampatter iti vākya-śeṣaḥ . . . yena karmaṇā śarīram ārabdhaṃ tasyopabhogena kṣayād deha-pāto yāvad ity arthaḥ / atha tadaiva sat sampatsye sampatsyata (*ChUŚ* 6.14.2).

67. siddho mokṣo 'ham (*UpSā* [metrical portion] 2.18.209). See also vs. 2.18.206, 211, 214.

68. kiṃtu vidvān sa ihaiva brahma yadyapi dehavān iva lakṣyate sa brahmaiva san brahmāpyeti / yasmān na hi tasyābrahmatva-pariccheda-hetavaḥ kāmāḥ santi tasmād ihaiva brahmaiva san brahmāpyeti na śarīra-pātottara-kālam (*BUŚ* 4.4.6).

69. The Upaniṣads and the *BS* do not always express the radical non-dualism that Śaṅkara espouses. The texts provide ample instances of an earlier, pre-Advaitic outlook that is more realistic than he as a non-dualist would wish to embrace. Most to the point, we often find in these primary sources—especially in the *ChU*—an inclination toward the commonsense idea of liberation as a post-mortem, heavenly state to which the soul, leaving the body behind, has to travel (see *ChU* 8.1.6; 8.2.1–10; 8.4.1–3; 8.12.3, and so forth). Bādarāyaṇa, the author of the *BS*, seems

to have been fond of the *ChU*, and it is likely that he thought of liberation as a heavenly state (see *BS* 4.4).

70. One of the great difficulties in interpreting Śaṅkara is that we almost always, except in the *UpSā*, see him as a commentator constrained by the texts rather than as the author of independent treatises. The degree to which he is so constrained is not always easy to determine.

71. Potter 1981: 35. (See Note 6.)

72. *ViCū* 453–463, *Aparokṣānubhūti* 90–97 (Swami Vimuktananda, ed. and trans., *Aparokṣānubhūti or Self-Realization of Śrī Śaṅkarācārya* [Calcutta: Advaita Ashrama, 1977]); see also *VS* 219. These texts are late, and with the exception of the *VS*, their authorship is highly dubious. While their probing of the *prārabdha* doctrine ought not for these reasons to be dismissed out of hand, they do belong to a more popular strand of the Advaita tradition than we are considering here. See Potter 1981: 320, 335, 560, reference in Note 6.

73. *The Naiṣkarmyasiddhi of Sureśvara* (Madras: University of Madras, 1988), 384. Satchidānandendra Sarasvatī expresses a similar view (*The Method of the Vedānta*, trans. A. J. Alston [London: Kegan Paul, 1989], 819). Compare Ramana Maharshi: "For those who ask it is said that a Realized Man with a body is a *jivanmukta* and that he attains *videhamukti* when he sheds the body, but this difference exists only for the onlooker, not for him. His state is the same before shedding the body and after" (Osborne 1978: 192). (See Note 46).

74. Eliot Deutsch, *Advaita Vedānta: A Philosophical Reconstruction* (Honolulu: East-West Center Press, 1969), pp. 69, 73.

75. mokṣam ekaṃ varjayitvā anyasyāvidyā-viṣayatvāt (*BUŚ* 4.5.15).

76. See *MāUKŚ* 4.73.

77. avidyādhyāropitasya śeṣānupapatteḥ (*BhGŚ* 18.48).

78. Arapura 1986: 130. (See Note 3.)

79. vimuktaś ca vimucyate.

80. He says: "This state is celebrated as 'living liberation'" (sā ceyam avasthā jīvanmuktir iti gīyate, *BSdh* 3, p. 132). It seems from the tone of this remark that others were using the term prior to Maṇḍana. Who exactly this might have been is an interesting question.

81. *BSdh* 3, pp. 131–133.

82. prārabdha-bhoga-śeṣābhāsa-mātra-sampādana-paṭīyo 'jñāna-śeṣaḥ (*IS* 1.9).

83. vidyā-prārabdha-bhogayor avirodhitvam / ata ā prārabdha-bhoga-kṣayāt vidvac charīram api tiṣṭhaty eva / tatra yathā vidyā bhogaṃ na bādhate, tathā bhogo 'pi na vidyāṃ bādhate (*IS* 1.9).

84. pratīteḥ / . . . tasmin arthe svānubhūtiḥ praṃāṇam (*SŚ* 4.43). This is a reference to Śaṅkara's commentary on *BS* 4.1.15, discussed above, which by Sarvajñātman's time had become the authoritative basis for the *saṃskāra* theory.

85. *TP* 4, pp. 385, 388.

86. *SLS* 4.

87. *PD* 6.54–56; Madhusūdana Sarasvatī uses this argument at *AS* 4.

88. *AS* 4, pp. 890–892; *SŚSS* 4.40–46. Compare: *SŚ* 1.20; *PD* 4.12, 6.26, 6.33; *SLS* 4; *VPBh* 9.54.

89. *BSdh* 3, p. 130.

90. na . . . adagdhaṃ . . . ajñānam asti (*NS* 4.58).

91. The complete text:

> [It might be ojected:] How, pray, can you assert that the intuition of Brahman and the experience of duality exist simultaneously? But we do not say [that they exist] simultaneously! Sometimes, there is the experience of the oneness of the unconditioned Self. At others, there is the experience of duality, caused by the defect created by the commenced *karma*.
>
> nanu brahmātmānubhava-dvaita-darśanayoḥ kutaḥ sāhityam ucyate? / na vayaṃ sāhityaṃ brūmaḥ / kadācid asamprajñātātmaikatva-darśanaṃ kadācid ārabdha-karmopasthāpita-doṣa-nimitta-dvaita-darśanaṃ ceti (*PPV*, p. 786).

But compare Śaṅkara:

> There is no possibility that, after being uprooted by the realization of unity, the perception of duality (*dvaita-vijñāna*) could arise again.
>
> na hy ekatva-vijñānenonmathitasya dvaita-vijñānasya punaḥ saṃbhavo 'sti (*BSŚ* 1.1.4, p. 11).

92. māyā-leśo jīvanmuktasyānivṛttaḥ samādhy-avastāyāṃ tirohito 'nyadā dehābhāsa-jagad-ābhāsa-hetutayānuvartate / prārabdha-karma-phalopabhogāvasāne tu nivartate (*TP* 4, p. 386).

93. na caivaṃ jīvanmuktasyātmaikyānubhava-dvaita-darśanayoḥ viruddhayoḥ sāhityaṃ prasajyeta iti mantavyam / na hi vayaṃ tayor yaugapadyaṃ brūmaḥ, kiṃ tu paryāyeṇodbhavābhibhavau (*VPS* 9.32).

94. bhikṣāṭanādi-pravṛttis tu ārabdha-karma-doṣa-mūlā (*VPS* 9.32).

95. tattva-darśinas tu ārabdha-karma-nimitta-doṣodbhavasya deśa-kāla-niyamābhāvena prārabdhānuṣṭhāna-samāpti-paryantam avasthānāyogāt (*VPS* 9.32).

96. brahma-vid-variṣṭha (*Gūḍhārthadīpikā* on *BhGŚ* 3.18). This scheme is also given in *Jīvanmuktiviveka* 4 (S. Subrahmanya Sastri and T. R. Srinivasa Ayyangar, eds., *Jīvanmuktiviveka of Vidyāraṇya* [Adyar, Madras: The Adyar Library and Research Center, 1978], 135–137).

97. *AS* 4, p. 885.

98. *Gauḍabrahmānadī* (*Laghucandrikā*) on *AS* 1, p. 3.

99. I find a hint of the two-level approach at *PD* 7.258–259. But this passage seems incompatible with the views (see above) of *VPS* 9.31–32 and other passages in the *PD* itself (for example, 6.263 and 7.245–246).

100. See *Sāṃkhya Kārikā* 66–68.

101. *Śvetāśvatara Upaniṣad* 4.10; *BSŚ* 2.1.33; *SŚSS* 2.181.

102. na hy anyatvaṃ jīvasyeśvarād upapadyate . . . ananya eveśvarāj jīvaḥ saṃdeha-yogāt tirohita-jñānaiśvaryo bhavati (*BSŚ* 3.2.6).

103. mithyā-jñāna-kṛta eva jīva-parameśvarayor bhedo na vastu-kṛtaḥ (*BSŚ* 1.3.19).

104. dehādi-saṃghātopādhi-saṃbandhāviveka-kṛteśvara-saṃsāri-bheda-mithyā-buddhiḥ (*BSŚ* 1.1.5). Compare:

> [Scripture] aims to establish, by removing its transmigratory condition, that the transmigrating soul has Īśvara as its Self.
>
> saṃsārinaḥ saṃsāritvāpoheneśvarātmatvaṃ pratipipādayiṣitam (*BSŚ* 4.1.3).
>
> The real nature of the embodied being is none other than the Supreme Lord; its embodiment is created by limiting adjuncts.
>
> pārameśvaram eva hi śārīrasya pāramārthikaṃ svarūpam / upādhi-kṛtaṃ tu śārīratvam (*BSŚ* 3.4.8).

105. īśvaro 'smi; aham īśvaraḥ (*UpSā* [metrical portion] 2.3.1, 2.10.8). Śaṅkara allows the latter expression also at *BSŚ* 4.1.3.

106. For this reason, Appayya held that the ultimate salvation of any one soul could not be attained until all *jīvas* were liberated (which would mean that all *pratibimbas* would be destroyed) and the universe finally dissolved along with its Lord. Hence this teaching is referred to as the doctrine of *sarva-mukti* ("universal

salvation"). See *SLS* 4, pp. 111–115. The difficulty with this doctrine is that, since the universe is eternal and *jīvas* are infinite in number, such a universal liberation can never occur.

107. Perhaps because Appayya's Śaiva-influenced model of *Īśvaratva* disallows the idea of a post-mortem *kaivalya*, which—I am arguing—is the real goal of classical Advaita.

108. See *BU* 3.7; *BhG* 3.27–28, 5.8–9.

109. See *BU* 4.4.7, *BhG* 5.10 and 18.61, and Śaṅkara's comments.

110. parameśvara-prerita-prāṇa-vāyu-vaśāt (*Gūḍhārthadīpikā* on *BhGŚ* 3.18).

111. Eliade 1969: 155. (See Note 5.)

112. na me pārthāsti kartavyaṃ triṣu lokeṣu kiṃcana / nānavāptam avāptavyaṃ varta eva ca karmaṇi (*BhG* 3.22).

113. yadi punar aham iva tvaṃ kṛtārtha-buddhir ātma-vid anyo vā tasyāpy ātmanaḥ kartavyābhāve 'pi parānugraha eva kartavyaḥ . . . evaṃ lokasaṃgrahaṃ cikīrṣor mamātmavido na kartavyam asti anyasya vā lokasaṃgrahaṃ muktvā tatas tasyātmavida idam upadiśyate (*BhGŚ* 3.24, 26).

114. yathā bhagavato vāsudevasya kṣātra-karma-ceṣṭitaṃ . . . tadvat phalābhisandhy-ahaṃkārābhāvasya tulyatvād viduṣaḥ (*BhGŚ* 2.11).

115. sa ca bhagavān jñānaiśvarya-śakti-bala-vīrya-tejobhiḥ sadā saṃpannas triguṇātmikāṃ vaiṣṇavīṃ svāṃ māyāṃ mūla-prakrtiṃ vaśīkṛtyājo 'vyayo bhūtānām īśvaro nitya-śuddha-buddha-mukta-svabhāvo 'pi san sva-māyayā dehavān iva jāta iva lokānugrahaṃ kurvan lakṣyate (*BhGŚ* 1.1).

116. vidvān sa ihaiva brahma yadyapi dehavān iva lakṣyate (*BUŚ* 4.4.6). No doubt the Advaitin must hold that all cases of embodiment are, strictly speaking, only apparent. But the liberated sage is distinctive in that, like Īśvara, he is *aware* of the "as if" nature of his embodiment.

117. See *BSŚ* 4.4.17, though on Śaṅkara's interpretation this text applies to those who have attained *brahmaloka* through worship of the *saguṇa* Brahman.

118. evam avidyā-kṛta-nāma-rūpopādhy-anurodhīśvaro bhavati, vyomeva ghaṭa-karakādy-upādhy-anurodhi / . . . tad evam avidyātmakopādhi-paricchedāpekṣam eveśvarasyeśvaratvaṃ sarvajñatvaṃ sarvaśaktitvaṃ ca (*BSŚ* 2.1.14). At *BSŚ* 4.4.19, Śaṅkara tells us that there are two forms of the Lord, the *saguṇa* and the *nirguṇa*. He characterizes the latter as "an eternally liberated form of the Supreme Lord (*nitya-muktaṃ pārameśvaraṃ rūpaṃ*)." Does this mean that the *saguṇa* form is *not* eternally liberated? The later tradition, at any rate, tends to reduce Īśvara to the conditioned, *saguṇa* aspect only. See the following note.

119. In the interest of preserving the absolute transcendence of Brahman, many later Advaitins tend to consign Īśvara to the realm of phenomenality. Thus they define Īśvara as Brahman reflected in, or even constructed by, *māyā*. For example, read *PD* 6.212: "Īśvara and *jīva* are created by *māyā* (īśvara-jīvakau māyayā kalpitau)." See also *SŚ* 3.277; *PD* 1.16; 3.37; 6.155; 8.61–64, 68; *SLS* 1, pp. 13–17; *VS* 37–38.

120. The full text reads:

> Although there is no question of He [Himself] being in ignorance (*ajñatva*), there is, even in Īśvara, the ignorance that is the cause of the world. In the *mukta*, this does not exist. This is the difference.
>
> asty eveśvare 'pi jagan-nidānam ajñānaṃ tathāpi na tasyājñātvam ity uktam / mukte tu tad api nāstīti viśeṣaḥ (*SŚSS* 2.181).

Sarvajñātman suggests further that, when the Lord assumes embodiment as an *avatāra*, the Lord may possess ego-sense (*ahaṃkāra*) and may even voluntarily subject himself to ignorance for a limited period of time, as in the case of Lord Rāma, who experienced anxiety and grief after the abduction of Sītā, his queen (*SŚ* 2.179, 2.182).

121. Prof. Veezhinathan sees in certain verses of the *SŚ* an interesting application of the doctrine of the two powers of *avidyā*, the projective (*vikṣepa*) and the concealing (*āvaraṇa*). Īśvara, we are told, though he experiences the world appearance as created by the *vikṣepa-śakti*, is not subject to the influence of *āvaraṇa*. This explains why he never loses awareness of his identity with Brahman, why he is never taken in by his own phenomenal magic (*SŚ*, p. 110). This application of the theory of the two powers of *avidyā* to Īśvara is, in fact, to be found in the text only implicitly (see *SŚ* 2.165, 168, 175, 183–186). I have not been able to find it stated explicitly anywhere in the classical literature. Nevertheless, it is noteworthy because it is the very device that, we have seen, Madhusūdana and others use to explain the limited mode of being of the *jīvanmukta*. The same model, then, is used to explain the experience of both Īśvara and the *jīvanmukta*.

122. See Note 3 above.

123. See Note 2 above. Consider also, in this light, the import of *ViCū* 2:

> For all beings, birth as a human is difficult to obtain. Next [in order of difficulty] is birth as a male; following that, as a Brahmin. Even more [rare] is devotion to the path of the Vedas. Following this, come knowledge [of the scriptures], discrimination between Self and not-Self, direct realization, and abiding in the Self which is Brahman. Liberation is not to be obtained except through the merits earned by millions of lives of good deeds.

jantūnāṃ nara-janma durlabham ataḥ puṃstvaṃ tato vipratā tasmād vaidika-dharma-mārga-paratā vidvattvam asmāt param / ātmānātma-vivecanaṃ svanubhavo brahmātmanā saṃsthitir muktir no śata-janma-koṭi-sukṛtaiḥ puṇyair vinā labhyate.

124. *PD* 7.143. Compare the attitude of Nisargadatta Maharaj, a highly regarded modern exponent of Advaitic realization: "For a *jnani*, what benefit of any kind can he expect by existing in the world even one more minute? So the only thing that would be nice is for the (vital) breath to leave quietly and not make a fuss" (Robert Powell, ed., *The Ultimate Medicine: As Prescribed by Sri Nisargadatta Maharaj* [San Diego, CA: Blue Dove Press, 1994], 128).

125. The experience of the world as Absolute is an important theme in later Tantric Advaita and especially in Kashmir Śaivism and Mahāyāna Buddhism. The idea that Śaṅkara's Advaita envisions "non-dual perception" of the world as identical with the Absolute has been suggested (for example, by David Loy, *Nonduality: A Study in Comparative Philosophy* [New Haven: Yale University Press, 1988], chap. 2). I find it difficult to support. See my "Reverence for Nature or the Irrelevance of Nature? Advaita Vedānta and Ecological Concern," *Journal of Dharma* 16 (July-Sept. 1991): 282–301.

126. *BSŚ* 4.1.15. But compare:

> The knower, once ignorance is dispelled by knowledge, is able to give up action entirely, for there can be no question of any remnant of what was superimposed by ignorance. For, when the disease causing double vision is cured, no remnant of the two-moons superimposed by the diseased eye can remain.
>
> vidvāṃs tu punar vidyayā 'vidyāyāṃ nivṛttāyāṃ śaknoty evāśeṣataḥ karma parityaktum avidyādhyāropitasya śeṣānupapatteḥ / na hi taimirika-dṛṣṭyādhyāropitasya dvi-candrādes timirāpagame 'pi śeṣo 'vatiṣṭhate (*BhGŚ* 18.48).

127. yathā guḍasya mādhurya-viniścaye 'pi pittopahatendriyāṇāṃ tiktatāvabhāsānuvṛttiḥ, āsvādya thūtkṛtya tyāgāt (*Bhā* on 1.1.1, p. 80).

128. paśyāmi dagdha-raśanām iva ca prapañcam . . . śarīram ahi-nirvlayanīva vīkṣe (*SŚ* 4.54–55). Compare *BU* 4.4.7.

129. The idea of Īśvara's omniscience (*sarvajñatva*) is stated (for example, at *MuU* 1.9), but it is hardly developed.

130. See Loy 1988, chap. 1, reference above in Note 123.

CHAPTER 2

Is the Jīvanmukti State Possible? Rāmānuja's Perspective

Kim Skoog

Introduction: Rāmānuja's Three Arguments

Within the Vedānta school of Indian philosophy, a dispute eventually developed concerning whether liberation can occur while the aspirant is still in an embodied condition (*jīvanmukti*) or only when the aspirant has left the physical body at death (*videhamukti*). In his *Śrībhāṣya* (*BSR* 1.1.4), a commentary on the *Brahma Sūtras*, Rāmānuja (belonging to the Viśiṣṭādvaita or Modified Nondualist school of Vedānta) attacks the doctrine of *jīvanmukti* as held by Śaṅkara and the Advaita or Nondualist school of Vedānta. In this essay, I will examine Rāmānuja's criticisms and assess how successful he is in his attempt to discredit the *jīvanmukti* doctrine. Additionally, I will speculate on what considerations lead Rāmānuja and Śaṅkara to their respective positions regarding the *videhamukti* and *jīvanmukti* state.

Rāmānuja's critique is given in the traditional dialectic method of disputation in Indian philosophy. The author gives an argument against a particular view and then entertains various replies or objections (*pūrvapakṣa*) from an opponent. The author then attempts to refute these rejoinders, and when s/he feels the issue has been sufficiently exhausted, presents a final conclusion (*uttarapakṣa or siddānta*). Rāmānuja's attempted refutation can be divided into three sections: (1) Rāmānuja's initial argument against the doctrine of *jīvanmukti*; (2) the Advaitin's reply to this argument (i.e., a clarification of the definition of the *jīvanmukti* state) and a second argument given by Rāmānuja refuting this modified Advaitin position; and (3) the Advaitin reply to this refutation, given in the form of an argument by analogy,[1] and Rāmānuja's refutation of this Advaitin response. Rāmānuja's final conclusion, *or uttarapakṣa*, has been deleted from this excerpt, since it includes matters outside the *jīvanmukti-videhamukti* issue:

> And what is this *jīvanmukti*? If it be argued that it is liberation even while in an embodied condition, then this explanation is incoherent (*asaṃgata*) in meaning; it is non-different from statements like, "my mother is barren." You [Advaitin] have even declared by means of scripture (*śruti*) that to be embodied is to be in bondage, and to be unembodied is to obtain release.
>
> [The Advaitin responds], "but, the *jīvanmukti* state is the cessation (*nivṛtti*) to embodiment in the sense that the appearance of embodiment is present, albeit the *jīvanmukta* is aware of the unreality of that appearance." [I reply], "no, for if the awareness of the unreality of the body puts an end (*nivṛtti*) to embodiment, how can you say that *jīvanmukti* means release while still in the body? Since liberation after death [i.e., *videhamukti*] is also defined as the cessation of the false appearance of embodiment, I ask, what is the distinction of this from the *jīvanmukti* state?"
>
> [If the Advaitin says], "a *jīvanmukta* has the appearance of embodiment even though s/he has annulled (*bādhita*) [its deceptive effect] like the case in which two moons persist even when one knows [one moon is illusory in nature]." [I reply], "no, because the annulling knowledge (*bādhakajñāna*) has for its object everything other than Brahman. Ignorance and its effect—*karma*, impurities, etc.—which are the causes of bondage, are annulled by the knowledge itself along with the appearance of embodiment; and so, it is not possible to speak of the persistence of the annulled. In the case of the two moons, however, the defect, which is the cause of the false appearance [of the two moons], is not the object of the annulling knowledge—i.e., that there is only one moon; and thus, it is not annulled. Consequently, the appearance of the two moons persists."[2]

Let us now proceed, section by section, to clarify and analyze this philosophical exchange. Rāmānuja, in my reading of this passage, has put forth three distinct arguments: (1) the self-contradictory argument; (2) the verbal-dispute argument; and (3) the disanalogy argument. I will reconstruct the various arguments and rejoinders found in these three sections and then assess the significance and success of each argument.

Rāmānuja's First Argument

Rāmānuja begins by asking his Advaitin opponent what precisely is the *jīvanmukti* state? When the basic definition is given, i.e., liberation while still in an embodied condition, Rāmānuja proceeds to give a *reductio-ad-absurdum* argument (to use the Western logical classification) against the Advaitin's doctrine of the *jīvanmukti* state. This initial argument attempts to show that the concept of *jīvanmukti* is self-contradictory. Roughly it asks, If liberation is defined as 'being without a body,' then how can one coherently speak of liberation 'while in a body'? Here is a formal construction of Rāmānuja's argument.

1. The *jīvanmukti* state is liberation while remaining in an embodied condition.
2. Liberation [according to scripture] necessarily entails the annulment of the embodied condition.
3. Thus, a *jīvanmukta* both has a body and does not have a body (1,2).
4. It is incoherent (that is, it is not possible) to both have a body and not have a body.
5. Therefore, the doctrine of the *jīvanmukti* state is incoherent in meaning [that is, the *jīvanmukti* state is self-contradictory] (3,4).

In this argument, Rāmānuja uncovers an apparent contradiction between two different aspects of Advaita's doctrine of liberation (*mokṣa*). The Advaita contention (based on scriptural text) that liberation is the cessation of embodiment contradicts his acknowledgment of an embodied state of liberation; thus, the *jīvanmukti* doctrine is incoherent, or more specifically, self-contradictory.

Rāmānuja's Second Argument

After Rāmānuja has given his initial argument, the Advaitin opponent responds with a clarification to the definition of *jīvanmukti*. The opponent states that the *jīvanmukti* state is a liberated state in which there is a "cessation of embodiment" but only in the sense that the aspirant is aware of the unreality of the body while still perceiving the body. That is, the expression "cessation of embodiment" is to be understood only in the sense that the aspirant is *aware* of the unreality of the body.

Rāmānuja objects, however, that this modified account does not avoid the problem raised in his argument, for if one is aware of the unreality of the appearance of the body, then this in itself means the end to embodiment. Thus there is no difference between the *jīvanmukti* and *videhamukti* states of liberation. A reconstruction of this second argument can be formulated as follows:

1. *Jīvanmukti* is defined as a state of personal liberation in which the liberated self is aware of the unreality of the body.
2. *Videhamukti* is defined as the cessation of the false appearance of embodiment as liberation occurs.
3. Since *jīvanmukti* is defined as "awareness of the unreality of the body," just as *videhamukti* is defined as cessation of the false appearance of embodiment, there is no semantic difference between these two terms (1,2).
4. Hence, [Advaita's] definition of liberation is *de facto* the definition of *videhamukti*, and the concept of *jīvanmukti* does not have any meaning or importance aside from a different name for the *videhamukti* state (3).

Rāmānuja's Third Argument

The third section of the passage also begins with an an expanded Advaitin account of the *jīvanmukti* state. The Advaitin opponent once again senses that Rāmānuja has misconstrued or unduly simplified the *jīvanmukti* position. In an effort to clarify and establish his position, the Advaitin opponent makes reference to the often used analogy of the "two moons." This analogy is used as a real-life example of how a misperception persists even after one learns of a mistake. Two variants of this analogy are used by Advaitins. The metaphysical version involves the reflection of a "second" moon in a calm body of water, while the psychological version involves an eye disorder that leads one to see two moons in the sky. Advaitins use the second version (interpretation) of the two-moon analogy to explain how *jīvanmukti* can occur. Hence, this is the version that concerns us.[3]

The second version of the analogy is based on a person suffering from double vision or diplopia (Skt: *taimirika*).[4] Such a person sees two moons in the evening sky due to the defect in the visual organs. Even when learning of this perceptual disorder, the distorted perception of the moon continues. In this case, the person will continue to see two moons in the sky—though now recognizing that only one moon really exists. In the same fashion, a *jīvanmukta* continues to perceive the world of multiplicity even though s/he knows that it is based in ignorance (*avidyā*) and is not real.

Rāmānuja criticizes this argument through analogy by pointing to a disanalogy between the nature of the "discerning knowledge" found in the two examples. In the case of the discernment of the illusory nature of the second moon caused by the eye disorder, the individual simply gains a new understanding of the double image perceived: there is a psychological modification in the agent's idea about the nature of the two moons perceived, while the causal factor that produces the image (the eye disorder) is not affected. However, in the case of the discernment of the falsity of embodiment—and this is what is crucial here—everything other than Brahman is annulled. This annulment includes the destruction of ignorance and all of its effects, such as *karma*, desire, fear, and so forth. Since these afflictions (*kleśas*) are held to be the cause of embodiment, embodiment cannot persist after attaining liberation. Unlike the case of the "two moons," not only is the illusion discerned, but also the *cause* of the illusion is annulled, thus destroying the illusion itself. Below is a formal rendering of this polemical interchange, beginning with the Advaitin argument by analogy and then Rāmānuja's argument against its cogency.

1. We can come to know how the *jīvanmukta* can at once be liberated and yet maintain the appearance of an embodied condition by comparing it to such cases as the persistence of the perception of two moons even after one recognizes that there is only one actual moon.
2. When one discovers that the second "perceived" moon is not a real moon, still the moon continues to appear. In the same way, when the *jīvanmukta* realizes his/her true nature is the cosmic Self, identical with Brahman, the appearance of the body continues [until the fructifying karma is burned off].
3. In response, one can observe that this analogical inference is flawed due to the central dissimilarity between these two cases (that is, the *jīvanmukti* state and the appearance of the two moons):

    • These cases are *not* similar with regard to the *mechanism* responsible for the persistence of the illusory phenomenon.
    • The factors responsible for the second moon's appearance (the diseased eye organs) exist, regardless of the perceiver's interpretation of the two-moon image; yet the factors giving rise to the appearance of the embodied self (ignorance, desire, fear, and so forth) are dependent on the attitude or awareness of the observer.

- Once the causes of embodiment/bondage are annulled through knowledge, embodiment ceases due to its dependence on the ignorant state of the self. However, the second moon persists since the cause of its appearance (eye defect) is not linked to the awareness of the observer.

4. Hence, the two-moon analogy fails to establish how embodiment is possible once liberation is attained.

In this third and final exchange, Rāmānuja attempts to show that the Advaitin has failed to give a relevant example for illustrating how embodiment can persist after liberating knowledge arises. It is now our task to determine the effectiveness of these three arguments directed against the Advaitin account of the *jīvanmukti* state.

Analysis of the First Argument: *Jīvanmukti* as Self-Contradiction

Rāmānuja's first argument rests on the apparent contradiction between premises one and two attributed to the Advaita position, rendering the concept of *jīvanmukti* self-contradictory. As observed in premise three, one cannot define liberation as the "annulment of the embodied state" and at the same time recognize that liberation occurs while still maintaining a body; this position is clearly contradictory. As presented, Rāmānuja's argument is clearly valid and devastating. One need only determine whether he has misrepresented or misconstrued the Advaita account of liberation. If he has done so, then his first argument is unsound and hence ineffective. On the other hand, if the premises are true, his argument stands. Let's consider the writings of Śaṅkara on this matter.

As Śaṅkara is well documented to have held premise one,[5] premise two needs to be scrutinized. Śaṅkara does make reference to passages in scripture that equate unembodiment with liberation. For example, in his commentary on the *Brahma Sūtra* Śaṅkara remarks:

> Having also annihilated the other meritorious and sinful acts which have already started to bear fruit, by experiencing their fruit, identification with the Supreme Self (*ātman*) is attained [that is, death], on the authority of the scriptural passages, "He is delayed [from liberation] only so long as he is not relieved of the body and then he becomes one with Brahman" [*Chāndogya Upaniṣad* 6.14.2], and "Himself being brahman, he merges into Brahman . . . " [*Bṛhadāraṇyaka Upaniṣad* 4.4.6] (BSŚ 4.1.19.)

In passages such as this one, Śaṅkara appears to be equating liberation with unembodiment, and it is quite possible that Rāmānuja had this passage—or one similar in content—in mind when he formulated his argument. However, what Rāmānuja has failed to consider is that Śaṅkara recognizes that liberation occurs either in an embodied or disembodied state. Śaṅkara holds that upon realization of Brahman, the aspirant maintains physical form in a state of embodied liberation and continues in that state until death occurs, at which point s/he "merges" into Brahman (disembodied liberation). Both passages cited above refer to a final merging into Brahman, but they do not deny or mitigate the occurrence of Brahman knowledge (*brahmavidyā*) and liberation prior to death. Śaṅkara's main point in his commentary on these passages is that death and the final merging of the liberated person into Brahman can only occur when the fructifying (*prārabdha*) *karma* of the present life has been annihilated. *Videhamukti* occurs after a *jivanmukta* has exhausted all the *karma* designated to bear fruit in the present life.

It should be observed that premise two is a clear statement that only *videhamukti* is possible. While Advaitins recognize the *videhamukti* state, they would not accept the explicit, exclusive restriction connoted in this formulation. In analyzing this argument one can observe that Rāmānuja is guilty of assuming the consequent, or begging the issue that is in dispute. This argument assumes what is at issue between the Viśiṣṭādvaita and Advaita positions; namely, whether there is both embodied and disembodied liberation. For those who do not assume that all instances of liberation are of the *videhamukti* type—that there is a state of embodied liberation for some aspirants occurring *prior* to disembodied liberation—there is no absurdity or self-contradiction in speaking of liberation while possessing a body. While Rāmānuja and other *videhamukti*-only advocates take as an analytical inference the conclusion that a liberated person cannot exist in a (mundane) embodied condition, other philosophers, i.e., *jīvanmukti* advocates such as Śaṅkara, do not. Since Rāmānuja has obviously encountered such philosophers, who have challenged his definition of liberation, it is incumbent upon him to at least acknowledge and address the reasons for their *jīvanmukti* position—which he actually does later in this passage. But as long as the Advaitin does not recognize the *jīvanmukti* and *videhamukti* state as occurring simultaneously, there is no contradiction. Hence, Rāmānuja's argument does not prove to be an effective refutation of the Advaitin position. Premise two of Rāmānuja's argument, then, is not true; consequently, Rāmānuja's first argument is not successful in demonstrating the contradictory nature of the Advaitin account of liberation or *jīvanmukti*. In this passage Rāmānuja goes on to argue that the dispute over embodied liberation versus unembodied liberation is only verbal in nature.

Analysis of the Second Argument: The *Jīvanmukti-Videhamukti* Dispute is Verbal in Nature

Rāmānuja's second argument against the Advaitin account of the *jīvanmukti* state is contained in premise three. He contends that the *jīvanmukti-videhamukti* dispute is reducible to a verbal issue, since the Advaitin definition of *jīvanmukti* is applicable to the *videhamukti* state as well. Therefore, even if Śaṅkara and other Advaitins wish to call liberation "*jīvanmukti*," in fact they are speaking of *videhamukti*.

Evaluating this argument, *prima facie*, Rāmānuja seems to be confused in failing to distinguish between two distinct propositions: "*S* has a body," and "It seems to *S* that *S* has a body." The first proposition is a metaphysical statement, while the second is a psychological one. The Advaitin position is of the latter sort; it connotes only that the liberated person is psychologically aware of the illusory nature of his or her physical embodiment. In contrast, the *videhamukti* position demands that one's body no longer exist. Thus, this is no mere verbal disagreement, for each expression denotes a radically different state of affairs.

Yet, I think there is a more fair and accurate way to construe Rāmānuja's argument. It must be recognized that Rāmānuja ascribed a doctrine of subjective idealism to Śaṅkara and Advaitins in general. Śaṅkara is linked to the doctrine that the world is illusory and has no reality apart from its temporary existence based on ignorance (avidyā). Rāmānuja's argument now takes on a different character, given this metaphysical presupposition that he attributes to Śaṅkara.

Rāmānuja is arguing that when a *jīvanmukta* realizes in attaining liberation the illusory nature of his or her body, there is no possible way that such an illusion (the *jīvanmukta's* body) can continue to exist. If the world—including the appearance of one's body—is illusory, then discovery of the illusion should bring about an instantaneous discontinuation of all illusory appearances. Hence, liberation in an embodied state (*jīvanmukti*), automatically leads to a disembodied existence (*videhamukti*), as the phenomenal universe—including one's body—ceases to exist. Consequently, it is not accurate to treat these "two" states of liberated existence as distinct, since they amount to the same state. Thus, it must be determined if Śaṅkara and Advaitins on the whole are subjective idealists. This concern will be discussed after we look at Rāmānuja's final argument.

Analysis of the Third Argument: Disanalogy in the Two Moons Analogy

The subjective-idealist interpretation and Advaita is also the basis of Rāmānuja's third argument. The analogy of two moons is meant to explain how one can recognize the unreal nature of some phenomenon and still continue to perceive its "occurrence." Just as one suffering from double vision continues to see a second moon even when that person knows the "second moon" is a product of diplopic vision, so too the *jīvanmukta* continues to experience the phenomenal world even though s/he now realizes it to be but the product of ignorance or *avidyā*. Rāmānuja—again, assuming a subjective-idealist interpretation of Advaita Vedānta—quickly points out a fundamental difference between these two phenomena. In reference to the person suffering from diplopia, the physical and biological phenomena creating the second moon image are real and, hence, continue to produce the image after discernment arises. That is, the disease that afflicts the sight of the perceiver produces the double image of the moon in the mind of the perceiver, regardless of that person's assessment of the image's metaphysical status. By comparison, when liberation occurs, the *jīvanmukta* now recognizes the mistaken attribution of "reality" ascribed to the world, now *knowing* that Brahman is the *sole* reality. As a consequence, all that is said to have given rise to the appearance of the world (that is, ignorance, the power of cosmic illusion, influence of past *karma*, and so forth) no longer exists for the liberated person; hence, the world and even the person, him/herself, cease to exist. Rāmānuja observes that it is not possible to speak of someone physically surviving liberating knowledge—at least liberating knowledge as defined by Advaita.

To discern the effectiveness of this line of argument, then, we must determine whether Advaitins uphold a position of subjective idealism. If Śaṅkara is not committed metaphysically to subjective idealism and can offer an account of some independent mechanical process responsible for the appearance of the embodied state, only then can the "two moon" analogy be accepted as plausible. It is generally recognized that Śaṅkara and most Advaitins[7] do not wish to classify their metaphysical position as subjective idealism; though the world is a product of cosmic illusion (*māyā*) and ignorance (*avidyā*), it still has some ontological status. Śaṅkara does not view the world as completely unreal, but rather appears to ascribe to the world a degree of reality and sense of autonomous existence independent of any one person's ignorance or liberation. Śaṅkara himself attacks the subjective idealist school of Buddhism (Vijñānavāda) on the grounds that one can never perceive that which is non-existent, and since we perceive external objects they must exist (*BUŚ* 2.2.28).

Advaitins define the world as either *sadasadvilakṣana* which literally means "characterized as other than real or unreal," or simply *anirvacanīya*, "ineffable, beyond verbal or conceptual expression."[8] Their position seems to be that one cannot deny that the world ever existed or say that it has no reality as one clearly experiences it daily; however, because it is fundamentally based in an error (*avidyā*), it can hardly be called reality—particularly in comparison with Brahman. Thus, Advaitins have created a middle category in their ontology and epistemology—between reality and illusion, truth and falsehood. Given that the world and body have some ontological status, they allow themselves the capacity to recognize the occurrence of a *jīvanmukta*.[9] Maintaining some semblance of a realist position is critical for Śaṅkara, since he emphatically holds that self-knowledge cannot arise without the medium of the body (*BUŚ* 4.1.15).

Advaitins explain the persistence of the body by assuming that (1) there is a type of bondage (specifically, fructifying *karma*) responsible for the creation and sustenance of the body and worldly self; (2) this type of bondage is not affected by liberating knowledge; and (3) ignorance and knowledge are correlative principles that interact with each other in a mutually exclusive fashion. The Advaitin explanation and justification for embodied liberation lies in the distinction that there is a form of bondage that continues to maintain the body even after ignorance is removed.

The relation between bondage (*bandha*) and ignorance (*avidyā*) can be distinguished according to the following points. Bondage is the process that "binds" the universal self (*ātman*) to the transmigratory cycle of worldly existence (*saṃsāra*). There are a number of components or factors that contribute to this process—for example, *karma*, superimposition (*adhyāsa*) of the worldly, ego-identity (*jīva*) upon one's real universal-identity (*ātman*) and vice versa, limiting adjuncts (*upādhis*), desire (*kāma*), attachment (*rāga*), aversion (*dveṣa*), and fear (*bhaya*). Ignorance is portrayed as the failure on the part of the true Self to recognize its universal, boundless nature. Ignorance is considered the root cause of bondage.[10] Yet ignorance of the true reality of things cannot *by itself* bind the self to worldly existence and transmigration; it is only through its effect, *karma*, that a self undergoes the cycle of rebirth (*BUŚ* 1.4.10).

If we die in a condition of ignorance (that is, an afflicted state with desires), then our stored *karma* from previous actions will bring about the development of a new body or physical existence to inhabit in the next life (*BUŚ* 3.3.1). And in this process of rebirth, a certain amount of *karma* is "activated" to bear fruit in this next life. This *karma* will determine one's type of birth (*jāti*), the duration of one's life (*āyus*), and the nature of one's experiences (*bhoga*) in the next rebirth. *Karma*, as a type of bondage, is particularly significant because it is *not* ignorance per se (for example, desire, superimposition, fear, delusion, grief), but a *product* of ignorance. Though it is caused to bear fruit in the above mentioned way through desire, it itself cannot be recognized as a type of ignorance (psychological affliction). The key point here is that although all forms of bondage are *due to ignorance*, not all forms of bondage are *forms of ignorance*. Hence, since there is a type of bondage that is not a form of ignorance, the destruction of ignorance does not remove all forms of bondage; thus, the body can remain even after attaining liberation.[11]

In his commentary on the *Bṛhadāraṇyaka Upaniṣad*, Śaṅkara gives a further explanation of why even knowledge cannot destroy this type of bondage (*BUŚ* 1.4.10). He holds that a particular phenomenon can be destroyed only by its opposite. For example, darkness is removed only by light, and light can illuminate that which is in darkness. In the case of knowledge, it can dispel only its opposite, ignorance. *Karma*, again, is not a type or form of ignorance; it is simply a mechanical system of retribution for actions performed. Knowledge destroys only its opposite, ignorance, and does not affect fructifying *karma*, which continues to sustain the embodied existence until it is exhausted.[12]

Let us return, now, to our earlier question regarding the ontological status of the world according to Advaita. From what has just been said, we can observe that (1) there is a type of bondage that is responsible for the creation and sustenance of the body and worldly self; (2) this type of bondage is not affected by the liberating knowledge; and (3) knowledge can annul only its correlative opposite, ignorance (that is, knowledge cannot cure a stomach ache, while it can "relieve" a math problem). Śaṅkara and most Advaitins, then, do not view the world as completely unreal, but rather ascribe to the world a degree of reality and a sense of autonomous existence independent of any one person's ignorance or liberation. Given that the liberated person reaches such a state in a body and existed as an individual self (*jīva*) before this awakening, it is plausible that s/he could continue in such a state even if s/he dispelled the false identification with the ego. In such a situation, past friends would continue to experience the newly liberated person's physical existence in the same way as before, so long as the body continues to maintain itself. However, the jīvanmukta no longer identifies with the worldly ego-self, even though outwardly s/he projects a continuous identity linked with the pre-liberated identity. The world, then, for Śaṅkara is not purely an illusion or fiction; it is just not as real as Brahman.

We can observe that Śaṅkara and most Advaitins do not appear to be subjective idealists; further, Śaṅkara has given an explanation for the persistence of embodiment (that is, fructifying *karma*). Hence, Rāmānuja's second and third arguments have failed, due to misrepresentation of the

Advaitin position. Yet even if Rāmānuja's arguments have not proved damaging to the Advaitin position, it is of significance that exponents of the same school of thought (Vedānta) disagree on such a central issue as liberation. It is important to come to some understanding of why this divergence of thought came about. In the next section I will speculate on why Rāmānuja rejects the *jīvanmukti* state and why most Advaitins chose to recognize its occurrence.

Basis for the *Jīvanmukti* and *Videhamukti*-Only Positions

Classical Indian thought characterizes all life as undergoing a transmigratory existence (*saṁsāra*), which is frequented by experiences of suffering and pain. Death offers little relief from suffering (*duḥkha*), since rebirth into yet another body is soon to follow; hence, true release from suffering must occur only when the process of rebirth is stopped. Consequently, the genesis of the notion of release or liberation must stem from a pressing need to discover a way to end this cycle of rebirth into a life of suffering.[13] Then liberation would appear to occur at the point of death, when one's present embodied condition ceases and no further incarnation is possible. That is, if embodiment entails experience of the world of suffering, it follows that liberation must occur only when this present life of suffering has come to an end and there is a permanent cessation of any future rebirths into this world. Hence, as Rāmānuja observes, it appears contradictory to speak of liberation while still surviving in the saṃsāric transmigratory sphere; that is, one is liberated from suffering (embodiment) while at the same time existing in a condition of suffering (embodiment). So why would anyone choose to speak of liberation while still maintaining a body?

Scriptural Basis

As Advaita Vedānta is an orthodox Indian school, it must attempt to incorporate Vedic doctrines in its philosophical position. There are several Upaniṣadic verses that appear to make reference to a state of spiritual attainment akin to the *jīvanmukti* state. Consider the following representation of Upaniṣadic verses indicating embodied liberation (with my italics added):

> On this point there is this verse:
> When are liberated all
> The desires that lodge in one's heart

> Then a mortal becomes immortal!
> *Therein he reaches Brahma[n]*!
>
> As the slough of a snake lies on an ant-hill, dead, cast off, even so lies this body. But this incorporeal, immortal Life (*prāṇa*) is Brahma[n] indeed, is light indeed (*Bṛhadāraṇyaka Upaniṣad* 4.4.7).
>
> Verily, *while we are here* we may know this [nature of the Self]. If you have known it not, great is the destruction. Those who know this become immortal,
> But others go only to sorrow (*Bṛhadāraṇyaka Upaniṣad* 4.4.14).
>
> If *one has known [It] here*, then there is truth.
> If one has known [It] not here, great is the destruction.
> Discerning [It] in every single being, the wise,
> On departing from this world, become immortal (*Kena Upanisad* 2.5).
>
> He, verily, who knows that supreme Brahma[n], becomes very Brahma[n]. In his family no one ignorant of Brahma[n] arises.
> *He crosses over sorrow. He crosses over sin*. Liberated from the knots of the heart, he becomes immortal (*Muṇḍaka Upaniṣad* 3.2.9).
>
> When through self, by the suppression of the mind, one sees the brilliant Self which is more subtile than the subtile, *then having seen the Self through one's self, one becomes self-less* (*nir-ātman*). Because of being selfless, he is to be regarded as incalculable (*a-saṃkhya*) without origin—the mark of liberation (*mokṣa*). This is the supreme secret doctrine (*Maitri Upaniṣad* 6.20).[14]

It should be noted that nowhere in the Upaniṣads do its authors use the term "*jīvanmukti*." The passages given above do seem to indicate embodied liberation but they are vague in nature, allowing for alternative (contrary) interpretations such as might be put forth by a *videhamukti*-only adherent. Indeed, we can just as easily quote other passages in the Upaniṣads that appear to support the *videhamukti*-only position.[15] Nevertheless, such passages as given above do suggest to subsequent listeners the occurrence of embodied liberation and provide authoritative references to support their contention that the *jīvanmukti* state exists.

Empirical Evidence for Jīvanmukti

Instrumental to the development and propagation of Indian philosophical and religious speculation is the institution of the *guru* or teacher. A usual criterion for establishing the authority of the *guru* is that s/he is a realized person, meaning that s/he knows the true nature of Reality. Advaita, being an orthodox school, anchors the correctness of its teachings to a chain of enlightened teachers stretching all the way back to the original *ṛṣis* who expressed the Vedas.[16] Advaitins emphasize that their teachings are based on the insights gained by these enlightened persons who continue to convey their wisdom to devotees for as long as their bodies continue to exist.[17] Stated baldly, one of the principal reasons Advaitin philosophers have developed the *jīvanmukti* position is because they have literally met individuals who they believe to be enlightened. Consider the passage below, taken from the *Upadeśasāhasrī*, which indicates the required characteristics for a teacher of Advaita, including reference to the liberated state of awareness:

> . . . [T]he teacher is able to consider the pros and cons [of an argument], is endowed with understanding, memory, tranquility, self-control, compassion, favor and the like; he is versed in the traditional doctrine; not attached to any enjoyments, visible or invisible; he has abandoned all the rituals and their requisites; *a knower of Brahman, he is established in Brahman*; (italics added) he leads a blameless life, free from faults such as deceit, pride, trickery, wickedness, fraud, jealousy, falsehood, egotism, self-interest, and so forth; with the only purpose of helping others he wishes to make use of knowledge (*UpSa* 2.1.6).

Doctrinal Considerations

Philosophically, it is not sufficient to simply observe that a particular individual appears to be liberated. There must be some doctrinal or theoretical account explaining the nature of bondage and liberation and how embodied liberation is possible. When considering the philosophy of Advaita, one finds that the acceptance of embodied liberation is a natural ramification of the philosophy itself. That is, it is not the case that Advaita must develop *ad hoc* justification for the *jīvanmukti* state, but rather, embodied liberation is a consistent and necessary correlate to the fundamental tenets of this religio-philosophical system of thought.

It might prove informative at this point to examine in more detail the doctrinal bases upon which Advaita and Viśiṣṭādvaita Vedānta developed their conflicting views on liberation. I will compare their positions on the nature of Self, significance of (religious) actions, and function of fructifying *karma*; additionally, there will be a comparison of selected metaphysical and theology doctrines.

View of the Self

By and large, schools of Vedanta begin with the characterization of the individuated self (*jīva*) self as the seat of consciousness and basis of personal identity and experience of the world; morally and spiritually the self is that dimension of human existence that survives death and it accumulates merit and demerit. Yet in its essence, the higher Self (*ātman*) is eternal and spiritually pure. But even given these common presuppositions, within the context of the *jīvanmukti* dispute, one can observe significant differences between each side's account of self.

Exemplifying the two sides of this dispute, we find that Rāmānuja views the self (*jīva* or *ātman*) as an immanent, active agent (*karaka*), whereas Śaṅkara perceives the Self (that is, the higher Self or *ātman*) as a transcendent observer that only vicariously participates in the thoughts and actions of the embodied agent (*jīva*). For Rāmānuja, the self is atomic in size, dwells in the heart of the body, remains conscious of all activities in the body, and is the real agent of all actions (*BSR* 2.3.24,25,33). In contrast, Śaṅkara describes the Self (*puruṣa, ātman*) as a witness (*sākṣin*) to the activities of the world (*BUŚ* 3.4.2; *BSŚ* 1.1.4; 2.2.28 and *passim*). Forever pure and unbounded, it only *appears* to have an association with the agent self (*jīva*) responsible for the actions in the world.

To maintain the transcendental character of the self and yet account for the conscious workings of mundane existence, Advaita uses a bicameral model of the self. Basic psychological modalities such as ego (*ahaṃkāra*), mind (*manas* or *citta*), and intellect (*buddhi*) or internal agency (*antaḥkaraṇa*) are designated as foreign entities to the true Self (*ātman* or *puruṣa*). These conscious phenomena exist on a level of reality distinct from the Self proper. The lower self or *jīva* is a mere reflection (*pratibimba*) or apparent entity (*vivarta*) of the true Self, having no ontological status on its own.[18]

Rāmānuja chooses to adopt a monolithic model: there is but one self, and it partakes in the activities of the world as a doer (*Vedāntasāra* or *VS* 2.2.42) and knower (*VS* 1.1.1). Rather than view mental modalities as foreign or subsidiary activities, Rāmānuja defines them as actual qualities of the self when in a state of bondage (*VS* 1.1.1). Though the self is always eternal and "untouched" (*asprṣa*) by faults occurring to the body, still the self is literally bound and must be freed by specified means (*VS* 1.1.1). For Śaṅkara the true Self is never "really" bound; it is only erroneously identified with the lower self and its activities, so no "actual" damage or "real" bondage takes place. Hence, from the Advaitin perspective, a sudden influx of knowledge about the true nature of things is sufficient to "clear up" this misidentification of the Self—technically the superimposition (*adhyāsa*) of lower self upon higher Self. But for the Viśiṣṭādvaitin, release is not quite so simple, as the self must be freed from the bondage (fructifying *karma*) that *literally* has bound it to a physical body.

Metaphysics

The quasi-idealist metaphysics of Advaita that portray the world in some way as less than real, naturally tends to lead to the *jīvanmukti* position. If the world is based in ignorance, then one need only remove its cause, ignorance, to reach liberation. Since the world is based in one's psychological state of ignorance, the influence and control of mundane existence upon the individual is greatly diminished once one has removed ignorance. As a *jīvanmukta*, one's body is still sustained as a residual product of ignorance, the bondage of fructifying *karma*; yet, psychologically one is no longer under the deluding influence of ignorance and suffering. In contrast, Rāmānuja cannot support the *jīvanmukti* position. For if the world is real and human involvement in it is real and substantial, then simply discovering one's true spiritual nature and recognizing the forces behind its existence (God), does not free a person from the substantial forces that initially bind someone. As long as a person is in a body, s/he is subject to the demands and dangers of mundane existence and is responsible for all of his/her thoughts and deeds.

Performance of Actions

The process or means to liberation takes on distinctive qualities, given the initial account of Self and its condition of bondage. If the Self is never (really) entangled in the world and does not "literally" exist in a state of bondage, then its release occurs simultaneously with the correcting knowledge. That is, since the Self is viewed as only "appearing" to be bound and undergoing a case of misidentification of its own identity, one need only correct this error and all is well: the self (*jīva*) is then released from its unfortunate situation. However, if one takes the *videhamukti*-only position that the self is indeed bound and enmeshed with worldly events and *karmic* residues, the task of freeing the self is much more involved and time-consuming. One must engage in a process of removing the (real) contaminants or qualities that have entangled the self. The liberative procedure involves ritualistic, devotional, penitential, and moral acts that purify the self, mitigating the influence of contaminants.

Both Rāmānuja and Śaṅkara stress the instrumental role that action plays in the quest for liberation. Śaṅkara outlines four general qualifications (*sādhana catuṣṭaya*) that must be satisfied for attaining liberation. These requirements include: (i) discrimination (*viveka*) between what's real and unreal; (ii) indifference (*vairāgya*) toward all petty and sensuous desires—the central cause of immoral activity; (iii) acquiring mental tranquillity (*śama*), self-control (*dama*), dispassion (*uparati*), endurance (*titikṣā*), focus of mind (*samādhāna*), and faith (*śraddha*); and finally, the relentless desire for liberation (*mumukṣutva*) (*BSŚ* 1.1.1). Rā phasizes that liberation can only come about through rigo mance of duties with complete detachment (*karma yoga*). A states in his commentary on the *Bhagavad Gītā*:

> Not by non-performance of the acts prescribed by the scriptures, does a person attain freedom from *karma*, i.e., *jñāna yoga*; nor by ceasing to perform such actions as are prescribed in the scriptures and are already begun by him . . . Hence devoid of it (*karmaniṣṭhā*), one does not achieve perfect knowledge (*jñānaniṣṭhā*). . . . By those persons who have not worshipped Govinda by acts done without attachment to fruits and whose beginningless and endless accumulation of evil has not been annulled thereby, constant contemplation on self is not possible (*BhGR* 3.4).

Differences in Advaitin and Viśiṣṭādvaitin attitudes toward action can be explained in terms of the role action plays in the actual liberating process. All agree that performance of moral and ritualistic duty serves to remove selfish and greedy attitudes that are integral to bondage. Further, specific yogic and devotional activities provide a means to calm the mind and root out mental afflictions (*kleśas*) that continue to cause the Self (*ātman*) to misunderstand its true nature and keep the self (*jīva*) preoccupied with egoistic desires for mundane wealth and power.

Śaṅkara views these actions as functioning in a preparatory capacity; they serve only to create a situation in which the true Self is able to reflect upon itself and discover its true identity. He states, "But final release is something not to be effected at all . . . works may subserve final release mediately. For in so far as furthering knowledge, work may be spoken of as an indirect cause of final release." (*BSŚ* 4.1.16). These actions are required only as a means to allow the mental faculties to "inform" the Self of its true nature (*UpSa* 2.1.4). Once this awakening is complete, the value of actions is nullified, and they no longer have a specific function. Śaṅkara is adamant on this point. He argues that the effect of action is either a production, modification, purification, or attainment of something previously unachieved. Liberation cannot properly be identified as any of these effects, principally because all of them occur as a finite action; liberation is an eternal state, so it could not be the result of such a finite event (*UpSa* 1.1.4). Rāmānuja in contrast adds an additional purpose to these sorts of actions, namely, to remove the effects of ignorance that still bind the Self. Continued observance of proper conduct (when done in a detached manner) serves to "burn up" the existing *karma* and provides further knowledge that removes the afflicted qualities attached to the self (*BSR* 4.1.15–16). For Rāmānuja bondage is a physical condition that requires real actions to overcome. A mere thought or clarification by the Self will not undo the existing effects of bondage and ignorance.

Fructifying Karma

Throughout this study, a reoccurring factor in the bondage-liberation scheme has been fructifying *karma*. Both Śaṅkara and Rāmānuja recognize that it is responsible for the continuation of the body after true knowledge is gained (*BSŚ* and *BSR* 4.1.14–16, 18, 19). But Rāmānuja views it as responsible for delaying liberation until death, while Śaṅkara maintains its presence does not warrant such status and holds that liberation can be attained even while the body still persists. What is the basis then for such radically different interpretations of fructifying *karma*? The answer to this central question lies in the differences found in Śaṅkara's and Rāmānuja's accounts of liberation and bondage previously discussed.

If the factors that bind the self due to fructifying *karma* are actual and real contaminants that "adhere" to the self (as espoused by Rāmānuja), then merely being aware of their nature does not free the self from its predicament; it only allows one to recognize what must be done to remove them. But if the factors that bind the self are only "apparent" and lie in the confusion of the Self itself—and not in the actual effects of *karma*—then fructifying *karma* is not going to be seen as a force capable of forever continuing to bind the Self once the misconception has been removed. Presumably the reason the Self in the Advaitin account must continue its relationship with the mind-body complex is because fructifying *karma* is a force of nature already set in motion and must continue its course until it is exhausted.[19] Nevertheless, the Self is no longer "fooled" into identifying with mundane activity and sees itself as distinct from the activities of the worldly mind and body.

Thus far we have seen that Śaṅkara's recognition of the *jīvanmukti* state is a natural ramification of his metaphysical, epistemological, and psychological positions. In contrast, Rāmānuja did not acknowledge the *jīvanmukti* state due to his views in these same areas. Yet, there is another, overriding concern that causes Rāmānuja and all other Viāsiṣṭādvaita Vedāntins to reject the *jīvanmukti* account of liberation. There are strong theological considerations that rule out the occurrence of a *jīvanmukta*.

Theological Considerations

A basic difference between the Viśiṣṭādvaita and Advaita expressions of Vedānta centers on the role of God in their respective systems of thought. For Rāmānuja, salvation or liberation is to lose the physical body and allow the self to reach the abode of Vaikuṇṭha (*BSR* 4.3.3). Within the worldly sphere, the highest that a person can aspire to while in the body is the state of *sthita-prajñā*, or equanimity. Such a person has discovered the true nature of self as well as its relation to God and the world, and is headed toward liberation upon death;[20] yet s/he is still under the influences and control of fructifying *karma*. Only at death does the self become completely free from the influences of virtuous and vicious deeds (*BSR* 4.4.2). At this stage (*videhamukti*) the self, closely resembling Brahman, remains in an eternal proximity with God, separate though in a relation of intimate association (*VG* 117–121).

In contrast, Śaṅkara offers a philosophy of startling simplicity and symmetry, reducing all existence (including God) to an *apparent* manifestation of an unmanifest absolute, Brahman. As God is only an apparent manifestation of Brahman, there is no concern for continued devotional obedience (*bhakti*) to Him once liberation is attained. The *jīvanmukta* has realized his or her non-duality with all of existence, including God Himself, so it is not appropriate to maintain a duality between oneself and Him. Yet from a *theistic perspective*, what good is liberation embodied or unembodied, if one cannot be in loving appreciation of God? The Advaitin *jīvanmukti* state, even if possible, is nihilistic and destructive of the supreme relationship we are given with God: one seems to be condemned to a state of perpetual isolation and solitude, or worse self-nihilation.[21]

Rāmānuja is in opposition to Śaṅkara not only in regard to the goal and nature of liberation/salvation, but also in the specific means necessary to attain liberation. As discussed in the previous two sections, Rāmānuja contends that attention to obligatory devotional, social, and moral actions are indispensable for liberation (*BhGR* Introduction to Chapter 3; *BSR* 4.1.16). In fact, self-knowledge, performance of obligatory actions, and devotion to God are all necessary for liberation. One of Rāmānuja's fullest statements of the requirements for liberation is contained in his *Vedārthasaṃgraha*:

> Now this supreme Brahman, the Supreme Person is to attained. The pathway through which He is to attained is as follows: By an accumulation of the greatest merit, the sins of the past [*sañcita karma*] gathered through all past lives, are destroyed. A person, whose sins are thus destroyed through great merit, seeks refuge at the feet of the supreme Person. Such self-surrender begets an inclination toward Him. Then the aspirant acquires knowledge of reality from the scriptures aided by the instruction of holy teachers. Then by a steady effort he develops in an ever-increasing measure the qualities of the soul, like the control of the mind, the control of the senses, austeritiy, purity, forgiveness, straightforwardness, discrimination as to what is to be feared and not feared,

> non-violence. He is devoted to the performance of *nitya* and duties [daily ethical observances and occasional obligations] to his *varṇa* [caste] and *āśrama* [4 stations of life], and avoids hibited, such a course of conduct being conceived as the worship of the supreme Person. He offers his all and his very self at the lotus-like feet of the supreme Person. Actuated by a loving devotion to him, he offers perpetual praise and obeisances, engages in perpetual remembrance of Him, bows down before Him in adoration perpetually, exerts himself always in the godward direction, always sings His glories, always listens to the exalted accounts of His perfections, meditates upon him continuously, ceaselessly worships him and dedicates himself once for all to him. The supreme Person, who is overflowing with compassion, being pleased with such love, showers his grace on the aspirant, which destroys all his inner darkness. *Bhakti* [spiritual devotion] develops in such a devotee toward the supreme Person, which is valued for its own sake, which is uninterrupted, which is an absolute delight in itself, and which is meditation that has taken on the character of the most vivid and immediate vision. Through such *bhakti* is the Supreme attained (*VG* 126).

As to how these specific factors leading to liberation function, we can summarize the following points in regards to Rāmānuja's position. Performance of action has the dual function initially of preparing for self-knowledge through the purifying influence of righteous acts (*nityakarma*) and, secondly, of preventing future demeritous *karma* through omissions or misdeeds which could lead to rebirth (*BSR* 3.4.27; *BhGR* 10.13; 12.2; 18.62). Self-knowledge is necessary because it renders impotent all stored meritous (*dharma*) and demeritous (*adharma*) *karmas* that could cause future birth on earth. Yet Rāmānuja views the understanding of the nature of self as only a "subsidiary" or "accessory" to the actual process of attaining liberation. Such study allows one's mind to be freed from distractions and afflictions, so as to be able to engage in unwavering focus toward God/Brahman (*BhGR*, Introduction to Chapter 3). Rāmānuja emphasizes that it is not until one reaches a state of total devotion or meditation on God that final release is possible. One begins this process while in the body, and upon death this state of ecstasy reaches final fruition (*BhGR*, Introduction to Chapter 3).

The previously quoted passage shows that Rāmānuja also wishes to recognize that liberation is possible only with the assistance and compassion of God—that is, grace (*BhGR*, Introduction to Chapter 3; 10.10; 18.56). God is characterized as having immense love for His devotees who have proved themselves worthy; this love is manifest in His granting liberation to the devotee who has adopted devotional meditation as a means to reach Him. Rāmānuja states, "One blessed with such *bhakti* attains the fitness to be chosen by the supreme Self" (*VS* 128).[22] Release, then, is a gift (*prasāda*) from God, but it falls upon only those individuals who have undergone careful and dedicated preparation toward liberation.

This redeeming knowledge is to be distinguished from the Advaitin Self-realization acquired through knowledge alone. Knowledge of the Self is not sufficient or fulfilling, since one ultimately should strive for the attainment and awareness of God. This intimate relationship between God and His aspirants is reflected in Rāmānuja's account of the afterlife and the disembodied state of liberation. This relationship with God differs strikingly from the sort of relationship available in the world, due principally to the nature of the heavenly environment (as compared to that on earth) and the increased capacities of the liberated Self existing in heaven.[23] A person who gains Brahman knowledge is still restricted by his/her physical existence, such that liberation (living in the direct presence of God) cannot be attained until one reaches the domain of God, the only place where total divine communion (*sayūjya*) is possible. Neither the Advaitin account of *jīvanmukti*, nor even its explanation of *videhamukti* ("merging into Brahman") fulfills this goal.

Advaitins recognize that such an alternative (devotion-based) liberation path exists. Referred to as gradual liberation (*kramamukti*), which is spoken of in Upaniṣadic texts (for example, *Chāndogya Upaniṣad* 5.10.1–10), it occurs for an aspirant who has been a devotee of God (in Advaita, *saguṇa-brahman*); this afterlife is either for one who has attained realization of qualified (*saguṇa*) Brahman or for one is spiritually devoted to God. Yet Śaṅkara views this realization as incomplete (*sāvaśeṣa*) and, hence, one must continue in one's spiritual path, unlike one who has attained total and absolute liberation with non-dual Brahman (*niravaśeṣa*) and attained non-separateness (*avibhāga*) (*BSŚ* 4.2.16). The *kramamukta*, after the body dies, travels through the way of gods (*devayāna*) toward the assorted worlds (*loka*) of the gods, onward to the World of Brahma-the-effect (*kārya-brahman*) passing the cosmic spirit of Hiraṇyagarbha (*BSŚ* 4.3.3). Yet according to Śaṅkara's interpretation of these accounts, ultimate salvation or liberation (*amṛtatva*) is not attained by these dwellers in the domain of the world of Brahman (*kārya-brahman*); they will not gain final and complete liberation until dissolution (*pralaya*) of the mundane world, the world of Brahman, and God Himself occurs (*BSŚ* 4.3.10). Śaṅkara views gradual liberation as inferior and limited compared to immediate liberation. As the world of Brahman is based in ignorance and transmigration as much as the mundane world, it must be seen as an obstacle to complete release and must be avoided.

Conclusion

In the first section of this chapter, we have explicated the celebrated trio of arguments offered by Rāmānuja against the *jīvanmukti* doctrine. Through my analysis of the arguments, they were shown to be ineffective in refuting the plausibility of the embodied liberation view. Nevertheless, this attack on the *jīvanmukti* position is useful in further clarifying some of the key differences between Advaita and Viśiṣṭādvaita Vedānta. In the second part of this study we have explored the fundamental polarity between the Advaita and Viśiṣṭādvaita strains of Vedānta. The transcendental, monistic, and illusionist tendencies in Advaita Vedānta have resulted in a portrayal of liberation in which the Self "discovers" its existing identity with Brahman. Accounts of a tantalizing heavenly after-world cannot be recognized as reflecting reality or providing final resolution to the primeval ignorance that defines the human condition. Yet for the realist, nonmonistic, and devotional tendencies of Viśiṣṭādvaita Vedānta, liberation cannot be anything but complete participation in the domain of God. The state of bondage and suffering are real, as are the activities necessary for attaining knowledge of Brahman, or God. These accounts express two distinct mind sets, reflecting two different attitudes toward life and the hereafter. In spite of all the heated arguments generated over the centuries—some of which we examined at the beginning of this study—the *jīvanmukti-videhamukti* dispute seems to have boiled down to the recognition of two internally consistent yet distinct systems of thought, each with particular spiritual goals and philosophical preoccupations that lead them to divergent positions on the nature of liberation.

Abbreviations

BhGR — *Gītā Bhāṣya of Rāmānuja*. Translated by Swāmī Ādidevānanda. Madras: Sri Ramakrishna Math, n.d.

BhGŚ — Gītā Bhāṣya of Śaṅkara. Translated by Alladi Mahadeva Sastry. Madras: Samata Books, 1988.

BUŚ — *Bṛhadāraṇyaka Upaniṣad with Śaṅkara's Bhāṣya*. Translated by Swāmi Mādhavānanda. Calcutta: Advaita Ashrama, 1975.

BSŚ — *Brahma Sūtra with Śaṅkara's Bhāṣya*. Translated by Vasudeo Mahadeo Apte. Bombay: Popular Book Depot, 1960.

BSR — *Brahma Sūtra with Rāmānuja's Bhāṣya*. Edited and translated by R. D. Karmarkar. Part I-III. Poona: University of Poona Sanskrit and Prakrit Series, 1962.

UpSa — *Upadeśasāhasrī of Śaṅkara*. Translated by Sengaku Mayeda. Tokyo: University of Tokyo Press, 1979.

ViCu — *Vivekacūḍāmaṇi of Śaṅkara*. Translated by Mohini M. Chatterji. 2nd ed. Adyar: Theosophical Publishing House, 1947.

VG — *Vedārthasaṅgraha of Rāmānuja*. Translated by S.S. Raghavachar. Mysore: Sri Ramakrishna Ashrama, 1978.

VS — *Vedāntasāra of Rāmānuja*. Edited by V. Krishnamacharya. Translated by M.B. Narasimha Ayyangar. Madras: Adyar Library and Research Centre, 1979.

Notes

1. The use of analogies, particularly when using an empirical phenomenon to explain a transcendent phenomenon, is found throughout Vedāntic literature. This use of "analogical argumentation" (*sāmānyadṛṣṭānumāna*) is not considered a proof of the veracity of a theory, but a demonstration of the plausibility or workability of the relationship or process explained. When attempting to explain the functioning of imperceptible natural forces or entities—for example, *karma*, cosmic ignorance, liberating knowledge, *dharma*, Brahman, and so forth—examples of natural occurrences are given that analogized these phenomena. Still the success of the analogy to support the account or theory depends on the relative degree of similarity versus dissimilarity between the two compared phenomena.

2. *Brahma Sūtra with Rāmānuja's Bhāṣya (BSR 1.1.4)*, my translation:

> kā ceyaṃ jīvanmuktiḥ? saśarīrasyaiva mokṣa iti cet—'mātā me vandhyā' itivat asaṇgatārthaṃ vacaḥ; yataḥ saśarīratvaṃ vandhyaḥ, aśarīratvameva mokṣa iti tvayaiva śrutibhirupapāditam. atha saśarīratvapratibhāse vartamāne yasyāyam pratibhāso mithyeti pratyayaḥ, tasya saśarīratvanivṛttiriti. na, mithyeti pratyayena saśarīratvaṃ nivṛttam cet, katham, saśarīrasya muktiḥ? ajīvato 'pi muktiḥ saśarīratvamithyāpratibhāsanivṛttireveti ko 'yaṃ jīvanmuktiriti viśeṣaḥ. atha saśarīratvapratibhāso vādhito 'pi yasya dvicandrajñānavadanuvartate, sa jīvanmukta iti cet—na; brahmavyatiriktasakalavastuviṣayatvād bādhakajñānasya. kāraṇabhūtā (to') vidyākarmādidoṣaḥ saśarīratvapratibhāsena saha tenaiva bādhita iti, bādhitānuvṛttir na śakyate vaktum. dvicandrādau tu tatpratibhāsāhetubhūtadoṣasya bādhakajñānabhūtacandraikatvajñānāviṣayatvenābādhitatvāt dvicandrapratibhāsānuvṛttiryuktā.

3. The metaphysical version is used principally to illustrate the relation between the relative self (*jīva*) and the supreme self (*ātman*). Specifically, the "two moon" analogy nicely mirrors the reflection (*pratibimba*) theory of personal identity. This variant of the analogy observes that, at times, when looking upon a calm

lake in the evening, one sees a "moon" shining in the lake. An ignorant person looking at the lake and then looking into the sky may think that two moons exist, one in the sky and one in the lake. This, of course, is an erroneous view, as the moon shining in the lake is only a reflection of the moon in the sky. Similarly, people who are ignorant of their true nature identify themselves with their empirical self (*jīva*), when in reality it is only a "reflection" of their supreme cosmic Self (*ātman*) which is non-different from Brahman. One of the most detailed accounts of the metaphysical version of this analogy can be found in the *Vivekacūḍāmaṇi* (*ViCu 220–221*), though its uses a slight variation involving the sun reflecting on the surface of water in a jar. One can find reference to accounts of the moon reflected in water in the *Brahmasiddhi* (1.17), the *Ātmabodha* (16), and *Chāndogyopaniṣad Bhāsya* (2.23.1).

4. Some specific texts that use the psychological version of the two-moon analogy include: *Brahmasiddhi* 1.35; 3.58; *Taittirīyopaniṣad Bhāṣyavārttika* 1.1.151; *Pañcīkaraṇavārttika* 65; *Pañcapādikā* 8.21; 20.66; 16.54; and *Upadeśasāhasrī* (*UpSa*) 1.40.

5. Technically Śaṅkara uses the term "*jīvanmukti*" only once in his commentary on the *Bhagavad Gītā* (*BhGŚ*), at 6.27, so it must not have been a technical term he employed; however, he frequently speaks of the persistence of the body after the occurrence of realization of Brahman or *brahmajñāna*: for example, *Saṅkara's bhāṣyas* of the *Brahma Sutra* (*BSŚ*) 4.1.15; 4.1.19, and *Bṛhadāraṇyaka Upaniṣad* (*BUŚ* 1.4.10). Further, Śaṅkara states, "the realization of Brahman is not confined to any specific condition such as that of final release" (that is, *videhamukti*) (*BSŚ* 2.1.14).

6. *BSŚ*, p. 810. Cf. Chapter 1 in this volume in reference to Śaṅkara's *apparent* link between liberation and disembodiment.

7. Perhaps the most notorious Advaitin who accepts a subjective idealist metaphysics is Prakāśānanda. Accordingly, he is but one of a handful of Advaitins who argue against Śaṅkara and other Advaitins' doctrine of *jīvanmukti*. For those Advaitins (for example, Prakāśānanda, Dharmarāja, Sarvajñātman, etc.) who are extreme *māyāvādins* (the world is a complete illusion) or *ekajīvavādins* (there is only one Self—even in the *māyā*–based world), it is logically impossible to uphold the *jīvanmukti* position. Yet, we need to remember that Rāmānuja intended his argument to apply to all Advaitins and not to just this fringe group of Advaitins; further, his argument has no detrimental effect against the latter group, since they have dismissed the *jīvanmukti* position already.

8. See Eliot Deutsch, *Advaita Vedānta: A Philosophical Reconstruction* (Honolulu: University of Hawaii Press, 1969), p.32; *UpSa* pp. 22–26; Karl H. Potter, ed. *Advaita Vedānta up to Śaṃkara and His Pupils* (Princeton: Princeton University Press, 1981), 78–88.

9. Even though the above analysis appears to show that this second argument is based on a misrepresentation of mainstream Advaita metaphysics and, hence, is

not effective, it is clear that this line of attack bothered Advaita philosophers a great deal; consequently, a number of doctrinal "innovations" were developed either to supplement the fructifying *karma* explanation or present an alternative. Assorted metaphors were utilized to help conceptualize how the *jīvanmukti* state occurs. The persistence of the body due to fructifying *karma* is compared to the continuing momentum of a potter's wheel after the potter has ceased to propel the wheel or the continued forward motion of an arrow after it has left the archer's bow. Additionally, Advaitins explained the persistence of the body as the product of a trace of ignorance which remains (*leśāvidyā*), the persistence of the projective (*vikṣepa*) mode of *māyā* while the concealment (*āvaraṇa*) mode has ceased, or the choice of the *jīvanmukti* to continue to project his/her worldly appearance so as to help other seekers of truth (a corollary to the Buddhist concept of *bodhisattva*). Alternatively, if one cannot accept that there remains *any* form of *karma* once there is Brahman knowledge, then it is suggested that the *jīvanmukta's vāsanās* or dispositions maintain the physical appearance for a time. The complexity and variation of these accounts can hardly be even summarized here. For further reference to these options and the reasoning behind them, see A.G. Krishna Warrier's *The Concept of Mukti in Advaita Vedānta*, (Madras: University of Madras, 1961), 480–508 and the footnote discussion 85 and 86 in S.S. Suryanarayana Sastri's translation of the *Vedāntaparibhāṣā* by Dharmarāja Adhvarin (Madras: Adyar Library, 1971), 216–218.

10. Śaṅkara actually fluctuates among naming ignorance, desire, or the limiting adjuncts (*upādhis*) as the "root (singular) cause of bondage and transmigration." However, ignorance and its prevalent manifestation, desire, seem to be singled out as the "paramount" cause of bondage. See Śaṅkara's commentary on the *Bṛhadāraṇyaka Upaniṣad* 5.4.6 for an example where, in a single passage, he refers to all three factors as the root of bondage.

11. The reason the *jīvanmukti* does *not* create a new body after the exhaustion of the current body upon death is that liberation *does* destroy the other two types of *karma* (besides fructifying *karma*) which are responsible for continuing the process of rebirth. All the *karma* from past lives (*saṃcita karma*), and all the *karma* to be incurred from future actions (*āgāmi karma*) are rendered impotent. Latent *karma* that is not destined to bear fruit in the present life is rendered impotent because one's desires (which are necessary for this *karma* to create a new body) have ceased. Further, future actions will not cause the accumulation of *karma* because only ego-based intentional actions create desires and additional *karma*. (*BSŚ* 4.1.19).

12. It should be noted that some Advaitins do use the expression "trace of ignorance" (*avidyāleśa*) in reference to fructifying *karma*. However, the intent is to identify a "remnant" of the influence of *karma*. If we were to interpret this expression to mean that there literally was some element of ignorance remaining after attaining knowledge of Brahman, then this liberating knowledge appears to lack effectiveness in removing ignorance. Concerns about whether liberation is actually possible and the prospect of backsliding would now become a concern.

13. This observation has been widely utilized and accepted. See John M. Koller, *Oriental Philosophies*, 2nd ed. (New York: Charles Scribner & Sons, 1985), pp. 8ff; Deutsch, *Advaita Vedānta*, pp. 103–104; Potter, *Advaita Vedānta*, p. 32; Surendranath Dasgupta, *A History of Indian Philosophy*, vol. 1 (Cambridge: Cambridge University Press, 1969), pp. 54–61.

14. All quotations from the Upaniṣads are from the translation by Robert E. Hume, *The Thirteen Principal Upanishads* 2nd ed. (London: Oxford University press, 1931).

15. One need only consider the two passages given earlier in our analysis of Rāmānuja's first argument against Śaṅkara—*Chāndogya Upaniṣad* 7.14.6 and *BUŚ* 4.4.6. Other examples of Upaniṣadic passages appearing to recognize the *videhamukti*-only position include:

> So the knower, being liberated from name and form, Goes unto the Heavenly Person, higher than the high (*Muṇḍaka Upaniṣad* 3.2.8.).
>
> By knowing God (*deva*) one is released form all fetters . . . They who know Him, have left the body behind (*Śvetāśvatara Upaniṣad* 5.13–14).
>
> Attaining Him [*ātman*] who is the universally omnipresent, those wise devout souls (*yuktātman*) into the All [Brahman] do enter. (*Muṇḍaka Upaniṣad* 3.3.8. All from translation by R.E. Hume, Note 14).

16. Consider the following passage from the *Vivekacūḍāmaṇi* attributed (dubiously) to Śaṅkara. Here the teacher—identified as being liberated—stressed that the information about to be shared that will take the student to liberation is derived from Upaniṣadic scriptures.

> Such a person [having satisfied prepatory requirements] must approach the teacher (*guru*) through who freedom from bondage is attainable; [this teacher] is one who is wise, well versed in the scriptures, sinless, free from desire, knowing the nature of Brahman (*brahmavid*). (34)
>
> How shall I cross this ocean of birth and re-birth? What is my destiny, what means exist, O Lord, I know not. O Lord, kindly protect me, lighten the sorrows arising from birth and re-birth. (42)
>
> The Master said: Fear not, wise man, there is no danger for you; there exists a means for crossing the ocean of birth and re-birth—that by which yogis have crossed. I shall point it out to you. (45)
>
> It is directly pointed out by the sayings of the scriptures that faith (*śraddhā*), devotion (*bhakti*), meditation (*dhyāna*), and discipline (*yoga*),

are the causes which bring about emancipation. Whoever abides by these, attains emancipation from the bondage of incarnated existence (*ViCu* 48).

17. A potential advantage for the *jīvanmukti* position lies in the fact that it recognizes that the originators of the tradition are fully realized and liberated individuals who are then inspired to share their insights with the unenlightened, suffering beings in the world. Given the *videhamukti*-only position, that no one can attain liberation until death, one might argue that such teachings are not derived from those possessing true knowledge, since no one who is living in a body can be recognized as having such insights. Yet, as *videhamukti*-only advocates do recognize that one can have Brahman-knowledge while still embodied (even though not liberation), this line of argument does not prove dangerous to their position.

18. It must be noted that this account is a generalization, though one that best suits the Advaitins' *jīvanmukti* position. An alternative theory of Self, at times referred to as *avacchedavāda* or theory of limitations, is less conducive to the transcendental account of Self. It theorizes that the Self undergoes a process of contamination as the *upādhis* or limiting adjuncts prevent the Self from perceiving its true nature. It is significant to note that these limiting adjuncts consist of psychological dispositions such as egoism, anger, selfishness, and so forth, rather than actual physical factors. Within the Advaita schools, some openly attacked the *upādhi* position (associated with the Bhāmati school) for the reasons just noted—that the Self should not be portrayed as undergoing any actual transformation or contamination.

19. Arguably, the *jīvanmukti* position appears to be having it both ways here, as on the one hand fructifying *karma* cannot prevent the Self's liberation, yet it still is responsible for maintaining the body and the Self's linkage with the body until it is exhausted. As summarized in footnote 10, there are assorted attempts by Advaitins to explain how *karma* can continue to control one's physical, worldly existence while not preventing one's capacity to realize Brahman.

20. It is significant to note that several post-Rāmānuja Viśiṣṭādvaitins acknowledge that it is possible for someone who has obtained knowledge of Brahman to backslide from the path to liberation before death (*videhamukti*). As indicated earlier, one must continue to perform prescribed rituals until death to ensure liberation and ascent to heaven. Rāmānuja doesn't explicitly state this concern, though one might argue that he implicitly is committed to this view given his insistence on performance of religious duty even after Brahman-knowledge has dawned. Regardless of whether Rāmānuja espoused this view or not, I question the plausibility of this entire line of concern. If one knows God/Brahman and embodies total devotion, nay near union with God, how could such an individual neglect religious obligations? Presumably the mental afflictions that would cause one to neglect the performance of one's duties are no longer present in one possessing Brahman-knowledge; hence, there is no basis for such demeritous behavior. For

further reference on this Viśiṣṭādvaita account of spiritual backsliding, see A. K. Lad, *A Comparative Study of the Concept of Liberation in Indian Philosophy* (Burhanpur: Girdharlal Keshavdas, 1967), 141.

21. The *Bhagavad Gītā* (3.8) recognizes two attitudes or separate paths leading to freedom from rebirth: nonaction (*jñāna yoga*) and action (*karma yoga*). The former aims at isolation (*kaivalya*) through the desire to know the Self, whereas the latter aims at the realization of God through devotion and service. There is no doubt that Rāmānuja sees the path leading to knowledge of the self (*avyakta*) as highly inferior to the path leading to communion with God (*BhGR*, Introduction to Chapter 12). He points out in his commentary on this passage (3.8) that the path of knowledge is difficult and dangerous, as it is not natural and familiar, and its inactivity can lead to a failure to properly nourish one's body, which is needed to attain liberation. As described by some later Viśiṣṭādvaitins, the path of non-action is a state devoid of God and, once attained, condemns the aspirant to eternal isolation, barred from ever knowing the bliss found in love for God. One appears to be in a state of identification with oneself, and not with Brahman or God. In other words, one is mistaken in thinking that one's self is Brahman, whereby one perceives the boundlessness of the self as the boundlessness of Brahman. As to where this isolated state actually takes place, Rāmānuja is vague, though later Vaiṣṇava theists engage in a dispute over whether it is in the material sphere or in a remote part of heaven (*Vaikuṇṭha*). Krishna Datta Bharadwaj in his book, *The Philosophy of Rāmānuja* (New Delhi: Sir Shankar Lall Charitable Trust Society, 1958), attempts to outline these differences among later Vaiṣṇavites. He states, "According to the Vadagalais, *kaivalya* is enjoyed somewhere in the material universe, whereas the Tengalais hold that *kaivalya* is trans-material so that its proper place is in the spiritual universe. The freed soul of a *jijñāsu* resides, according to the latter, in isolation in a distant part of Vaikuntha just as a woman forsaken by her husband lives away from him" (pp. 217–218).

22. See also *BSR* 1.1.1.

23. Rāmānuja gives some detail regarding this new enlightened existence in heaven (*Vaikuṇṭha*). The released Self has unlimited knowledge now that it is freed from the influence of *karma* (*VS* 4.4.2). Such a person, being forever freed from the influence of *karma* (*VS* 4.9), no longer has a body and so is capable of enjoying the sport or play created by God for the Self's pleasure (*VS* 4.9). Yet it can create a body so as to enjoy experiences in heaven similar to that found on earth (in a dreamlike fashion) (*VS* 4.4.13). Limited only in the power to rule over the worlds, the liberated Self beholds the pure Brahman, the Supreme Person, in all His glory. (*BSR* 4.4.18) One lives free from fear, since one is constantly conscious of the changeless highest Brahman (*BSR* 4.4.19). One's existence is characterized as living in union (non-division) with God (*BSR* 4.2.15) in the highest Brahman—beyond the Brahma-world and Hiraṇyagarbha (*BSR* 4.3.13). For eternity, the released Self experiences an infinity of bliss, hidden previously while in an embodied condition under the influence of ignorance and bondage (*BSR* 4.4.1).

CHAPTER 3

Direct Knowledge of God and Living Liberation in the Religious Thought of Madhva

Daniel P. Sheridan

Introduction

It is sometimes said that the Hindu concept of the *jīvanmukta*, the person who is liberated while living, usually associated with the teachings of Sāṃkhya, Yoga, and the Advaita Vedānta taught by Śaṅkara (C.E. eighth century), is not acknowledged in Dvaita Vedānta, the religious thought of Madhva (C.E. 1238–1317). For example, S. Radhakrishnan asserts that for Madhva, "absolute liberation and embodied life are not compatible."[1] Likewise A. K. Lad states: "Śaṅkara is the only Vedāntin who believes, and emphatically maintains, that jīvan-mukti is possible."[2] M. Hiriyanna states: "Madhva also rejects the ideal of *jīvanmukti*."[3] It is true that the term *jīvanmukti* is not found in the writings and that he clearly rejects the concept as taught by Śaṅkara's Advaita and his school up to Madhva's own time.[4] However, care must be taken that judgments such as Radhakrishnan's, Lad's, or Hiriyanna's not miss important nuances of historical interpretation and comparative insight. Although Madhva rejects the notion of *jīvanmukti* as understood by Advaita up to the fourteenth century, the concept of "liberation while living," in the broadest sense of contemporary scholarship and of this volume, is quite compatible with Madhva's teaching. Madhva's teaching of *aparokṣa-jñāna*, the direct and immediate knowledge of God, is functionally equivalent to Advaita Vedānta's teaching of *jīvanmukti*. The two concepts, when compared, are substantively quite different, but they will be shown to function in a similar way in these two distinct systems of Vedāntic thought.

The term *jīvanmukti*, as well as the reality ostensibly signified by the term, has had a long and varied history within the schools of Hindu religious thought. A good deal of the contemporary discussion of "living liberation" by historians of religion and Indologists is confused by a lack of precision about the meaning of the concept in its historical context and within the system of each thinker or school of thought. Furthermore, the concept of "living liberation," when used as a general interpretative category by contemporary scholars, is open to confusion with the specific historical usages of *jīvanmukti*.[5]

Śaṅkara and Madhva each teach two different versions of what liberation means. As Vedāntins, of course, both rely on Bādarāyaṇa's *Brahma Sūtra (BS)*. According to Śaṅkara and his Advaita interpretation of the *BS* of *Bādarāyaṇa*, the state of liberation from *saṃsāra*, the cycle of rebirth, is the state of one's absolute ontological identity with Brahman. This state is the result of immediate knowledge and may occur while living. According to Madhva's understanding of Vedānta and his Dvaita interpretation of the *BS* of Bādarāyaṇa, liberation from *saṃsāra* is the state of immediate knowledge of one's dependent difference from Brahman. This state must occur out of the body and after death in order to be truly a liberation from the cycle of rebirth and from obscuring ignorance, the cycle's immediate cause. On this point, according to most contemporary scholars, Madhva is in line with Bādarāyaṇa, and it is Śaṅkara who diverges from the original teaching of the *BS*.[6] For Madhva, Advaita's teaching of liberation while living, *jīvanmukti*, both is contrary to the proper import of the *Upaniṣads and the BS*, Vedānta's primary scriptural sources, and is self-contradictory. According to Śaṅkara's Advaita, *jívanmukti* means (1) that state of having true transforming knowledge of one's self as non-different from Brahman, (2) while still embodied. Madhva rejects both of these dimensions of Śaṅkara's teaching: (1) the substantive identification of liberation as a transforming knowledge of one's self as non-different (*abheda*) from Brahman, and (2) the fact that such a liberation occurs while embodied. It is obvious that, given Madhva's rejection of the first dimension, the rejection of the second automatically follows. But is there not for Madhva some sort of transforming, liberating knowledge possible while embodied and living, even if substantially different from that which Śaṅkara has described?

Madhva and Śaṅkara are interpreting a common body of Vedāntic scriptural texts, which to some extent constrain them. Madhva is not just rejecting Śaṅkara's doctrine, but he is also rejecting Śaṅkara's interpretation of those texts upon which he bases his teaching of Advaita. Yet Madhva, even while disagreeing with Śaṅkara's interpretations, must present his own interpretations of the authoritative texts. These texts indicate that liberation is from the cycle of rebirth (*saṃsāra*) caused by ignorance (*avidyā*), and that liberation has some relationship to events that occur while embodied. Hence Madhva, even in disagreeing with Śaṅkara, will teach with Śaṅkara that liberation is from *saṃsāra* and *avidyā*, and that it has a relationship to events that occur during embodiment.

Although Śaṅkara explicitly uses the term *jīvanmukti* only once, he clearly teaches the doctrine represented by the later Advaitin use of the term.[7] The term came into general use after Śaṅkara in the developed teaching of his school of Advaita. In order to defend its teaching, the Advaitin school of Vedānta resorts to the *BS* assertion: "But only those past [virtues and vices] get destroyed that have not begun to bear fruit, for death is set as the limit of waiting for liberation. . . . But having exhausted by enjoyment the other two works [good and evil works that have begun to bear fruit], he becomes one with Brahman" (*BS* 4.1.15 and 19). Although most *karma* has been annihilated by the event of liberation, *prārabdha-karma, karma* that has begun to bear fruit, continues its final course until exhausted and death occurs. For Śaṅkara, this explains why a liberation from the cycle of the embodied states of rebirth and redeath can occur during a state of embodiment. The difference between *jīvanmukti*, the state of embodied liberation, and *videhamukti*, the state of being liberated without a body, is thus explained by this reference to Bādarāyaṇa's teaching about *prārabdha-karma*. That which is common to both states of liberation is that both are constituted by the transforming and liberating knowledge of the non-duality of Self and Brahman. That which is different between the two states is that for *jīvanmukti, prārabdha-karma* must bear its fruits in a state of embodiment even after the dawn of liberating knowledge, while *videhamukti* is free from that embodiment caused by *karma*. These teachings are tied quite tightly to the general propositions of Śaṅkara's doctrine, although the specific view on *prārabdha-karma* is derived from Bādarāyaṇa's *BS*.[8]

Madhva also relies on the teaching of the *BS* IV.1.15 and 19 about *prārabdha-karma*. He even tends to cite in support of this teaching the same texts from the *Upaniṣads* as does Śaṅkara. However, he and Śaṅkara differ in the use to which they put Bādarāyaṇa's teaching on *prārabdha-karma*. Madhva and his school charged, at the substantive level, that the Advaitin view of liberation as the transforming knowledge of the non-duality of Self and Brahman, whether while embodied or not, was inconsistent on its own grounds, and inconsistent with the clear import both of the scriptures and of Bādarāyaṇa's *BS*. Nevertheless, at the functional level, Madhva and his school use the teaching of the *BS* on *prārabdha-karma* in a way similar to the use made of it by Śaṅkara; that is, to support the idea that there are two stages in the process of liberation, with the second stage being delayed by *prārabdha-karma*.

We will see that the polemical background of this dispute about the nature of liberation and about the proper interpretation of the *BS* may explain why the term *jīvanmukti* was not used by Madhva himself, although it was later equated with his teaching of *aparokṣa-jñāna* by his commentator Vyāsatīrtha (1460–1539). In the fourteenth century Madhva would not have used the term without seeming to agree with the Advaitin concept of liberation as the transformation brought about by the liberating knowledge of the non-duality of the Self and Brahman.

The concepts of *jīvanmukti* and "living liberation" may be used by contemporary scholars in a broader comparative sense as hermeneutical categories, not specifically tied to the postulates of Śaṅkara's Advaitin teaching. This is the case with the title of this very volume, *Living Liberation*. Such terms would then refer to that state of being in one's final, or almost final,[9] life, wherein the ultimate and final human goal is achieved but, because of the continued working of *prārabdha-karma*, life in the body continues until *karma* is exhausted and a final death without rebirth is occasioned. The person who will be liberated at death is assured of that liberation and that new karmic input has ceased. Such a person is liberated while living. This more general statement of "living liberation" is consistent with the semantic range of the Sanskrit term *mukti*. In this sense too Madhva may be said to espouse *jīvanmukti* or "living liberation."[10] However, this broader use of *jīvanmukti* must be employed very carefully in Madhva's case, lest it mask the finer details of Madhva's philosophical and theological teaching and be confused with the Advaitin teaching of *jīvanmukti*.

The role *jīvanmukti* plays in the thought of Śaṅkara and his followers is functionally similar to the role *aparokṣa-jñāna* plays in the religious thought of Madhva and his followers. At the same time, the two concepts are substantively different, because the two thinkers disagree so profoundly about the substantive meaning of liberation. This disagreement is itself driven fundamentally by their differing views about the nature of Brahman and about the nature of what knowledge of Brahman produces. Śaṅkara's and Madhva's views about *prārabdha-karma* are both based on Bādarāyaṇa's *BS*,[11] and thus converge in explaining why liberation from the cycle of rebirth (*saṃsāra*) is delayed and embodiment continues.

We will explore this functional similarity and substantive difference (1) by situating Madhva within the context of the Advaitin teaching about *jīvanmukti*, as it had developed by the fourteenth century, (2) by explaining what Madhva meant by bondage and the state of liberation, (3) by reviewing Madhva's teaching about the means to liberation, and (4) by explaining the relationship between the direct and immediate knowledge of God (*aparokṣa-jñāna*) and liberation.

Madhva in the Context of Thirteenth- and Fourteenth-Century Advaita

Madhva was born in 1238 of Brahmin parents in the village of Pājaka near Uḍipi, not far from Śṛṅgeri, in the present Indian state of Karnataka. He died in 1317.[12] At the age of sixteen Madhva was initiated into the Tīrtha order of Śaṅkara by Acyutaprekṣa (Puruṣottama Tīrtha). Under him Madhva studied the *Iṣṭasiddhi (IS)* of Vimuktātman, an Advaitin who flourished possibly between C.E. 850–1050. Madhva's insight into Advaita and his understanding of it was shaped by his early study of Vimuktātman. This particular study with his *guru* was terminated when Madhva pointed out thirty-two errors in the work's first verse: "I salute that Brahman that is unborn, unknowable, infinite, is the Self, is of the nature of Bliss, the canvas of the illusory picture of the universe beginning with *mahat*, etc." (*IS*, p. 1) Madhva and his Advaitin *guru* thus had a basic disagreement concerning the Advaitin teaching about the nature of Brahman. In its place Madhva introduced his own authoritative teaching about the import of the Vedānta scriptures. He claimed in his writings to be an appearance of Viṣṇu's son, Vāyu, who had appeared in this latter age to combat the mistaken teachings and interpretations of scripture promoted by Śaṅkara, an *avatāra* of the demon, Maṇiman.[13]

A review of early Advaitin views on *jīvanmukti* will help clarify Madhva's position. Especially significant is Vimuktātman's interpretation of Śaṅkara on the possibility of *jīvanmukti* since we know that Madhva had studied Vimuktātman's work. Vimuktātman's *Iṣṭasiddhi* (*IS*), an important treatise of the post-Śaṅkara school of Vedānta, includes a discussion of *jīvanmukti*, a topic much debated within Advaitin schools from the seventh through thirteenth centuries. During these early centuries, Advaita developed three different supporting arguments in defense of its concept of *jīvanmukti*. The first, based on *prārabdha-karma*, closely follows Śaṅkara's own teaching. The second, based on the *saṃskāras* of *avidyā*, stems from the teaching of the early Advaitin, Maṇḍana Miśra. The third is Vimuktātman's alternative position that *prārabdha-karma* is a *leśa* of *avidyā*, not a *saṃskāra*. All three deal with *avidyā*, the ignorance that causes bondage, which ceases at liberation through a knowledge that does not immediately cause embodiment to cease. Why does not the disappearance of the cause occasion the disappearance of the effect?

According to Śaṅkara (first half of the eighth century), the realization of Brahman completely annihilates only *saṃcita-karmas*, those accumulated past *karmas* that have not yet begun to produce effects. It also prevents any further accumulation of *kriyamāṇa-karma*. It does not destroy the *karmas* that have been producing the effect of the current life, *prārabdha-karma*, but allows them to work themselves out. The realizer, free from unfructified *karma* and from the possibility of any new *karma*, but not free from *prārabdha-karma*, is the one Śaṅkara's tradition calls the *jīvanmukta*. The persistence of the body for the *jīvanmukta* does not in any way constitute a state of bondage, but merely a working out of *prārabdha-karma*. Thus the state of realization of the *jīvanmukta* is a true liberation that will be completed at the death of the body since, "when the effect already produced wears away, liberation comes inevitably to the man of knowledge" (*BSŚG* 4.1.19).

However, Maṇḍana Miśra (fl. C.E. 690), an Advaitin contemporary of Śaṅkara, attributes the persistence of the body in the realizer to the *saṃskāras*, the remaining latent and residual impressions of *avidyā*, ignorance, which is the cause of immersion in *saṃsāra*. The *saṃskāras* remain even after their cause in ignorance has been removed. This is illustrated by the analogy of the continuation of the fear of the serpent for some time after the removal of illusion of the snake caused by confusion with a rope. Embodiment continues even after the removal of its cause. Although these latent impressions are unable to occasion the further mental and physical bondage of *saṃsāra*, they are real enough to bring about a semblance of continuing bodily experience. This is why knowledge itself does not immediately bring about the immediate liberation from the illusory experience of the self's relation to a body:

> Even though the truth is known through the means of knowledge, illusory cognitions do not disappear in all cases. There is the continuance of the illusion due to the capacity of the powerful impressions which have accumulated on account of the repetition of the beginningless erroneous cognition for one who has known the reality of the Self through Scripture which is free from doubt. . . . Even though the knowledge of the truth has taken place, so long as its impression has not grown strong, while the impression generated by the erroneous cognition is strong, even the valid cognitions do not begin their work in the same way as the cognitions that the objects are illusory do not. . . . So even a person who has known with certainty the non-difference of Brahman and the Self is in need of other aids in order to remove that (continuance of illusion). Just as release does not become an effect which is accomplished when the nature of its reality is manifested by the means of knowledge. . . .[14]

While explaining the role of *prārabdha-karma*, Śaṅkara himself in his comments on *BS* 4.1.15 had introduced the role of *saṃskāras*, latent impressions, in delaying final liberation from *saṃsāra*. In his commentary an opponent objects to Śaṅkara that "if this realization that the Self is not an agent annihilates all results of work by its own intrinsic power, how can it demolish only some leaving behind others?" Why are not all the effects of *karma* annihilated by liberating knowledge? Śaṅkara's answer is that "it cannot be that knowledge can arise without the help of some residual results of actions that have begun to bear fruit" (*BSŚG* 4.1.15). These residual effects continue in existence along with *prārabdha-karma*. Underlying all *karma* is *avidyā*, wrong knowledge, which also underlies the arising of liberating knowledge in the first place: "This false ignorance, even when sublated, continues for a while owing to past tendencies [*saṃskāra*]" (*BSŚG* 4.1.15). Thus, as Lance Nelson explains in Chapter 1 of this book, Saṅkara's admitting this continuation of *karma* implies in some sense the continuation of *avidyā* as its support.

Vimuktātman two centuries later had carefully reasoned through both Śaṅkara and Maṇḍana Miśra. He rejected Śaṅkara's and Maṇḍana Miśra's explanation that the latent impressions or effects (*saṃskāras*) of ignorance are the sufficient reason for the continuing bodily existence of the *jīvanmukta*. For Vimuktātman, the latent impressions of ignorance are effects of ignorance (*avidyā*), and if ignorance itself has been removed by realization, then its effects also must be removed, since for all types of effects a material cause is necessary.[15] Vimuktātman instead states that "the appearance of the body, etc., for the knower of Brahman is only from the residuum [*leśa*] of ignorance" (*IS*, p. 79 modified). The *leśa*, residuum or small amount, of *avidyā* is *avidyā*, whereas a *saṃskāra* is not. Thus a small amount of *avidyā* can coexist with liberation and so also the effect of *avidyā* which is embodiment. For Vimuktātman, a *saṃskāra* cannot exist after its cause in *avidyā* has been removed, "because of the impossibility of latent impression in the absence of nescience as the latent impression and their locus both form the body of nescience" (*IS*, p. 79).

But a *leśa* or a small amount of *avidyā* can continue to exist and thus provide the material cause for embodiment. For Vimuktātman, the form that the residuum of ignorance, *avidyā-leśa*, takes is *prārabdha-karma*. *Prārabdha-karma*, for Vimuktātman, is not a continuing hidden latent impression of *avidyā*, since an effect cannot exist without its cause. If *prārabdha-karma* persists after liberation, there must be a *leśa* of its material cause still present. At the final death of such a realizer of Brahman there is no further *karma*—that is, residuum of ignorance that can produce a rebirth within *saṃsāra*—and thus liberation is complete. For the *jīvanmuktas*, who have realized themselves to be non-dual with Brahman, the continuing reality of the body, occasioned by *prārabdha-karma*, which is *avidyā-leśa*, has no effect on the realized state of being non-dual with Brahman. The continued bodily existence of the *jīvanmukta* precludes all further selfish and binding actions. Thus Vimuktātman's distinction between *leśa* and *saṃskāra*, as well as his rejection of the theory of *saṃskāras*, harmonizes and advances the teaching of Maṇḍana Miśra and Śaṅkara.[16] His use of *leśa* is more logically consistent than either Maṇḍana Miśra's or Śankara's use of *saṃskāra* in order to distinguish *prārabdha-karma* from *avidyā*. It was this form of Advaitin teaching on *jīvanmukti* with which Madhva was acquainted.

Bondage and Liberation in Madhva's Teaching

Madhva disagreed with Vimuktātman and the entire Advaitin teaching on *jīvanmukti*. Madhva's central dispute with Advaita is, of course, the nature of Brahman and thus what it means to know Brahman. The metaphysical basis for Madhva's views on liberation is his Dvaita teaching on the *pañca-bheda*, the five fundamental differences or distinctions: between God/Brahman and the individual self, between God and matter, between the individual self and matter, between one individual self and another, and between one form of matter and another. For Madhva only Brahman is *svatantra*, independent or Self-existent. All other realities, although ontologically different from God, and precisely by being different from God, are dependent (*paratantra*) upon God for their reality and the nature of their existence. That which is *svatantra* is that which is able to be, to know, and to act of its own accord, and this applies to God alone. Only God is *svatantra*. Everything else exists eternally as dependent, and yet as eternally different, subject to the will of the only *svatantra* reality, God.

The difference between God and the individual selves, and between God and material beings, does not imply the absolute, exclusive, and total transcendence of God. For Madhva, that which is *svatantra*, self-existent, must of necessity be immanent within that which is different, but dependent, *paratantra*. There is a dualism between God and all else, but it is not the kind of absolute dualism that would result if God and all else were equally self-existent. Thus, Madhva's Vedāntic Dvaita must be correctly understood. There are two kinds of reality: the Self-existent (Brahman/God), and everything else, where everything else depends on God for its existence. Brahman is that which is non-dual. For Madhva, there is no non-dualism between Brahman and everything else.[17] The Self-existence of Brahman and the dependence of everything else on Brahman directly influence Madhva's views on liberation and on bondage, that from which one is liberated, since it precludes the Advaitin teaching that ignorance and bondage have been superimposed on the Self and are unreal, *mithyā*. As Madhva states: "Since the texts state thus, it is not true that liberation depends on the falsehood of bondage. The falsehood of bondage is contradicted by perception."[18]

There is one catechetical refrain throughout Madhva's writings: "Him on account of whom there are creation, maintenance, and destruction, and also regulation, destiny, knowledge, ignorance, bondage, and release . . . by Viṣṇu these are divided and pervaded . . . He lacks all defects, is full of joy and is imperishable."[19] Madhva is a Vaiṣṇava theist. For him beginningless bondage has its origin in God. Although not the material cause of anything, God is the remote and efficient cause of bondage; that is, the individual self's union with the subtle and the gross bodies. This union obscures the individual self's true relationship to God. Beginningless ignorance, the immediate cause of bondage in the person, is also ultimately from Viṣṇu and Viṣṇu alone. This ignorance hides from the individual self its true nature of being ontologically dependent on God. As Jayatīrtha (C.E. 1365–1388), one of Madhva's commentators, states: "The power of the Supreme Lord is the principle means of obscuring the essential form of the individual self. But *avidyā* is only his instrumental cause."[20] Ignorance is a positive reality, a *tattva*, an evolute of the immanent worldly quality of *tamas*, obscuring darkness. Ignorance veils from the individual self its true nature of being, consciousness, and bliss which are dependent upon God and reflective of God's being, consciousness, and bliss. At its worst, ignorance leads the individual self demonically to think itself non-different (*abheda*) from God. This, of course, was what the demon Śaṅkara taught. Madhva states: "The thief thinks that the self is the Supreme Self, which is truly different."[21]

The individual self in its dependent difference from God is a true reflection, *pratibimba*, of God's independent, quality-full reality, while the *bimba* is that which reflects. However, ignorance, although metaphysically derived from God, causes the individual self to be unaware of its dependence upon God and to fail to see its *pratibimba*-to-*bimba* relation to God. Here Madhva's statement is relevant: "Brahman is that from whom the origin, subsistence, dissolution, order, enlightenment, nesicence, bondage, and liberation proceed."[22] This God-derived ignorance has the function of veiling and obscuring God from the individual self, of obscuring the true nature of the individual self, and the true nature of its relation to the world and to God. Real ignorance is the cause of real bondage. The subtle and gross bodies are the proximate means by which this bondage works: "The individual self is under His control for ever and is His reflection. . . . The principal Prāṇa [dependent creative deity], the senses and also the body arise from Him" (*AṇB* 1.6–7).

Thus being positively and really bound by the subtle and gross bodies, the individual self is subject to the cycle of rebirth with all its sufferings. Forgetful of its true nature, the individual self identifies itself as a self-existent "ego." This false identification brings about desire, anger, lust, and so forth, as the driving forces of the individual self's activities. These activities, in turn, prevent the individual self from achieving its true destiny of liberation, since they further attach the individual to sensible objects that are not God. Thus, actions based on desire are not conducive to liberation. Identifying itself with its ego, the individual self imagines itself to be independent from God, acting as if its actions were its own.

All of these activities of bondage and ignorance are *karma*; they will inexorably produce their effects in the cycle of death and rebirth. Bondage, for Madhva, implies an inevitable and heavy burden of sinful actions carried through the individual self's passage through this cycle of rebirth. As long as it is in *saṃsāra*, the individual self cannot, without the aid of God, become detached from actions with these evil and painful results. Created by God's efficient will, bondage is a cosmic, a psychological, and a moral reality, affecting every single individual self in a different way. Since bondage is caused by God's efficient will, the individual self does not bear the ultimate responsibility for its status. Some selves are destined by God's will for liberation; their bondage and ignorance, although real, do not affect the deepest levels of their individual selves. Others are destined by God for eternal *saṃsāric* rebirth; their evil actions outwardly manifest the deep, inner wickedness of their own self-being, *svabhāva*. This predestination has been severely criticized by some. For S. Radhakrishnan "the theory of election is fraught with great danger to ethical life."[23] B. N. K. Sharma vigorously replies that a "gloomy truth is a better companion through life than a cheerful falsehood" such as the doctrine of liberation for all, *sarvamukti*."[24] Nonetheless, although Madhva has no satisfactory answer to the question of why Viṣṇu elects some and not others, he is consistent with his premises.

In considering the efficient will of God ultimately responsible for human bondage, Madhva must also consider God responsible for liberation from bondage. Citing the *Skānda Purāṇa*, Madhva states: "Viṣṇu gives knowledge to the ignorant and he gives liberation to those who have knowledge and he, Janārdana, gives bliss."[25] Negatively, liberation will be release from desire, anger, attachment; from birth, death, and rebirth; from the effects of *karma*; from the subtle and gross bodies; and from positive and real bondage and ignorance. Positively, liberation is occasioned by the direct vision and knowledge of God, *aparokṣa-jñāna*, which is allowed by God's grace. *Aparokṣa-jñāna* delivers one from *saṃcita-karma* and from undesirable (*aniṣṭa*) *anārabdha-karma*. This vision may occur in the embodied state to one who is still subject to *prārabdha-karma*; it will then result inexorably in the state of final liberation, where one is no longer subject to the cycle of birth and death. No one can know and see the true independent form of God and remain bound to the bondage of the cycle of birth and death. As Madhva states: "The liberation of each one is due to the vision of the very form of the Supreme Self, not from the qualities (of God) which are everywhere identical; this same vision of God in God's own reality causes the liberation."[26] The direct and immediate vision and knowledge of God's form causes the individual self to realize the truth of its dependence upon and difference from God. It undoes, or will eventually undo, all the negative effects of *karma*, which will be explained more completely later in this chapter.

The Practical Means to Liberation According to Madhva

According to the teaching of Madhva, the practical means, *sādhanas*, by which an individual self reaches liberation are progressively: (1) *vairāgya*, detachment from the body and the pleasures of the body based on a true knowledge of God; (2) *bhakti*, loving devotion to God as a means to liberation; (3) *śravaṇa*, listening to, or study of, the authoritative scriptural texts, usually under a guru's direction; (4) *manana*, critical reflection about the import of the texts; (5) *nididhyāsana* or *dhyāna*, meditation on the attributes of God as presented through the scriptures and as present in all that is not God, primarily in the various deities mentioned in the scriptures; and (6) *sākṣātkāra-* or *aparokṣa-jñāna*, direct and immediate knowledge or vision of God.

The early stages of *sādhana* lead toward an indirect knowledge of God mediated by symbols, images, and created concepts. *Vairāgya* is the process of detachment from a sensual life, wherein the individual is an end to itself, as if it were self-existent (*svatantra*) and not actually dependent (*paratantra*). *Vairāgya* leads to a deep-rooted love for God, *bhakti*, which builds on *vairāgya*. This stage of *bhakti*, love for God, is a preliminary form and must be carefully distinguished from *parabhakti*, supreme love for God. *Śravaṇa* is the careful study, under the guidance of competant teachers, of the true import of the scriptures, both *śruti* and *smṛti*, that reveals the true nature of God and of the individual selves. *Manana* is the reflection that leads to conviction about the correct interpretation of the scriptures.

Dhyāna, meditation, is the next to last stage on the road to liberation. It continues the removal of obstacles to the final direct vision of God and produces a *parokṣa-jñāna*, an indirect and mediated knowledge of God: "Just as Brahman is distinct from the bliss, etc., of the individual self, so He is different from that which is produced in the mind during meditation" (*BSMR* 3.2.37). *Dhyāna* produces a form of God before the mind of the seeker. This form, however, is mediated, a construct of the mind and not God's very Self. In Madhva's own words:

> Decisive ideas of all that is true, and the conclusive understanding of all scripture that such and such is the meaning and no other, are both quite different from the direct perception of Brahman. . . . The consequence of study, etc., is the removal of obstacles to seeing Brahman, such as ignorance, wrong knowledge, doubt, *etc*. (*BSMR* 3.3.43).

Since the individual is a *pratibimba*, a reflection of God, a mental construct of God within a self that is a real reflection of God is nonetheless a real knowledge of God, but this mediated knowledge is not a knowledge of God in God's very own, *bimba*, reality.

These first five stages lead up to a knowledge that would liberate, an immediate knowledge and a direct intuition that delivers the self-existent reality of God without any mediation. None of these first five *sādhanas*, though necessary, will produce the direct vision of God whose fruit is liberation, since final liberation comes from God's grace alone. With *dhyāna* the individual self approaches the *aparokṣa-jñāna*, which brings liberation and, indeed, constitutes what liberation is in the positive sense. *Dhyāna* and all five stages of *sādhana* are necessarily bound to *bhakti*. Madhva uses the term *bhakti* in at least two ways–first, as a means to liberation, and, second, as constituting liberation itself. *Bhakti* in this second meaning is virtually equivalent to *aparokṣa-jñāna*, the immediate and direct vision of God. *Bhakti* can then be understood as the supreme goal and as a term summing up all the means to such a liberation. Madhva states: "As the Supreme Being of his own accord shows himself in consideration of the individual self's devotion and bestows upon it final beatitude; devotion becomes the foremost of all means, and consequently it is spoken of as the only means" (*BSMR* 3.3.54).

In this broad sense, for Madhva, *bhakti* includes all the practical means to liberation. Knowledge, *jñāna*, is a principal constituent of *bhakti*. Thus *bhakti* is often referred to in the basic texts of Vedānta as *jñāna*. This equation enables Madhva in his vast exegetical writings to connect all the scriptural references to *jñāna* with the primacy he gives to *bhakti*. Where attachment to God is discussed, Madhva uses the term *bhakti*. Where dispelling ignorance is discussed, he generally uses the term *jñāna*. Initially, love for God begins when the ignorance that the individual self is independent from God is dispelled by means of a conscious knowledge of the error. Subsequently, love for God, *bhakti*, increases and grows from this positive knowledge of the majesty of God. As Madhva states, citing the *Māyā Vaibhava*:

> This is also said in the *Māyā Vaibhava*: "The Supreme Being Viṣṇu is in devotion, and by devotion brings him under His influence and in consid-

> eration of devotion He discovers Himself and bestows final beatitude. The intense love, which proceeding from a knowledge of His greatness becomes the tie between the Lord and the individual self, is called devotion; and that indeed is the instrument of the Supreme Ruler" (*BSMR* 3.3.54).

Knowledge is thus indispensible for, and is identical with, love for God. Negatively, it delivers one from the bondage of ignorance of God's true nature and from the mistaken knowledge that the individual self is independent from God. Positively, it delivers a vision of God as God is. Knowledge reveals to the individual self one's dependent (*paratantra*) relation to God, and fosters *bhakti,* to which God responds with liberation. Madhva defines *bhakti* as "that firm and unshakable love of God, which rises above all other ties of love and affection, based upon an adequate knowledge and conviction of His great majesty."[27] Thus adequate knowledge must be knowledge of the reality of God and is intimately connected with love for God. This connection is explained by Jayatīrtha as follows:

> In this work wherever it is stated that *jñāna* is the means to liberation, it must be understood that *bhakti* is also conveyed by it through the secondary significatory power of the word. This is because of the intimate relationship that exists between them insofar as *jñāna* is a constituent factor of *bhakti* which has been defined as a blend of knowledge of the Lord's majesty with an absorbing love for Him. This part and whole relationship between them explains the implicit reference by one constituent factor to the other.[28]

The Direct Knowledge of God while Living

Madhva's polemic against Advaita Vedānta conditions all of his teaching and all of his commentaries.[29] In his commentary on Bādarāyana's *BS*, it is Madhva's judgment that the prevailing *pūrvpakṣa,* primary objection, is Advaitin. The description of Madhva's school as *dvaita* carries a direct anti-Advaita overtone. However, he is not teaching "dualism" pure and simple. Since God is self-existent, and everything else dependent upon God (*paratantra*), the "two" of *dvaita* are not symmetrical. The eternal and dependent relation, even to the point of intimacy, of the individual selves upon God is a metaphysical dependence of both being and becoming. The individual self is dependent upon God, although this true nature of dependence is obscured by God's will while the individual remains enmeshed in *saṃsāra*. However, the individual self's dependence upon God is inherent, and not a conditional result of ignorance; thus dependence remains in the state of liberation. The obscurance of this relationship of dependence is what results from ignorance, but that ends when true knowledge of God dawns. Madhva states: "There is only liberation by his grace, born of knowledge, issuing itself from the desire to know."[30]

For Madhva, the individual self's intrinsic relation of dependence upon God is based on its metaphysical nature as a reflection of God's own being. As dependent the individual self is different from God, but as a reflection it is related to (that is, similar) to God's own being. For Madhva, the eradication of the ignorance of this relation is always by means of the grace of God. It is not required or produced by anything in human nature itself. With the eradication of ignorance of this dependence by means of the indirect and mediated knowledge produced by the first five *sādhanas*, an added possibility arises of not merely being delivered from the cycle of birth and death, but of actually experiencing God directly and immediately (*aparokṣa-jñāna*). By God's grace, this possibility can become actual during the embodied state when all negative forms of *karma* are eradicated, and when only *prārabdha-karma* is left to work itself out. The direct and immediate knowledge of God is a far more valuable grace from God than its secondary effect, deliverance from the cycle of birth and death.

For Madhva, this direct and immediate knowledge of God is not merely intellectual. Being a form of *bhakti, aparokṣa-jñāna* involves an inherent, loving attraction and attachment to God. Knowledge and loving attachment combined, subject to God's grace, bring an end to bondage. There is no self-liberation for Madhva because the bondage is not due to the individual self in the first place; rather it is due to God's efficient causality. What God gives God can take away. What God gives in the early five stages of *sādhana*, a mediate knowledge of God, God can enhance and build upon, resulting in the sixth stage of direct and immediate knowledge of God. This is a direct intuition of the being of God (*bimba*) of which the individual self has a reflection (*pratibimba*) at the core of its own being.

Since God is in God's own being *avyakta*, unmanifested, the direct vision of God is beyond one's own efforts. Nevertheless, it can be granted while living through God's grace. As Madhva succinctly states in the *Aṇubhāṣya*, his thirty-two verse summary of the *BS*: "Worshipful meditation of Viṣṇu as 'Brahman' must be practiced always, even in affliction. Brahman comes to be directly and immediately perceived" (*AṇB* 4.1). Liberation from *saṃsāra* is assured upon the initial arising of *aparokṣa-jñāna* but, first the *liṅga-śarīra*, the subtle body, which has been produced by *karma* must disintegrate. Madhva distinguishes several stages that take place after *aparokṣa-jñāna*: (1) *karma-nāśa* or *karma-akṣaya*, the eradication of *prārabdha-karma*, (2) *utkrānti*, the arising of the self from the last physical body, (3) *mārga*, the journey of the disembodied self to the realm of Brahman, and (4) *bhoga*, the enjoyment of the liberated state.[31]

After *aparokṣa-jñāna*, the individual self goes on living through the stage of *karma-nāśa*, for the effects of *prārabdha-karma* continue while they are being eradicated and eliminated. This is the state in Madhva's thought that corresponds to the state of *jīvanmukti* as taught in Advaita. This state would then be a state of "living liberation" in the sense meant by the title of this book. In fact this stage may last through more than one life. In this stage of liberation from *saṃsāra*, the various *sādhanas* should be continued, since they partake of the nature of liberation itself. With *aparokṣa-jñāna*, most *karmas* perish or no longer cling: "On seeing Brahman, the sins that may be committed thereafter do not cling to the *jñānin*; and all the previous sins that have been committed become destroyed" (*BSMR* 4.1.13). The ties that bind one to an embodied state begin to fall away. Of the three kinds of karma that bind the individual self, the first, *saṃcita-karma*, the accumulated *karma*, is destroyed by the direct vision of God. Of the second kind of *karma, anārabdha-karma, karma* that has not begun to produce results, there are two forms: *iṣṭa*, the desirable, and the *aniṣṭa*, the undesirable. The desirable *karma* is accounted to the individual self in view of a more profound degree of *mokṣa* after liberation. The undesirable *karma* is destroyed. The third form of *karma* is *prārabdha-karma, karma* that has begun to bear fruit. The amount is fixed, and no more *karma* is accumulated. Liberation from the cycle of birth and death is delayed as long as *prārabdha-karma*, both meritorious and demeritorious, works itself out. Madhva explains that this may take several lives:

> Only in the absence of *prārabdha-karma*, immediately on casting off the body in which knowledge is obtained, heavenly existence is attained; but if there be *prārabdha-karma*, there are other lives to be lived . . . The following is said in the *Nārāyaṇādhyātma*: "He who knows Brahman obtains heaven, and there is no question about it; and he attains heaven after the fall of the same body, if *prārabdha-karma* is exhausted; if not, having gone through several births, he will at the end doubtless attain to heaven" (*BSMR* 3.4.51).

Two further post-*aparokṣa-jñāna* stages precede the final culmination of liberation that is the enjoyment of God. The stage of *utkrānti* is the exit of the soul and its divestiture of the final body at the final death when *prārabdha-karma* has worked itself out. It is the final liberation from the bonds of *prakṛti* and from *saṃsāra* itself. This definitive divestiture of the body, *dehakṣaya*, or final death, obviously differs from the usual death followed by rebirth during the cycle of *saṃsāra*: "The lighting up of the top of his abode takes place; and by the path so lighted up the individual self departs by virtue of his knowledge as well as with the help of the memory of the path resulting from that knowledge, and by the grace of

Him that dwells in the heart, issues out by the Naḍi which is in excess of the hundred" (*BSMR* 4.2.17). For the next to the last stage, Madhva teaches, without elaborating, in his commentary on the *BS* IV.4.19 that the liberated self travels through four worlds of the gods, assimilating the qualities of the gods, before reaching the state of liberation appropriate to the unique nature of each individual self.[32] Liberation in its most complete sense follows the journey, *mārga*, of the individual self through these worlds.

Bhoga, enjoyment of the Lord, is the last stage and the highest state of liberation. Madhva is emphatic that this experience of God in liberation is personally and individually blissful. This supreme bliss, the direct and immediate knowing of God as God with full consciousness, is the culmination of *aparokṣa-jñāna* already begun while embodied. As Madhva states: "From *bhakti* one reaches knowledge, then again *bhakti*, then vision, then *bhakti* again. Then comes liberation and thereby *bhakti* again, which is of the essence of bliss and an end in itself."[33] At this final stage, the individual self, while in dependent communion with the independent divine person of God, is able to find complete Self-expression, Self-manifestation, and Self-realization. Every false sense of either separateness or independence from God is removed. The liberated Self sees God with the God-given eyes of God. Purely voluntary *bhakti*, loving God, is the essence of the bliss and enjoyment of final liberation. Worship goes on without end. Sacrifices may still be offered in this heavenly realm, but they are no longer obligatory. There are no longer any injunctions: "Only when compulsion to do and liability to punishment for omission are absent, the state of being released, i.e., heavenly existence, would be an end worth seeking and accomplishing; otherwise it would be no release at all" (*BSMR* 3.3.30). Love for God, which during the process of *sādhana* was a means to liberation, is now the essence of liberation. The person who has sought Brahman enjoys God. As *pratibimba* to the *bimba* of God's bliss, *ānanda*, the liberated Self finds its own *svarūpānanda*, essential bliss. Thus Madhva quotes the *Jābāla Śruti*:

> And this released individual self who has attained to Brahman in this world of heaven has no birth, no death, no decrease, no increase, but is always in the same unshaken state of blessedness, always seeing Brahman as the highest, and contemplating Him as the Lord; for this one who thus sees and contemplates Brahman forever, there is neither increase nor decrease (*BSMR* 4.4.21).

Conclusion

For Madhva liberation is not the characterless state of being that he considers the liberated state of the Advaita teaching to be. Liberation is a state of communion that preserves the essential difference between God/ Brahman and the individual self. It is not a union based on the essential non-difference between Brahman and the individual self. To make this point, Madhva cites the *Parama Śruti* :

> The unity of the individual self with the Lord consists of sameness of thought or it may mean dwelling in the same place. Such sameness of habitation is relative to some particular manifestation of the Lord. It is not unity of essential being, for even the released individual is different from Him. The difference between the two lies in the Lord being independent and infinite and the individual being finite and dependent (*VTN* 301, translation modifed).

This, according to Madhva, is the teaching of Vedāntic scriptures: "the difference between the individual self and the Lord is not a matter established otherwise than through scriptures. Therefore the scripture cannot aim at the teaching of identity [*abheda*] between individual self and the Lord" (*VTN* 436).

Two centuries after Madhva, his teaching of *aparokṣa-jñāna* was called the equivalent of *jīvanmukti* by Vyāsatīrtha (C.E. 1478–1539), one of his most authoritative commentators: "When *bhakti* has not reached its supreme capacity—whose cause is the inherent supreme bliss—for the grace of the liberating Lord has not yet been given to this seeker, that state is *jīvanmukti* due to the course of *saṃsāra* based on *prārabdha karma*."[34] This fact implies that the term *jīvanmukti* by that time had widened its semantic range beyond the confines of Adviatic usage. The conditions of polemic were different from Madhva's time. The kinds of Advaitin teaching of *jīvanmukti* that were being presented also differed. Madhva himself did not make this identification or equation of *aparokṣa-jñāna* and *jīvanmukti*, for it was inappropriate to do so given the state of his polemic with the *jīvanmukti* teaching of the thirteenth century Advaitins like Vimuktātman and his understanding of their position.

According to Madhva, it is the clear sense of scripture that the direct and immediate vision or knowledge of God, based on the difference between God and the individual self, is possible while living a *saṃsāric* life. It may begin during the embodied state. This knowledge, subject to God's grace, also constitutes the essence of the state of being liberated from the embodied life in *saṃsāra*. His objection to the Advaitin position on *jīvanmukti* is both metaphysical and exegetical. It centers not so much on the *jīvan* as on the *mukti*, and hence also on what constitutes bondage. Madhva's primary and fundamental objection is to the Advaitin understanding of liberation as the positive realization of the non-difference between Brahman and the individual self and the negative removal of an illusory ignorance. His objection only in a secondary way addresses the fact that such a liberation can take place in the embodied state. This kind of *jīvanmukti*, in Madhva's mind, was a key point in the demonic teaching of Śaṅkara and of his followers like Vimuktātman. The purpose of his life was to refute and correct such an understanding.

For Madhva the essence of liberation, and that which freed one from the cycle of death and rebirth, was the direct and immediate knowledge of God, possible while embodied. Madhva thus taught "living liberation" as understood in the title of this volume. In addition, at another level of understanding and interpretation, Madhva's teaching is functionally comparable to the Advaitin teaching of *jīvanmukti*. For Madhva, the direct and immediate knowledge of God, which is the blissful essence of liberation, and which he carefully distinguished from what the Advaitins considered the essence of liberation, begins during this life, while supreme bliss is granted in the next. But since his teaching that the individual self perdured in the state of *videhamukti* was so dramatically contrary to that of the teachers of the Advaitin *jīvanmukti* doctrine, it is understandable why he steered clear of the term *jīvanmukti* itself and all that it seemed to imply for the Advaitins.

Abbreviations

An — Madhva, *Anuvyākhyāna* in *SMG*, Vol. 1.

AṇB — Madhva, *Aṇubhāṣya*. Translated by S. S. Raghavachar. Bangalore: Dvaita Vedānta Studies and Research Foundation, 1974.

BhG — *Bhagavad Gītā*. See *BhGS*.

BhGS — *The Bhagavad Gītā with the Commentary of Śrī Śaṅkarācarya*. Edited by Dinkar Visnu Gokhale. Poona: Oriental Book Agency, 1950.

BhTN — Madhva, *Bhāgavata Tātparya Nirṇaya* in *SMG*, Vol. 3.

BS — Bādarāyaṇa, *Brahma Sūtras*. See *BSM*.

BSM — Madhva, *Brahmasūtrabhāṣya* in *SMG*, Vol. 1.

BSMR — *The Vedānta-Sūtras with the Commentary of Śrī Madhvācarya: A Complete Translation*. Translated by S. Subha Rau. Madras: Minerva Press, 1904.

BSS — Śaṅkara, *The Brahmasūtrabhāṣya*. Edited by Ram Acharya. Bombay: Satyabhamabai Pandurang, 1948.

BSŚG — *Brahma-Sūtra-Bhāṣya of Śaṇkarācarya*. Translated by Swami Gambhirananda. Calcutta: Advaita Ashrama, 1965.

IS — *Iṣṭa Siddhi of Vimuktātman*. Translated by P. K. Sundaram. Madras: Swadharma Swaarajya Sangha, 1980.

SMG	Madhva, *Sarvamūla Granthāḥ*. Edited by Bannaje Govindacharya. 4 volumes. Bangalore: Akhila Bharata Madhva Maha Maṇdala, 1969–1980.
VTN	Madhva, *Śrimad Viṣṇu-Tattva Vinirṇaya*. Translated by S. S. Raghavachar. Mangalore: Sri Ramakrishna Ashrama, 1959.

Notes

1. S. Radhakrishnan, *Indian Philosophy*, Vol. 2 (London: George Allen & Unwin, 1929), 748.

2. A. K. Lad, *A Comparative Study of the Concept of Liberation in Indian Philosophy* (Chowk, Burhanpur: Girdharlal Keshavdas, 1967), 121.

3. M. Hiriyanna, *Essentials of Indian Philosophy* (London: George Allen & Unwin, 1949), 199.

4. For Śaṅkara's thought, see Andrew O. Fort, "Knowing Brahman While Embodied: Śaṅkara on Jīvanmukti," *Journal of Indian Philosophy*, 19 (1991):369–389.

5. Much of the early Buddhist teaching about *saṃsāra, karma*, and *nirvāṇa* is also relevant to this discussion. Compare the Buddhist teaching of the four major stages through which a person on the way toward enlightenment advanced: stream-entrant (*śrota-apanna*), once-returner (*sakṛdagāmin*), non-returner (*anagāmin*), and one who will reach enlightenment and *nirvāṇa* in this life (*arhat*). See Hirakawa Akira, *A History of Indian Buddhism: From Sakyamuni to Early Mahayana*, translated by Paul Groner (Honolulu: University of Hawaii Press, 1990), 57.

6. See Hajime Nakamura, *A History of Early Vedānta Philosophy* (Delhi: Motilal Banarsidass, 1983), 1: 531: For Bādarāyaṇa, "This realm of liberation is to be achieved after death, and it cannot be reached in this present life. The attainment of the world of Brahman is the ultimate liberation, and no other forms of liberation exist; thus the liberation conceived by the author of the *Sūtra* is only of one type. There is no idea of such distinctions of later Vedānta as liberation in this life (*jīvanmukti*), gradual liberation (*kramamukti*), and ultimate liberation." See also B. N. K. Sharma, *The Brahma Sūtras and Their Principal Commentaries (A Critical Exposition)* (Bombay: Bharatiya Vidya Bhavan, 1978), 3, xxvi: "We have, therefore, to look for a different pattern of thought in place of Śaṅkara's to help us in understanding the true nature of Bādarāyaṇa's teaching"; Surendranath Dasgupta, *A History of Indian Philosophy* (Cambridge: University of Cambridge Press, 1922), 1, 421: "I am myself inclined to believe that the dualistic interpretations were probably more faithful to the Sūtras than those of Śaṅkara"; and S. Radhakrishnan, *Indian Philosophy* (London: George Allen & Unwin, 1923), 2, 440: "There is strong support for the view that Bādarāyaṇa looks upon the difference between Brahman

and the individual soul as ultimate, i.e., something which persists even when the soul is released."

7. In Śaṅkara's Commentary on the *BhG* 6.27 he says one who "'has become one with Brahman' means the one who has become a *jīvan-mukta*" (*brahma-bhūtaṃ jīvanmuktaṃ, BhGS*, p. 110). Thus Dasgupta is not quite accurate when he says: "*Jīvan-mukti*, or emancipation while living, is considered by Śaṅkara also as a possible state, though he does not seem to have used the term in his works." See Dasgupta, 2: 246, reference in Note 6.

8. See A. G. Krishna Warrier, *The Concept of Mukti in Advaita Vedānta* (Madras: University of Madras, 1961), 475–487.

9. As taught by Bādarāyaṇa according to Madhva's interpretation. Compare *BSMR* 3.4.51:

> Hence release does not necessarily follow . . . The following is said in the Nārāyaṇādhyātmya: 'He who knows Brahma does obtain heaven, and there is not question about it; and he attains to heaven after the fall of the same body, if *prārabdha-karma* is exhausted; if not, having gone through several births, he will at the end doubtless attain to heaven.

Śaṅkara also teaches this. See Andrew O. Fort, "Knowing Brahman while Embodied: Śaṅkara on *Jīvanmukti*," p. 378 (reference in Note 4): "In BS III.4.51, however, Śaṅkara suggests release might be delayed for an embodiment or two, as some texts indicate."

10. See Surendranath Dasgupta, *A History of Indian Philosophy. Volume IV. Indian Pluralism* (Cambridge: At the University Press, 1949), 88: "It cannot be urged that with the rise of knowledge all *karmas* are destroyed and salvation comes by itself; for knowledge can remove only the unripe (*aprārabdha*) *karmas*. The fruit of the *prārabdha* or ripe *karmas* has to ripen till they are exhausted. Thus Madhva favours the doctrine of *jīvanmukti*." Dasgupta seems to be one of the few scholars of the older generation who read carefully Madhva's teaching on *prārabdha-karma* and thus noticed its implications for *jīvanmukti*. See also Ignatius Puthiadam, *Viṣṇu the Ever Free* (Madurai: Dialogue Series, 1985), 293: "The '*samyagjñānin*' or '*aparokṣajñānin*' of Madhvism corresponds to the 'jīvanmukta' of other Hindu schools."

11. See Bādarāyaṇa's *BS* 4.1.15–19, and both Śaṅkara's and Madhva's commentaries.

12. I accept the dates proposed and defended by B. N. K. Sharma, *History of the Dvaita School of Vedānta and Its Literature*, revised edition (Delhi: Motilal Banarsidass, 1981 [1961]), 77–79.

13. See Daniel P. Sheridan, "Vyāsa as Madhva's Guru: Biographical Context for a Vedāntic Commentator," in Jeffrey R. Timm, ed., *Texts in Context: Traditional Hermeneutics in South Asia* (Albany: State University of New York Press, 1992).

14. Mandaṇa Miśra, *Brahmasiddhi*, cited in Eliot Deutsch and J. A. B. van Buitenen, *A Sourcebook of Advaita Vedānta* (Honolulu: The University Press of Hawaii, 1971), 238–39.

15 See *IS*, p. 49 : "Indeed, the origination of the effect is not from the instrumental cause alone; and hence the material cause too is to be sought."

16. My interpretation of Vimuktātman differs from B. N. Jha, "Vimuktātman . . . has chosen to follow Mandaṇa's position on the problem of Jīvan-mukti" in *Lights on the Vedānta: A Comparative Study of the Various Views of the Post-Śaṃkarites with Special Emphasis on Sureśvara's Views* (Varanasi: The Chowkhamba Sanskrit Series Office, 1959), 249.

17. See M. Hiriyanna (Note 3) p. 190: "It is on this basis of God's complete supremacy or, to state it differently, on the basis of not numerical but teleological unity that the Dvaita sometimes explains Upanishadic statements of monistic import like 'All this, indeed, is Brahman.'"

18. ityukterbandhamithyātvaṃ naiva muktirapekṣate/ muthyātvamapi bandhasya na pratyakṣavirodhataḥ (*An* 1.1.16).

19. sṛṣṭisthityapyayehāniyatidṛśitamobandhamokṣāśca yasmādasya (*BhTN* 1.11).

20. Jayatīrtha, *Nyāya Sūdha* I.1.15: parameśvaraśaktir eva jīvasvarūpāvaraṇaṃ mukhyam/ avidyā tu nimittamātram. Cited in Suzanne Siauve, *La Doctrine de Madhva* (Pondichery: Institut Francais d'Indologie, 1968), 338, translation mine.

21. anyaṃ santaṃ paramātmānaṃ svayamiti manyamānaḥ stena eveti; (*VTN* 221, translation mine).

22. sṛṣṭisthitisaṃhāraniyamanajñānājñānabandhamokṣā yataḥ (*BSM* 1.1.2).

23. S. Radhakrishnan 2:750. See Note 6.

24. B. N. K. Sharma, *Philosophy of Śrī Madhvācārya* (Bombay: Bharatiya Vidya Bhavan, 1962), 213.

25. ajñānāṃ jñādo viṣṇuḥ jñānināṃ moksadaśca saḥ/ ānandadaśca muktānāṃ sa evaiko janārdana iti ca (*VTN* 110).

26. na ca paramātmanaḥ sarvatra guṇasāmyāt yasya kasyāpi rūpasya darśanāt sarveśāṃ muktiḥ/ samo'pi bhagavān svabimbadarśana evainaṃ mocayati (*Nyāya Vivaraṇa*). My translation of the Sanskrit text cited in Sharma, 1962, p. 426. See Note 24.

27. Madhva, *Mahābhārata Tātparya Nirṇaya* I.85, cited in B. N. K. Sharma, trans., *Madhva's Teaching In His Own Words* (Bombay: Bharatiya Vidya Bhavan, 1970), 91.

28. Jayatīrtha, *Nyāya Sudhā*, cited and translated in Sharma, 1962, 405. See Note 24.

29. For a treatment of the polemics of the later Madhva school with the later Advaitins, see K. Narain, *A Critique of Mādhva Refutation of the Śamkara School of Vedānta* (Allahabad: Udayana Publications, 1964) and Dasgupta, 4: 204–319, cited in Note 10.

30. jijñāsotthajñānajāt tatprasādadevamucyate (*An* 1.1.1.16).

31. Madhva discusses these stages in *BSM* 4.1–4.

32. See also Madhva's commentary on the *Bṛhadāraṇyaka Upaniṣad* 3.5.4 and 6.4, in *SMG*.

33. bhaktyā jñānaṃ tato bhaktistato dṛṣṭastataśca sā/ tato muktistato bhaktiḥ saiva syāt mukharūpiṇī (*An* 3.4.215).

34. aparokṣajñānino'pi svayogyaparamānandahetuparamakāṣṭhāpannabhaktyabhāve tatsādhyasya mocakasyeśvaraprasādasyābhāvena prārabdhakarmaṇā saṃsārānuvṛttyā jivamuktih. (Nyāyāmṛta 4.4, cited in Sharma, 1962, p. 440, translation mine. See note 24.)

PART II

Yoga and Renunciation in Living Liberation

CHAPTER 4

Living Liberation in Sāṃkhya and Yoga

Christopher Key Chapple

Introduction

The notion of being liberated while alive has come to be closely associated with the Vedānta, Yoga, and Sāṃkhya schools, among others. In this chapter, I will explore metaphors for liberation in the *Sāṃkhya Kārikā*, and then turn to some later Sāṃkhya texts that make mention of the term *jīvanmukta*. The second portion of the chapter will examine notions related to living liberation in the *Yoga Sūtra*. Both traditions emphasize the importance of non-attachment, identified with the cultivation and actualization of a knowledge or discernment (*jñāna* in Sāṃkhya and *viveka khyāti* in Yoga) that frees one from compulsive thought and action. In the concluding section I explore differences in the liberated state as described in each text, especially on the issue of purification, with comparative reference to the Jaina tradition, which contains many parallel concepts.

The *Sāṃkhya Kārikā* of Īśvarakṛṣṇa and the *Yoga Sūtra* of Patañjali, both of which probably appeared around the fourth or fifth centuries of the common era,[1] provide extensive categorized analyses of the nature of bondage and, in the case of Yoga, numerous means of escape from that bondage. In these root texts of Yoga and Sāṃkhya, the terms *jīvan* and *mukta* are not used, separately or in tandem, though the *Sāṃkhya Kārikā* does use verbal forms derived from the root *muc*, to liberate. Neither text waxes eloquent on the qualities one exhibits after the escape has taken place. The *Sāṃkhya Kārikā* merely affirms that the body continues to exist after release just as a potter's wheel continues to spin by prior momentum;[2] it makes no attempt to describe the nature of that state. The *Yoga Sūtra* is hardly more descriptive, saying only that one dwells without impurity in a "cloud of *dharma*."[3]

One possible reason for this brevity of description is that the genre in which these texts were written does not allow for the sort of narrative and poetic embellishment found in the epics and Purāṇas. Another reason might be that a deliberate attempt has been made to guarantee that the recognition of a liberated person remains in the hands of a spiritual preceptor. The teachings of Yoga and Sāṃkhya traditionally have taken place in the context of an *āśrāma*, a community closely regulated by its *guru*. The largely oral and highly personalized lineage tradition maintained by the *guru* helps to ensure the authenticity and integrity of the tradition. Without the authority of the main teacher, whose task it is to discern the spiritual progress of an *āśrāma*'s inhabitants, it would be relatively easy for impure persons to claim advanced spiritual status based on his or her misinterpretation of written texts. A third reason for brevity could hinge on the logical contradiction that arises due to the fact that the notion of self is so closely identified with *ahaṃkāra*, the mistaken ego sense that is fraught with impure residues of *karma*. It would be an oxymoron for a person to say "I am liberated." According to the *Yoga Sūtra*, it is impossible for the Self to see itself (see *YS* 4:19). The liberative experience is by definition ineffable, with no content, no activity, no mark.

Despite the brevity of their descriptions, both texts present an ideal state in which a person has uprooted the causes of bondage, and hence embodies a perspective that lies beyond attachment. Though the *Yoga Sūtra* and *Sāṃkhya Kārikā* speak sparingly and metaphorically of what later is called living liberation, their definitions are indeed helpful for understanding subsequent discussions.

Sāṃkhya

The Sāṃkhya system affirms the manifestations of *prakṛti* as providing experience to be enjoyed by pure consciousness. Although deemed to be fraught with threefold suffering (*duḥkha*),[4] the purpose of experience is to provide both enjoyment and liberation for *puruṣa*. The Sāṃkhya path to liberation emphasizes that through release from mental conditionings, one becomes free. However, this can take place only through *prakṛti*; there is no escape from *prakṛti* until the point of death.

Sāṃkhya describes human experience as an interplay between an unconscious realm of manifestation as expressed through the many constituents (*tattva*) of *prakṛti* and a silent witness (*puruṣa*) for whom all this is performed. Anything that can be spoken of in concrete terms is in the realm of *prakṛti*, which is pervaded and instigated by the three *guṇas*. By definition, *puruṣa* is inactive and is not creative; hence *puruṣa* cannot strive for liberation. All experience, including the drive to become liberated, is performed for *puruṣa*, yet *puruṣa* remains aloof. Activity is performed by *prakṛti*, and it is *prakṛti* only that can claim "I am free," though, as we will see, she does this negatively by stating "I am not, this is not mine, there is no self of me." By seeing how and why she operates, she paradoxically unravels herself, allowing for liberation.

To describe this function, Īśvarakṛṣṇa writes that "as the unknowing milk flows to nourish the calf, so the *pradhāna* (*prakṛti*) functions for the sake of *puruṣa*'s liberation" (*SK* 57). The association of *puruṣa* and *prakṛti* is also compared to the relationship between a blind person and a lame person: *puruṣa* cannot act or move and *prakṛti* cannot see; hence *puruṣa* climbs on the back of the blind person (*prakṛti*) and the two together operate within the world, with *prakṛti* clearly doing all the work for *puruṣa* (*SK* 21). Liberation takes place when knowledge (*jñāna*) arises, the unique modality (*bhāva*) within *prakṛti* that allows the mind to realize its actions are not for itself but for the unseen master. At this point, *prakṛti* ceases her yearning, and the pure consciousness attains a state of repose.

In order for living liberation to be attained, the nature of bondage due to desire must clearly be discerned and then eliminated. Īśvarakṛṣṇa states that *prakṛti* operates so that desires may be fulfilled, hence releasing *puruṣa* (*SK* 58). Once this has transpired and *prakṛti* has done her job, so to speak, *puruṣa* loses interest, and the dancer (*prakṛti*) ceases to dance. The lame one who sees no longer needs the blind one because the desire to "get around" has ceased. The cessation of *prakṛti* and the loss of interest on the part of *puruṣa* constitute the raw liberating event that suspends compulsive attachment driven by desire.

Verses sixty-four through sixty-eight summarize the process of liberation as follows:

> From the study of the constituents of manifest reality (*tattvas*), the knowledge arises that "I do not exist, nothing is mine, I am not." This [knowledge] leaves no residue, is free from ignorance, pure, and is singular (*kevala*).
>
> Then *puruṣa*, with the repose of a spectator, sees *prakṛti*, whose activity has ceased since her task has been fulfilled and who has abandoned her seven modes [that perpetuate bondage: ignorance, virtue, nonvirtue, attachment, indifference, power, and weakness].
>
> The seer (*puruṣa*) says "I have seen her." The seen (*prakṛti*) says "I have been seen." Though there is closeness of the two, there is no incentive for further creation.
>
> Upon gaining this singular knowledge (*kevalajñāna*), virtue

> (*dharma*) and the other [modes of bondage or *bhāvas*] no longer constitute reasons [for action]. Yet the body abides due to the force of *saṃskāras* like the spinning of a potter's wheel.
>
> When separation from the body is attained, and when *prakṛti* ceases, her task fulfilled, then complete and unending isolation (*kaivalyam*) is attained (*SK* 64–68).

The negation of self, the abandonment of all modalities (*bhāvas*) except for discriminative knowledge (*jñāna*), and the image of the wheel that continues to spin, all indicate that the liberation in Sāṃkhya hinges on non-attachment.

Knowledge and Non-attachment in Sāṃkhya

In an uncharacteristically personal and poignant verse, Īśvarakṛṣṇa states, "In my opinion, there is nothing as delicate as *prakṛti* who says, 'I have been seen' and then does not again come into the view of *puruṣa*" (*SK* 61). The sentiment conveyed here is that *prakṛti* undergoes a dignified form of embarassment, and that her retreat clearly results from the dawning of the knowledge that any further action would be utterly inappropriate. This transformation is perhaps comparable to a scenario wherein a person with a harmful or irrational behavioral habit continues to perform this behavior until stopped in his or her tracks in an embarassing moment. Such a jolt, which certainly need not be experienced as pleasant, can carry with it enough impetus to reshape future actions.

In his commentary, Gauḍapāda describes this process as follows:

> As people being influenced by some favorite desire engage in actions of various kinds like going and coming for the gratification and fulfillment of that desire and stop from their activity when that is accomplished, so Prakṛti too, active for the purpose of liberating Puruṣa, ceases from its activity, after having accomplished its twofold purpose for Puruṣa (*SKGB*, p. 58).

Once this reordering has taken place—that is, once the dance of *prakṛti* has been arrested by knowledge (*jñāna*)—the manifestations of *prakṛti* no longer hold any interest for the witness (*puruṣa*). The motivating intent has been eradicated. The text states that "though the two are still in proximity, no creation (emerges)" (*SK* 66), indicating that the propensity to enter again into attachment has been rendered sterile. This is perhaps the closest direct acknowledgment of "living liberation" in the *Sāṃkhya Kā-*

rikā. The text strongly implies that the compulsive activities dominated by the residue of past impulses no longer gnaw at one's being, though the body remains. Knowledge (*jñāna*) prevents a resubmersion in that which has proven futile. The body and mind and so forth go on, but due to the direct knowledge that the Self has nothing it can call its own (*SK* 64), not even *dharma* obtains as a compulsive call for action. The individual moves on through life in a detached manner, until the moment of death when final separation takes place (*SK* 68).

In this phenomenological or process reading of Sāṃkhya, *puruṣa* is not a soul or thing, and *prakṛti* is not dead materiality. *Puruṣa* is defined by Īśvarakṛṣṇa as "consciousness, inactive, noncreative, witness, nonreactive, neutral, not created, free" (*SK* 9). It is not mind in the conventional sense: mind is governed by past impulses and is inseparable from the world that it first construes and then conceives and then perceives. Residues of past action contained in the intellect (*buddhi*) congeal into a fixed notion of self that then defines and construes the world. Suffering results because the world does not cooperate with one's notions of the way it should be. The world is not at fault; the source of discomfort is to be found in firmly held expectations and anticipations (*saṃskāras* or *vāsanās*), which are far removed from a pure consciousness that merely witnesses the unfolding of things.

Sāṃkhya invites the re-examination of the notion of self in such a way that the patina of inappropriate, self-generating interpretation is stripped away, leaving one free. Gauḍapāda employs a business analogy in describing this state of freedom:

> An analogy is of the debtor and creditor, between whom a contract exists for receiving [payment back on a] loan; but after the repayment of the loan, there is no money transaction between them, even if their contract continues. In a similar manner, Puruṣa and Prakṛti have no motive (*SKGB*, p. 66).

Any necessity or compulsion for further action has been eliminated.

This intermediary state between becoming established in the mode of spiritual knowledge (*jñāna bhāva)* and final liberation (*kaivalyam*) is very similar to what the Jainas refer to as the thirteenth of the fourteen stages (*guṇasthānas*) of spiritual development (which will be discussed briefly at the end of this chapter), and what the Vedāntins refer to as knowledge of Brahman. However, the intra-traditional commentators make scant reference to this transitional state, leaving its full discussion to later Vedāntins. Various questions remain unanswered if one looks solely at the Sāṃkhya system. What sorts of action does a person engage in as the "wheel goes on spinning?" Can a "backsliding" into ignorance and the other seven detrimental modes occur? If so, what can be done to prevent it?

Later Vedāntic Interpretations of Sāṃkhya

By the time of both the major and minor commentaries on the *Sāṃkhya Kārikā*, Vedānta had gained ground as the preeminent basis for philosophical discourse, eclipsing the other major schools of thought.[5] Hence, the views analyzed below show evidence of syncretism that automatically draws from assumptions established by Vedāntins. For instance, though the *Sāṃkhya Kārikā* does not mention *jīvanmukta*, several authors discuss it as if it were part of Īśvarakṛṣṇa's system. In his gloss on the *Sāṃkhya Sūtra*, Aniruddha, who probably flourished in the early sixteenth century, describes *jīvanmukta* as a "middle-level" accomplishment prior to the total dissolution of *prakṛti* at the time of death. He claims that *jīvanmukti* "allows for the teaching of the tradition" and that it is supported in the Vedas. Without persons in the status of *jīvanmukta*, there would be no standard for liberation; any spiritual quest would be the blind leading the blind.[6]

The descriptions of the *jīvanmukta* given in Vijñānabhikṣu's *Sāṃkhyasāra* (ca. late 16th century) seem to have been influenced by the *Bhagavad Gītā* and *Yogavāsiṣṭha*:

> (Such a one) neither rejoices nor hates . . . . never fails to remember the existence of the transcending self . . . . possesses an even and unshaken mind and acts without any attachment . . . . devoid of passion and aversion . . . being free from duties, attains liberation . . . . the same in honor and dishonor . . . . lust, greed, anger, etc., have dwindled and erroneous awareness has come to an end forever . . . . he abides in the fourth state.[7]

In commenting on Aniruddha's gloss cited above, Pramathanātha Tarkabhūṣana (1865–1941) has provided an interesting description of how *saṃskāras* or *karmic* influences operate for a *jīvanmukta*, saying they are "without sting."[8] Another modern Sāṃkhya commentator, Rāmeśacandra Tarkatīrtha (1881–1960), underscores that liberative knowledge (*jñāna*) provides both liberation while living and liberation from rebirth after death.[9] These later commentarial traditions clearly have embraced the vocabulary of "living liberation," and seemingly presume that the *saṃskāras* that remain active for bodily maintenance no longer sway the liberated one from the transcendent state of *puruṣa*, defined by Īśvarakṛṣṇa as a "free, nonaligned witnessing, a state of nonreactive looking on" (*SK* 19).[10]

In summary, the *Sāṃkhya Kārikā* provides a philosophical basis for the discussion of liberation within life, although it is not extensively described, and later commentaries seem to pattern their descriptions on other sources. The text clearly states that the force of past impressions will cause one to continue to live. Does this mean that defilement remains but that the liberated one is non-attached within the defilement? When Vijñānabhikṣu and others wax eloquent about the personal qualities of the *jīvanmukta*, is the perdurance of *saṃskāra* being whitewashed? Or are they assuming that the only remaining *saṃskāras* would be those cultivated during the course of achieving *jñāna*? For a more complete perspective on the difficult issue of the influence of past impressions, we need to turn to the *Yoga Sūtra* of Patañjali and look at its statements regarding the diminution of *karmic* effects and its descriptions of what may be considered the state of *jīvanmukta*.

Yoga

In this section, we will examine the discussion of liberation found in the *Yoga Sūtra* of Patañjali, which relies upon the view of reality asserted in the Sāṃkhya system, but augments Sāṃkhya by articulating in greater detail the nature of suffering and offering several alternative paths to liberation.

The Yoga system places greater emphasis than Sāṃkhya on the processes of purification that accompany the cultivation of liberative knowledge. The term that perhaps best describes the Yogic path to liberation is subtilization (*pratiprasava*): the aspiring Yogi strives to lessen his or her attachment first to the gross world and then to the subliminal influences that shape perception of the gross, until he or she finally enters a liberated state wherein all obscurations are burned away. In order to understand the context for this state of liberation, we will briefly discuss Patañjali's view on the nature of afflicted action and then turn to three of the means by which it is purified: concentration, eightfold Yoga, and the reversal of the mind's going forth (*pariṇāma*). Each of these culminates in *samādhi* and, as T.S. Rukmani has noted, "*Samādhi* is not only a means to the end but is also the end itself. For it is in *samādhi* that the final truth is realized."[11]

The path to *samādhi* requires that the Yogic practitioner overcome the influences of past action that are fraught with impurity or affliction. The *Yoga Sūtra* identifies five afflictions (*kleśa*) as the root causes of bondage that must be overcome in order for living liberation to take place. These afflictions, listed as ignorance, egoism, attachment, revulsion, and clinging to life (*avidyā, asmitā, rāga, dveṣa, abhiniveśa*), according to Patañjali, are inextricably linked to *karma*, and are to be avoided through meditation (*YS* 2.11). Whenever *karma* occurs, it is fraught with one of these five. With the suppression of these five through the processes of meditation and purification, the practitioner attains a state of equilibrium. In the *Bhagavad Gītā*, Kṛṣṇa states that "Supreme bliss comes to the Yogi whose mind is peaceful, whose passions are calmed, who is free from sin. . . ." (*BhG* 6.17). The discriminating one sees the sorrow and difficulty (*duḥkha*) inherent in worldly involvement (*YS* 2.15) and seeks to avoid the difficulty in the future (*YS* 2.16) through understanding the world-generating process of the seen (*YS* 2.18). As in the Sāṃkhya system, once the Yogi sees that all activity is performed only for the sake of the seer, then the need to perpetuate that action is quelled. At this point, the culmination of the subtilization process, a state of liberating wisdom, is achieved: "From following the limbs of Yoga, on the destruction of impurity there is a light of knowledge, leading to discriminative discernment" (*YS* 2.28). This discernment (*viveka khyāti*) provides a way to prevent the predominance of ignorance and the other four afflictions (*kleśas*), and can be equated with a state of living liberation.

The hierarchy of concentrations (*samāpatti* and *samādhi*) given in *YS* 1.44–51 is ordered according to increasing levels of subtlety designed to progressively minimize attachment. The concentration process begins with focus on gross objects, first with the object present (*savitarka*) and then using the mind alone (*nirvitarka*). One then focuses on subtle objects, first with imagery (*savicāra*) and then without imagery (*nirvicāra*). At each stage, a greater degree of purification and refinement is attained, finally culminating in *nirbīja*, or seedless, *samādhi*, which reverses and replaces the impulses of prior *saṃskāras* (*YS* 1.50). This hierarchy of concentrations progressively purifies the mind of the practitioner.

The eightfold Yoga path (*YS* 2.29–3.8) outlines a more detailed program for the attainment of liberation through overcoming the influences of afflicted past action (*kliṣṭa karma*). The first phase is a series of vows of abstinence (*yama*) that involve a conscious retreat from the habits of violence, lying, stealing, lust, and possessiveness. Each of these involves turning away from attachment to the gross. Next, in the practice of observances (*niyama*), one cultivates new interactions in the world based on purity, contentment, austerity, self-study, and dedication to Īśvara (the Lord). Having thus stabilized one's social intercourse, one then focuses on the outer layer of one's immediate self, the body. Through postures (*āsana*), comfort and steadiness are gained (*YS* 2.46); through breath control, the internal and external are appeased (*YS* 2.51). This then allows, in the final four phases of Yoga, the taking on of the most subtle aspects of the *citta*. *Pratyāhāra*, the first of these four, is specifically defined as the withdrawal from objects of sense; it is followed by the inner limbs of concentration, meditation, and *samādhi* as mentioned above.

The path to liberation is also discussed by Patañjali in yet another way that again emphasizes subtilization (*pratiprasava*) as the means, but using a terminology focused more directly on mental processes. This approach hinges on the notion that the source of ignorance and suffering is to be found in the sullied going forth or transformation of the mind (*citta-pariṇāma*), and that this process can be stopped. Patañjali states that the powers of mind can be directed either outward toward manifestation (*YS* 3.13) or called back to the point of restraint or *nirodha* (*YS* 3.9), which, when applied consistently, leads to the mental state identified with liberation or *samādhi* (*YS* 3.11). In going outward and involving and identifying oneself with objectivizing processes, the *saṃskāras* fraught with impurity or affliction (*kleśa*) that bind one to compulsive action are strengthened. The reversal of this process through its transformation (*pariṇāma*) into a state of *samādhi* causes seeds of deleterious action to diminish and eventually vanish. Things arise because of the solidification of mind processes (*YS* 4.2,14); Yoga reverses the process. At the conclusion of *pariṇāma* (*YS* 4.32,33), wherein the compulsive generation of the world ceases, one becomes liberated.

Distinctions between Sāṃkhya and Yoga

Sāṃkhya and Yoga can be read in tandem. Both systems bring one to the point of overcoming ignorance, associated with the modes (*bhāvas*) of Sāṃkhya and the residues of afflicted action (*kliṣṭa karma* or *saṃskāra*) in Yoga. No further binding action is created once this state has been achieved; in later traditions, such an adept would be referred to as a *jīvanmukta*. However, whereas Sāṃkhya almost fatalistically states that the "wheel continues to turn" after the initial liberating experience, Yoga develops and advances a "post-graduate" course for eradicating *saṃskāras* through the continued application of *samādhi*, leading to a state known as "seedless" (*YS* 1.50–51). Through the subtilizing techniques of Yoga, one can steadily deepen the detachment that originally arises with knowledge. In the practice of Yoga, the *karmic* residues or *saṃskāras* that cause bondage become subtilized: first they are meditated upon in external form, next they are internalized, and finally, according to Vyāsa's commentary of the seventh or eighth century, they become roasted (*dagdham*) like a seed of winter rice. (See Vyāsa's comments in *YSVB Bhāṣya* on 2.2 and 4).[12] Such a seed, once burned, is rendered sterile; it can produce no sprout. Analogously, a specific *saṃskāra* can no longer exert influence that would cause further action after it is burned through meditation and *samādhi*; one becomes freed of its sway and, according to the modern Yoga commentator Hariharananda Aranya, one enters into the state of *jīvanmukti*.[13]

Although this description of liberation in many ways can be seen as parallel to the description of liberation given in the *Sāṃkhya Kārikā*, it could be argued that the emphasis on dissolution of *saṃskāra* in Yoga allows for the emergence of the *jīvanmukta* state, while in Sāṃkhya, the persistence of *saṃskāra* until death without any description of a lasting purified state seems to indicate a slightly different interpretation of liberation. In Sāṃkhya, there seems to be an almost "fatalistic" unfolding of *saṃskāras* until the point of death; Yoga advocates an active path to their dissolution. Both systems emphasize knowledge, though Sāṃkhya does not specify the outcome of this knowledge in as much detail as does Yoga.

Yogic Liberation as the End of Afflicted Action

Of particular interest is the notion that in the practice of Yoga, afflicted action (*kleśa-karma*) ceases (*nivṛtti*) (*YS* 4.30) and an active, clarified mode of perception (*citi śakti*) emerges (*YS* 4.34). Patañjali does not state that all action comes to an end, but that action becomes devoid of afflicted impulses. Impure motives and results cease, and presumably only purified action can be performed. The seventh-century commentator Vyāsa states that "when afflicted action ceases, that wise person is liberated, even while living" (*kleśa-karma-nivṛttau jīvanneva vidvan vimukto bhavati YSVB* 4.30). This sentence is the earliest extant account of the notion of *jīvanmukti* in the classical Yoga tradition, and is specifically linked to how action is performed. One is reminded that the performer of such activity is described in the *Bhagavad Gītā* as one who has "cast away desire, fear and anger" (*BhG* 5.28), has renounced attachment, and knows "I am not doing anything at all" (*BhG* 5.8).

The quality of being free from afflicted action is also associated with Patañjali's description of Īśvara or God, defined as "a distinct *puruṣa* untouched by afflicted action, fruitions, or their residue" (*YS* 1.24). Patañjali states that Īśvara is the teacher or *guru* or all that are wise (*YS* 1.26) and associates the deity with the sacred syllable *OM* (*YS* 1.27). By devoting oneself to the ideal put forth by Īśvara, the paradigm for what is later described by Vyāsa as *jīvanmukta*, success in *samādhi* is guaranteed (*YS* 2.45). This relationship between Īśvara and the *jīvanmukta* as defined in Advaita Vedānta is fully explored in Chapter One of this book. In the *Yoga Sūtras*, what the two have in common is the absence of afflicted actions. The difference is that Īśvara has never been associated with afflicted action, whereas the liberated one has struggled to undo the afflictions.

The state of liberation is achieved when the generation and identification of the false self mired in afflicted activities ceases and one enters into association with the highest *sattva*, or purity (*YS* 4.25). In this state, the five afflictions (*kleśas*) of ignorance, egoism, attachment, revulsion, and clinging to life cease. Patañjali offers other definitions of Yogic accomplishment that also imply freedom from afflicted *karma*, such as "clarity of authentic self" (*adhyātma prasāda, YS* 1.47). Actions that proceed from this modality are said to be "seedless" (*YS* 1.51) or nonproductive of further compulsory, afflicted action. In this state of purification, the purpose of the manifest world (*prakṛti*) has been fulfilled, and the seen no longer is compelled to spin forth her manifestations in the previous sullied manner. The seen as characterized and determined by the afflictions disappears (*YS* 2.21, 22), leaving the seer pure (*YS* 2:20). Patañjali describes this final state of isolation (*kaivalyam*) as seeing the distinction between the purity of *sattva* and the *puruṣa* (*YS* 3.35, 49, 55). Simultaneous with this liberated moment, "discriminative discernment" and "cloud of *dharma samādhi*" (*YS* 4.29) are said to arise, along with the "cessation of afflicted action" (*YS* 4.30), which, as noted above, is the only state directly characterized by Vyāsa as the state of living liberation.

The culmination of Yoga is given in the final *sūtra* as follows: "The return to the origin of the *guṇas*, emptied of their purpose for *puruṣa*, is *kaivalyam*, the steadfastness in own form, and the power of higher awareness" (*YS* 4.34). This final description indicates that the dance of the manifested mind has ceased with "the return to the origin of the *guṇas*," and that the seer or pure witness has prevailed, exhibiting both "steadfastness in own form," and the "power of higher awareness" (*YS* 4.34). These descriptions seem to equate living liberation with quiescence and nonattachment but not total negation. The term "higher awareness," although somewhat ambiguous, seems to indicate that some life endures, but that this life is lived within an ongoing path of discernment (*viveka khyāti*) and lightness (*sattva*). Otherwise, as I have noted elsewhere, the only good Yogi would be a dead one![14]

The action of the accomplished Yogi is free from affliction; the *Yoga Sūtra* says such a person enters into a form of *samādhi* characterized as "cloud of dharma" (*dharma megha*). Does this phrase mean that the undertakings of the Yogi are permeated with duty or have the form of virtuous actions? Patañjali does not clearly define the meaning of *dharma megha samādhi,* and the commentators do little to resolve this question. Vijñānabhikṣu, a sixteenth-century commentator, writes that the one who is "established in the state of *dharma megha samādhi* is called a *jīvanmukta*."[15]

Perhaps Patañjali's use of this obscure term might have been inspired by Mahāyāna Buddhism.[16] In the *Daśabhūmika Sūtra*, a Mahāyāna Buddhist text from the early third century (and hence within a century or so of Patañjali), *dharma megha* is the name of the tenth and highest level of attainment for the *bodhisattva*. At this phase, the *bodhisattva* "acquires a glorious body . . . he emits some rays which destroy the pain and misery of all living beings . . . He especially cultivates the perfection of knowledge (*jñāna*) without neglecting others."[17] Although the texts of Yoga and Sāṃkhya do not include such standard Mahāyāna Buddhist ideas as compassion and bodily perfection normally associated with the *bodhisattva*, all three traditions emphasize knowledge (usually referred to as *vidyā* in Buddhism). Another similarity can be found in the fact that both the *bodhisattva* and the *jīvanmukta* attain the stage of *dharma megha* within the realm of human birth.

A Comparative Analysis of Living Liberation in Sāṃkhya and Yoga

The various descriptions of Yogic liberation offer an interesting complement to the Sāṃkhya notion of liberation. As we saw above, Yoga claims that afflicted past impressions (*saṃskāras*) are sequentially attenuated and replaced by unafflicted *saṃskāras* generated by *samādhi* experiences. This process starts with the arising of knowledge (*jñāna*) or discriminative discernment (*viveka khyāti*), accompanied with the performance of purified action. For Sāṃkhya, it seems acceptable that past *saṃskāras* will continue to operate; according to the potter's wheel analogy, the world spins on, but one's investment in it has ceased. In Yoga, discernment results in the cessation of afflicted action (*YS* 4.30). Sāṃkhya states that the embarassed *prakṛti* runs away, but that life somehow goes on, perhaps unaltered, save for the new, detached perspective. In Yoga there is said in liberation to be a cloud of *dharma* (*dharma megha*); in Sāṃkhya, it is said that there is no longer any further reason for *dharma* and the like (*dharmādinam akaraṇāpraptau*, *SK* 67). Yoga appears to be somewhat more rigorous in its definition of the liberated state, demanding its adherents to follow any one of a number of paths of purification, and asserting that only unafflicted action can remain for the truly liberated. Sāṃkhya, on the other hand, does not specifically address the question of performing action following the knowledge event, except to imply that one develops a sense of detachment.

This difference between the two systems, whether seen as contrasting or complementary, can be found in many aspects of the traditions. The adept within Sāṃkhya is said to have achieved a state of knowledge (*jñāna*) that results in a sublime detachment from things of the world. It allows one to watch life go by without becoming invested or interested in life's affairs. The relative absence of emphasis on purity and virtue within the Sāṃkhya system,[15] though not highlighted by prior commentators and scholars, seems striking. In Yoga, the liberated being also displays discriminative discernment that seemingly results not only in a detached perspective but also involves the cultivation of virtue and the elimination of deleterious activity. In Sāṃkhya, one knows that one is not the doer, regardless of what is done; in Yoga, only virtuous actions remain as possibilities. Sāṃkhya seems to emphasize only one moment of knowledge that brings about the destruction of the seven modes (*bhāvas*) and a state of liberation. In this living state, the wheel turns due to past momentum; the body persists and *saṃskāras* continue to operate to produce life experience until death. Nothing is said in Sāṃkhya about this, though it is stated that the individual remains detached from it all. Yoga, as mentioned earlier, provides a program for ongoing purification.

Another key to understanding the differences between Sāṃkhya and Yoga might be gleaned from the nature of the texts to which each tradition is tied. Though both systems are concerned with the prospect of human liberation, the *Sāṃkhya Kārikā* of Īśvarakṛṣṇa is a brief philosophical poem that clearly conveys the centrality of knowledge as the means to release. Its message is conveyed in a few dozen tightly constructed verses that focus quite pointedly on the centrality of knowledge in the quest for liberation. The *Yoga Sūtra* of Patañjali comes from another literary genre and, according to some scholars, is a patchwork of several different theories and practices regarding Yoga.[16] This text consists not of verses, but of 195 extremely short aphorisms divided into four "books" that provide a catalog of methods designed to attenuate the effects of afflicted action and to promote the adoption of a lifestyle that is conducive to a purified way of life. Sāṃkhya clearly communicates the excitement of liberation on a theoretical level, whereas Yoga meticulously outlines how the sort of knowledge gained in moments of insight can be applied in an ongoing manner. One is reminded of the encounter near the end of the *Mahābhārata*, where Kṛṣṇa is asked what happened to Arjuna following his enlightenment in the *Bhagavad Gītā*. Kṛṣṇa replies that Arjuna forgot the knowledge he had gained, and as a result suffered the consequences of attachment in his later life. It might be that the practice of Yoga as outlined by Patañjali is needed to help people remember and cultivate moments of insight.

Possible Jaina Elements in the Yoga System

Some of the contrast between Sāṃkhya and Yoga can perhaps be understood by juxtaposing certain aspects of Vedānta and Jainism. When one reads the texts of Vedānta such as the *Atmabodha*, the metaphysical tidiness of the author's system makes one almost able to taste the experience of liberation; by gaining knowledge that all this is merely illusion, dialectically one becomes free.[20] This reading of Vedānta in some ways resembles our discussion of Sāṃkhya above, which emphasizes the cultivation of knowledge alone as the path to release. When one studies Jainism, the path appears much more rigorous, requiring monasticism and in some instances total renunciation of all possessions, even one's clothes, in the case of the Śvetāmbara sect. Bondage is taken much more seriously, and the path to release seems much more arduous. Knowledge alone is merely the beginning of true liberation. All afflicted *karma* must be exhausted, and the job cannot be finally finished until the body is left behind.

Possible Jaina influence on the Yoga tradition might provide an explanation for the greater emphasis on purity within the Yoga tradition. The first practices within the eightfold path of Yoga—non-violence, truthfulness, non-stealing, chastity, and non-possession (*ahiṃsā, satya, asteya, brahmacarya,* and *aparigraha*)—are listed in the Jaina *Ācārāṅga Sūtra* also.[21] This emphasis on the observance of vows indicates that Yogis take moral behavior and worldly renunciation very seriously. In the Jaina system, these practices are undertaken to purge (*nirjarā*) the accumulated (*āsrava*) *karma* that has attached itself to one's life force or *jīva*. This *jīva* in its pure state is characterized as possessing boundless consciousness, energy, and bliss. However, due to its having committed countless acts of violence throughout its repeated births in the four realms of elemental/botanical/animal, demonic, divine, and human life forms, the *jīva* has become clouded over and unable to experience or express its highest nature. Only in the human realm (*gati*) can the *jīva* hope to proceed in the process of purging fettering *karma* accrued by violence and ultimately enter the state of freedom or enlightenment. This final state of perfect aloneness (*kevala*) is referred to metaphorically as the vantage point one assumes when sitting in solitude on the top of a great mountain.

In Jainism, the *karmas* that bind one to ignorance are found in eight fundamental species (*mūla-prakṛti*). Five *karmas* obscure knowledge; four *karmas* obscure insight; five cause different forms of sleep; two cause feelings of pain and pleasure; three pervert religious views; twenty-five disrupt proper conduct, subdivided into sixteen passions, six "non-passions," and three forms of sexual desire; four *karmas* determine the nature of one's birth; ninety-three *karmas* determine the composition of one's body; two establish one's family status; and five hinder one's energy. In total, Jainism analyzes 149 *karma-prakṛtis*[22] that must be overcome in order to gain liberation.[23]

Unlike Sāṃkhya but similar to Yoga, the process that leads to Jaina liberation is progressive. In Jainism, fourteen levels or *guṇasthānas* are said to comprise the path to liberation.[24] In the first stage (*mithyā-dṛṣṭi*), one dwells in ignorance, disbelieving any statements of a spiritual nature. One is said then to proceed directly to the fourth level (*saṃyak-dṛṣṭi*), a state of liberating insight that is said to last from one instant in duration up to forty-eight minutes. In this state, vast numbers of binding *karmas* are said to depart. P.S. Jaini comments that the fourth state

> . . . allows the soul to progress quickly. . . . It withdraws attention from the possessions, body, and psychological states with which it had formerly identified itself; gaining thereby a certain distance or detachment from passions, it attains the pure and peaceful state called *viśuddhi*.[25]

However, this experience, though an important rite of passage, is clearly temporary: one is expected to then fall back to the second or third level, though not to the first level of utter ignorance (*mithyā-dṛṣṭi*).

The path to final liberation in Jainism truly "gets started" after one experiences the fourth *guṇasthāna*. The insight gained in *samyag-darśana* is said to prompt the purposeful adoption of the five basic vows of Jaina religious life: *ahiṃsā, satya, asteya, brahmacarya*, and *aparigraha*. This occurs in the fifth *guṇasthāna*. In the sixth stage, one eliminates anger, pride, deceit, and greed. In the seventh, one quells all forms of carelessness. In the eighth, ninth, and tenth stages, one banishes such sentiments as laughter, pleasure, displeasure, sorrow, fear, disgust, and sexual cravings. After a little backsliding, allowed for in the eleventh *guṇasthāna*, one then annihilates the last particle of greed in the twelfth stage.[26]

The critical phase for the purposes of our discussion of *jīvanmukta* is found in the thirteenth stage (*sayoga-kevala-guṇasthāna*). P.S. Jaini summarizes this state as follows:

> This is the state of enlightenment, where the aspirant will become an *Arhat* or *Kevalin*, endowed with infinite knowledge, infinite perception, infinite bliss, and infinite energy. . . . The *Kevalin* because of his omniscience has no use of the senses or the mind that coordinates their functions; but he still is not free from the vocal and physical activities such as moving place to place.[27]

In terms of the Sāṃkhya and Yoga systems, this would mean that all eight or fifty *bhāvas* and all five *kleśas* have been destroyed. All three traditions refer to this state with terminology that resembles the Jaina state of *kevalajñāna*: Sāṃkhya actually uses the term *kevala* and Yoga uses the term *kaivalyam*. In this state, one is released from all psychological fetters; only the body remains. The *kevalin* or *jina*, the Jaina equivalent of a *jīvan-*

mukta, is one who has achieved the level of the thirteenth *guṅasthāna*, free of all passions, carelessness, and obscurations. This person is referred to as *sayoga-kevalin*, which in the Jaina tradition means that although liberated from destructive *karmas*, one is still joined (*sayoga*) to the body.

For the Jainas, *karmas* cannot be entirely eliminated until the moment of death, at which point one moves into the state of *ayoga*. The final and fourteenth level is said to occur at the moment just prior to death; at this point all *karmas* that have kept a person alive but are not necessarily deleterious (feeling, name, life span, and family identity) now dissolve. With the dissolution of these four, the drive to continue with life (also referred to in the *Yoga Sūtra* as clinging to life or *abhiniveśa* [2.9]) ceases and, therefore, death follows, often preceded by a ritual final fast. As an interesting sidenote to this discussion, both the Digambara and the Śvetāmbara schools of Jainism teach that the last person to achieve liberation was a monk called Jambū, who died in 463 B.C.E., 64 years after the death of Mahavira.[28]

I would like to discuss some of the implications of the phase in which religious insight first dawns, the state known as *saṃyag-dṛṣṭi*, the fourth *guṇasthāna*. The entry into this fourth level is compared to the experience of a blind man who is suddenly able to see. It perhaps is not unlike that critical moment in *Sāṃkhya Kārikā* 64, when the seer consciousness realizes "I am not, nothing is mine." In Jainism, this moment of first insight is preliminary to a long and arduous path of purification, along which many pitfalls and setbacks are expected. This contrasts with the state described in the Sāṃkhya system, which considers this insight to be final and does not discuss any possibility of falling back. Sāṃkhya states that the modes (*bhāvas*) no longer have any effect, though the body continues to live, due to the force of prior *karma*. The difficulty here is that Sāṃkhya does not specify which type of *karma* continues on. Is it the *karma* of personality? Or is it merely the breath and body that lives on, perpetually unattached? Sāṃkhya does state that one *bhāva* persists, that of knowledge (*jñāna*). The persistence of knowledge implies that a disciplined form of discrimination continues to be applied. If, as I suggested earlier, this results in a constant state of psychological awareness that prevents one from entering into attachment and repeating old patterns, then some forms of *karma* that potentially could cause obscuration would in fact appear to be present, though the power of discernment helps to quickly dismiss it. If this hypothesis stands, then the moment of liberation described in the *Sāṃkhya Kārikā* would be followed with a life of mindfulness until the point of death, during which *karmas* would continue to be encountered but would be disassembled by the modality of knowledge. In many ways, this seems to be parallel to the ongoing path described in

Jainism. If only innocuous *karmas* remain, then the liberation described in Sāṃkhya would be equivalent to the thirteenth stage of the Jaina path, as described below. However, due to non-specificity of *karma* in Sāṃkhya, this point remains somewhat ambiguous. By contrast, in the Jaina tradition, as well as in Yoga as noted above, the varieties and potencies of various *karmas* are well described, along with methods through which they can be uprooted.

The long and detailed process of purifying the various destructive *karmas* in Jainism raises many questions when compared with the Sāṃkhya and Yoga traditions. Are these the same as the *saṃskāras* mentioned by Patañjali and Īśvarakṛṣṇa? In Sāṃkhya, remnants of *karma* do remain after the experience of liberation, and the wheel of *prakṛtic* existence does turn, implying the presence of some action, though, as noted above, this *karma* is neutralized by the application of knowledge. In Yoga, the seeds of *karma* are countered by the repeated practice of *samādhi* until, in the words of Vyāsa, the seeds are all burned up and hence incapable of bearing fruit (*YSVB* 2.2 and 4). At this point one's actions become unafflicted, which for Vyāsa qualifies one for liberated status (*YSVB* 4.30). One gets the sense that these *karmas* that continue to unfold until the point of death are a bit more "weighty" than the non-destructive *karmas* mentioned in Jainism that determine feeling, type of birth, family, and lifespan. Sāṃkhya emphasizes the insight experience; Yoga augments this by explicating various paths to reduce the effects of afflicted action (*kliṣṭa-karma*); and Jainism provides a complete catalog of the 148 forms through which *karma* becomes manifest. Both the Jaina and Yoga systems emphasize a commitment to the purification of *karma* through taking on vows; both acknowledge a sequenced hierarchy of spiritual attainment; and both claim that the true adept cannot engage in afflicted or harmful action.

Conclusion

In conclusion, and perhaps at variance with both traditional commentators and modern scholars, I would suggest that Sāṃkhya and Yoga might be read sequentially. Sāṃkhya describes a life-reordering, liberating breakthrough, perhaps corresponding to the fourth *guṇasthāna* of Jainism. Yoga, beginning with the Jaina-inspired practice of non-violence or *ahiṃsā*, provides tools for this insight wisdom to be cultivated and applied to quell attachments within *prakṛti*. Living liberation as hinted at in Sāṃkhya begins with a moment of transformative insight. This insight as described in Yoga can lead one to restructure and purify one's actions through the application of various Yogic disciplines designed to bring about the progressive elimination of residual karmic influences. Stemming from the critical insight that "this is not the self of me," one important practice to sustain living liberation is common to both systems: discriminative discernment (*viveka-khyāti*) or knowledge (*jñāna*), which are to be applied until the moment of death, when even the desire to live ceases.

The *jīvanmukti* concept provides inspiration for one to seek knowledge. Although the qualities of this person are not discussed as such in the root texts of Sāṃkhya and Yoga, both systems are designed to lessen the effects of bondage and lead one to a knowledge that allows living liberation. Sāṃkhya offers a single method, described in terms of one single metaphor: the allures of manifestation (*prakṛti*) cease when the knowledge dawns that "I am not really this, nothing really is mine," allowing entry into the highest mode of human consciousness (*puruṣa*), a "free, nonaligned witnessing, a state of non-reactive looking on" (*SK* 19). Yoga offers multiple paths to the unafflicted action of *dharma megha samādhi*, emphasizing the cultivation of dispassion and virtue. Although Yoga does not contradict Sāṃkhya, it does emphasize the need for ongoing purification both on the path and at the penultimate phase of the quest for liberation.

Abbreviations

BhG — *Bhagavad Gītā*. Translated by B. Srinivasa Murthy. Long Beach: Long Beach Publications, 1991.

SK — *Sāṃkhya Kārikā* of Īśvara Kṛṣṇa. Text and translation in Gerald J. Larson, *Classical Saṃkhya: An Interpretation of its meaning*. Delhi: Motilal Banarsitass, 1979. Translations here are those of the author.

SKGB — *Sāṃkhyakārika of Īśvarakṛṣṇa with the Commentary of Gauḍapāda*. Translated by T. G. Mainkar. Poona: Oriental Book Agency, 1972.

YS — *The Yoga Sūtras of Patañjali*. Translated by Christopher Chapple and Eugene P. Kelly, Jr. Delhi: Sri Satgura Publications, 1990.

YSVB — *Yoga Sūtra of Patañjali with the Commentary of Vyāsa*. Edited and translated by Bengali Baba. Delhi: Motilal Banarsidass, 1976.

Notes

1. Gerald Larson dates Īśvarakṛṣṇa at C.E. 350–450 and Patañjali at C.E. 400–500. See *The Encyclopedia of Indian Philosophies, Volume IV: Sāṃkhya, Dualist*

Tradition in Indian Philosophy. (Delhi: Motilal Banarsidass, 1987), 15. Hereafter abbreviated as Larson.

2. See *SK* 67.

3. See *YS* 4.29.

4. According to sixth century commentator Gauḍapāda, this pain is internal (both psychological and physical), external (caused by living beings other than oneself), and from "above" (in modern parlance, acts of God). See his commentary on the second *kārikā* in *SKGB*.

5. See Larson, 29ff.

6. Larson, 353.

7. Larson, 411.

8. Larson, 482.

9. Larson, 574.

10. For related Advaitin views, see Lance Nelson's chapter in this volume.

11. T.S. Rukmani, "Samprajñāta Samādhi in the Patañjala Yoga System—Difference in Interpretation between Vācaspati Miśra and Vijñānabhikṣu," Appendix 3 in *Yogavārtikka of Vijñānabhikśu* (New Delhi: Munshiram Manoharlal, 1989), 159.

12. See also James Haughton Woods, *The Yoga System of Patañjali* (Delhi: Motilal Banarsidass, 1977 [first published in 1914]), 105–108.

13. Swami Hariharananda Aranya, *Yoga Philosophy of Patañjali* (Albany: State University of New York Press, 1983 [first published in 1963]), 119.

14. See "*Citta-vṛtti* and Reality in the Yoga Sūtra" in *Sāṃkhya-Yoga: Proceedings of the 1981 IASWR Conference* (Stony Brook, New York: The Institute for Advanced Studies of World Religions, 1983), 103–119.

15. . . . dharmameghaḥ samādhiḥ . . . asyāmavasthāyāṃ jīvanmukta ityucyate, as found in Vijñānabhikṣu, *Yoga-Sara-Sangraha* (Madras: Theosophical Publishing House, 1933), 17.

16. For other references to the relationship between Yoga and Buddhism, see Émile Senart, "Bouddhisme et Yoga" in *La Revue de l'histoire des religions*, Vol. XLII (1900), 345–364, and Louis de la Vallée Poussin, "Le Bouddhisme et le Yoga de Patañjali" in *Mélanges Chinois et Bouddhiques*, Vol. V (1936–37), 232–242.

17. Har Dayal, *The Bodhisattva Doctrine in Buddhist Sanskrit Literature* (New York: Samuel Weiser, 1932), 291.

18. Īśvarakṛṣṇa states that "by virtue (*dharma*) [one obtains] ascent to higher planes" (*SK* 44), interpreted by Vācaspati Miśra to be heaven. This attainment is clearly at variance with the goal of liberation, which achieved only through knowledge (*jñāna*).

19. For a summary of these views, see my Introduction in *YS*.

20. See *Self-Knowledge* (*ātmabodha*), Swami Nikhilananda, tr. (New York: Ramakrishna-Vivekananda Center, 1970), pp. 117–172.

21. The very first verse of the *Acārāṅga Sūtra* indicates Jainism's commitment to *ahiṃsā*; the second section of the text is devoted to a detailed description of the practices of *satya, asteya*, and *aparigraha*, all of which find direct parallels in *YS* 2:30–39. The earliest sections of the *Acārāṅga Sūtra* date from the third or fourth century B.C.E., several centuries before the *Yoga Sūtra*. See Christopher Key Chapple, *Nonviolence to Animals, Earth, and Self in Asian Traditions* (Albany: State University of New York Press, 1993), 10, 17–18, 71.

22. It is interesting to note that the Jainas use the term *karma-prakṛti*. One possible way to interpret the Sāṃkhya tradition in light of Jainism would be to see Sāṃkhya's *prakṛti* not as a universal or cosmological principle but as a discrete *karmic* pattern. Perhaps it could be conjectured that the insight mode of Sāṃkhya allows one to quell a particular *karmic* configuration, but that this insight or knowledge must be used repeatedly according to new *karmic* circumstances that arise.

23. Helmuth von Glasenapp, *The Doctrine of Karman in Jain Philosophy* (Bombay: Bai Vijibai Jivanlal Panalal Charity Fund, 1942), pp. 5–19. Hereafter abbreviated as von Glasenapp. See also Muni Shivkuman, *Doctrine of Liberation in Indian Philosophy* (New Delhi: Munshiram Manoharlal, 1984), 66–72.

24. See Padmanabh S. Jaini, *The Jaina Path of Purification* (Berkeley: University of California Press, 1979), 141–156. Hereafter abbreviated as Jaini.

25. Jaini, 142.

26. von Glasenapp, 76–92.

27. Padmanabh S. Jaini, *Gender & Salvation: Jaina Debates on the Spiritual Liberation of Women* (Berkeley: University of California Press, 1991), 95.

28. Jaini, *Gender and Salvation*, 98.

CHAPTER 5

Liberation While Living in the *Jīvanmuktiviveka*: Vidyāraṇya's "Yogic Advaita"

Andrew O. Fort

Introduction

When considering the possibility and nature of *jīvanmukti* (liberation while living) in Indian thought, few texts are as thought-provoking as the *Jīvanmuktiviveka* (*JMV*)[1] (*Discerning Liberation While Living*), a syncretic fourteenth-century work by Vidyāraṇya.[2] The *JMV* outlines the nature of living liberation and teaches the path to liberation via a combination of knowledge, yogic practice, and renunciation.[3] This text is especially interesting because of the author's attempt to weave together a number of strands of Indian thought to create what I will call "Yogic Advaita." While primarily an adherent of Advaita (non-dual) Vedānta, Vidyāraṇya also emphatically enjoins following the ascetic path, and refers far more often and more favorably than does Śaṅkara to the yogic practices of Patañjali and the *Bhagavad Gītā*. In a way rarely seen in Śaṅkara's "mainstream" Advaita, Vidyāraṇya claims that yoga and ascetic renunciation (*saṃnyāsa*) together both lead to *and* express the liberating knowledge (*jñāna, vidyā*) of Brahman. In fact, the text uses the terms "*yogin*," "*saṃnyāsin*," and "*mukta*" (with appropriate qualifiers) to identify the same person—one with full knowledge of non-dual Brahman.

Another indication of Vidyāraṇya's Yogic Advaita is his repeated citation of the *Laghu* (short or abridged) *Yogavāsiṣṭha* (*LYV*); at times the *JMV* virtually becomes a commentary on the *LYV*. This latter text is an abridgement of the *Yogavāsiṣṭha*, an eleventh-century work structured as the teachings of the sage Vasiṣṭha to world-weary Rāma. The text blends poetry, Purāṇic mythology, and philosophical teachings of Advaita, Sāṃkhya/Yoga, and Vijñānavāda Buddhism. While deeply influenced by the *LYV*, the *JMV* is more respectful of Vedic and *saṃnyāsa* traditions linked with mainstream Advaita, while the *LYV* has an even greater complement of Sāṃkhya, Purāṇic, and Buddhist ideas.

The significant differences in emphasis and focus in Vidyāraṇya's Yogic Advaita and Śaṅkara's Advaita rarely lead to direct opposition or contradiction—both are still Advaita. For example, Vidyāraṇya does not dispute Śaṅkara's (and most later Advaitins') view on the importance of ending identification of self and body and on bodily continuity due to currently manifesting (*prārabdha*) *karma*,[4] but he does not focus on them. He spends much more time than does Śaṅkara on yogic issues relating to the mind and its manifestations (*citta-vṛtti*) and the importance of renunciation to make suffering cease. While Vidyāraṇya talks of Ātman/Brahman more than of *puruṣa/prakṛti*, he describes the Sāṃkhya evolutes at some length and makes far more use of Sāṃkhya-Yoga terminology and analysis than does Śaṅkara. The *JMV* cites Śaṅkara, and other Advaitins like Sureśvara,[5] but references to the Sāṃkhya-Yoga influenced *LYV* and *Bhagavad Gītā* are far more extensive. Unlike Śaṅkara, who takes a dialectical approach (stressing reasoning and debate), Vidyāraṇya seems to be a syncretist. Where Śaṅkara excludes or disputes Sāṃkhya-Yoga notions of mental activity or world evolution, Vidyāraṇya wants to be inclusive, or at least omit opposition. In his Yogic Advaita, as in all Advaita, knowledge of nondual Brahman is the *sine qua non* of *jīvanmukti*. However, while Śaṅkara holds that yogic practice is at best merely a preparatory form of action, Vidyāraṇya claims it is central in attaining and safeguarding Brahman-knowledge. We shall see that this perspective further shapes Vidyāraṇya's views on the relationships between embodiment and liberation, and renunciation and living in the world.

The Nature of *Jīvanmukti*

As stated above, Vidyāraṇya holds that knowledge of non-duality is the fundamental cause of liberation while living, but yogic practice is necessary to gain and safeguard this knowledge. Both aspects can be seen in his definition of liberation while living. In the *JMV* he writes that "bondage exists for a living being since the nature of affliction [is] having mental notions consisting of joy and sorrow, being enjoyer and doer, and so on. Living liberation is the cessation of this."[6] When such dualistic notions as "I am doer/enjoyer" cease due to knowledge of Brahman, one is liberated while living. Vidyāraṇya then immediately adds a Yogic component to this

Advaitin claim; he writes that ultimately all mental modifications (*citta-vṛtti*) which cause this bondage can be overcome by repeated yogic practice (*yogābhyāsa*) (*JMV* 10, 195). Here and throughout the text, Vidyāraṇya's view seems to be that the *jīvanmukta* must, first and foremost, realize non-dual Brahman and thereby gain Advaitin serenity; but he must also concomitantly work to end suffering by destroying the mind and its impressions (*vāsanā*) by means of renunciation (*saṃnyāsa*) and yogic enstasis (*samādhi*). According to Vidyāraṇya, then, attaining living liberation requires personal renunciation and yogic body mastery as necessary complements to non-dual knowledge.

One of Vidyāraṇya's main reasons for emphasizing yogic practice for the *jīvanmukta* is related to yoga's role in removing *karma* currently bearing fruit (*prārabdha karma*) (*JMV* 10, 195). Śaṅkara argues that knowledge of Brahman eradicates all *karma* except that which is currently manifesting (*prārabdha*); *prārabdha-karma* thus causes the body to continue after Brahman-knowledge, and its cessation puts an end to the *jīvanmukta's* embodiment forever.[7] Śaṅkara and later mainstream Advaitin thinkers discuss *prārabdha-karma* at some length, because all *karma* is a result of ignorance, and ignorance is supposed to end completely after Brahman-knowledge. Śaṅkara's tradition argues that the entire mass of previously accumulated (*saṃcita*) *karma*, which are not yet manifesting, and all *karma* productive of future fruits (*āgamī*) cease by knowledge. However, they also hold that a trace of ignorance, consisting of *karma* currently bearing fruit, remains. This trace is not removed by knowledge, and it temporarily causes continued embodiment after liberation, like a potter's wheel continues spinning at a slowly diminishing pace for a time even after the potter departs. In the same way, one may continue trembling for a time even after realizing an imagined snake is only a rope; the delusion ends before the effect on the body does.

Vidyāraṇya follows mainstream Advaita in holding that the fruits of currently manifesting (*prārabdha*) *karma* obstruct ignorance-destroying knowledge and cause the body and senses to continue. However, he parts company with the mainstream tradition by claiming that one can overcome the necessity of experiencing the fruits of actions by making personal effort—specifically, repeated yogic practice. Vidyāraṇya here argues (unlike Śaṅkara) that even though *prārabdha-karma* is stronger than ignorance-destroying knowledge, yogic practice is strong even than *prārabdha-karma* (*JMV* 11, 196). He repeatedly declares the necessity of human effort to overcome being controlled by mental modifications and preexisting *karma*. These efforts include Advaitin means, such as following the sacred texts (*śāstra*) and associating with the wise (although he does not here mention the fourfold *sādhana* Śaṅkara discusses in *Brahman*

Sūtra Bhāṣya 1. 1. 1), as well as yogic efforts—such as resisting desires and controlling the mind. He cites approvingly the *LYV's* claim that all results—hell, heaven, or liberation—derive from human effort, and only right effort can bring the highest goal (*JMV* 12, 197–8). He also endorses the *LYV's* claim that strong and repeated personal effort will allow one to guide the everflowing stream of mental impressions (*vāsanā*) into the right channel, creating waves of good (*śubha*) impressions, which wash over impure ones (*JMV* 13, 199).[8] Śaṅkara, on the other hand, carefully separates the effort of yogic practice from knowledge, which alone brings liberation.[9] Thus, unlike mainstream Advaita, yogic effort is necessary to both foster and sustain knowledge of non-dual Brahman in Vidyāraṇya's Yogic Advaita.

However, Vidyāraṇya curiously changes course at this point (*JMV* 15, 201). He agrees with the *LYV's* statement that after accumulating enough good impressions, one then gives up *all* impressions and desires, including the desire to follow a sacred text and master. When the highest goal is realized, even the effort to give up all desires is abandoned. Put another way, the supreme effort takes one to a state beyond any effort. Vidyāraṇya concludes that *jīvanmukti* is indisputably due to the disappearance of all desire through yogic practice. Vidyāraṇya could be clearer here. He is perhaps suggesting that efforts and practices, even yogic ones, indicate that one still sees the world dualistically, as if there is something left to do or someplace to get to. Ultimately, however, the *jīvanmukta* is content with whatever comes his way—and "whatever" comes, of course, only from currently manifesting (*prārabdha*) *karma*, since the *jīvanmukta* no longer initiates any efforts of his own. We will return to this point when we discuss the highest renunciate, the *paramahaṃsa yogin*.

The *Jīvanmukta* as One with Firm Wisdom (*Sthita-Prajña*)

We can also find Yogic Advaita in Vidyāraṇya's interpretation of the *Bhagavad Gītā*, particularly in his consideration of the *jīvanmukta* as one having firm wisdom (*sthita-prajña*) (*JMV* 20, 211ff.). It is significant that the *Gītā*, with its extensive use of Sāṃkhya/Yoga categories like qualities (*guṇa*) and mental manifestations (*citta-vṛtti*), is second only to the *LYV* in number of references throughout the *JMV*. This suggests not only the authority that the *Gītā* held for Vidyāraṇya and his audience, but also its congeniality to his views. Vidyāraṇya wants to show that the existence of living liberation is established through the many scriptural references not only to the *jīvanmukta* per se, but also to one having firm wisdom, one who is devoted to the Lord (*bhagavad-bhakta*), to one who has gone beyond the three qualities (*guṇātīta*), to one who is a true *brāhmin*, and to one who has transcended caste and life stage (*ativarṇāśramin*). According to Vidyāraṇya, all these persons are (at least potentially) liberated while living.

Vidyāraṇya spends considerable time elaborating on the description in *Gītā* 2: 54–72 of the one with firm wisdom, the *sthita-prajña*. He explains that firm wisdom gives knowledge of the real (*tattva-jñāna*, the highest end of *jīvanmukti*), and one with firm wisdom, abandoning all desires, attains the highest renunciation by repeated yogic practice. The *sthita-prajña's* mind never budges from the truth, and (in an image that is surprising, given the text's misogyny) the sage's focus on truth is compared to a woman whose mind is constantly on her lover, forgetful even of her household duties (*JMV* 20, 211). Vidyāraṇya holds to the mainstream Advaitin position that knowing the Self brings supreme satisfaction and a bliss higher than any bliss from mental manifestations, including those in concentrated (*saṃprajñāta*) *samādhi*. The *sthita-prajña* is detached from joy and sorrow, attraction and repulsion, craving, anxiety, and anger. These attachments arise from actions currently bearing fruit, and especially from dull, ignorance-filled (*tāmasic*) mental impressions (*vāsanā*). Such impressions are impossible for a sage (*JMV* 22, 214).

While the *sthita-prajña* is also an exemplar of the liberated being to Śaṅkara, his description emphasizes the *sthita-prajña's* renunciation and knowledge of Brahman. Vidyāraṇya again adds a strong Yogic component: by the repeated practice of meditative enstasis (*samādhi*), the *sthita-prajña's* senses are restrained and mastered, and Brahman is "seen" (*JMV* 23, 216). Before knowledge arises, pursuing it by means like *samādhi* takes effort, but such means become natural for one with firm knowledge. Put another way, efforts (like *samādhi*) bring and safeguard knowledge; after the arising of firm knowledge, *samādhi* is natural. Knowing the Self by unbroken Self-illumination is in fact called *jīvanmukti* (*JMV* 25, 217).[10] Again we see Vidyāraṇya's ambivalence about the necessity of unceasing yogic efforts for a *jīvanmukta*. He seems to want to hold both that unceasing efforts are necessary and that the one who reaches the highest goal is beyond any effort.

The Threefold Means to Obtain *Jīvanmukti*

So far we have seen how Vidyāraṇya describes the nature of living liberation; we next consider his views on how to reach this *mukti*. The largest portion of the *Jīvanmuktiviveka* (37, 232ff.) is devoted to describing and analyzing the threefold means for obtaining liberation while living: knowing the truth (*tattva-jñāna*), extinguishing the mind (*mano-nāśa*), and destroying mental impressions (*vāsanā-kṣāya*). While Vidyāraṇya holds that priority must be given to knowing the truth (the highest end in Advaita), he also claims that without practicing all three means, liberation while living is impossible. These means are mutually reinforcing and should be practiced simultaneously. Both the focus on the mind and its impressions and the model of threefold means are central to Vidyāraṇya's Yogic Advaita, and references to the *LYV* and the *Gītā* abound in this section. On the other hand, the threefold means to liberation do not appear in Śaṅkara's Advaita, which holds that yogic practices of any sort are a form of action, and thus are ultimately part of the lower, dualistic realm.[11]

Vidyāraṇya analyzes the relationship of these three means by discussing the continuity and discontinuity among them.[12] Throughout this section he seems to be both descriptive and normative. For example, he claims that destroying impressions and extinguishing the mind must take place simultaneously (*JMV* 40, 237). Impure impressions (*vāsanā*) generate anger and other mental forms (*ākāra*); destroying such impressions prevents anger from arising (even when it is "justified"), since it implants pure impressions—like self-restraint and equanimity born of right discrimination (another way of saying *tattva-jñāna*). When mental manifestations (*vṛtti*) cease (*mano-nāśa*), new, impure impressions will not arise, and when impure impressions are destroyed, mental transformations will cease.

Mental manifestations also cease by the first means, knowing the truth (*tattva-jñāna*); that is, knowing that apparent diversity is illusory and the Self alone is real. Until non-duality is known, mental forms continue as a fire constantly fed with fuel continues. These ever-arising forms then reaffirm the experience of apparent diversity, creating a never-ending cycle. Thus, knowing the truth of non-duality destroys mental impressions like anger, whose destruction, with the concomitant rise of equanimity, reveals non-dual Brahman. Vidyāraṇya is suggesting that practicing any one means reinforces the others. His emphasis on the importance of repeated human effort, particularly to counter impure mental impressions by developing pure impressions, shows the influence of Patañjali's Yoga. Impressions are not destroyed all at once, nor is liberation gained with one insight. Knowledge and yogic practice are linked, for discerning non-duality aids the cessation of mental activity, and ceasing mental activity through yoga helps one experience non-duality.

Vidyāraṇya's entire chapter on extinguishing the mind (*mano-nāśa*) indicates his Yogic Advaita; the chapter's theme is controlling and restraining the mind by yogic discipline, particularly Patañjali's eight-limbed Yoga.[13]

Vidyāraṇya claims that while the mind is extinguished when mental impressions are destroyed, only repeated practice of *mano-nāśa* secures permanent destruction of mental impressions. In fact, he begins the chapter by saying, "Extinguishing the mind is *the* means to living liberation (*atha jīvanmukti-sādhanam manonāśam*)"—for only extinction of the mind keeps destroyed impressions from ever rising again (*JMV* 86, 303).

This Yoga-oriented emphasis on extinguishing the mind is not found in Śaṅkara or later mainstream Advaitins, yet Vidyāraṇya's exegesis of *mano-nāśa* still affirms the centrality of knowledge of Brahman, a point absent in the Yoga school. Yogic practices, while crucial on the path to *jīvanmukti*, must still be informed by knowledge of the non-dual Self. For example, Vidyāraṇya notes that some *yogins* attain supernatural powers (*siddhis*) like flying, which are not obtained by *jīvanmuktas*. However, even one ignorant of the Self can get such powers, which are not the object of Self-knowledge. The pursuit of powers only indicates one's ignorance and doesn't help one attain the highest end. All desires must cease, so desiring powers is ultimately an obstacle. Further, since such wonderful powers come from the Self, any one who knows the Self could achieve them (*JMV* 103, 327).[14] This passage echoes a common Indian refrain that Brahman-knowers can certainly gain and use supernatural powers, but they are too wise and detached to do so. Such claims affirm the ultimacy of the path of knowledge over yogic mastery.

Throughout the chapter on extinguishing the mind, Vidyāraṇya examines types of meditative enstasis (*samādhi*) which aim to still the mind and urges the cessation of the activity of Sāṃkhyan evolutes through yogic practice. However, he says, even the highest (*nirodha* or *asaṃprajñāta*) yogic *samādhi* is not the final goal; it leads to the highest goal—knowledge of the Self (*JMV* 114, 344). Here Vidyāraṇya clearly indicates a limitation of Yoga: texts of the Yoga school focus only on stilling the mind by *samādhi* and do not explicitly mention the Advaitin realization of the Self (*ātma-darśana*), which is, of course, the ultimate goal. He claims that even after one attains the highest *samādhi*, another mental manifestation (*vṛtti*), called knowledge of Brahman (*brahmavidyā*), must arise in order to reach identity with Brahman. This *vṛtti* appears by hearing the Upaniṣadic great statements (*mahāvākya*), like "you are That" (*tat-tvam-asi*). Thus, one can realize one's Self, the "basis of you" (*tvaṃpadārtha*), by either the highest meditative enstasis (Yoga) *or* by Sāṃkhyan discrimination of consciousness (*cit*) and gross matter (*jaḍa*), but one realizes the highest (Advaitin) teaching that the Self (the "basis of you") is Brahman only by the Upaniṣadic great sayings (*JMV* 115, 345). Once again we see Vidyāraṇya's "Yogic Advaita" holds both that meditation is vital *and* that the path of knowledge is higher.

Vidyāraṇya makes this point again in a passage that addresses the relative status of a *yogin* and a knower (*JMV* 147, 391). He considers whether the *yogin* concentrated (*samāhita*) in meditation is better than the truth-knower involved in the world (*loka-vyavahāra*). He quotes *LYV* 25. 5-9, which states that they are equally good, if both keep their "inner cool" (*antaḥśītalatā*). This inner cool takes the form of both destruction of impressions and extinction of the mind. For Vidyāraṇya the key to liberation is mental quiescence, not action (or lack thereof) in the world.

He continues by arguing that at one level the *yogin* concentrated in meditation is better than a person involved in the world, although ultimately knowing the truth is the highest goal. Generally, *samādhi* is better than worldly involvement. If one lacks knowledge and still has mental impressions, *samādhi* practice is better, because it leads to heaven (*uttama-loka*). However, worldly involvement without mental impressions is better than *samādhi* with them—and such a *samādhi* isn't really the highest *samādhi* anyway. Once knowledge is fully established and impressions are absent, *samādhi* is then also superior to worldly involvement, for it preserves liberation while living (*JMV* 148, 392-3). Again, in Vidyāraṇya's Yogic Advaita, liberation is beyond mere yogic practice, but liberation is at risk without it.

Jīvanmukti and *Videhamukti* in the *Jīvanmuktiviveka*

Like other Advaitins, Vidyāraṇya discusses the relationship between liberation while living (*jīvanmukti*) and bodiless liberation (*videhamukti*). While he argues that one certainly gains liberation here (in life), Vidyāraṇya sometimes suggests that embodied liberation is not quite equal to liberation without a body. His reservation appears in two not completely congruent claims, to be documented more fully below. Apparently influenced by the yogic notion that embodiment (with its inevitable suffering) is a limitation, he seems at times to claim that *videhamukti* is a greater achievement than *jīvanmukti*, precisely because one then has no body. In other places, he follows mainstream Advaita, asserting that liberation while living and after death are essentially similar, as both lack any notion of duality, and in both only pure self-luminous consciousness remains. From this view, merely dropping the body, without the liberating knowledge of the unconditioned Self, will inevitably bring re-embodiment. One is fully liberated even while living, since the body and senses are merely adventitious adjuncts of the Self.

Both these claims can be seen in his very first reference to living versus bodiless *mukti* (*JMV* 15, 202ff.). He here interprets *Kaṭha Upaniṣad*

5. 1, which says "having been liberated, he is released," to mean that one liberated from present bondage (like desire) while living is further liberated from future bondage at the fall of the body (*dehapāta*).[15] This implies that *videhamukti* is beyond *jīvanmukti*, because one then has no body and this state lasts forever. However, he goes on here to say one is liberated when all mental manifestations (*dhi-vṛtti*) cease after knowledge, citing the claim in *Bṛhadāraṇyaka Upaniṣad* 4. 4. 7 that the desireless sage realizes Brahman even here. He explains (following Śaṅkara) that one should not aim merely to drop the body, since without liberation one will soon again be embodied in another birth. Only knowledge of the unconditioned Self brings permanent liberation (*JMV* 16, 203). In the most important way, says Vidyāraṇya, liberation while living and after death are similar, as neither contain any notion of dualism. They are differentiated "merely" by the presence or absence of the body and senses, both adventitious adjuncts of the Self (*JMV* 16, 204).

In the most interesting passage on this topic (*JMV* 45, 245ff.), Vidyāraṇya introduces a new solution to this difficult issue of the relationship between full liberation and embodiment. He begins by saying that knowledge alone brings release or perfect isolation (*kaivalya*), and release means being bodiless (*videha*). Destroying impressions and extinguishing the mind without studying the knowledge-texts (*jñāna-śāstra*) will not bring release, since only knowledge destroys the subtle body (*liṅga-deha*) and all bondage (*JMV* 46, 246).[16] Bodiless liberation is therefore simultaneous with the rise of knowledge. However, as seen above, he repeatedly claims that one can have knowledge while living (i.e., embodied). An implicit but obvious question then arises: how can this be so if bodilessness is simultaneous with the rise of knowledge? Vidyāraṇya clarifies this point here with an interesting definitional maneuver: he claims one can have bodiless liberation while living! This view does not contradict mainstream Advaita, but is a novel articulation of it. He points out (accurately) that the term "*deha*" (body) has been understood in many ways (*JMV* 47, 247).[17] Here *deha* refers just to *future* (*bhāvi*) bodies; the present body is a prior acquisition, so it can't cease even with knowledge. Bodiless liberation is thus freedom from future (not present) embodiment, and knowledge is simultaneous with *this* freedom. Dropping the present body is no mark of knowledge, for death will be reached eventually by even the most ignorant person.

Here, Vidyāraṇya, like other Advaitins, hold that knowledge removes only uncommenced (*anārabdha*) *karma*, not actions bearing fruit now (*prārabdha*) (*JMV* 47, 248). Knowledge is thus the necessary but not sufficient cause of bodilessness. Only when *prārabdha-karma* ceases will the body/sense world cease. A fire must burn out its current fuel, and knowledge is not water, but absence of fuel. So knowledge and embodiment *this time around* are not related, allowing Vidyāraṇya to state that "bodiless" liberation and knowledge arise simultaneously. Thus the *jīvanmukta*—who will take no future body—is also a *videhamukta*.[18]

However, Vidyāraṇya elsewhere seems to suggest that *videhamukti* is actual bodilessness, not living liberation with no future births (128, 365). He cites *LYV* 28. 15–27, which says that the extinguished mind has two modes: with form (*sarūpa*), belonging to the *jīvanmukta*, and without form (*arūpa*), belonging to the *videhamukta*. The *jīvanmukta's* "formed" mind (*sarūpa-citta*) contains the quality of purity (*sattvaguṇa*), full of attributes like friendliness. The extinguished mind of the *videhamukta* is beyond even this, however; it is formless, for even purity (*sattva*) is dissolved there. This apparently "bodiless mind" is pure bliss, taking all space itself (*ākāśa*) as its body. Thus, Vidyāraṇya seems to argue that while *jīvanmukti* is full liberation, bodiless (or space-embodied) *videhamukti* is a little fuller.

The Purposes of Attaining Liberation While Living

Vidyāraṇya's Yoga-influenced Advaita is also evident in his description of the five "purposes" (*prayojana*) of attaining living liberation: guarding knowledge (*jñāna-rakṣā*), austerity (*tapas*), non-disputation (*visaṃvādābhāva*), destroying suffering (*duḥkha-nāśa*), and manifesting serenity (*sukhāvirbhāva*) (*JMV* 130, 367ff.). One should note that Vidyāraṇya's usage of *prayojana*—translated by Sastri and Ayyangar as "purpose" or "aim"—can be taken a number of ways. *Jīvanmukti* would not seem to have any purpose beyond itself, for realizing non-dual Brahman while living is itself the ultimate aim of existence. Neither are the five "purposes" simply causes or benefits of living liberation. The difficulty can be partly clarified by the lack of distinction in the text between means and end. Vidyāraṇya seems to regard these "purposes" both as the practices of one who wants to reach liberation and the identifying marks of one who has already achieved it. Put another way, one practices these means to attain the highest end, and the achiever of the highest end is recognized by his constant practice of these means. Further, Vidyāraṇya is here describing the prescription for liberation (or better, prescribing his description).

Both the Yogic and Advaitin influences on Vidyāraṇya are apparent in his exposition of the five aims. Consistent with his claim that knowledge is the central, but not sole, characteristic of *jīvanmukti*, Vidyāraṇya makes clear that guarding (or preserving) knowledge is the primary purpose and mark of attaining liberation while living. However, he adds that unless the *jīvanmukta* guards his knowledge by practicing yogic pacification of mind, doubt (*saṃśaya*) and error (*viparyaya*) may arise, even after the truth is known (*JMV* 130, 367).[19]

Vidyāraṇya then differentiates knowers (*jñānins*) and *jīvanmuktas*, a distinction foreign to Śaṅkara but significant for Yoga-influenced Advaita, for it suggests that "merely" knowing the truth is somehow less than the fullest liberation—which is brought by yogic practice. He describes types of Brahman knowers (*brahmavid*)[20] based on the stage of knowledge each has achieved (134, 373). One becomes a knower of Brahman, but not yet a *jīvanmukta*, in the stage (fourth of seven) which brings the direct realization of Brahman/*ātman* unity through the Vedāntic great sayings. The next three stages, Vidyāraṇya writes, are subdivisions (*avāntarabheda*) of *jīvanmukti*. They derive from differing degrees of repose (*viśrānti*), which arise from repeated practice of unconditioned (*nirvikalpa*) *samādhi* (*JMV* 136, 375). Thus, Vidyāraṇya holds that there are even degrees of *jīvanmukti*, and these degrees arise from yogic practice. Unlike Śaṅkara, who makes no distinction between a Brahman-knower and a liberated being, Vidyāraṇya finds knowledge of Brahman a necessary, but not sufficient, cause for *jīvanmukti*. How can one be a Brahman-knower, but not a *jīvanmukta*? According to Vidyāraṇya, only in the *jīvanmukti* stages does no doubt or error arise, since all appearance of duality has vanished. Only after one gains the repose from the highest *samādhi* is knowledge completely safeguarded (so *jīvanmukti* attained) (*JMV* 137, 377).

Vidyāraṇya also discusses how it is possible for a Brahman-knower to have attachments, such as pride in learning, if the knowledge which ends in *jīvanmukti* supposedly allows for no pride (*JMV* 73, 285). Vidyāraṇya first claims the knower has only the semblance (*ābhāsa*) of attachment, and he recognizes its mere seeming, like recognizing the rope's appearance as a "snake." But what then of the sage Yājñavalkya, proud, greedy for cows, and even cursing Śākalya to death (*Bṛhadāraṇyaka Upaniṣad* 3. 1)? Vidyāraṇya says Yājñavalkya is not a *jīvanmukta*, even though he is a knower of Brahman (*JMV* 74, 287). Brahman-knowers (unlike *jīvanmuktas*) have impure impressions, like jealousy and anger. This point reinforces Vidyāraṇya's emphasis on the need to continue to extinguish the mind and mental impressions even after knowledge of the real has dawned. Further evidence is his distinction between a knower (*jñānin*) or seeker (*vividiṣā*) renunciate and a *jīvanmukta* or realized (*vidvat*) renunciate (*JMV* 51, 254).[21] The "mere" knower must renew his efforts of destroying impressions and extinguishing the mind to become fully realized. Due to currently manifesting (*prārabdha*) *karma*, even one with knowledge cannot permanently remove impressions and mental manifestations without practicing yoga steadily. Doubt, error, and other attachments fully disappear only when (by yoga) the mind is pacified (*JMV* 51, 255).

The four latter purposes or marks of attaining liberation while living reinforce and reflect the first—guarding knowledge. Austerity (*tapas*) focuses on yogic practice and detachment from works (*JMV* 137, 377ff.).[22] According to Vidyāraṇya, the third aim, non-disputation (*visaṃvādābhāva*), arises because the sage has no concern with the world, so no reason for argument or censure arises. As he is without anger and talks only of the Self, how could anyone dispute with him (*JMV* 143, 385)?[23] The last two aims, destroying suffering (*duḥkha-nāśa*) and manifesting serenity (*sukhāvirbhāva*) combine knowledge, following dharmic regulation, and renunciation (*JMV* 145, 388ff.). Serenity, described in terms also used by Śaṅkara, manifests in three ways: obtaining all desires, completing all duties, and attaining all that is attainable (*JMV* 146, 389). Also like Śaṅkara, Vidyāraṇya affirms that the *jīvanmukta* realizes he is Brahman, and not a body. Thus, in Vidyāraṇya's Yogic Advaita, these aims and practices taken together both point to and demonstrate having reached and safeguarded the highest end, *jīvanmukti*.

Renunciation and *Jīvanmukti*

Throughout the text, Vidyāraṇya closely connects liberation while living with renunciation (*saṃnyāsa*).[24] While knowledge of non-dual *ātman*/ Brahman is the defining feature of liberation, renunciation (which includes yogic practice) both leads to and follows knowledge. Vidyāraṇya's description of the practice (*sādhana*) of the renunciate (*saṃnyāsin*) is in line with mainstream Advaita. The *saṃnyāsin*, he says, renounces the worlds of the not-Self to experience the Self alone, abandons desire-impelled actions, and studies the *Veda* (*JMV* 3, 181). The realized renunciate (*vidvat saṃnyāsin*) specifically has attained the truth by having renounced worldly desires for offspring and wealth, and by having heard, reflected, and meditated on the Veda (*śravaṇa-manana-nididhyāsana*) (*JMV* 4, 183).

While virtually all Advaitins endorse *saṃnyāsa*, few emphasize it as much as Vidyāraṇya. He repeatedly prescribes rejecting the world's temptations. Attachment to wife and children is bad: women's bodies are tempting but disgusting, and parenting is a misery (*JMV* 77, 291ff.). Isolation and indifference, on the other hand, bring many benefits. For example, the renunciate should not greet nor bless others, because such acknowledgement demands the mental agitation of attending to proper word choice for salutation (*JMV* 29, 223). Following Śaṅkara (in *Upadeśasāhasrī* 17. 64), Vidyāraṇya asks: When established in the non-duality beyond names, who would one greet (*JMV* 30, 224)? The *saṃnyāsin* should remain alone, focused on meditation; three mendicants together are a village, and more are a city. Solitude allows uninterrupted meditation, but a place full of people hinders realizing the bliss of the Self (*JMV* 33, 228). Again we see Vidyāraṇya's close intertwining of knowledge of non-dual Brahman with renunciation and yogic practices, like solitary meditation.[25]

Vidyāraṇya recounts the *jīvanmukta's* way of life most clearly in the final chapter of the *JMV*, which forms a commentary on the *Paramahaṃsa Upaniṣad*. The chapter, devoted to describing the supremely ascetic (*paramahaṃsa*) *yogin* or realized renunciate (*vidvat-saṃnyāsin*), interweaves renunciation, yogic practice, and knowing non-duality. We here find the terms *yogin*, *saṃnyāsin*, and *mukta*, with their respective qualifiers (*paramahaṃsa*, *vidvat*, and *jīvan*), all identifying the same being. This discussion illustrates both the path to, and "lifestyle" in, living liberation. While Vidyāraṇya's understanding is undergirded by Advaitin metaphysics and ethics, it is certainly not narrowly Śaṅkaran, for it includes notions of yogic practice and transcending dharmic duties unexpressed by Śaṅkara.

To Vidyāraṇya, a *paramahaṃsa-yogin* (that is, *jīvanmukta*) combines the best qualities of the knower and the *yogin*: a mere *yogin* does not have knowledge of the real and desires supernatural powers like flying; a mere *paramahaṃsa*, while knowing reality (Brahman), spurns Vedic injunctions and prohibitions (*vidhi-niṣedha*). A *paramahaṃsa-yogin*, however, neither desires powers nor disregards injunctions (*JMV* 150, 395).[26] Thus, this *yogin* still follows both the Vedāntic and yogic paths. He removes ignorance (of non-duality) by realizing the meaning of the great sayings (*mahāvākya*), and removes impressions (*vāsanās*) arising from ignorance by repeated yogic practice (*JMV* 159, 412). Only together can these paths bring eternal awakening (*nitya-bodha*).

What then, Vidyāraṇya asks, is the worldly manner (dress, speech, and so forth) of this rare bird of a *yogin*? And what is his internal condition (*sthiti*)? Sometimes Vidyāraṇya simply argues that the *paramahaṃsa-yogin* treads the path of total renunciation, including the abandonment of dharmic regulations: he departs from family and friends and ignores even Vedic study and ritual action. He gives up all that brings worldly *or* heavenly rewards (*JMV* 155, 405). All rules and injunctions are abandoned, since such everyday conventions breed attachment (*JMV* 27, 221).[27] Clothed or unclothed, he roams anywhere and eats anything, recognizing neither good nor bad—for separating these two (or seeing *any* opposites) is itself a flaw.

Vidyāraṇya goes on, however, to claim that the renunciation of the knower (*vidvat-saṃnyāsa*) has another dimension: while ultimately unconcerned with actions and injunctions, the Brahman-knower also continues to perform them. Performing duties is necessary, since even after the Self is known, adventitious adjuncts (*upādhi*) remain in the *yogin's* "mind" (*antaḥkaraṇa*). Although knowing the truth, he still has not achieved the satisfaction (*tṛpti*) and mental repose which comes from completing every duty (*JMV* 154, 402-3).[28]

Vidyāraṇya's inclination toward synthesis and perhaps purposeful ambiguity are apparent here. He could certainly say more about the need to perform duties after knowledge (which is not the same as continuing yogic practice so often emphasized elsewhere), but he nowhere explicitly explains why the *dharma*-transcending *jīvanmukta* will live in accord with the *dharma*, a topic briefly discussed by Sureśvara and other later Advaitins. One possible reason is that since the *dharma* is the cosmic structure and law, a detached *jīvanmukta* (despite being beyond the *dharma*) will "instinctively" follow the nature of things.[29]

While renunciation and knowledge go together for Vidyāraṇya, knowing the non-dual Self ultimately takes one beyond conventional *saṃnyāsa*. Ordinary renunciation affects the body, not the ever-detached Self. For the *paramahaṃsa-yogin*, body-based injunctions, such as wearing a loincloth and using a bamboo walking stick (*daṇḍa*) are not essential, for thinking about them could perturb his one-pointed mind (*JMV* 156, 407-8). Renunciates in the lower stage of merely desiring knowledge (*vividiṣā*) hold on to the bamboo stick and the performance of Vedic injunctions, while the *paramahaṃsa-yogin* carries no stick—or, rather, carries only the "stick" of knowledge. The true ascetic is not one who literally holds a triple staff (*tridaṇḍin*), but one who shows threefold control of speech, mind, and action (*JMV* 163, 419). He needs no blanket, as he is beyond feeling any heat or cold. And he is certainly beyond slander, pride, greed, anger, and so on. He disputes with no one, knowing no other truly exists. Clearly then, the highest knowledge takes one beyond mechanical adherence to Vedic ritual and the ascetic path. Still, how can anyone, even the *paramahaṃsa-yogin*, give up all material goods and worldly feelings while embodied? Vidyāraṇya, citing the *Paramahaṃsa Upaniṣad*, states that the *yogin's* body is now merely like a corpse (*kuṇapa*), since it is known as other than the Self which is pure consciousness (*caitanya*). Feelings like slander and pride can be abandoned while living when the body (different from consciousness) is seen as a corpse (*JMV* 158, 411).[30] Thus, detachment from the body ultimately comes from knowledge, not renunciation.

The text concludes by reaffirming Yogic Advaita, that is, maintaining the importance of yogic practice and renunciation in both leading to *and* expressing knowledge of non-dual Brahman. The liberated being (*jīvanmukta*, *vidvat-saṃnyāsin*, or *paramahaṃsa-yogin*), with sense activity at rest and unobstructed meditative enstasis, abides in the Self. Blissfully realizing "I am Brahman," he has completed all duties (*JMV* 172, 431). Thus, in Yogic Advaita, repeated human effort (via yogic practice) and renunciation are necessary to end all desires and gain Brahman knowledge. The liberated being is also recognized by his yogic practice and renunciation. However, the true *jīvanmukta* is no longer bound even to *samādhi* or a ritually pure life (which presupposes duality). His effortless non-dual bliss both results from and perfects *samādhi* and purity.

Conclusion

Let us close by reviewing Vidyāraṇya's key arguments. First, and most important, is his claim that to be liberated while living, one must have the knowledge (*jñāna*) that Brahman and *ātman* are one. Such knowledge, which comes from hearing and studying the Vedānta texts, is the necessary basis for *jīvanmukti*. However, one who knows (that is, the *jñānin*) is not automatically a *jīvanmukta*. Vidyāraṇya points out that even a sage like Yājñavalkya was jealous and proud, and that even a Brahman-knower can have doubt and error. Due to currently manifesting (*prārabdha*) *karma*, one must also practice *yoga* repeatedly to destroy the mind and mental impressions (which produce doubt and error). *Karma* currently bearing fruit are stronger than knowledge, but yogic practice can overcome even the necessity of experiencing *prārabdha-karma*.

Vidyāraṇya repeatedly stresses the importance of yogic techniques in destroying mental impressions (*vāsanā-kṣāya*) and extinguishing the mind (*mano-nāśa*) while seeking knowledge of the truth and even after finding it; this is a key reason for calling his view "Yogic Advaita." Yogic influence also appears in his concern about the "mental state" and *samādhi* level of the *jīvanmukta*. However, Vidyāraṇya makes it clear that yoga alone cannot make one a *jīvanmukta*. To be liberated while living, one needs both discernment (*viveka*, or *brahma-jñāna*) and sense-restraining "unconditioned" (*asaṃprajñāta* or *nirvikalpa*) *samādhi*. A concentrated *yogin* without knowledge may have supernatural powers and may go to heaven, but he is not liberated, nor is he better than a knower acting in the world. This *yogin* reaches the insight of the "basis of you" (*tvaṃpadārtha*), but not of the unity of Ātman and Brahman. Again, we see Vidyāraṇya's central claim that both Vedāntic knowledge and yogic enstasy are necessary to gain and sustain full liberation. Further, Vidyāraṇya's discussion of both the threefold means to liberation and the five marks or purposes of *jīvanmukti* indicate that the means to reach liberation are also the way of life after liberation. They not only lead to and safeguard liberation; they are the expressions of the achievement of *mokṣa*.

Vidyāraṇya also holds that one can be fully liberated while embodied—if liberation means knowing the non-dual Self, extinguishing the mind and its impressions, and never taking another birth. The embodied knower of Brahman is already dead to the world—a corpse—so in a sense "without a body" (*videha*). However, he also suggests that *videhamukti* only exists when one is literally without a body, and this *mukti* is the fuller liberation. Thus, for Vidyāraṇya, liberation does occur while embodied, but he also considers bodilessness to be a sign of the highest release.

Finally, Vidyāraṇya points out that renunciation is critical to *jīvanmukti*, both as a path to and as an indicator of liberation. However, he suggests that the path to *jīvanmukti* goes beyond conventional *saṃnyāsa*, which calls for living in solitude and renouncing desires and all that consists of worldly "householding," such as gaining wealth or offspring, or even performing Vedic ritual actions. Knowledge of non-dual Brahman leads ultimately to a renunciation higher than conventional world renunciation. In a sense, renunciation of Vedic *dharma* affirms the existence of the world of duality by rejecting it. The realized (*vidvat*) renouncer (and *paramahaṃsa yogin*) is not bound by (yet does not transgress) all Vedic prohibitions and "good" or "evil": he is both a brāhmin and beyond any caste or life-stage. As the *Bhagavad Gītā* says, mental detachment is more important than worldly action (or non-action). The highest *yogin* is not one with a loincloth and staff, but one who keeps his "inner cool" (*antaḥśītalatā*), destroying the mind and its impressions. He thus lives "in the world" competing karmic duties, and as a truly free being, passing beyond disgust for, and rejection of, everyday human existence.[31]

To conclude, let us again briefly contrast Vidyāraṇya's Yogic Advaita with Śaṅkara's mainstream Advaita. While there views are rarely directly opposed, their emphases and interests are often dramatically different. Vidyāraṇya's Yogic Advaita is linked, both by philosophical commitment and by extent of textual references, more to the views of the *LYV* and the *Gītā*, with their Sāṃkhya/Yoga emphases than to the Śaṅkaran mainstream.[32] Both Vidyāraṇya and Śaṅkara hold that the primary mark of the *jīvanmukta* is knowing non-dual Brahman, but only Vidyāraṇya claims that such knowledge cannot be gained or sustained without repeated yogic practice. With such practice, liberation can be achieved while embodied; and with the highest knowledge, the *jīvanmukta* can live in the world while detached from it. Vidyāraṇya's emphases on yogic practice, cessation of mental activity, and the distinction between the *jīvanmukta* and Brahman-knower are not shared by Śaṅkara. On the other hand, Vidyāraṇya rarely explores some of Śaṅkara's central concerns, such as discriminating between body and Self, or the utter separation of knowledge and activity.

Also unlike mainstream Advaitins, who focus on the role of *prārabdha karma* (or any remnant of ignorance) in the continuity of embodiment, Vidyāraṇya instead emphasizes the importance of yogic practice now to remove remaining *karma*. Vidyāraṇya and Śaṅkara do not disagree on "bodiless" liberation, but Vidyāraṇya's understanding is far more refined and clearly articulated. Śaṅkara does argue that one is bodiless while embodied when one knows that the Self is not the body and that embodiedness itself is a false notion (*Brahma Sūtra* 1. 1. 4). However, he never uses the term *videhamukti*, much less employs Vidyāraṇya's specification of *videhamukti* as freedom from future (versus present) embodiment, nor does he discuss the relationship between *jīvan*- and *videhamukti* (or Vidyāraṇya's occasional suggestion that the latter is "more" free). Vidyāraṇya's examination of the purposes or marks of attaining *jīvanmukti*, which describes a non-disputatious and actively world-purifying liberated being, is also expanded far beyond any of Śaṅkara's descriptions. Finally, both argue that renunciation is central to liberation, but Vidyāraṇya's intense focus on *saṃnyāsa* and his claim that the renouncer passes beyond all dharmic duties would be disputed by Śaṅkara. Thus, Vidyāraṇya, while Advaitin, is his own kind of Advaitin—a Yogic Advaitin.

Abbreviations

JMV *Vidyāraṇya, Jīvanmuktiviveka*. Edited and translated by S. Subrahmanya Sastri and T. R. Srinivasa Ayyangar. Madras: Adyar Library and Research Centre, 1978. (Translations cited are mine).

LYV *Laghu-Yoga-Vāsiṣṭha*. Translated by K. Narayanaswami Aiyer. Madras: Adyar Library and Research Centre, 1971.

Notes

1. References that follow indicate pages in text and translation, i.e., (*JMV* 33, 178).

2. There has been some debate about the relationship of the *JMV* author to Sāyaṇa, Mādhava, Bhāratītīrtha, and Vidyāraṇya of the *Pañcadaśī* (including whether they are different people or the same person at different stages of life). For purposes of this essay, the most important point to make is that it is unlikely that the Vidyāraṇya of the *JMV* is the same Vidyāraṇya who authored the *Pañcadaśī*. When considering *jīvanmukti*, the *Pañcadaśī* author follows the Śaṅkaran tradition of Advaita more closely than does the *JMV* author: there are more references to key Upaniṣadic passages (such as *Chāndogya* 6. 14. 2, *Kaṭha* 6. 14–5, and *Muṇḍaka*

3. 2. 9) and far fewer to the *Laghu Yogavāsiṣṭha*. Unlike the *JMV*, the *Pañcadaśī* also emphasizes knowing the world's unreality, *cidābhāsa* ("ego") versus *kūṭastha* (self), and the role of *prārabdha-karma* in causing bodily continuity. On the other hand, key aspects of the *JMV*, such as types of renunciation, extinguishing the mind (*mano-nāśa*) and destroying mental impressions (*vāsanā-kṣaya*), and the purposes of *jīvanmukti* are mentioned rarely or not at all.

3. For an excellent summary and analysis of this text, one can consult J. F. Sprockhoff's two part article on the *Jīvanmuktiviveka*, "Die Weg zur Erlösung bei Lebzeiten, Ihr Wesen and Ihr Wert, nach dem *Jīvanmuktiviveka* des Vidyāraṇya." *Wiener Zeitschrift für die Kunde Süd- und Ost-asiens* 8 (1964): 224–62 and 14 (1970): 131–59. A more recent work focusing on living liberation in the *JMV* is L. K. L. Srivastava's *Advaitic Concept of Jīvanmukti* (Delhi: Bharatiya Vidya Bhavan, 1990). This book is less satisfactory than Sprockhoff's work, as it is heavily neo-Vedāntin and lacking in critical analysis.

4. See my article "Knowing Brahman while Embodied: Śaṅkara on *Jīvanmukti*." in *Journal of Indian Philosophy* 19 (1991): 369–89.

5. See for example pp. 30, 224; 72, 285.

6. Jīvataḥ puruṣasya kartṛtva-bhoktṛtva-sukhaduhkhādi-lakṣaṇaś citta-dharmaḥ kleśa-rūpatvād bandho bhavati, tasya nivāraṇaṃ jīvanmuktiḥ." (*JMV* 10, 194)

7. For Śaṅkara's views, see Lance Nelson's discussion of *Brahma Sūtra Bhāṣya* 4. 1. 15 and 19, and *Bṛhadāraṇyaka Upaniṣad Bhāṣya* 1. 4. 7 and 10.

8. Vidyāraṇya discusses mental impressions at some length, devoting an entire chapter to the destruction of impressions (*vāsanā-kṣaya*) as a means for attaining *jīvanmukti*. He adopts the *LYV* definition of *vāsanās* as an intense binding to a thing, which, because of strong attachment, causes one to think one's delusory impression is the real thing (*sadvastu*) (*JMV* 52, 256). The rest of the chapter describes various kinds of pure (*śuddha*) and impure (*malinā*) *vāsanās*. Pure *vāsanās* are sense activity that merely keep the body alive, without causing rebirth (*JMV* 56, 261). Impure mental impressions are of three types: *loka* (desire for the world's praise), *śāstra* (addiction to, and pride in, mere textual study and ritual observance) and *deha* (the threefold illusion that the body is the Self, that it can be beautified, and that its flaws can be removed) (*JMV* 56, 261ff.).

9. Lance Nelson points out that Śaṅkara does, on rare occasions, speak of the value of mental concentration as a preparatory stage encouraging the rise of knowledge.

10. Still following the *Gītā*, Vidyāraṇya goes on to describe the *jīvanmukta* as a detached and content devotee of the Lord (*bhagavad-bhakta*) and as one who has gone beyond the threefold qualities (*guṇātīta*) (*JMV* 25, 218ff.). Here we see Vidyāraṇya's commingling of devotional, yogic, and non-dualistic strands of Indian thought. He writes that the discriminating *guṇātīta* is beyond activity or superim-

posing the "I" on action. The one beyond qualities aims to serve the Self by knowledge, repeated meditation, and unswerving devotion (a theme clearly emphasized in the *Gītā*).

11. For a discussion of this point, and the role of yoga and meditation in Śaṅkara's thought, see J. Bader's *Meditation in Śaṅkara's Vedānta* (New Delhi: Aditya Prakashan, 1990).

12. The technical term for this is "positive and negative concomitance" (*anvaya-vyatireka*).

13. Sprockhoff (1964, Note 3) has a detailed analysis of this portion of the text, and points out that Vidyāraṇya, while following Patañjali in many ways, has his own version of yogic limbs (p. 251).

14. The passage quoted is from *LYV* 28. 1–9. See also *Yogavāsiṣṭha Upaśama khaṇḍa* 89. 9–21.

15. Jīvanneva ḍṛṣṭabandhanāt kāmāder-viśeṣeṇa muktaḥ san dehapāte bhāvibandhanād-viśeṣaṇena mucyate (15, 202).

16. He here gives many examples of Upaniṣadic *jñāna-śāstra: Muṇḍaka* 2. 2. 8 and 10, 3. 2. 9; *Kaṭha* 3. 8; *Bṛhadāranyaka Upaniṣad* 1. 4. 10, and so forth.

17. Śaṅkara's discussion of *aśarīratva* (bodilessness) in *Brahma Sūtra Bhāṣya* 1. 1. 4 is exemplary here.

18. To this mainstream Advaitin position, he adds a familiar Yogic Advaitin point: knowledge of the truth is the main, direct means to *mukti* (here "bodiless"), while destroying the mind and impressions are means to knowledge. Though inferior, they are still necessary (*JMV* 49, 252).

19. Vidyāraṇya argues that doubt is even worse than error (such as the erroneous belief that ritual action can bring release). One can at times be happy when ignorant or in error, but doubt prevents worldly enjoyment as well as liberation, thus allowing no satisfaction on either level.

20. This categorization of Brahman-knowers is based (as usual) on *LYV* 13. 113–23.

21. For more on the two types of *saṃnyāsa*, see note 24.

22. The most interesting aspect of this section is Vidyāraṇya's suggestion that austerity (*tapas*) provides for the welfare of the world (*loka-saṃgraha*). Here we may glimpse what a *jīvanmukta* does for others—his "social ethics" and role in society. Austerity here has a transpersonal, or even cosmic, potency.

Vidyāraṇya suggests that the *yogin* performs a most important activity or service by allowing others to follow, serve, and worship him. His presence is a great favor. For example, those who take the *yogin* as teacher (*guru*) attain knowledge rapidly. Devotees who provide his food and shelter are doing the equivalent of austerity by such service. Believers (*āstika*) merely observing him begin to follow the right path (*san-mārga*), and even unbelievers are freed from evil when seen by him. Thus, the opportunity to serve or even see the *yogin/jīvanmukta* arises from his grace (*upakāritva*).

There is another way that the *yogin's* personal (but not body-based) austerity affects many. Appealing to *Sūtasaṃhitā* 2. 20. 45, Vidyāraṇya says that the *yogin*, by knowing Brahman, saves his ancestors from rebirth, sanctifies his entire family, and purifies the whole earth. By transforming his own consciousness, he transforms his entire lineage.

23. Non-disputation is certainly not a goal of mainstream Advaita, nor an attribute of Śaṅkara, himself often called a *jīvanmukta*.

24. He distinguishes two kinds of renunciation: the renunciation of one who possesses knowledge (*vidvat*), which is the cause of liberation while living, and the renunciation of one who merely desires knowledge (*vividiṣā*), which causes liberation only after death (1, 177). How exactly they "cause" liberation and how any liberation can happen after death go unexplained.

25. Vidyāraṇya's emphasis on renunciation also diverges from the *Yogavāsiṣṭha's* stress on detached action in the world. The *JMV* repeatedly speaks of isolation and abnegation, while the *Yogavāsiṣṭha* puts more emphasis on the non-difference between bondage and liberation and the ease of completely detached action in the world. For the latter text, abandonment of any activity is virtually optional.

26. Mainstream Advaita gives even less attention than Vidyāraṇya to either yogic powers or freedom from Vedic injunctions. To Śaṅkara, the highest renunciation is that of the "I-notion," not action.

27. It does not seem that one can be so detached about women, however. Vidyāraṇya claims they are forbidden (*pratiṣiddha*) and disgusting (*jugupsita*) like corpses. They overcome men by causing desire, despite having vaginas like oozing sores, and so forth (*JMV* 32, 227).

28. Still, Vidyāraṇya states, after liberation, completing these duties will not cause future births. Injunctions to study, meditate, and assimilate remove obstacles to *brahma-jñāna* but do not add *karma* (*JMV* 154, 403).

29. Further, as Vidyāraṇya indicates in his discussion of austerity (*tapas*), at this highest level of detachment, the *jīvanmukta* can allow others to follow and serve him, freeing them and purifying the world by his injunction-transcending austerity.

30. Asceticism is prescribed through the rest of this chapter, and a mendicant is described as being beyond *mantra* or *dhyāna*, beyond textual debates and the distinction of "I" and "you." One with the stick (*daṇḍa*) of knowledge is abodeless, only skyclad, greets no one, and does not propitiate ancestors (*JMV* 166, 422).

Abodelessness is important because even living in a monastery reinforces the "I," as does possession of utensils and plates. This renouncer shuns students, rejects gold, and remains always detached. He simply rests in Brahman, avoiding all mixing with the world.

31. Vidyāraṇya's views here represent a common theme in religious literature: after rejecting the world, one can return, "in" but not "of" the world. When ignorant, one thinks one must get from "here" (the world of suffering and attachment) to "there" (liberation). From the liberated viewpoint, however, the duality of "here" and "there" is an illusion. *Jīvanmukti* is in part predicated on the idea that you can be both here *and* there.

32. Though, as mentioned earlier, the *JMV* is not as free from concerns with performing dharmic duties following the path of *saṃnyāsa* as are both forms of the *Yogavāsiṣṭha*.

CHAPTER 6

Modes of Perfected Living in the *Mahābhārata* and the Purāṇas: The Different Faces of Śuka the Renouncer

C. Mackenzie Brown

Introduction

For Western students one of the more startling claims made by Indian religions has been that a state of perfected living is possible even in this life. The notion of perfection, or liberation while still living, commonly referred to as *jīvanmukti* by Hindus, appears in radical opposition to the traditional Western predilection for an exclusively postmortem salvation. For the empathetic outside student, then, there is the intriguing question of what such an alleged state of perfected living is like. Or put another way, how might one go about recognizing a person who has attained such perfection? Such questions have been raised, of course, by Hindus themselves, and this chapter will look at some of their answers.

Many Hindus have argued that *jīvanmuktas* (those liberated while living) transcend all empirical categories and distinctions so much so that they cannot be recognized, except by those who have themselves become perfected. Despite this, Hindu thinkers have spent much effort analyzing and describing the various subtle stages of consciousness through which a being on the way to perfection passes. Regrettably, most such treatments, dealing in highly abstruse concepts, provide scant assistance for the average, non-enlightened person, Western or Hindu, trying to come to terms with perfection as it might manifest itself in the workaday world.

At the same time, in more popular literature, such as the epics and Purāṇas, there are numerous portrayals of sages and saints who, the tradition maintains, have attained the perfected state. In these stories we find dramatically displayed the psychological or mental outlook and consequent social behavior of such enlightened beings. These stories seem to presuppose that even the average layperson, given the right attitude and provided with certain essential clues, can come to recognize, at least in a tentative way, the distinctive features and actions of a *jīvanmukta*, however concealed these may at times be to ordinary perception.

Within the epic and Purāṇic stories, one especially intriguing and enigmatic figure is Śuka, son of the famous Vedic arranger, Vyāsa. While Vyāsa's spiritual authority is beyond question in the tradition, as he is not only the editor of the Vedas but also the author of the great *Mahābhārata* (*Mbh*) epic and the major Purāṇas as well, these very texts attribute an even higher sanctity to his son. Śuka is universally recognized as a model of human perfectibility, an ideal renunciate with complete knowledge of the Absolute.

The tradition, however, does not have one monolithic image of Śuka. The differing portrayals of this saint reflect diverse views on the nature of enlightened consciousness and perfected living. The tradition as a whole, for instance, is ambivalent regarding the extent to which "householding" and procreation are compatible with renunciation. A closely related issue is the problem of what sort of model a perfected being should provide for others still "in the world," that is, for those attempting to uphold the responsibilities of *varṇāśrama-dharma* (the duties pertaining to class and stage of life). And is action performed for the welfare of the world compatible with the dispassionate state of mind that is regarded as a *sine qua non* of liberation? The various answers to these questions have clearly shaped the ways in which the popular texts have painted the worldly career of our sage.

We shall focus on three portrayals of Śuka: one from the *Śānti Parva (ŚP)* of the *Mbh* and two from important later Purāṇic texts which build upon the epic's picture. The first of the Purāṇic texts, the *Bhāgavata Purāṇa (BhP)* (ca. C.E. tenth century), only briefly alludes to Śuka's life story, assuming the reader is already familiar with the details as provided in the *ŚP*. Yet Śuka plays a critical role in the *BhP*, as he is the reciter of that Purāṇa to King Parīkṣit during the latter's last week of mortal existence. The other Purāṇic text is the *Devī-Bhāgavata Purāṇa (DBhP)* (ca. C.E. twelfth–fifteenth centuries), composed in part as a response by the Śākta community to the growing popularity of the Vaiṣṇava *BhP*. The Śākta composer of the *DBhP* gives an extended account of Śuka's life, following the general outline of the *ŚP's* version. But he recasts the specific details in an imaginative reconstruction that pointedly contradicts the ideals of perfection reflected in the *BhP's* image of Śuka.

At least a thousand years separates the earliest and latest accounts with which we will be concerned. Over the course of the intervening millennium, three important religious and philosophical developments occurred: the explosion of the *bhaktic* or devotional schools, the systematic elaboration of the non-dualist, Advaita philosophy, and, near the end of the period, the flourishing of Tantric ideas and practices. An investigation of Śuka in our three stories, then, should provide us with some insight into how these major movements transformed the popular perception of the ideal of perfected living.

These three stories have been chosen both for their historical and their religious interest. Thus, while keeping in mind the historical concerns just mentioned, we will not forget our original question of how to recognize a perfected being. We will pay special attention to the ways these texts reveal—not only to the other characters within the narrative drama itself, but also to us, the reader or audience—Śuka's liberated consciousness. For instance, how do the reactions of enlightened and unenlightened beings to the behavior and antics of Śuka in these stories help the devout listener transform his or her own understanding of perfection?

Before we commence our enterprise proper, one observation regarding terminology is in order. The Hindu tradition at times makes a relatively sharp distinction between *videhamukti*, literally "disembodied liberation," or liberation fully realized only in a state beyond death, on the one hand, and *jīvanmukti* on the other, a distinction emphasized in some of the other chapters in this book. Here, however, we shall not assume any such clear-cut demarcation. There are two reasons for this. First, our texts are popular and quite unsystematic works whose interest often lies in telling a good story, without great regard for philosophical niceties. For instance, none of the texts actually applies either of the above terms to Śuka's spiritual attainment, though the *DBhP* frequently refers to the ideal of *jīvanmukti* and explicitly considers Śuka's teacher, Janaka, to be a *jīvanmukta*. In any case, it is often impossible, or at least quite arbitrary, to give a systematic and terminologically precise definition of what constitutes full, complete, or essential liberation in these accounts.

The second reason is of greater philosophical import, as it concerns our understanding of how Hindus themselves have interpreted liberation. According to the modern Hindu philosopher M. Hiriyanna, *videhamukti*, or "*mokṣa* in the eschatological sense

> . . . is a relic from earlier times when it was believed that the consequences of a good or bad life led here were to be reaped elsewhere in a state beyond death; and the retention of it by any school does not really affect its philosophic standpoint."[1]

Thus, Hiriyanna argues that, even in schools in which the *jīvanmukti* ideal is formally denied, as in Viśiṣṭādvaita,

> "there is clearly recognized the possibility of man reaching here a state of enlightenment which may justifiably be so described because it completely transforms his outlook upon the world and fills with an altogther new significance the life he thereafter leads in it."[2]

Hiriyanna's conclusion is supported by other essays in this volume.

The notion of *videhamukti* may at times presuppose, as Hiriyanna suggests, a postmortem compensation in other worlds, but it may also rest upon a sharp ontological division between spirit and matter, such as is found in the ancient Sāṃkhya. Salvation of the spirit, in this system, consisted of the complete disentanglement of the soul from matter. With the gradual erosion of the belief in the full, separate reality of matter under the influence of Upaniṣadic monism, culminating in the non-dualist philosophy of Śaṅkara, embodied existence, being a kind of illusion, could hardly function as a major impediment to liberation. Accordingly, *videhamukti* itself lost much of its significance, being based on a somewhat unreal distinction, and thus largely irrelevant.

Only in our oldest text, the *ŚP*, does the idea of *videhamukti* play a significant role. Here alone does Śuka cast off his physical body in his quest for the Supreme. The Purāṇic accounts pay little attention to his post-embodiment destiny, focussing instead on his spiritual sojourn in this world. Nonetheless, all three of our texts portray Śuka in his various guises as exemplifying the ideals of supreme enlightenment and perfected living. We are now ready to begin our investigation of the diverse faces of Śuka, starting with the story of his life as found in the epic.

The "Empty Form" of Śuka in the *Mahābhārata*: The Revelation of Inscrutable Indifference

According to the account in the *ŚP*, Śuka's career as a renouncer is presaged early in his life.[3] After his miraculous birth from two firesticks rubbed together by his father, Vyāsa, the infant sage receives from heaven the emblems of celibate life: the ascetic's staff, an antelope skin, and a water pot. He is also invested with the sacred thread by one of the gods. Śuka studies the Vedas under the sage Bṛhaspati, returns home to practice austerities, intent on the life of a celibate student (*brahmacārī*). He takes no delight in the following stage of life as a householder, for he is absorbed in the pursuit of *mokṣa*.[4]

Vyāsa oversees his son's further studies and one day tells him to visit the learned king of the Videhas, Janaka of Mithilā. Janaka is a patron of Vyāsa and a great authority on matters of liberation, from whom Śuka can discover all that remains to be known about this business of *mokṣa*. After a long journey Śuka arrives in Mithilā neither hungry, thirsty, nor tired in any way. Despite the heat, he looks upon shade and sun as equal. Upon reaching Janaka's court, Śuka is treated rudely by the gatekeepers, yet he harbors no resentment. Janaka's minister next leads Śuka to a beautiful garden, where a party of expert courtesans awaits to entertain the young guest. As one would expect from an earnest *yogin*, Śuka is not attracted by their passionate dalliance. But unlike so many ascetics famous for their wrathful outbursts when confronted with such "obstacles" to spiritual practice, Śuka is not angered by the attentions of the women. Instead, he simply spends the night in meditation, briefly dropping off to sleep.[5]

The next morning Śuka meets with Janaka and inquires of the king the path to *mokṣa*, whether it is to be gained through action or inaction (*pravṛtti* or *nivṛtti*), through knowledge or asceticism. Janaka's basic answer is that a person should follow progressively the order of the four stages (*āśramas*) of life, performing the duties appropriate to each, including the procreation of sons as a householder, in order to achieve the final goal. Śuka wonders, however, if it is necessary for one to go through all the stages if he has already attained the knowledge necessary for liberation.[6]

Śuka hereby raises one of the long-standing questions in the Hindu tradition regarding the interrelation of the *āśramas* as a whole. According to the point of view known as *samuccaya* (orderly progression), the four stages must be passed through in order, with no possibility of skipping or reverting to an earlier stage. Janaka, in response to Śuka's further questioning, rejects the *samuccaya* view he suggested above, in favor of the *vikalpa* (optional) view. According to the *vikalpa* interpretation of the *āśramas*, the fulfillment of duties in each of the four stages is merely for the maintenance of society, and that for a soul purified in the course of many births, *mokṣa* can be attained even in the first stage, at which point the remaining three stages become irrelevant.[7]

Janaka goes on to describe in rather traditional terms the fundamental characteristics of a liberated person, or of a person nearing liberation—the text is not clear whether the qualities are a means to liberation, or a consequence of Self-realization, or both. Janaka points to both privative and positive aspects of the liberated outlook. The privative mode manifests itself in diverse forms of non-attachment: to physical comfort, to social status and wealth, to personal friendship, and to life itself. This non-attachment is expressed in terms of indifference to the various dualities or opposites of existence: heat and cold, happiness and misery, praise and blame, gold and iron, success and failure, dear and despised, life and death.[8] Śuka, we have seen, manifests many of these qualities in his reactions to the hardships of his journey, as well as in his encounters with the gatekeepers and courtesans.

On the positive side, liberation involves an internal and an external realization: insight into one's Self-identity and awareness of one's identity with all creatures. As Janaka says, using time-honored phrases, "Ever abandoning faults arising from passion and sloth, adhering to the path of goodness, one should see the Self by the Self; and seeing all beings in the Self and the Self in all beings, one should remain unaffected."[9] Such well-known positive characteristics, in themselves, would be hard for an observer to verify. Fortunately, Janaka adds a kind of corollary and helpful clue regarding the behavioral implications: "He then attains the supreme who neither inspires others with fear nor fears others himself, and who neither desires nor hates."[10]

Janaka concludes his instructions by encouraging the youthful seeker in his quest for *mokṣa*, pointing out Śuka's non-attachment and indifference to several of the pairs mentioned above, as well as his lack of fear. The only thing that seems to be wanting in Śuka's spiritual attainment is simply a self-recognition of his own attainment. Janaka repeatedly tells the lad that his knowledge (*vijñāna*) and power (*aiśvarya*) are greater than he realizes.

Listening to Janaka's words, Śuka becomes "Self-perfected (*kṛtātmā*) with his aims fulfilled, having established his Self in his Self and realizing his Self by his Self."[11] One might now assume that Śuka is fully liberated, but the older, eschatological ideas of a postmortem emancipation enter in at this point. Śuka returns home where his father, knowing his son to have cognized the Self by the Self, instructs him in the ancient, Upaniṣadic notion of the two paths of the soul departing from the world: the path of the gods (*devayāna*) and that of the "fathers" (*pitṛyāna*). These paths, loosely correlated with the solar (steady) and lunar (waxing and waning) courses, lead to emancipation and rebirth, respectively.[13]

Śuka eventually decides to enter the solar path without going through the usual stages of life. Believing that children and a wife are of no use to him, and that he must renounce the world, including his own body (*gṛha-kalevara*) by the power of *yoga*, he intends to become mere breath or wind, enabling him to rise up and enter the resplendent mass of the sun. Having merged with the effulgent solar orb, ever steady and unchanging, Śuka will at the same time enter all beings in the universe. When Śuka goes to take leave of his father to begin his celestial journey, Vyāsa at first is quite pleased. But then he requests his son to linger for just a while for the pleasure of his eyes. Śuka, however, is quite indifferent (*nirapekṣa*) and without affection (*niḥsneha*), intent on *mokṣa* alone, and so departs at once.[14]

Soon through his yogic power Śuka enters into space, freed from all attachments, including his gross physical body. He is still endowed with some sort of perceptible body (*kāya*) and visage (*vaktra*),[15] though, as he is viewed with amazement by the various beings he passes in his ethereal excursion. Some even guess that Śuka is liberated, as it were (*vimuktam iva*).[16] Others recognize his exceptional achievement in a reverse sort of way, by their non-response. As he flies over the Mandākinī River, a host of *apsarases* or celestial nymphs, bathing in the waters below, behold Śuka of "empty form" (*śūnyākāra*).[17] The maidens, though without clothes, remain unperturbed (*nirākāra*, a term that also suggests modesty)[18] and continue their play while he speeds on.

It is doubtful that Śuka's "empty form" means that he is absolutely "without form" or completely "bodiless,"[19] as Śuka is clearly visible in some sense. Such a rendering in any case would blunt the basic point of the incident, especially when we take into account the reaction of the nymphs to Śuka's father (see below). While the exact meaning of Śuka's "empty form" is unclear, it presents a number of intriguing interpretive possibilities. The phrase *śūnyākāra* at least hints at Śuka's bare or naked figure, a meaning emphasized later in the tradition, as we shall see. At the same time, *śūnyākāra* suggests that Śuka has a face void of expression, unmoved by the potentially erotic display of the nymphs. In both senses, as naked and as void of expression, Śuka's *śūnyākāra* appearance plays nicely off the unembarrassed, self-effacing modesty or *nirākāra* demeanor of the maidens.

Returning for a moment to Śuka's bereft father, we find Vyāsa overcome with paternal affection. He sets out after Śuka, following the same path by dint of his own yogic powers, and calling for his son. But he receives only an echoed monosyllable, "Bho," in response from Śuka, who has become the omnipresent Self of all. Here, by the way, in Śuka's echoed reply, is the only indication of some vestigial compassion left in the son, and it seems prompted primarily by a lingering sense of filial obligation. Otherwise, Śuka in his perfected consciousness appears entirely indifferent to both the physical and social world.

The father, though appreciating the achievement of his son, nonetheless laments his absence and sits down on a mountain peak overlooking the Mandākinī River. The *apsarases* still sporting there, on seeing Vyāsa, are at once perturbed: some plunge back into the water, others hide behind trees, and others hastily put on their clothes. Vyāsa, knowing how differently they had responded to Śuka, now begins to understand the true extent of his son's liberation and the persistence of his own attachment.[20] Thus, Śuka's non-arousing of embarrassment in the maidens constitutes an intriguing counterpart to the non-arousing of fear mentioned by Janaka as a mark of the liberated person.

The non-threatening appearance of Śuka raises a perplexing question:

what is the actual, observable difference between Śuka and his father? Vyāsa possesses many of the same yogic powers as his son, but he is still bound by affection and thereby fails the nymph-test. Clearly, the possession of yogic powers is no sufficient mark of the fully perfected soul. Non-attachment is the key, but exactly how the non-attachment of the son is manifested and recognized by the nymphs is only half explained. The text simply tells us that the maidens observe his empty visage, his *śūnyākāra*. But at the same time, that blank expression gives no real clue to Śuka's inward thoughts or feelings. Intuitively, the maidens seem to sense from Śuka's unmoved expression that they have nothing to fear, nothing to hide from, even while the sage himself remains hidden. His empty visage (*śūnyākāra*) thus both reveals and conceals. This double aspect of the perfected being, inscrutable yet partially cognizable, is merely hinted at in the epic; it takes on interesting twists in the Purāṇic texts.

From this epic story it is easy to see how Śuka became the epitome of continence and renunciation. Śuka appears here not simply as a *saṃnyāsī* (a renouncer in the last stage of life), but as a *brahmacārī* who totally bypasses the normal progression through the later three stages. The story thus evokes a tension between two modes of life, that of the celibate and that of the householder, a tension resolved in opposite ways in the Purāṇic texts to be considered below.

Śuka and His Models in the *Bhāgavata Purāṇa*: Enlightened Idiots of Dazzle and Dirt

The epic view of Śuka as a lifelong celibate clearly appealed to the author of the *BhP*. In introducing Śuka as the narrator of the Purāṇa, the author refers briefly to Vyāsa's sorrow of separation from his son and his frustrated attempt to follow his son after the latter's departure.[21] Śuka leaves home apparently without being initiated with the sacred thread (*anupeta*),[22] as he has no responsibilities (*apetakṛtya*). The Purāṇa thus seems to go even further than the epic in its portrayal of Śuka as transcending entirely the order of *varṇāśrama-dharma*, for evidently he does not even receive the emblem (sacred thread) of the first stage of life.

That such a radical renouncer is chosen as one of the main reciters of the Purāṇa underscores the basic attitude of the *BhP* to the stages of life and especially the position of the householder. In general, the Purāṇa finds great peril in home life, with its attachments to spouse, children, and wealth. Śuka is thus portrayed as leery of the domestic sphere, resting at the door of householders for no longer than it takes to milk a cow.[23] Indeed, it is proof of the remarkable sanctity of the *BhP* that Śuka is willing to stay one week in the same place in order to recite it to King Parīkṣit.

But why should a person so indifferent to the world concern himself with reciting the *BhP* in the first place? In the epic, Śuka appears emotionally indifferent, both to his father (with one slight exception) and to society at large. In the Purāṇa, Śuka's compassionate concern for those mired in *saṃsāra* is a crucial aspect of his character. Here, in the rejection of an extreme, isolationist asceticism, we see clearly the impact of *bhakti* ideals, especially the synthesis of non-attachment and social action as propounded in the *Bhagavad Gītā (BhG)*.[24] The *Gītā's* ideal of disinterested action performed for the welfare of the world (*loka-saṃgraha*) in a spirit of selfless surrender to God is reflected in the *BhP's* ideal of motiveless devotion (*ahaitukī bhakti*).

Such pure devotion entails, among other things, listening to the virtues and exploits of the Lord (*Kṛṣṇa*). Even those realized sages who delight only in the Self still practice motiveless devotion and enjoy hearing the stories of the Lord. Śuka is portrayed in the Purāṇa as just such a disinterested devotee and one who eagerly studied the *BhP*.[25] Śuka's selfless devotion culminates in his newfound empathy for those suffering in the world, reflected in his eagerness to share the stories of the *BhP* with others. As the bard Sūta says, "I take refuge in that teacher of sages, Vyāsa's son, who out of compassion for sentient beings . . . recited this mysterious Purāṇa."[26] A disinterested devotee wishes to bring others to God as well.

Perhaps the most intriguing innovation in the *BhP's* portrayal of Śuka concerns his hidden identity. The sage Śaunaka describes Śuka not only as an orthodox *mahāyogin* who "sees all things equally (*sama-dṛś*)," but also as "hidden or disguised (*gūḍha*)" and "appearing bewildered (*mūḍha*)."[27] Śaunaka at this point mentions the encounter of the clothed father and the naked son with the celestial damsels and the different reactions provoked.[28] Śaunaka adds a few interesting details to the story: Vyāsa is perplexed by the deportment of the *apsarases* and inquires of them the reason for their varied responses. The maidens reply that Vyāsa still is cognizant of male and female, while his son is not. But Śaunaka does not explain how the damsels perceived this non-differentiating consciousness in Śuka. Indeed, Śaunaka himself is puzzled as to how one could recognize Śuka's true character, given the latter's somewhat bizarre and deceptive behavior, including apparently his wandering about naked.

In specific terms, Śaunaka asks Sūta how Śuka was recognized when he came to Hastināpura (Parīkṣit's capital), wandering about the city as if "mad (*unmatta*), dumb (*mūka*), and dull-witted (*jaḍa*)."[29] Relevant here is the detailed account of Śuka's arrival at the banks of the Ganges where King Parīkṣit was sitting in meditation awaiting death:

> There Vyāsa's blessed son came by chance during the course of his wanderings, indifferent to the world (*anapekṣa*), devoid of any marks [of caste or stage of life],[30] content in the realization of his Self. He was surrounded by [curious] children and women, [as he was] clothed in the garb of an *avadhūta* [an ascetic that goes about naked]. He was sixteen years old, beautiful in limbs and features . . . naked (*digambara*), his disheveled hair around his face . . . dark complexioned (*śyāma*), ever of charming appearance (*apīcya*) and youthful, captivating the hearts of the women by his beauty and smile. The sages rose from their seats, recognizing his distinctive features, even though his splendor was hidden (*gūḍha-varcasa*) [behind a crazy appearance].[31] Parīkṣit bowed to the guest, honoring him, and the ignorant women and children turned back.[32]

Parīkṣit then asked Śuka what a dying man should do in order to attain the final goal (*saṃsiddhi*), referring to the sage as one who is himself perfected (*saṃsiddha*),[33] though of inscrutable condition or doings (*avyakta-gati*).

How are we to account for the puzzling, new features of Śuka's already enigmatic personality? From where comes his fresh, erotic charm? And from where his idiotic demeanor? What do the sages know, that the curious women and children do not, that enables them to recognize the full significance of such paradoxical attributes? To answer these questions, it will be helpful to look at other saintly and perfected figures in the *BhP* who display some of the same remarkable qualities.

One important aspect of the *BhP*'s description of Śuka is the similarity of his persona to that of the Lord Kṛṣṇa himself. Like Kṛṣṇa, the sage is ever youthful, beautiful, swarthy, and alluring to women, in apparent contrast to his non-arousing, non-erotic impact in the epic. The word *apīcya* as applied to both Śuka and Kṛṣṇa is especially suggestive, for it means not only charming but also concealed or hidden.[34] Kṛṣṇa's concealed identity is noted by Bhiṣma in a deathbed scene parallel to Parīkṣit's: when Kṛṣṇa appears before the dying general, Bhīṣma refers to the Lord's living incognito (*gūḍha*) in the world, and that his hidden glory is known only to a few.[35] Kṛṣṇa's true essence is overpoweringly awesome, and thus he obscures his real nature during his worldly sojourn, often to increase the bonds of human affection between Himself and others, such as His mother and the *gopīs* or cow maidens. Kṛṣṇa's basic facade is His very humanity.[36] Within the *bhaktic* context of the *BhP*, Kṛṣṇa's ideal human beauty, reflected in His ideal devotee Śuka, serves to attract those humans to God, who might otherwise be unprepared for an unmediated encounter.

Śuka's hiddenness, however, is of a rather different sort from Kṛṣṇa's. Śuka's inner, effulgent nature, though irrepressibly manifesting itself in a charming appearance, is disguised behind a facade of imbecility that only the wise can pierce. Yet even here, the sage is not lacking for a divine role model: the eighth incarnation of the Lord is the crazy king Ṛṣabha.[37] Śuka's madness in the *BhP* is patterned in many ways upon the antisocial antics of this strange *avatāra* of God.

The Purāṇa tells us that Ṛṣabha, in order to illustrate the *pāramahaṃsya-dharma* (mode of life of those ascetics known as *paramahaṃsas*), after installing his son Bharata on the throne for the benefit of the world, left his country as a wandering recluse, as if mad, sky-clad, with disheveled hair. He acted like a dumb, blind, mute, and deaf idiot, wearing the garb of an *avadhūta*, and not responding when spoken to. He allowed himself to be insulted by any and every passerby: men beat him, spat on him, urinated on him, threw stones and feces on him, and farted in his face, so indifferent was he to the body. And yet through all the grime and dirt, he appeared dazzling, with lotus-like eyes, graceful smile, wonderful limbs, all captivating the hearts of women! This strange combination of the repulsive and alluring reaches its apex when Ṛṣabha, adopting the lifestyles of such creatures as pythons, bulls, and deer, takes to lying in his own waste.[38] The wind, perfumed by the excrement smeared on his body, gives a sweet scent to the surrounding countryside for a distance of eighty miles.[39]

This juxtaposition of beauty and pollution transcends the norms of everyday society and points to the divine union of opposites that constitutes God's nature. It is to be understood only through the mystical insight that God is all, and in all. Śuka's portrayal in the Purāṇa, though not drawn in quite such dramatic terms as Ṛṣabha's, reflects the same paradoxical quality of aversion and attraction. Śuka, too, can be fully recognized only by those who are indifferent to social status and have transcended the worldly distinctions of sane and insane, pure and impure. Yet there is the danger that some ardent spiritual seekers with only a partial understanding will misconstrue the import of such unconventional saints. The *BhP* cautions us that in the corrupt *Kālī Yuga*, certain people will be led astray and abandon the proper standards of personal purity by falsely imitating Ṛṣabha's example.[40]

Despite such dangers, the *BhP* recounts that Ṛṣabha's own son, Bharata, eventually adopted a similar mode of life, appearing dumb, stupid, and crazy, his spiritual glory covered by dirt.[41] Bharata, or Jaḍabharata as he came to be known, was entirely unresponsive to the demands of life in the world. His bizarre behavior prompted one exasperated observer to blurt out that Bharata was "dead though living" (*jīvanmṛta*),[42] an interesting alternative or parallel to the notion of a *jīvanmukta*.[43]

Ṛṣabha, Jaḍabharata, Śuka and other unconventional models of the "living dead" illustrate what the *BhP* designates as *pāramahaṃsya-dharma*, also referred to as *jaḍa-yoga*. While *jaḍa* in this context may suggest something of the motionless *yogin* lost in trance, it specifically refers to "the *yoga* of idiocy." This "path of idiots" is briefly mentioned in the *Jābāla Upaniṣad*, where various sages, including Jaḍabharata, are called *paramahaṃsas*.[44] These sages are said to be of unmanifest marks (*avyakta-liṅga*) and inscrutable behavior (*avyaktācāra*), reminiscent of Parīkṣit's description of Śuka as *avyakta-gati*. They have renounced even the signs of renunciation, such as the water pot and trident, and wander like madmen, even though not mad (*anunmattā unmattavad*).

It is noteworthy that this portrayal of *paramahaṃsas* in the *Jābāla Upaniṣad* is provided shortly after a discussion of renunciation and the four stages of life.[45] The sage Yājñavalkya advises Janaka that (normally) one progresses through the first three stages before renouncing, yet, if one becomes disgusted with the world (*virajet*) at any stage, even as a student, whether having completed vows or not, he may renounce right then all worldly attachments (*pravrajet*). We can see, then, where Janaka learned of the *vikalpa* (optional) view of the *āśramas*. In any case, the *BhP*'s emphasis on Śuka's lifelong celibacy, as well as on his imbecilic facade, has the highest Vedic endorsement.

Where the *BhP*'s portrayal of Śuka and other *paramahaṃsas* goes beyond the *Jābāla Upaniṣad* is in its synthesis of the ancient ascetic ideal of dispassion with the *bhaktic* ideals of intense love for God and compassion for fellow devotees, conjoined with Advaitic notions of non-dual knowledge. The *BhP* itself describes the *pāramahaṃsya-dharma* as characterized by devotion, knowledge, and dispassion (*bhakti-jñāna-vairāgya*).[46] It is the conjunction of disinterested devotion and non-dual knowledge that underlies many of the paradoxes manifest in the perfected renunciates of the Purāṇa. There is the physical paradox of the outward dazzle breaking through the crust of dirt, a visible reflection of the psychological incongruity between enlightened consciousness and imbecilic behavior.

As we may recall from Janaka's description of the perfected being in the epic, there are privative and positive modes of liberated consciousness. In the *BhP*, these modes are developed along both *jñānic* and *bhaktic* lines, culminating in various types of inner realization and corresponding outward manifestations. Liberated consciousness in the context of non-dual knowledge results privatively in an indifference to the body as something of an illusion (*māyā*) and less real than the Self. Thus, the body is submitted to all kinds of neglect and abuse, symbolized by the naked *avadhūta* covered with dirt.[47] In the context of disinterested devotion, the privative mode results in an indifference to the world and its laws, as these are distractions from God. Such *bhaktic* dispassion expresses itself in nakedness as a sign of indifference to worldly opinion. But here the nakedness shines with the fervent fire of devotion, the devotee reflecting the Lord's own dazzling beauty that attracts rather than repels.

On the positive side, non-dual knowledge that sees all things impartially reckons not just dirt and gold as equal, but also, in the *BhP* at least, feces and gold. Such equanimity of vision, manifesting itself in a non-discrimination of pure and impure, praise and blame, is readily perceived as imbecility. In the devotional context of the *BhP*, the positive realization that God is in all (and/or all is in God) finds expression in compassion towards all beings and the desire to bring others to God through imparting the stories of his deeds and virtues.[48] These various modes of liberated consciousness and their outward manifestations are schematized in Figure 1. It is the intricate intertwining of the various *bhaktic* and *jñānic* strands that results in the *BhP's* images of the enlightened and compassionate idiots of dazzle and dirt.

These paradoxes of transformed consciousness, partly revealing, partly concealing, are most easily maintained outside the normal social structures of hierarchy and caste, of stages of life, of communal rules and moral consequences. To the ignorant, expecting the saintly person to appear somehow in conformity with the accepted social norms, the perfected soul will pass by unrecognized, though not unnoticed. To the wise, the perfected soul as envisioned in the *BhP* may well be known, in part, by his

Figure 1
Modes of Liberated Consciousness in the Bhāgavata Purāṇa

		Inner Realization	Physical/Psychological Manifestation
Consciousness Transformed by Non-Dual Knowledge	Privative Mode	Indifference to body as not self	Nakedness covered with dirt
	Positive Mode	Seeing all as equal	Non-discrimination and idiocy
Consciousness Transformed by Disinterested Devotion	Privative Mode	Indifference to world as not God	Nakedness that dazzles
	Positive Mode	Seeing all as God	Compassion and teaching

non-conformist opposition to the ways of *varṇāśrama-dharma*. Such at least seems to be a key mark by which Parīkṣit and his seers recognize the itinerant storyteller and madman, Śuka.

Śuka in the *Devī-Bhāgavata Purāṇa*: The Reluctant Householder

The epic fame of Śuka as a youthful renouncer who opted to bypass the householder stage did not prevent a somewhat different picture of the sage emerging in some of the Purāṇas. Thus, in the *Kūrma Purāṇa* we find reference to Śuka's fathering five sons and a daughter, and similarly in the *Matsya Purāṇa* we find mention of Śuka's wife, Pīvarī, who gives birth to four sons and a daughter.[49]

The Śākta composer of the *DBhP* took cognizance of this alternative view of Śuka and developed it in great detail in rewriting the epic's version.[50] The Śākta author, and many in his community in the centuries immediately following the composition of the *BhP*, were distressed by the seeming breakdown of brahminical ideals of the *varṇāśrama-dharma*.[51] Such a breakdown was, in their eyes, due in part to the growing popularity of Kṛṣṇa and his apparent message of disregard for family responsibilities under the pretext that these belong solely to the realm of *māyā*. The Śāktas shared with the Vaiṣṇavas certain Advaitin ideals of non-dual knowledge, including the notion of *māyā*. But for the Śāktas, *māyā* is not just the *saṃsāric* realm of delusion and the illusory power of God, but the very essence of the Supreme; that is, the Goddess Śakti or Devī, Mother of the universe. The world itself, from the Śākta perspective, is a manifestation of the Devī's loving essence. Thus the world as *māyā* becomes radically revaluated, becoming more a means than an obstacle to liberation, a view reinforced by the Tantric currents of the day. The Śākta/Tantric revaluation of the world transformed along with it the ideal of the perfected life in the material realm. Such revaluation is beautifully illustrated in the *DBhP's* version of the Śuka story.

The *DBhP* follows the epic's basic account in its narration of Śuka's birth and his receiving the ascetic's staff, antelope skin, and water pot. Vyāsa himself performs the son's *upanayana*.[52] The major break with the epic is first signaled in Vyāsa's request to Śuka to secure a wife and beget children.[53] Śuka, however, opposes his father, seeing the life of a householder as in total conflict with the ideal of liberation from the world. Vyāsa praises the householder stage, regarding it as superior to all other *āśramas*, and encourages his son to adopt the stages in orderly progression (*samuccaya*). Śuka remains obstinate, and eventually the father suggests that his son go visit King Janaka: "If you are not satisfied by my words, son, go to Mithilā where Janaka reigns . . . He is the soul of Dharma and [known as] Videha (literally, "disembodied"). . . . Remove your doubts (*sandeha*): enquire of him, son, about the *varṇāśrama-dharma*. He is a *jīvanmukta*, a royal sage, a knower of Brahman, and pure."[54]

In the epic, Vyāsa initially encourages his son in his quest for *mokṣa*, sending him to the wise Janaka simply to remove any lingering doubts about the appropriate path. In the *DBhP*, Vyāsa has a different motive in sending his son to the king: the father hopes that his son will change his mind about renunciation after talking with Janaka, who is fully liberated while still discharging his duties as a king. In short, Janaka as a royal *jīvanmukta* is an ideal role model for Śuka, in Vyāsa's eyes. Śuka, though, is very doubtful that Janaka is truly liberated, for despite his name, Videha, he is still in physical form, and thus in Śuka's mind a hypocrite.[55] Śuka seems to believe only in the possibility of *videhamukti*. In any case, the Purāṇa delights in the punning contrast between Janaka's liberated state suggested by the name Videha, and Śuka's bound state manifested in his doubt (*sandeha*).[56]

The essence of the *DBhP's* views of renunciation and *jīvanmukti* is given in the dialogue between Śuka and Janaka.[57] In response to Śuka's query about what he must do to attain *mokṣa*, Janaka replies, as in the epic, with the notion that a person should follow the course of the four stages of life, enjoying in particular life as a householder and earning his livelihood in an appropriate manner. Then, with dispassion arising, he has the right to enter the stage of *saṃnyāsa*. Moreover, Janaka says, the Vedas proclaim forty-eight *saṃskāras*—forty for householders and eight for those desiring *mokṣa*. Janaka repeats that a man should go from one *āśrama* to the next, thereby implying that all the *saṃskāras* are to be performed.[58]

Śuka then asks if progression through the stages is necessary if one already has dispassion and knowledge in one's heart. Janaka's answer now is quite different from what the *Mbh* reports. The king points out that the senses are very powerful and not [readily] disciplined on the part of one who is immature, and these senses, though seemingly controlled, can later cause all sorts of disturbances in such a person. Thus, if one takes the vow of *saṃnyāsa* and later discovers that he still has desires for the world, he is lost.[59] It is much safer to go gradually, stage by stage, and in any case, even a householder can acquire *mokṣa* through steadiness in pleasure and pain, performing actions regardless of fruits, and realizing the Self. Janaka declares: "Look! I am a *jīvanmukta* even while engaged in kingship. . . . Neither the body, the soul (*jīvātman*), nor the senses but just the mind (*manas*) is the cause of bondage and liberation. Pure and liberated always is the *ātman*; it is never bound."[60] Janaka adds one final argument: for the protection of the world the rules of propriety fixed in the Vedas should be observed, or else *dharma* will perish, along with the proper conduct of the social classes.[61] Janaka in the *DBhP* thus rejects for various reasons the *vikalpa* (optional) perspective of his teacher in the *Jābāla Upaniṣad,* in favor of the *samuccaya* view.

Śuka is hardly convinced and turns to questioning Janaka's spiritual qualifications: how can Janaka as king be a true *jīvanmukta* if his mind still desires royal pleasures and victory in battle? And since Janaka's intellect still discriminates between thief and saint, how can he be truly detached and disembodied? In contrast, Śuka himself insists that he has no desire for home, spouse, companion, or anything else. All he wishes is to wander alone in the forest like a deer, subsisting on fruits, roots and leaves.[62] Underlying Śuka's objections to Janaka's teaching is his fundamental disbelief that a person can be free from desires and from dualistic (and thus deluded) discrimination while experiencing the pleasures and pains of worldly existence and being involved in worldly actions.

There is a certain inconsistency in Śuka's views, though, which Janaka hastens to point out. Even in the forest Śuka will not be alone, as he will be accompanied by deer and the natural elements. Nor will he be completely free of all concerns, for he will still have to think about securing food. Thus, the concern for the ascetic's staff and antelope skin is not essentially different from the king's concern with ruling.[63] Further, Śuka is besieged with doubt (*vikalpa*), while Janaka is free of such (*nirvikalpa*).[64] The term *nirvikalpa* not only contrasts with Śuka's spiritual uncertainty, but also suggests Janaka's supreme Yogic achievement of exclusive concentration upon the absolute, i.e., *nirvikalpa-samādhi*. Janaka concludes:

> I sleep easily and enjoy happiness constantly, O wise one. Thinking "I am not bound," I am ever happy, O sage. You, however, are constantly pained, thinking "I am bound." Abandon this false belief and live happily and composed. Thinking this body is mine is bondage. Realizing it is not mine is freedom. Thus this wealth, home, and kingdom surely are not mine.[65]

Here we see the true significance of the name Videha: Janaka is indeed bodiless because he knows that his true Self is not the body.

Śuka's mind is at last satisfied and he takes his leave of the royal *jīvanmukta*. Returning home, he attains the highest repose (*nivṛtti*) while staying in his father's ashram. He then takes the beautiful and auspicious Pīvarī as his wife, at the same time adopting the path of Yoga. Pīvarī then gives birth to four sons and a daughter. At this point, the *DBhP* reverts to the *Mbh*'s basic account, with Śuka finally leaving his father to fly through the heavens and become united with the Supreme, entering into all beings.[66]

In the *DBhP* Janaka appears as a *jīvanmukta* who is both a model householder and a model renunciate. His renunciation does not entail the abdication of socially responsible action, but rather any sense of ownership either of the body or of material wealth. Janaka's renunciation is thus in the same spirit as the *BhG*'s ideal of engaged detachment. It is of interest that in the *Gītā* Kṛṣṇa himself points to Janaka as an example of one who attained perfection while still engaged in action for the benefit of the world.[67] Śuka in the *DBhP* follows this "worldly" model, however reluctantly, in clear contrast to his portrayal as a radical renouncer in the *BhP*.

Also noteworthy in the *BhP* is the role, or rather lack of it, of King Janaka. He has been replaced, as it were, by the royal householder Parīkṣit. But Parīkṣit in the *BhP* is merely a listener and the disciple of a renunciate, while Janaka in the *DBhP* teaches even ascetics and would-be renunciates. That is, the renunciate Śuka teaches the king (Parīkṣit) in the *BhP*, but learns from the king (Janaka) in the *DBhP*. Put another way, the ideal householder and the ideal renunciate in the *BhP* appear as two distinct figures, while in the *DBhP*, with its *Gītā*-like ideal of renunciation, the two are conjoined (see Figure 2 below), first in Janaka, and later emulated by Śuka.

The *DBhP*, in retelling the story of Śuka and Janaka, is primarily concerned with countering the *BhP's* view of the sage as a radical renouncer who evaded the responsibilities of the householder stage. Perhaps for this reason, the Purāṇa gives little attention to the devotional side of Śuka's life, though we are told his son-in-law becomes a worshipper of the supreme Goddess.[68] Elsewhere, however, the text makes clear the connection between *bhakti* and liberation: by worship (*bhajana*) of the Devī, one attains the state of living liberation (*jīvanmuktatva*).[69] As in the *BhP*, the *DBhP* conjoins the ideals of *bhakti* and *jñāna*. In a passage reminiscent of Janaka's description of the realized person in the epic, the Śākta Purāṇa declares: "One should meditate upon the Self in all beings, and all beings in the Self. When one sees the Self of all beings, then one sees the auspicious Devī. . . . Then everything, beginning with *māyā*, becomes burnt up, with only *prārabdha-karma* remaining so long as the body lasts. One has become a *jīvanmukta*."[70] The *DBhP* also recommends that one should meditate in the following manner:

> "I am Devī, I am not another. I am Brahman, free of sorrow. I am the Self, having the form of *saccidānanda*," thus should one reflect. . . . By realizing the oneness of *jīva* and Brahman, one immediately becomes a *jīvanmukta*.[71]

Such realization, we may assume, was attained by Śuka.

The nature of devotion in the two *Bhāgavatas*, while occasionally described in similar terms, is also quite distinct. The differences in *bhaktic* orientation help to explain the diverse expression of perfected living in the two texts. Both Purāṇas espouse the ideal of an intense, personal love or affection for the Supreme, a form of *bhakti* known as *preman*. In the *BhP*, *preman* is clearly distinguished from *kāma* (lust, desire for sensual enjoyment). This distinction is dramatically manifested in the relation of the *gopīs* or cow maidens with Kṛṣṇa. Their ecstatic/erotic love for Kṛṣṇa has nothing to do with *kāma*, which is associated with the marital relationship and procreation.[72] It is hardly surprising, then, that the adult Kṛṣṇa, as the object of *preman*, is an intimate companion, a friend or lover, not a father. Śuka, likewise, is not a father in the *BhP*.

In the *DBhP* the Goddess as Mother is, by definition, involved with the continuation of the life-cycle and its associated *kāma*. The ideals of *varṇāśrama-dharma*, and especially of family life, are close to Her heart. Her love transcends the opposition between *kāma* and *preman*, and thus She grants both enjoyment and liberation, or as the Tantric formula puts it, She showers both *bhukti* and *mukti* on her children.[73] In the *BhP preman* is confined largely to an extra-social norm that makes for discontinuity not only between *preman* and *kāma*, but also between renouncer and non-renouncer. In the *DBhP* the *jīvanmukta* as loving devotee of the Goddess is both an enjoyer of the gifts of the Mother and a renouncer of any sense of ownership over those gifts.

Conclusion

In looking back at the three portrayals of Śuka, we may note that the first, epic account offers two models of enlightened sages; Janaka, the wise, householder teacher, and Śuka, his earnest, ascetic disciple who eventually outshines his master. The epic version, in its glorification of an extreme renunciation of the world, reflects a soteriological perspective that allows for full liberation only in a disembodied state. The two saints ultimately go their separate ways, and the tension between their respective lifestyles is left for later generations of Hindus to resolve.

The Purāṇic accounts, based on their particular *bhaktic* orientation, resolve the tension in opposite ways. Devotion in the *BhP*, with its model of God as intimate companion, legitimates renunciation and an anti-social asceticism that reinforces the discontinuity between the ideal householder and the homeless wanderer. The *DBhP*, with its model of the Divine Mother who espouses both *preman* and *kāma*, legitimates staying in the

Figure 2
Models of Jīvanmuktas in Itihāsa-Purāṇa

	Model Householder	Model Renunciate	Divine Model	Bhaktic Implications
Perfected Living in the Mahābhārata	Teacher of ascetics (Janaka)	Disem-bodied, wandering Yogi (Śuka)	NA	NA
Perfected Living in the Bhāgavata	Disciple of an ascetic (Parīkṣit)	Naked, wandering idiot (Śuka)	God as intimate companion	*Preman* vs. *kāma*
Perfected Living in the Devī-Bhāgavata	Teacher of = Married, w. ascetics children (Janaka and Śuka)		The Devī as Mother	*Preman* and *kāma*

world and supporting society. In the process, the *DBhP* retains the epic's model of the ideal householder as a teacher of ascetics, but discards the epic's eschatological perspective. The result is the convergence of the ideal householder and renunciate. These relationships between the three accounts are summarized in Figure 2.

In all three accounts, the problem of recognizing a perfected being is raised, though in the epic the issue is largely implicit. In the latter case, even Śuka himself at first does not recognize his own advanced progress toward perfection. By way of contrast, in the *DBhP* Śuka thinks himself more perfected than he truly is. In both texts, it is the wise householder Janaka, and not the career *yogin* Vyāsa, who awakens Śuka and the audience to the actual condition of the young saint. Moreover, in the epic, it is the nymphs—not noted for their yogic proficiency or ascetic training—who seem quicker than Vyāsa in recognizing the attainment of his son. The audience thereby understands that even spiritual professionals may have difficulty in recognizing perfection. Indeed, we realize that those who are themselves approaching perfection are subject to considerable confusion in these matters.

In turning to the *BhP*, we find that the perfected man has learned the appropriate social skills, or rather, asocial behavior, of renunciation, thereby keeping himself hidden from the eyes of the less discriminating. Perfection here is not to be judged by ordinary social conventions. Those who do judge by such conventional standards end up reviling and abusing the saints of God. Women and children, the Purāṇa suggests, are less tutored in social orthodoxy and thus more open to the enchanting allure of such men, even if only out of idle or romantic curiosity. Yet it takes sages of developed insight to recognize the real significance of the asocial paradoxes of Śuka and his kind.

In both *Bhāgavatas*, recognizing a perfected being is clearly not a matter of simple perception but of discriminating insight. This point is clearly made in the *DBhP*, when Janaka declares to Śuka that the Self is not perceptible (*pratyakṣa*) and can only be known by inference (*anumāna*).[74] Thus the enlightened or non-enlightened state of consciousness is equally imperceptible. While in the *BhP*, the perfected being hides behind an improbable facade confusing to conventional minds, the *jīvanmukta* of the *DBhP* is quite possibly even more difficult to recognize, precisely because he appears as an ordinary being. One can more readily learn to be suspicious of naked idiots than of your average-looking family man.

Abbreviations

BhG — *The Bhagavad-Gītā with the Commentary of Śrī Śankarācārya*. Critical edition by Dinkar Vishnu Gokhale. Poona: Oriental Book Agency, 1950. Poona Oriental Series, no. 1.

BhP — *[Bhāgavata Purāṇa.] Srīmad Bhāgavata Mahāpurāṇa (With Sanskrit text and English translation)*, 2 vols. Translated by C. L. Goswami. Gorakhpur: Motilal Jalan, 1971. (Translations cited are my own, not Goswami's.)

DBhP — *[Devī-Bhāgavata Purāṇa.] śrīmaddevībhāgavatam; mahāpurāṇam*. Varanasi: Ṭhākur Prasād and Sons, n.d.

Mbh — *The Mahābhārata*. 19 vols. Crit. ed. V.S. Sukthankar et al. Poona: Bhandarkar Oriental Research Institute, 1933–59.

ŚP — *Śānti Parva*, the twelfth book of the *Mbh* (see above).

Notes

1. M. Hiriyanna, *Outlines of Indian Philosophy* (London: George Allen & Unwin Ltd., 1932), 19–20.

2. Hiriyanna 1932:19. Cf. Arvind Sharma, "Jīvanmukti and Bhakti," *Saiva Siddhanta*, 19 (1984), 107–110.

3. The story of Śuka is found in 12.310–320 of the critical edition of the *Mbh*. All citations of the *Mbh* are to the critical edition unless otherwise noted.

4. Śuka's birth and childhood is recounted in *Mbh* 12.311.

5. Śuka's journey and arrival at Janaka's court is described in *Mbh* 12.312.

6. The interview between Janaka and Śuka, including portions still to be described, is the subject of *Mbh* 12.313.

7. There is a third view, *bādha* (annulment), that regards householding as the only *āśrama*. *Brahmācārya* in this perspective is seen as merely preparatory to the second, and the last two stages are set aside as inferior. For a discussion of the development of the *āśramas* and the different interpretations of them, see Pandurang Vaman Kane, *History of Dharmaśāstra (Ancient and Mediaeval Religious and Civil Law* 5 vols. (Poona: Bhandarkar Oriental Research Institute, 1930–62), vol. 2, 416–26.

8. These dualities are listed in *Mbh* 12.313.37–38.

9. rājasaṃstāmasāṃścaiva nityaṃ doṣān vivarjayet/
sāttvikaṃ mārgam āsthāya paśyed ātmānam ātmanā//
sarvabhūteṣu cātmānaṃ sarvabhūtāni cātmani/
saṃpaśyan nopalipyeta . . . // (*Mbh* 12.313.28–29.)

10. na bibheti paro yasmān na bibheti parāc ca yaḥ/
yaś ca necchati na dveṣṭi brahma saṃpadyate tadā//
(*Mbh* 12.313.33.)

11. etac chrutvā tu vacanaṃ kṛtātmā kṛtaniścayaḥ/
ātmanātmānam āsthāya dṛṣṭvā cātmānam ātmanā//
(*Mbh* 12.314.1.)

12. *Mbh* 12.315.30. Cf. *Bṛhadāraṇyaka Upaniṣad* 6.2 and *Chāndogya Upaniṣad* 5.3–10. (All references to Upaniṣads are to *The Principal Upaniṣads* [with Sanskrit text], edited and translated by S. Radhakrishnan. London: George Allen & Unwin, 1953. Reprint 1968.)

13. In the Upaniṣads, the paths lead respectively to the worlds of Brahmā and non-returning, and to continued rebirth in this world. Vyāsa's original explanation of the two paths differs somewhat from the Upaniṣadic: he states that the *devayāna* leads to heaven, the *pitṛyāna* to the infernal realm (*Mbh* 12.315.30). It is Śuka who later provides an interpretation more in line with the Upaniṣads (*Mbh* 12.318.54–56).

14. Śuka's decision to quit the world, his body, and his father's ashram is given in *Mbh* 12.318.46–63.

15. *Mbh* 12.319.16.

16. *Mbh* 12.319.19.

17. *Mbh* 12.320.17.

18. *Mbh* 12.320.17.

19. "Bodiless" is the translation given by Ganguli (12.34.17). (*The Mahabharata of Krishna-Dwaipayana Vyasa*. 12 vols. Translated by Kisari Mohan Ganguli. 3rd improved ed. New Delhi: Munshiram Manoharlal, 1972–75. Orig. pub. 1883–96.)

20. The account of Vyāsa's own yogic sojourn and his encounter with the nymphs is found in *Mbh* 12.320.18–30.

21. *BhP* 1.2.2. Unless otherwise noted, references to the *BhP* are to the Gorakhpur edition.

22. The commentator Śrīdhara gives two possible interpretations for *anupeta*: the first is as given above, namely, that Śuka never approached a teacher for the sake of receiving initiation (and the thread); the second is that Śuka is unaccompanied. (*Bhāgavata Purāṇa of Kṛṣṇa Dvaipāyana Vyāsa, with Sanskrit Commentary Bhāvārthabodhinī of Śrīdharasvāmin*. Ed. J. L. Shastri. Delhi: Motilal Banarsidass, 1983.) The Dvaita commentator Vijayadhwaja Swami renders *anupeta* as having "no attachment to the body, etc., for without Upanayana Sanyasa cannot be resorted to." (Translated by S. Subba Rau in his *Bhāgavata Purāṇa* [Tirupati: S. Lakshmana Rao, 1928], vol. 1, p. 5.) Vijayadhwaja certainly represents the establishment point of view. I have, however, tentatively followed Śrīdhara's first interpretation, as it seems in line with the Purāṇa's general attitude towards the stages of life and its radical rejection of social orthodoxy. For the social significance of the lack of *upanayana*, see Kane 1930–62: vol. 2, 376–80.

23. *BhP* 1.4.8; 1.19.39.

24. See esp. *BhG* 3.17–30.

25. *BhP* 1.7.9–11. Cf. *BhG* 3.17, where the sage who delights in the Self alone is briefly described, without reference to any specific *bhaktic* practices.

26. yaḥ . . . saṃsāriṇāṃ karuṇayā ''ha purānaguhyaṃ taṃ vyāsasūnam upayāmi guruṃ munīnām// (*BhP* 1.2.3.)

This verse and the preceding are quoted in the "*Bhāgavata-Māhātmya*" (1.2–3), from the *Padma Purāṇā*. The author of the "*Māhātmya*," after honoring Śrī Kṛṣṇa in the first verse, then attests to Śuka's importance as narrator of the *BhP* by quoting the above verses. (The "*Bhāgavata-Māhātmya*" text is given in the Gorakhpur edition of the *BhP*.)

27. *BhP* 1.4.4.

28. *BhP* 1.4.5. The text refers to Vyāsa as *apy anagna* (even though not naked), implying a contrast with his son. Śrīdhara makes explicit the contrast, referring to Śuka as *nagna*.

29. *BhP* 1.4.6.

30. Śrīdhara glosses *alakṣya-liṅga* as "devoid of the marks of the *āśramas*, etc."

31. The words in brackets are the suggested interpretation of a modern translator, C. L. Goswami.

32. tatrābhavad bhagavān vyāsapūtro yādṛcchayā gāmaṭamāno 'napekṣaḥ/
alakṣyaliṅgo nijalābhatuṣṭo vṛtaśca bālair avadhūtaveṣaḥ//
taṃ dvayaṣṭavarṣaṃ sukumārapādakarorubāhvaṃ . . . /
. . . //
. . . /
digambaraṃ vaktravikīrṇakeśaṃ . . . //
śyāmaṃ sadāpīcyavayo 'ṅgalakṣmyā strīṇāṃ manojñaṃ rucirasmitena/
pratyutthithās te munayaḥ svāsanebhyas tallakṣaṇajñā api gūḍhavarcasam//
sa viṣṇurāto 'tithaya āgatāya tasmai saparyāṃ ''jahāra/
tato nivṛttā hy abudhāḥ striyo 'rbhakā . . . //
BhP 1.19.25–29.

33. The Dvaita commentator Vijayadhvaja glosses Parīkṣit's description of Śuka as "*saṃsiddha*" by the phrase, "you who are almost a *mukta*" (noted by S. S. Rau in his translation of the *BhP*, vol.1, p. 101). In general, while Advaita thinkers accepted the ideal of *jīvanmukti*, many non-Advaita, Vaiṣṇava theologians, including Rāmānuja and Nimbārka, did not. The exact position of the *BhP* is unclear. As D. Sheridan has written: "The *Bhāgavata*, indeed, is much clearer about what is not the goal or salvation of human beings than what is." (*The Advaitic Theism of the Bhāgavata Purāṇa* [Delhi: Motilal Banarsidass, 1986], p. 93.)

We may note, however, that some Hindu interpreters and devotees have seen *jīvanmukti* as inherent in the message of the *BhP*. For instance, Swami Tyagisananda, former president of the Ramakrishna Ashrama in Bangalore, asserts that the highest liberation as described in the *BhP* "is possible in this very life," an analysis consonant with his strong Advaitic interpretation of the text. ("Philosophy of the Bhāgavata," in *The Philosophies*, rev. ed., edited by Haridas Bhattacharyya [Calcutta: Ramakrishna Mission Institute of Culture, 1962. *Cultural Heritage of India*, vol. 2] p. 296.) And Sadguruswāmī, from the South Indian *bhajana* tradition, writes: "It has been said in the *Bhāgavata* that even sages, *jīvan-muktas* who delight in the bliss of *Ātman*, who have no further ends to achieve . . . show spontaneous reasonless devotion to Hari . . . ." (Quoted by T. K. Venkateswaran, "Rādhā-Kṛṣṇa *Bhajanas* of South India: A Phenomenological, Theological, and Philosophical Study," in *Krishna: Myths, Rites, and Attitudes*, ed. Milton Singer [Chicago: University of Chicago Press, 1968], 167.) While Sadguruswāmī cites Nārāda as an example of such a *jīvanmukta*, his description applies equally well to Śuka as portrayed in the *BhP*.

34. See BhP 1.12.8, where Kṛṣṇa is so called.

35. BhP 1.9.19–20.

36. Cf. *BhP* 1.1.18–20; 1.11.35–39.

37. The list of *avatāras* in *BhP* 1.3.6–25 mentions Ṛṣabha specifically as the eighth, whose purpose was to show the course of conduct of the wise and self-possessed (*dhīra* [1.3.13]), glossed by Śrīdhara as the way of the *paramahaṃsas*. In *BhP* 2.7.10, Ṛṣabha appears ninth in an unnumbered list, where he is said to practice *jaḍa-yoga*, equated with the state of *paramahaṃsas*. We shall consider these *paramahaṃsas* and their *jaḍa-yoga* below.

Ṛṣabha, interestingly, figures prominently in the Jain tradition as the first Tīrthaṅkara, who went about careless as to his clothed or naked state. In Jain tradition, he was the First Lord (*Adinath*) of the world and a cultural hero who introduced crafts and skills to his people. He eventually became a monk and endured the most severe austerities. See K.C. Lalwani, *Sramana Bhagavan Mahavira: Life and Doctrine* (Calcutta: Minerva Associates, 1975), pp. 12–13; and Padmanabh S. Jaini, *The Jaina Path of Purification* (Berkeley: University of California Press, 1979), 14, 61. The Vaiṣṇava story of Ṛṣabha seems to be a recast of the Jain accounts, though the motif of madness, so emphasized in the *BhP*, seems to come from Hindu sources.

38. The practice of taking vows to act like certain animals is quite ancient, being mentioned in early Buddhist literature. See Richard F. Gombrich, *Theravāda Buddhism: A Social History from Ancient Benares to Modern Colombo* (London: Routledge & Kegan Paul, 1988), p. 57.

For a helpful discussion of the seemingly lunatic behavior of renouncers in the Saṃnyāsa Upaniṣads (late medieval texts for the most part, though some may precede the *Bhāgavata Purāṇa*), see the section entitled "Courting Dishonor: Madness and Acting Like Animals," in Patrick Olivelle's Introduction to his translation, *Saṃnyāsa Upaniṣads: Hindu Scriptures on Asceticism and Renunciation* (New York: Oxford University Press, 1992), 107–15.

39. *BhP* 5.5.28–33.

40. *BhP* 5.6.9–11. The *BhP* seems to assume that those led astray are the Jains. Cf. H. H. Wilson, *The Vishnu Purana: A System of Hindu Mythology and Tradition*, 3rd ed. (Calcutta: Punthi Pustak, 1972. 1st ed., London: 1840), 133, n. 7.

41. *BhP* 5.9.9–10. In the Jain tradition, Bharata is the eldest son of Ṛṣabha and the first universal monarch (*cakravartin*). According to the Śvetāmbaras, he attained complete knowledge without taking monastic vows, a unique occurrence in the Jain canonical accounts. The Digāmbaras reject this interpretation, but still consider Bharata an ideal king who attained omniscience after becoming a monk. See P.S. Jaini, *The Jaina Path of Purification*, 61–62. Jaini makes no reference to

any imbecilic behavior on Bharata's part in his discussion of this legendary Jain saint.

42. *BhP* 5.10.7.

43. The remark was intended to be sarcastic and disparaging. Bharata, however, accepted the observation as containing truth, in the sense that all things subject to transformation, marked by a beginning and an end, are dead even if (for the moment) they are living (*BhP* 5.10.11). The comment does not apply, then, to the real Self, which is beyond life and death. Bharata's explanation of the term thus does not associate it with the ideal of *jīvanmukti*. Nonetheless, since the *jīvanmukta* is dead to the normal demands and desires of life, the observer's original meaning, however unintentionally, may well be more insightful than Bharata's own rather metaphysical interpretation.

44. *Jābāla Upaniṣad* 6 (Note 12).

45. *Jābāla Upaniṣad* 4. This is one of the earliest, explicit references to the four stages. See Kane 1930–62: vol. 2, p. 422.

46. *BhP* 5.5.28.

47. Kane points out (1930–62: vol. 2, p. 419), "In the Ṛg. X.136.2, there is a reference to *munis*, who are wind-girt and who put on brownish dirt (dirty garments)." Again, we find ancient Vedic sanction for Śuka's behavior.

48. Cf. *Bhagavad Gītā* 13.27–28, where insight into God's abiding in all beings leads to the practice of not harming others. In the *BhP*, such insight leads to the active desire to help others realize their own divine natures, as seen in Śuka's willingness to undertake the recitation of the Purāṇa.

49. *Kūrma Purāṇa* 1.18.26 (*The Kūrma Purāṇa [with English Translation]*. Crit. ed. Anand Swarup Gupta; translated by Ahibhushan Bhattacharya et al. Varanasi: All-India Kashiraj Trust, 1972), and *Matsya Purāṇā* 15.5–11 (*matsyapurāṇam*. Calcutta: Nandalāl More, 1954. Gurumandal Series, no. 13). I was alerted to these references by V. M. Bedekar, in his article, "The Story of Śuka in the Mahābhārata and the Purāṇas: A Comparative Study," p. 127 (*Purāṇa* 7 [1965], 87–127).

50. The story of Śuka is found in *DBhP* 1.14–19.

51. See C. Mackenzie Brown, *The Triumph of the Goddess: The Canonical Models and Theological Visions of the Devī-Bhāgavata Purāṇa* (Albany: State University of New York Press, 1990), 163–66.

52. Śuka's birth and childhood are recounted in *DBhP* 1.14.2–25.

53. *DBhP* 1.14.26–31.

54. na cen manasi te śāntir vacasā mama . . . /
gaccha tvaṃ mithilāṃ putra pālitāṃ janakena ha//

. . . /
. . . dharmātmā videhaḥ . . .//
. . . . sandehaṃ svaṃ nivartaya/
varnāśramāṇāṃ dharmāś tvaṃ pṛccha putra yathātatham//
jīvanmuktaḥ sa rājarṣir brahmajñānamatiḥ śuciḥ/
(*DBhP* 1.16.45–48.)

55. See, for example, *DBhP* 1.16.51 and 1.19.18.

56. See, for example, *DBhP* 1.16.46–47, 51, and 53.

57. *DBhP* 1.18.5–1.19.35.

58. Janaka's response is given in *DBhP* 1.18.15–22.

59. For a fascinating and amusing account of one such passion-filled *saṃnyāsa*, the king-renunciate Gopi Chand, see Ann Grodzins Gold, "The Once and Future Yogi: Sentiments and Signs in the Tale of a Renouncer-King," *Journal of Asian Studies*, 48 (1989), 770–786.

60. paśyāhaṃ rājyasaṃstho 'pi jīvanmukto yathā . . . /
. . . .
na deho na ca jīvātma nendriyāṇi . . . /
mana eva manuṣyāṇāṇ kāraṇam bandhamokṣayoḥ//
śuddho muktaḥ sadaivātmā na vai badhyate karhi cit/
(*DBhP* 1.18.33, 39–40.)

61. *DBhP* 1.18.46–47. Cf. *Bhagavad Gītā* 3.22–25, where Kṛṣṇa asserts that he himself, though beyond any need to act, still engages in action in order not to mislead the world.

62. Śuka's objections are found in *DBhP* 1.19.1–27.

63. *DBhP* 1.19.31. Cf. Janaka's question to the female renunciate Sulabhā in the epic:

> If there is *mokṣa* in the triple staff (symbol of the *saṃnyāsī*) by means of knowledge, why not also in the umbrella (symbol of the monarch) . . . ?
>
> tridaṇḍādiṣu yady asti mokṣo jñānena kena cit/
>
> chatrādiṣu kathaṃ na syāt . . . //
>
> (*Mbh* 12.308.42.)

64. *DBhP* 1.19.32.

65. sukhaṃ svapimi viprāhaṃ sukhaṃ bhuṃjāmi sarvadā/
na baddhosmīti buddhy ahaṃ sarvadaiva sukhī mune//

tvaṃ tu duḥkhī sadaivāsi baddho 'ham iti śaṃkayā/
iti śaṃkāṃ parityajya sukhī bhava samāhitaḥ//
deho 'yaṃ mama baṃdho 'sti na mameti ca muktatā/
tathā dhanaṃ gṛhaṃ rājyaṃ na mameti ca niścayaḥ//
(*DBhP* 1.19.33–35.)

66. The conclusion to the Śuka story is given in *DBhP* 1.19.36–60.

67. BhG 3.20.

68. In *DBhP* 1.19.45, the son-in-law, Aṇuha, attains complete knowledge through instruction in the *māyābīja*, the seed mantra sacred to the Devī.

69. *DBhP* 4.13.39–40.

70 . . . dhyāyec . . . /
sarvabhūtastham ātmānaṃ sarvabhūtāni cātmani//
yadā paśyati bhūtātmā tadā paśyati śivām/
. . . //
tadā māyādikaṃ sarvaṃ dagdhaṃ bhavati bhūmipa/
prārabdham karmamātraṃ tu yāvad dehaṃ ca tiṣṭhati//
jīvanmuktas tadā . . . /
(*DBhP* 3.12.55–58.)

71. ahaṃ devī na cānyo 'smi brahmaivāhaṃ na śokabhāk/
saccidānandarūpo 'haṃ svātmānam it ciṃtayet//
. . . .
jīvabrahmaikyatā yena jāyate tu niraṃtaram/
jīvanmuktaś ca bhavati tatkṣaṇād eva . . . //
(*DBhP* 11.1.46, 11.2.4.)

72. See Frederique Marglin, "Types of Sexual Union and Their Implicit Meaning" (the section on Kāma and Prema, pp. 305–7), in *The Divine Consort: Rādhā and the Goddesses of India*, edited by John Stratton Hawley and Donna Marie Wulff (Berkeley: Graduate Theological Union, 1982), 298–315.

73. For an extended discussion of these themes, see Brown 1990:31–32, 74–75, 172–76.

74. *DBhP* 1.18.36. From a somewhat different perspective, but one that is quite empathetic to Janaka's views, Wilfred Cantwell Smith writes: "A fundamental error of the social sciences, and a fundamental lapse even of some humanists, has been to take the observable manifestations of some human concern as if they were the concern itself. The proper study of mankind is by inference." "Comparative Religion: Whither—and Why?" 143, in *Religious Diversity; Essays by Wilfred Cantwell Smith*, edited by Willard G. Oxtoby (New York, Harper & Row, 1976), 138–157.

PART III

Living Liberation in Śaiva Traditions

CHAPTER 7

Aspects of Jīvanmukti in the Tantric Śaivism of Kashmir

Paul E. Muller-Ortega

> *O Lady with beautiful hips! The Heart is the subtle vibration of the triangle which consists of the incessant expansion and contraction of the three powers, and it is the place of repose, the place of supreme bliss. This very Heart is the Self of Bhairava, of that which is the essence of Bhairava, and of the Blessed Supreme Goddess who is inseparable and non-different from Him.*
>
> Abhinavagupta, Parātrīśikā-laghuvṛtti[1]

Introduction: Placing the Tradition

The elaborate and even baroque complications of the tantric *sādhanā* aim at the acquisition of a condition of embodied enlightenment—*jīvanmukti*.[2] The present essay explores the concept of *jīvanmukti* as the ultimate goal of Tantric *sādhanā*[3] for one particular branch of the Hindu Tantra known as the Trika-Kaula, that is, the non-dual Śaivism of Kashmir.

Given the relative obscurity within which this branch of the Hindu Tantra has languished for many centuries—and despite the recent rash of studies on "Kashmir Śaivism"—it would seem useful to begin by indicating very briefly the place that this complex of traditions has within the larger historical schema of the Indian religious and philosophical traditions. It might first be observed that the term "Kashmir Śaivism" (or as it is sometimes found, "Shaivaism") is fairly misleading and problematical. It seems to have come into usage with the publication (in 1914) of a book by J. C. Chatterji entitled *Kashmir Shaivaism*.[4] This title created the mistaken impression that there was a single, easily locatable tradition which was to be identified by the appellation "Kashmir Śaivism." Until fairly recently, scholars and others have uncritically followed suit in using this designation as if there were accepted agreement as to its meaning. Recently, however, the inappropriateness and distortive character of this appellation have been argued on at least two grounds.

First, the term seems to imply that there was a single tradition of Śaivism in Kashmir, whereas it is now well established that there were several varieties that were deeply divided both doctrinally and ritually. There were various forms of non-dualistic tantric Śaivism represented by a series of related preceptorial lineages: the Trika, Pratyabhijñā, Kaula, Krama, and Mata, which were by no means identical in practice or doctrine. In addition, there were also powerful lineages of a conservative, dualistic Śaiva Siddhānta in Kashmir, as well as the centrist cult of the worship of Svacchandabhairava. Of these, it is the first, by no means homogeneous, group that seems to have generally and imprecisely been referred to as Kashmir Śaivism. More over, it is by no means clear that the teaching of Śaivism as propounded by any of these groups originated wholly or exclusively in Kashmir.[5]

In what follows then, the slightly more precise formulation of "the non-dual Śaivism of Kashmir" will be employed. It might further be specified that the present essay draws from the textual materials of the non-dual Śaivism of Kashmir, and more specifically, from the particularly elegant expression of these teachings to be found in the writings of its most inspired exponent, the tenth century Śaivācārya, Abhinavagupta.[6] Abhinavagupta (ca. C.E. 950–1014) was a Kashmiri Brahmin and tantric Śaiva *guru* who until very recently was still probably best known for his contributions to the development of Indian aesthetic theory, particularly the exploration of the concepts of *rasa* and *dhvani*. However, as a result of work done in the last three decades by a small but growing group of scholars, the extent of his contributions to the development of the Hindu Tantra is finally being acknowledged. Abhinavagupta's synthesis may generally (though also not unproblematically) be termed the Trika-Kaula, because it skillfully and selectively melds together doctrinal and ritual elements drawn from these two preceptorial lineages. This synthesis is so compellingly and powerfully accomplished that, for all practical purposes, it subsequently becomes the definitive and normatively accepted formulation of what much later comes to be referred to as "Kashmir Śaivism." In a wider context, Abhinavagupta's Trika-Kaula synthesis must be located within the context of the early Hindu Tantra. His writings give voice to one of the most sophisticated, elegant, and enduringly definitive expressions of the then emerging Hindu Tantra.[7]

Nevertheless, it should be emphasized that the wider, historical placement of the non-dual Śaivism of Kashmir is no easy matter to accomplish. It remains a tradition whose historical lineaments are complex and still ambiguous. What is known is that the Trika-Kaula of Abhinavagupta inherits and reshapes the teachings of a series of multiply intersecting, initiatory lineages.[8] This occurs in the environment of Kashmir, a traditionally somewhat isolated and separate geographical region of India. Moreover, Abhinavagupta lives during a relatively "late" historical period in which much of the Indian religious and philosophical traditions of India have reached a certain established maturity. Because of this, and because of his subtle mind and immense erudition and training, Abhinavagupta writes from the perspective of one who surveys and incorporates into his writings much of the richness of the intellectual and religious resources that were available at this time.

From a doctrinal point of view, the non-dual Śaivism of Kashmir is to be distinguished philosophically and metaphysically by its assertion that what is termed "Śiva"—the absolute and primordial consciousness—is *advaya* or non-dual. Moreover, this is a non-dualism that differs in important ways from the Vedāntic *advaita*. For the Kashmiri non-dual Śaivites, the non-dualism or Kashmiri *advaya* of Śiva does not in any way imply that the world and all who dwell in it are in any way illusory. To the contrary, Śaivites assert that this world is real precisely because and insofar as it is only Śiva—the absolute consciousness. It should be emphasized that this philosophical assertion of the reality of the world does not fall into the position of a "naive" realism. Rather, it seeks to articulate the enlightened and transformed point of view of the mystic—the *jīvanmukta*—for whom the paradoxical omnipresence of Śiva has become a tangible reality. If the world is declared to be real, it is so only and insofar as it is all Śiva, the unitary reality of the absolute consciousness.[9]

The non-dual Śaivism of Kashmir is also to be distinguished by its emphasis on the *śakti*, or ultimate power that abides intrinsically and inseparably as and in the absolute consciousness. Adherents of this school are not afraid to state that Śiva is possessed of *śakti*—that is to say, that the ultimate consciousness is essentially possessed of an ultimate, and even transcendent power. Moreover, this teaching gives expression to a different kind of non-duality, the non-difference between Śiva and *śakti*.[10] This particular teaching resides very close to the core of the Śaivites' most fundamental assertions about the nature of reality. Much of what Abhinavagupta has to say about the nature of Śiva is couched in terms of an analysis of the nature of *śakti*. Historically, this posture is interesting, because it is precisely in the lineages of the Śāktas that the elegant and complex ideology confected by the Kashmiri non-dual Śaivites has survived to this day.[11]

Moreover, the Kashmiri non-dual Śaivites appropriate and further articulate a series of complex ritual performances linked to an elaborate pantheon of tantric deities. They do so, however, in a way that underscores the experiential and transformative nature of ritual. In the midst of the complex details of ritual, their emphatic focus never wavers from an understanding of ritual as an occasion for the experiential apprehension of the non-dual, *śakti*-filled, ultimate consciousness that is Śiva. It is not surprising, therefore, to find an articulation of the doctrine of *jīvanmukti* present in these traditions. For it is in asserting the possibility of this religious, spiritual, and ultimately mystical goal that this tradition focuses on the life-altering, individuality transcending state of life in which this ultimate consciousness of Śiva comes actually to awaken stably and relatively permanently as a breathing, living human being.

In terms of "placement" of this tradition, there remain manifold, interesting but vexing historical and philosophical questions about the relationship of the non-dual Śaivism of Kashmir to other philosophical and religious traditions in India. For example, it is clear that the non-dual Śaivism of Kashmir is aware of forms of Vedānta and has something to say about their disagreements with and critiques of this tradition.[12] As well, there are important problems to be studied with regard to the forms of Buddhism that were powerfully operative in Kashmir at this time. Nevertheless—and without underestimating the intricacy and importance of these and other historical relationships in the formation of the contours of the non-dual Śaivism of Kashmir—the autonomy and even self-sufficient creativity of the non-dual Śaivism of Kashmir must also be emphasized. Despite the fact that in some of his writings Abhinavagupta engages in the traditional intellectual polemics that typify a certain kind of Indian philosophical *śāstra* (and does so exceedingly skillfully), it can be argued that he was not ultimately interested in this kind of philosophical attack and self-justification. Rather, he was seeking to articulate a comprehensible and intelligible statement about the nature of Śiva. At the core of that statement lies the experiential journey by which the *jīvanmukta* achieves the established and permanent vision of Śiva, and it is to a consideration of this notion that we now turn.

The Problem of *Jīvanmukti*

In the religious texts of India, the term *jīvanmukti* encompasses a wide variety of spiritual and religious referents. It is not at all clear that what one tradition refers to as *jīvanmukti* is identical or even very close to that proposed by another. In addition, there is no single, systematic rendering of the meaning of *jīvanmukti* to be found in this specific body of tantric texts. They manipulate a concept that clearly resembles yet also distinctly differs from the uses the same term is put to elsewhere. Thus, in what follows are presented approximations extracted from a complex and not altogether uncontradictory body of teachings.

Moreover, it is clear that the concept of *jīvanmukti* as it develops in the Kashmiri Tantra represents a controversial innovation that runs directly counter to the more conservative formulations to be found in the early Śaiva Siddhānta then prevalent in Kashmir. These Northern Śaiva Siddhānta theoreticians claim that liberation occurs through the agency of the ritual of initiation (*dīkṣā*) which, however, manifests its full effects only after the death of the physical body.[13] By contrast and without explicitly contradicting the Kashmiri Siddhāntika formulations, the northern traditions of tantric Śaivism—of which Abhinavagupta stands as the most sophisticated exemplar—proclaim the availability for a few extraordinary practitioners of a state of liberation even while still alive.[14] Thus, at least in this textual and doctrinal environment, *jīvanmukti* forms the core religious goal for those yogic virtuosi of exceptional capacity who are endowed with a "descent of the energy" (*śaktipāta*) of sufficient strength to warrant the process of liberation manifesting its full fruit even before the death of the physical body.[15] The exploration of the ideology of *jīvanmukti* leads directly into the marrow of the highly experiential, yogic world of this particular branch of the Hindu Tantra. Here, while never denying the efficacy and importance of external ritual, Abhinavagupta and his successors will map the extraordinary mystical journey of inner transformations that will lead to the experience, indeed, to the permanent state of being, that is denoted by the term *jīvanmukti*.[16]

Abhinavagupta is one of the greatest geniuses of medieval India. The most illustrious teacher in the lineage of the Hindu Tantra known as the Trika-Kaula, he composed his sophisticated treatises in Kashmir in the tenth century. In one of his commentaries called the *Parātrīśikālaghuvṛtti (PTlv)* (roughly, *The Short Gloss on the Supreme, the Queen of the Three*) he expounds the nature of the yogic realization that will lead to the acquisition of liberation in this very life, saying:

> Even though [the absolute reality] shines [in the Heart], it has not truly become a conscious apprehension. Without conscious apprehension, even if a thing exists, it is as if it did not exist, just as leaves and grass and other things [might not be seen] when riding in a chariot. The question is thus appropriate, because contentment (*tṛpti*) is not possible without a conscious realization. Contentment is of two kinds. The first is effected

> by means of absorption (*samāveśa*) and consists of magical powers. The second is attained by reaching a condition of conscious heart-felt realization, and is the state of being liberated while still alive (*jīvanmuktatā*).[17]

The phrase "conscious heart-felt realization" translates the rather complex Sanskrit term *hṛdayaṅgamībhūta*. This term, the construction and meaning of which I have explored at length elsewhere, points us directly at the central, experiential argument of this particular tradition's interpretation of *jīvanmukti*.[18] In simplest terms, Abhinavagupta—echoing the epistemological argument of his philosophical predecessors in the Sāṃkhya[19] and elsewhere—argues that it is not sufficient simply to have intellectual comprehension of one's identity with Śiva to bring about liberation. To be soteriologically effective, knowledge must go beyond the purely speculative or logical. It must be rooted in yogic realization. While intellectual conviction is crucial for liberation, it must be an outgrowth of the kind of "conscious realization" that will make it existentially and spiritually authentic. Otherwise, as Abhinavagupta states, "Even if a thing exists, it is as if it did not exist." That is to say, the potency of the freedom already abiding as the truth of consciousness must bear fruit in the transformed quotidian experience of the practitioner. Otherwise, such a freedom remains meaningless. Hence, the conscious realization that is aimed at must transform the experience of the *yogin* to so great an extent that such a one may properly be said to have achieved a state of liberation even while still alive.

In another passage in the *PTlv*, Abhinavagupta links the achievement of such a state of freedom to an entry into the domain of the Heart, a term he uses for the absolute consciousness itself. He describes the entrance into the Heart thanks to the superb efficacy of the empowered Heart-*mantra*, *SAUḤ*, saying:

> He who obtains this seed-*mantra*, in the very moment he obtains it, is no longer a bound creature. Because, when this seed-mantra is obtained, for him this Heart is produced. This Heart is the very condition of Bhairava. For that reason, as long as he is not born from the union of the pair—from the union of Rudra and the *yoginī*—that is to say, as long as he has not opened his vision to the very Self, or in other words, until a "descent of energy" (*śaktipāta*) has fallen on him, how then could this Heart appear to him?
>
> He is united with this Heart as soon as this has appeared before him. In fact, the state of liberation of one who is still alive, characterized by an absorption into the pair of the Śrī Bhairava, is precisely this attainment of the Heart. Because, as soon as it appears, the Ultimate, which is formed of consciousness only, grants the highest *kaulika* perfection,

which is precisely a state of liberation while one is still alive (*jīvanmuktatā*).[20]

These statements are extremely rich and contain much that I have explored and unpacked at length elsewhere.[21] For the purposes of our current exploration into the condition of living liberation, it may be noticed that Abhinavagupta is here playing on two meanings of the term "Heart": both as referring to a particular *mantra*, as well as to the ultimate consciousness. In this passage, Abhinavagupta states that truly to receive the Heart-*mantra* constitutes the equivalent of "receiving" the Heart of ultimate consciousness itself. This is a clear expression of the power of this *mantra* to serve as a vehicle for the awakening of the impulse of *śaktipāta*. *Śaktipāta* is the initiatory and esoteric "descent of energy" of consciousness itself which serves to unfold the vision of the Heart—that is to say, of ultimate consciousness. It awakens the *kaulika-siddhi*, or *kaulika* perfection, or the inherent and self-revelatory power of consciousness, and it is this very power that is intrinsically contained in the Heart-*mantra*. Thus, Abhinavagupta is able to make the somewhat controversial assertion that the reception of this *mantra* constitutes, in its most powerful sense, an act tantamount to the achievement of *jīvanmukti*. Thus, this passage serves to exemplify Abhinavagupta's established conviction that at the end of the journey to the Heart detailed in his writings, the goal is indeed the achievement of the state of liberation while one is still alive.

Jīvanmukti in Early Texts

One of the foundational texts of the Kashmiri Śaivites is the collection of revealed aphorisms known as the *Śiva Sūtras* (*ŚS*).[22] It is interesting that we do not find the notion of *jīvanmukti* explicitly mentioned in this important text. Instead (in *sūtras* 3.25–34), we receive a picture of the one who has become "like Śiva" (*Śiva-tulyo jāyate*): such a one remains in the body as part of his religious vow (*ŚS* 3.26); the conversation of such a one is likened to *japa* or the repetition of the *mantra* (*ŚS* 3.27); such a one bestows the gift of knowledge and serves as the agency of wisdom (*ŚS* 3.28–29); the entire universe and its maintenance and reabsorption are the unfoldment of his power (*ŚS* 3.30–32); yet such processes do not interrupt the state of realization (*ŚS* 3.32) of such a one for whom even pleasure and pain are viewed as external (*ŚS* 3.33); such is the condition of the one who is isolated (*kevalī*) in the unitary state of the one consciousness (*ŚS* 3.34). While this sequence of *sūtras* is clearly liable to a variety of interpretations, it seems to demonstrate that the complex of ideas (later?) explicitly named by the term *jīvanmukti* is already present here.

Another important, early text in this tradition is the *Vijñāna Bhairava Tantra* (*VBhT*). Here one finds a series of meditation practices called *dhāraṇās*, which are clearly aimed at the yogic goal of uncovering the domain of the absolute consciousness. It is no surprise, therefore, that in this highly experiential text the notion of *jīvanmukti* surfaces as an explicitly named goal. In one of the last verses Bhairava addresses the Goddess as follows:

> O Goddess, the aspirant [who has become efficient in any one of the above *dhāraṇās*] gains freedom from old age and mortality, and becomes endowed with *aṇimā* and other powers. He becomes the darling of the *yoginīs* and master of all *melāpakas*. He is liberated even while living, and carrying on all of the activities [of life], he is not affected by them (*jīvann api vimukto*).[23]

Yet another fundamental text of the early Kashmiri Śaivite tradition is the compilation of verses on the concept of "vibration" (*spanda*) known as *Spanda Kārikā (SpK)*.[24] Kṣemarāja commenting on *SpK* 1.1 takes up the connection between meditative absorption into Śiva and the achievement of *jīvanmukti* already alluded to by his teacher, Abhinavagupta, in the passage quoted above that begins "Even though [the absolute reality] shines [in the Heart] . . . "[25] This connection is repeated again in various places in his comment, with an emphasis on the knowledge that everything is identical with the absolute consciousness.[26] Of even more interest is the references to *jīvanmukti* in the body of the *SpK* itself where we read:

> Or he, who has this realization [viz. identity of the his Self with the whole universe], being constantly united with the Divine, views the entire world as the play [of the Self identical with Śiva] and is liberated while still alive (*jīvanmukta*). There is no doubt about this.[27]

It is clear that in the examination of the early texts of the tradition, we find the notion of *jīvanmukti* first present as an unnamed idea, then elaborated—especially in the writings of Abhinavagupta—and then, in the writings of his disciple Kṣemarāja, accepted as a definitive and possibly no longer even controversial goal. Certainly, when Kṣemarāja composes his digest on *The Doctrine of Recognition (PHṛ)*, he includes the notion of *jīvanmukti* in his *sūtras* almost as a matter of course.[28] This survey of the presence of the concept in these texts allow us an initial entry into the baroque domain of the Hindu tantric worldview, especially as elaborated by

Abhinavagupta who, with great seriousness of intent and laudable completeness, confects an elite ideology of Hindu Tantric mysticism in terms of the ascending journey to the achievement of freedom in the Heart. The details of this path, which we now turn to examine, are both intrinsically interesting as well as capable of contributing importantly in the wider context of the comparative study of mysticism.

Kashmiri Constructions of Bondage and Liberation

In the *Parātriṃśikā-vivaraṇa (PTv)*, usually considered to be the most complex work of the great Kashmiri teacher, Abhinavagupta addresses himself to very advanced disciples as well as to those who have already achieved liberation.[29] In a passage that delineates the *prayojana* or purpose of his composition, Abhinavagupta says:

> The purpose of this text is the attainment of liberation while still living (*jīvata eva mukti*). The nature of this state of liberation is that it results from a profound absorption into the non-differentiated essential form of Bhairava, which is identical with the perfect egoity, the astonishment of the Self. The living being now consists of the entire group of principles conceived as being in connection with totality. The differences that compose it are luminous with the play that bestows the fragrance of the Self. This liberation occurs because of the heart-felt realization of the innermost Self. Thus, the living being becomes the Lord of all conscious subjects; among all beings he is a fit recipient for the knowledge of the Supreme. This liberation occurs because grace has entered into him; he has received the supreme descent of energy.[30]

The purpose of the text, says Abhinavagupta, is the attainment of *jīvanmukti*, embodied enlightenment. For Abhinavagupta, the primary characteristic of *jīvanmukti* involves not a Sāṃkhya-like introvertive *kaivalya*, but an extrovertive and open-eyed *samādhi*, the nature of which is clarified by the term *ekarasa*—the blissful and unitary vision of the all-pervasiveness of Śiva, the unitary structure of unbounded consciousness.[31] A concomitant factor in this form of tantric *jīvanmukti* is the acquisition of power—the *jīvanmukta* becomes one with the blissful Bhairava, at whose beck and call all of the *śaktis*, the various goddesses or powers of reality, respond.[32] The *jīvanmukta* is often termed a *siddha*, an ambiguous designation referring equally to spiritual perfection as well as to one's attainment of power.[33] The clear meaning of *jīvanmukta* is thus embodied enlightenment. What this means for tantric Saivism is that the *jīvanmukta* becomes coequal with Śiva as the possessor and wielder of the cosmic powers of creation, maintenance, and dissolution, and indeed, achieves in some cases a form of bodily divinization. Moreover, the *jīvanmukta* is considered to be beyond the reach and requirement of the *varṇāśrama-dharma*, and becomes, especially in the Kaula and Krama lineages of the Kashmiri Tantra, a deliberate transgressor of dharmic boundaries of social convention.[34]

The primary feature of *jīvanmukti* involves the unitive perception of the omnipresence of Śiva. From this extrovertive *samādhi* arises the celebrated Tantric attitude of non-renunciation. The senses and their objects are not to be abandoned. Rather, the process of sense perception becomes itself a channel for the discovery of that which is ordinarily beyond the reach of the senses—the infinity of Śiva.[35]

According to Abhinavagupta, *svātantrya* or freedom is the primary characteristic of Śiva.[36] In his freedom, Śiva mediates and transcends all opposites and polarities. Impelled by the descent of power and through the practice of absorptive meditation (*samāveśa*), at the culmination of *sādhanā* the practitioner finally achieves the extrovertive trance (*unmīlana-samādhi*).[37] Here the *jīvanmukta* enjoys the freedom of Śiva as the experience of unified perception (*ekarasa*). For such a liberated one, all of the usually constraining polarities—inner and outer, life and death, pure and impure, good and evil—no longer hold. In the direct perception (*anubhava*) of the Supreme in the Heart, the *sādhaka* becomes a *siddha*, a perfected one who wields the power of the Embodied Cosmos, the *kaulikī-siddhi*.[38] Thus, the *sādhaka* replicates the autonomous and paradoxical condition of Śiva. He is free, as a perfected creature who has recognized his or her identity with Śiva, to range beyond all constraining polarities. As the authoritative texts of the tradition insist, *all* that such a being says is to be considered *mantra*, while everything done by the *jīvanmukta* is a *mudrā*, a spiritual gesture expressive of his or her ecstatic and unconstrained perception of freedom.[39] Such a being is thought to dwell in the sacred Heart of reality.

In the radically left-handed Krama and Kaula tantric lineages of Kashmir, there occurs a redefinition of the nature of freedom that allows for deliberately transgressive rituals (*kula-yāga*) involving impure substances such as meat, wine, and various intoxicants, as well as orgiastic sexual intercourse. As graphic demonstrations of the relativity of *dharma*, these rituals also aim at displaying the absoluteness and transcendence of the state of the *jīvanmukta*.[40] The tantric *sādhaka*, even as he maintains outward conformity with the orthodox, brahminical formulations concerning purity, harbors a secret obsession with power, an obsession that leads him to perform a series of deliberately transgressive rituals. These complex and baroque performances serve to court the elusive *śakti,* the power of Śiva, and to invite the descent of this power into the awareness of the practitioner.

Thus, in the pursuit of a boundary-transcending freedom, the *sādhaka* binds himself to intense ritual and meditative practice. In contrast to his orthodox non-tantric brahminical counterparts who endlessly obsess about purity, the skull-bearing tantric *sādhaka* deliberately courts power through the most impure means: midnight meditations in the cremation grounds; the use of wine, drugs, meat, and orgiastic, caste-free sexual intercourse. These extreme left-handed practices belong to the secret ritual, the *kula-yāga,* which has often been mistaken by synecdoche as identical with the entire gamut of tantric practice.[41] Empowered by a *mokṣa* which demonstrates the purity of all things, the tantric *jīvanmukta* obliterates all traces of the brahminical obsession with purity in the overmastering power of the blissful, englobing consciousness of liberation tangibly present in the body.

It is in this condition that the practitioner will come to realize that purity and impurity are not qualities that reside intrinsically in objects themselves. The distinction between purity and impurity arises only in a consciousness in which differences and differentiations are present. But when the practitioner is overtaken by the non-dual consciousness of Śiva, there then arises a vastly different and unified perception of all objects and all experiences as continuously bathed in the purity of the ultimate light of consciousness.[42]

It is the context of this remarkable redefinition of one of the traditional categories of Indian thought that the transgressive elements of the Hindu Tantra may best be approached. Abhinavagupta's remarkable and encyclopedic work on the Tantra, *Tantrāloka (TĀ),* is based on the revealed literature of the older cults of Kashmiri tantric Śaivism. Most of these texts express the cremation-ground culture of heterodox and transgressive groups seeking power through the control of hordes of semi-divine, semidemonic blood-sucking goddesses (*śākinīs, mātṛs, yoginīs, yogeśvarīs, kālīs*) by means of complex rituals.[43] Abhinavagupta's authoritative exposition, permeated by a thoroughgoing non-dualism, transforms these older cults of controlled possession into a yogic, left-handed Tantra. Dominated by an overarching inquiry into the nature of the power of ultimate consciousness, his writings transmute the external goddesses into the mechanisms of the Ultimate Reality of Śiva, and the secret ritual into an occasion for the recognition of the true nature of reality which is Śiva.

The tradition synthesized by Abhinavagupta represents an idealistic and introvertive recasting of earlier extremist, antinomian cults. It retains much of the flavor of the original, but now recast in terms of a phenomenology of consciousness and its powers. The *kaulikī-vidhi* (the cremation-ground secret method of the initiated in-group), which originally served as the context for the mediumistic, quasi-shamanic adept's control, possession by, and exorcism of these female deities, becomes in Abhinavagupta's synthesis the context in which the disenfranchised and contracted atomic self discovers, recovers, and recognizes its own primordial condition. Described as the state of Bhairava (*Bhairavatā*), the awakened consciousness sought by the *sādhaka* transcends all possible boundaries. In this state adepts will find themselves released from the regulations of the *varṇāśrama-dharma* that structure the orthodox, brahminical conception of the person. As freedom comes to be experienced in the very physicality of the *siddha*, there is thought to take place an alchemical transmutation leading to the divinization of the body itself.[44]

To understand further about the nature of embodied enlightenment (*jīvanmukti*) according to the non-dual Śaivism of Kashmir, we must first inquire into the nature of the bondage that terminates with its achievement. In the religious thought of India, conceptions about bondage and freedom exist in a tangled, symbiotic web.[45] Because that which structures bondage gives its peculiar flavor to the tantric descriptions of embodied freedom, it is crucial to understand how notions of bondage and of the finite, transmigrating self are constructed in the Kashmiri Śaiva tradition. A crucial passage is to be found in the *PTlv*, where Abhinavagupta says the following with regard to the finite self:

> The knowing subject has as its essence the supremely subtle vibration of the Self. Its nature is one of contraction and expansion, that is, opening and closing. The more this combination of expansion and contraction becomes evident in the vibration of the Heart, of the triangle, etc., the more does the subjectivity become elevated, until it reaches the consciousness of Bhairava. Conversely, the more the expansion and contraction diminish, the more does the subjectivity fall until it becomes inert like a stone, etc. This expansion and contraction is the characteristic of the *visarga*, whose essence is freedom, that is, the very power of the Lord, of the Ultimate (*anuttara*).
>
> These are the four powers [the sheaths] which maintain the individual soul resting in the middle like Triśaṅku which would otherwise fall into the condition of complete inertia like a rock, or would ascend into the sky of consciousness like the supreme Lord.[46]

This passage highlights the fluid nature of the finite self by explaining its expansive-contractive core. As the subtle vibration of the finite self expands, it moves in the direction of the absolute consciousness, here termed Bhairava. As it contracts, it approaches the complete inertia of a stone. The archetypal mythological image that recurs in this passage is that of Triśaṅku, the ancient sage and king of Ayodhyā who hangs suspended in the mid-heavens as a constellation of stars. He is destined to stay there, neither able to ascend higher nor to descend back to earth, because he once attempted to enter heaven with his very body. Impelled by the power of the sacrifice performed by Viśvāmitra and all of the other great sages (except Vasiṣṭha), Triśaṅku began his ascent into the heavens. When Indra and the other gods hear of his imminent arrival, they turn him away, and so Triśaṅku remains forever hanging upside down, suspended between earth and heaven by the two equal but opposing forces of the sages' impelling sacrifice and the gods' repelling exclusion from heaven.[47] This image of the suspended self corresponds neatly to Kashmir Śaiva constructions of the trasmigrating self (*puruṣa*, *jīva*, *aṇu*, *saṃsārin*, *puryaṣṭaka*, and so forth).[48]

Because the Trika-Kaula is an emphatically non-dual school, like other non-dual schools, it lands itself on the horns of a dilemma. Whence ignorance, the world, *karma*, and transmigration? How to justify the nature of ignorance that will come to bind the transmigrating self? If it once succeeds in the task of rendering *saṃsāra* intelligible, then its very success renders the notion of enlightenment all the more difficult to explain.[49] The problem of the non-dual schools is how to account for the existence of the world and of the transmigrating, karmically entrapped self. Bondage is constructed during the primordial, cosmogonic process as part of the self-shadowing, self-concealment, and self-limitation that Śiva operates on Himself.[50] Employing His unlimited power of freedom (*svātantrya-śakti*), Śiva contrives to limit the great and fundamentally unconstricted light of consciousness so that the worlds of experience and transmigration may arise. We are familiar with the conceptualization and philosophical difficulties inherent in the notions of *avidyā* or world-constructing ignorance, and *māyā* or creative illusion, as found in other schools of Indian philosophical thought.[51] In the case of Abhinavagupta (as representative of most of the non-dual schools of Śaiva thought), the coagulation of a tangible, perceptible reality within the field of light and consciousness which is Śiva arises spontaneously due to the operation of Śiva's will, the *icchā-śakti*.

How then to account for the nature of enlightenment? Once again, this theological problem is "solved" in the non-dual Śaivism of Kashmir by the idea that enlightenment and liberation while still alive arise solely due to the operation of Śiva's will, this time manifesting itself in the form of the *śaktipāta*, the descent of the power of Śiva. Thus, both bondage and liberation are "explained" theologically, while remaining mysteries from a rational point of view.[51] Nevertheless, Abhinavagupta has a good deal to say about the nature of *jīvanmukti* in terms of the construction and deconstruction of ignorance.

The Seven Experiencers

To understand the nature of bondage and of liberation according to the Kashmiri Tantra, we need to inquire into the interaction of several important ideas: the thirty-six *tattvas* (clearly an adaptation of earlier, dualistic Sāṃkhya notions), especially the five levels of the pure path, and the five sheaths or *kañcukas*, the three impurities or *malas*, and all of this related to the seven experiencers or *pramātṛs*. (See Figure 3.) Essentially, the thirty-six Śaiva *tattvas*[53] represent the twenty-five *tattvas* of the Saṃkhya, to which have been added *māyā* and the five sheaths, and then the five levels of the so-called pure path (*śuddhādhvan*).[54] In a very general way, we might say that Śiva constructs a zone of contraction or limitation, through which He then forces himself to traverse, and the result is the finite, transmigrating self. By the continued operation of this zone of contraction, the self or *jīva* is maintained in a suspended and contracted condition, being allowed neither to ascend to the consciousness of Bhairava, nor to descend to the inertness of a stone.[55] The primary constituents of this zone of contraction are three impurities (*malas*): a subtlest impurity, the atomic (*āṇava-mala*), which gives rise to a fundamental and pervasive feeling of incompleteness; a subtle impurity, the constructive (*māyīya-mala*), which gives rise to notions of distinction and differentiation, and a crude impurity, the active (*kārma-mala*), which stands at the basis of all actions and sets up the polarity of pleasure and pain.[56]

Related to these are the five sheaths (*kañcuka*) generated by *māyā*, which reduce the fullness of Śiva to the incompleteness of the finite self. These are the limiting power (*kalā*), which limits the omnipotence of the universal Śiva consciousness to a limited efficacy and capacity for action; limited knowledge (*vidyā*), which similarly reduces the omniscience of Śiva to a limited knowledge; impelling desire (*rāga*); which reduces the unbroken plenum of fulfillment of the ultimate and sets in motion a desire for limited experiences of fulfillment; time (*kāla*), which breaks the eternity of Śiva into the sequential divisions of time: past, present, and future; and, finally, contingency (*niyati*), which limits the freedom and all-pervasiveness of Śiva and creates limitations with respect to extension and space.[57]

Another important set of concepts are the principles (*tattvas*) that correspond to what the tradition calls the pure path (*śuddhādhvan*). This divine superstructure contains *tattvas* named in descending order, *śiva*, *śakti*, abiding Śiva *(sadāśiva)*, the Lord (*iśvara*) and purified knowledge *(suddhavidyā*). This collection of principles represent what might be called

Figure 3
Abhinavagupta and the Heart of Śhiva: Aspects of Embodied Enlightenment in the Kashmiri Tantra

TATTVA PRINCIPLE		*PRAMĀTṚ* EXPERIENCER
	Parama Śiva Transcendent Supreme Śiva	
Śuddhādhvan: The Pure Path		
1. *Śiva*		Level 7. Śiva *AHAM*
2. *Śakti*	Power	
3. *Sadāśiva*	Eternal Śiva	Level 6. *Mantra-maheśvara* Great Lord of Mantra *AHAM-IDAM*
4. *Īśvara*	Lord	Level 5. *Mantreśvara* Lord of Mantra *IDAM-AHAM*
5. *Śuddhavidyā*	Purified Knowledge	Level 4. *Mantra AHAM-AHAM IDAM-IDAM*
Illusion and the five sheaths (*kañcukas*)		
6. *Māyā*	Illusion	Level 3. *Vijñānākala* Non-perception due to higher knowledge (*AM*)
7. *Kalā*	Limited Efficacy	Level 2. *Pralayākala* Devoid of perception due to dissolution (*AM,MM*)
8. *Vidyā*	Limited Knowledge	
9. *Rāga*	Desire	
10. *Kāla*	Limited Time	
11. *Niyati*	Limited Space	
12. *Puruṣa*	Infinite Knowing Subject	Level 1. *Sakala* Perceptional (*AM,MM,KM*)
13. *Prakṛti*	Primordial Materiality	
14. *Buddhi*	Intellect	
15. *Ahaṃkāra*	Ego	
16. *Manas*	Perceptual Mind	
17–21. *Buddhīndriya*	Five sense-capacities	
22–26. *Karmendriya*	Five action-capacities	
27–31. *Tanmātra*	Five subtle elements	
32–36. *Mahābhūta*	Five gross elements	
MALA-s Three Impurities		
Āṇava-mala	Subtest: "Atomic" impurity *(AM)*	
Māyīya-mala	Subtle: "Constructive" impurity *(MM)*	
Kārma-mala	Gross: "Action" impurity *(KM)*	

the plane of continuous cosmogony. Here, the expansive-contractive play of Śiva with His consort, Śakti, results in the continuous birthing of the universe of objective reality.[58] This pure path gives rise to the zone of contraction represented by *māyā* and the five sheaths, and out of this arises the soul (*jīva, puruṣa*) or finite, atomic self (*aṇu*), and then the usual twenty-four other principles *(tattvas)* as described in the Sāṃkhya philosophy. (See Figure 1.)

Having set up the zone of contraction we can now examine the process by which the soul attains embodied enlightenment. The ascent back to Śiva is sequentially narrated in terms of the seven perceivers or experiencers, seven states (*sapta-pramātṛs*), which ascend out of the zone of objective, dual reality as comprised by the *puruṣa-prakṛti,* traverse the zone of contraction, and, breaking out of it and entering into the pure path, complete the ascent of the Self and the recovery of its fundamental identity as Śiva.[59]

The first and lowest state, known as the *sakala,* the perceptional, corresponds to the finite and karmically entrapped self. Here all three impurities are operative as well as the full force of *māyā* and the five sheaths. It is important to note that the category of the *sakalas* includes not just human beings, but all ignorant transmigrating beings, including large numbers of gods.[60]

The second state is known as the *pralayākala,* devoid of perception due to dissolution. The name of this state is descriptive of a being who has been lifted out of transmigration not by liberation, but by the dissolution at the end of the time cycle which destroys all universes of experience. Here the transmigrating being has been freed of the crudest of the three bonds, the *kārma-mala,* but is still bound by the other two. Thus, the experience of this level is said to be one of a mere voidness or emptiness, that is, non-perception due to dissolution.[61]

The third level is known as the *vijñānākala,* non-perception due to higher knowledge, and here only the subtlest of impurities remains, that is, the *āṇava-mala*. The *vijñānākala* describes the *yogin* who is on the path towards liberation. The experience at this stage is described as consisting of distinct alternations between an ordinary extroverted awareness and an inward, appeased, meditative awareness (*turīya* or *samāveśa*).[62]

The fourth plane of experience in this ascending path corresponds to the level of the *śuddhavidyā-tattva,* and is known by the technical term *mantra*. Here the experiencer has emerged from the zone of contraction and has entered the pure path. From this plane up there are appropriate summarizing tags that characterize the nature of the experience at each level. The description of this stage is expressed as AHAM AHAM, IDAM IDAM, "I am I and This is This," that is to say, the expanded egoity of the consciousness of Śiva is experienced clearly, while at the same time awareness of the world has not been lost. The world of objectivity is seen as sharply different yet somehow connected to the pure "I" consciousness. Often, the image used to describe this state is that of the equally balanced pans of an evenly held hand-balance. This level is an intermediate stage that functions as the threshold of liberation.[63]

The fifth state is called the *mantreśvara*, the Lord of *mantras*, and it is linked to the *iśvara-tattva*. Its descriptive tag is *IDAM-AHAM*, "This am I," or "This (world) is the 'I' consciousness." In the previous state, the realization of the unbounded Self overshadows the objective universe to the extent that the world is experienced as false and illusory. In the *mantreśvara* state however, the true intrinsic reality of the objective universe begins to be perceived. Here, the objective universe is no longer evaluated as illusory but is rather experienced as an expansion of the intrinsic nature of consciousness.[64]

The sixth level is that of the *mantra-maheśvara*, the great Lord of *mantra* who experiences the *sadāśiva-tattva*. Its tag reverses the previous one and is *AHAM-IDAM*, "I am this," or perhaps more precisely, "the 'I' consciousness is this (world)." Here the unbounded Self has swollen to such dimensions as to almost completely overshadow the experience of the so-called objective universe which is gradually being devoured in the abyss of consciousness.[65]

The seventh and final level is called *śiva* and corresponds to the level of the *śiva-tattva*. Its plane of experience is nothing other than the great, limitless totality of Śiva. Its tag is very simple *AHAM*, or as it is sometimes rendered in the ecstatic cry of recognition, *ŚIVO'HAM*, "I am Śiva," or again, "It is Śiva which is the 'I' consciousness."[66] This plane corresponds to the complete emergence of consciousness from any form of contraction or limitation, and to the return of Śiva back to Himself completely.

It might be noted here that this survey of *jīvanmukti* demonstrates the complexity of referents and variety of meanings that appear to be implicit in the term for this particular tradition. While the notion of embodied enlightenment thus extends over several quite dramatically different levels of spiritual realization ranging from the plane of *mantra* to the level of *śiva*, it is clear that this last one represents the full and final realization. Says Abhinavagupta:

> The state of liberation while still alive (*jīvanmukti*) arises. Here the great entanglement of the sport of existence which is produced as a result of the astonishment experienced in one's own supreme consciousness, this great entanglement becomes filled with the great Lord, the blessed Bhairava. This state of liberation while still alive is a direct experience (*anubhava*) . . . which does not revolve around anything other than the perception of the Self.[67]

Embodied Enlightenment

The dry recital of a series of planes of spiritual realization does not adequately convey the remarkable astonishment and wonder that the practitioner experiences as he or she undergoes the radical changes that are entailed in the transit through the seven states. The *Śiva Sūtras* state, "*vismayo yogabhūmikāḥ*—The planes of yogic realization constitute wonder, astonishment."[68] While it is not possible adequately to convey the experiential content of *jīvanmukti*, it is possible to emphasize the primacy of bliss (*ānanda*) in the texts of this tradition. The one who experiences embodied enlightenment is said to experience the universal bliss, *jagadānanda*,[69] as he or she abides in the *bhairavīmudrā*, the spiritual posture in which consciousness is simultaneously completely introverted and completely extroverted. This posture represents an important description of the nature of *jīvanmukti*. It describes the tasting of the nectar of the bliss of Śiva (*śiva-ānanda-rasa*), which is discovered by the *siddha* both in the innermost depths of awareness, as well as at the outermost limits of sensory experience. Indeed, the *bhairavīmudrā* is important because it represents the fullest possible stretch of awareness, and in this condition what the *siddha* tastes in the innermost depths of consciousness is identical to that which is found as the essence of all sensory experiences of the so-called objective world.[70]

The ecstatic journey through the planes of *yoga* thus traverses a very wide range. It is in this context that the tantric definition of *bhoga* or enjoyment may be more properly understood. *Bhoga* does not refer to a crass or superficial enjoyment, which indeed is already available even to the *sakalas*.[71] Rather, it names the exquisitely refined enjoyment of all planes of experience as the ultimate consciousness of Śiva. All structures are inherently composed of the consciousness of Śiva. Enjoyment is in fact descriptive of this realization, which becomes the primary activity of the *jīvanmukta*. It is in this sense that this form of refined enjoyment is directly linked to a spontaneous state of devotion (*bhakti*). The *jīvanmukta* represents the inherently unified consciousness, a point of compressed but lively infinity moving coherently and blissfully through itself, through the field of infinity.[72]

Freedom is first touched in the so-called *nimīlana-samādhi* or introvertive absorption, the *turīya*, the fourth, which is the experience of the *vijñānākala*.[73] Here Śiva is experienced as the plane of pure, contentless consciousness absolutely isolated from all possible mental activities, which have completely, though temporarily, stopped (*nirodha*). However, due to the tradition's emphasis on the freedom of Śiva, it is inconceivable that Śiva would remain locked up in this perfect castle of transcendence. The transcending of transcendence gives rise to the experience of the *mantra-pramātṛ*. Here the totally stabilized unbounded awareness of Śiva begins to accompany all of the quotidian fluctuations of awareness involved in waking, dreaming, and sleeping. The level of the *mantra-pramātṛ* describes the continuous co-presence of the infinite point of freedom as it now consciously accompanies the field of bondage and transmigration. This is described in *ŚS* 1.7, which states: "Even during the three different states of awareness in waking, dreaming, and deep sleep, the rapturous experience of the I-consciousness, of the fourth state abides."[74]

What is curious about this condition of the *mantra-pramātṛ* is that it is a profoundly dualistic state. The image of the balanced pan denotes the evenly balanced condition between absolute consciousness and relative objectivity.[75] Whereas in the phase of the *sakala*, the objective world completely shadowed any experience of the unbounded consciousness, in the state of the *mantra-pramātṛ* the two have come into equilibrium. Nevertheless, this state describes a human experience that is severed into two separate domains. An apparently unbridgeable line of demarcation runs down the center of awareness. What is consciousness is consciousness, and it is entirely separate and different from the objective world. In fact, this is a state of complete renunciation of the world.

What will occur in the next three planes is the progressive swallowing and assimilation of all "objectivity" into the consciousness of Śiva. At the plane of the *mantreśvara*, this begins by the bewildering discovery that what was before evaluated as an object is somehow connected to consciousness. This subtle perception or tasting of consciousness in the world of objects is what Abhinavagupta describes when he says: "The differences that compose it are luminous with the play that bestows the fragrance of the Self."[76]

It is at this stage that the *jīvanmukta* will also begin to discover the multitude of gods, the plethora of *śakti*s that may be perceived at this subtle plane of existence. As this experience matures into the full-blown level of the *mantra-maheśvara*, the astonishing discovery is made that consciousness can be directly perceived moving, vibrating, sparkling within every object. Or more precisely, every object is now properly evaluated as existing within consciousness, as being simply a *parāmarśa*, a cognition, or an area of patterned activity within the patternless and unbounded consciousness of Śiva. The blissfulness of this experience is tasted by the *mantra-maheśvara* for as long as the desire for an objective world remains. Then, very gently, the world simply begins to fade away, and to leave the *jīvanmukta* completely immersed in the ocean of Śiva. This gradual fading of the "objective" world does not mean that the *jīvanmukta* necessarily dies or loses connection to the body, or is no longer able to communicate. Rather, from that point on, the overwhelming majesty of the Śiva consciousness has completely overtaken the experience of the *siddha*.

The *siddha*, therefore, has no need for an artificial attitude of renunciation of the world. The world has gently slipped away, even as it still remains. At this plane of the *śiva-pramātṛ*, the *jīvanmukta* serves as the staging point that enables the absolute consciousness to experience itself as Śiva. He or she serves to channel the unbounded abyss of infinity through the *bindu*, the point of self-referential consciousness, and outward into the finite self, body, senses, thoughts, and emotions. The descent of the power of Śiva, the entry of this total and radical *śakti* into the hitherto finite structure of individuality, works the magical and incomprehensible transformation of a finite being into a 'Śiva,' who utters the supreme *mantra* AHAM (I am). The abstract and inert absolute consciousness is thus made to live and breathe and feel and experience. At this stage the *jīvanmukta* functions as a totally free point of action, desire, and fulfillment within the great unboundedness of Śiva. Abhinavagupta ecstatically sings the praise of this state in the *Parātriṃśikā-vivaraṇa (PTv)*, where he says:

> That in which everything shines and which shines everywhere, O awakened ones, is the one brilliant quivering gleam, the Supreme Heart. That which is the abode of the origin of this world, expanding and contracting at the same time, he rejoices in his own Heart. He should worship the vibrating Heart which appears as cosmic manifestation; thus the Heart should be worshipped in the heart, in the *suṣumnā* passage where one will encounter the great bliss of the pair of Śiva and Śakti.[77]

Conclusion

While the conceptualization of embodied enlightenment in the Kashmiri Tantra has led into the abstruse thicket of Śaivite technicalia, it also presents us with a remarkable vision of the goal of the Hindu Tantric tradition. Here we see—as always in the Tantra—the coincidence of the unfolding cosmogonic narration and the yogic path. The cosmogony details the unfolding journey of descent. The yogic path mirrors and reverses this process and elaborates the ascending return to the primordial source which enfolds all that has emerged. Yet that source—Śiva—is neither far distant in space nor in any way removed in time. As close as the Self, it is, rather, the primordial unity eternally hidden beneath and inside the visible structures of space and time. The tantric *jīvanmukta* discovers this sacred abode of the absolute and proceeds to live within it as the only true reality, unimpeded by the presence of the body and unmoved by the functioning of the senses and the activities of the mind. All of these are finally seen to be no more than the modifications of a single, fundamental reality, the unbounded consciousness which is Śiva. In this way, the tantric *jīvanmukta*—radically transformed and reborn in the crucible of *sādhana*—lives this reality freely and completely without obstruction.

The elaboration of the seven states of the experiencer functions as a map for the rarefied territories of tantric enlightenment. Because of the obscurity that has enveloped this tradition until recent times, these precise and even somewhat intoxicated visions from the most esoteric of Hindu traditions have been little known. While I have not attempted any cross-cultural juxtapositions in this essay, I believe that the tantric map may be fruitfully employed in a great variety of comparative enterprises in the History of Religions.

Abbreviations

ĪPv — *Īśvara-pratyabhijñā-vimarśinī* of Abhinavagupta. Edited by Mukunda Rāma. Kashmir Series of Texts and Studies, nos. 22 and 33. Srinagar: Research Department, Jammu and Kashmir Government, 1918 and 1921.

MVv — *Mālinīvijaya-vārtika* of Abhinavagupta. Edited by Madhusūdan Kaul. Kashmir Series of Texts and Studies, no. 31. Srinagar: Research Department, Jammu and Kashmir Government, 1921.

PHṛ — *Pratyabhijñāhṛdayam of Kṣemarāja*. Edited by Mukunda Rāma. Kashmir Series of Texts and Studies, no. 3. Srinagar: Research Department, Jammu and Kashmir Government, 1918.

PHṛS — *The Doctrine of Recognition*. Translated and edited by Jaideva Singh. Albany: State University of New York Press, 1990.

PTlv — *Parātrīśikā-laghuvṛtti* of Abhinavagupta. Edited by Jagaddhara Zādoo. Kashmir Series of Texts and Studies, no. 68. Srinagar: Research Department, Jammu and Kashmir Government, 1947.

PTv — *Parātriṃśikā-vivaraṇa of Abhinavagupta*. Edited by Mukunda Rāma. Kashmir Series of Texts and Studies, no. 18. Srinagar: Research Department, Jammu and Kashmir Government, 1918.

SpKS	*The Yoga of Vibration and Divine Pulsation: A Translation of the Spanda Kārikās with Kṣemarāja's Commentary, the Spanda Nirṇaya*. Translated and edited by Jaideva Singh. Albany: State University of New York Press, 1992.
ŚS	*Śiva Sūtras: The Yoga of Supreme Identity*. Translated and edited by Jaideva Singh. Delhi: Motilal Banarsidass, 1979.
ŚSD	*The Aphorisms of Śiva: The Śivasūtra with Bhāskara's Commentary, the Vārttika*. Translated and edited by Mark Dyczkowski. Albany: State University of New York Press, 1992.
TĀ	*Tantrāloka* of Abhinavagupta. Edited by Mukunda Rāma and Madhusūdan Kaul. Kashmir Series of Texts and Studies, nos. 23, 28, 30, 35, 36, 29, 41, 47, 59, 52, 57, 58. Srinagar: Research Department, Jammu and Kashmir Government, 1918–1938.
TS	*Tantrasāra of Abhinavagupta*. Edited by Mukunda Rāma. Kashmir Series of Texts and Studies, no. 17. Srinagar: Research Department, Jammu and Kashmir Government, 1918.
VBhT	*Vijñāna-Bhairava Tantra*. With commentaries by Kṣemarāja and Shivopadhyāya. Edited by Mukunda Rāma. Kashmir Series of Texts and Studies, no. 8. Srinagar: Research Department, Jammu and Kashmir Government, 1918.
VBhTS	*The Yoga of Delight, Wonder, and Astonishment: A Translation of the Vijñānabhairava*. Translated and edited by Jaideva Singh. Albany: State University of New York Press, 1991.

Notes

1. bho bhagavati suśroṇi! viśrāntaparamānandamayadhāmaśaktitrayagatānavaratasaṇkocavikāsarūpatrikoṇaparispandanarūpam etad hṛdayaṃ bhairavātmano bhairavasya ātmabhūtatāyās tadavibhagāmayyāh bhagavatyāḥ śrīparādevyāḥ tattvaṃ bhavati (*PTlv* commentary, p. 10).

2. For a concise and felicitous statement on the Hindu Tantra, see Andre Padoux, "Tantrism," *The Encyclopedia of Religion*, ed. Mircea Eliade (New York: Macmillan, 1987). See the bibliography in Paul E. Muller-Ortega, *The Triadic Heart of Śiva: Kaula Tantricism of Abhinavagupta in the Non-Dual Shaivism of Kashmir* (Albany: State University of New York Press, 1989) for references to many of the recent studies on the Hindu Tantra and especially its Kashmiri literature and authors.

3. In a recently published study entitled *The Triadic Heart of Śiva: Kaula Tantricism of Abhinavagupta in the Non-Dual Shaivism of Kashmir*, I explored the concept of the Heart (*hṛdaya*) as forming the central symbolic focus for the tantric *sādhanā* prescribed by the great Kashmiri Śaivite master of the tenth century. As

the primary textual focus of this study I presented a translation of Abhinavagupta's *Parātrīśikā-laghuvṛtti (PTlv)*, the *Short Gloss on the Supreme, the Queen of the Three*. In my study of this text, I argued that the *PTlv* gives us direct access to the theoretical and practical bases of one of the most obscure yet influential lineages in the history of medieval "Hinduism": the Kaulas. This lineage, which is neither properly a "school," nor a separate "tradition," contributes most directly to tantric formulations focusing on the use of transgressive or antinomian forms of ritual. In addition, I attempted to show that the Kaula emphasis on the direct and unmediated experience of the reality of Śiva, as symbolized by the Heart, provides a key entry-point into an understanding of the tantric worldview, generally, and the theoretical formulations of Abhinavagupta, specifically. My study and translation of the *PTlv* aimed at reconstructing a coherent understanding of the Kaula lineage by examining a key term: *hṛdayaṅgamībhūta*, literally: "become something that moves in the Heart"; that is to say, conscious realization or, more interpretively, "experiential replication." This important concept was explored in relation to two other crucial ideas presented in the *PTlv*, the *visarga-śakti*: the Emissional Power of Śiva, and the *kula*: the Embodied Cosmos. All of these ideas stand in the foreground of any consideration of *jīvanmukti*. Moreover, much of what I have to say in the present essay is based on my understanding specifically of the *PTlv*, to which the interested reader is referred.

4. J.C. Chatterji, *Kashmir Shaivaism* (Albany: State University of New York Press, 1986), reprint of the first edition (Shrinagar: Kashmir State Research Department, 1914).

5. For more details, see Alexis Sanderson, "Śaivism and the Tantric Traditions," *The World's Religions*, eds. Stewart Sutherland, Leslie Houlden, Peter Clarke, and Friedhelm Hardy (London: Routledge, 1988), 692ff.

6. Abhinavagupta is usually counted as being the most illustrious representative of the tradition which includes Vasugupta (ca. 9th century), transmitter of the foundational text known as the *Śiva Sūtras: The Concise Aphorisms of Śiva* (*ŚS*); his disciple Kallaṭa, to whom are usually attributed the important *Spanda Kārikās: The Aphorisms on Vibration* (*SpK*); Somānanda, also ninth century, author of the influential text known as the *Śiva-dṛṣṭi: The Viewpoint of Śiva*; and his disciple Utpalācārya, author of what has come to be recognized as the foundational text for the philosophical explication of the tradition, the *Īśvara-pratyabhijñā-kārikās: Aphorisms on the Recognition of the Lord*.

In addition to these important intellectual forebears, the tradition which Abhinavagupta inherits, and comes eventually to synthesize, includes powerful influences from a number of celebrated *āgamic śāstras*. Of these, the *Mālinīvijaya Tantra*, is usually considered the most authoritative. Abhinavagupta studied these āgamic texts with his Kaula master, Śambhunātha, and he dedicates a large portion of his writings to an explication of the then developing Śaivite Hindu Tantra, including the lineage of the Kaulas.

Abhinavagupta was a prolific writer, and some forty-four works are attributed to him. In his *Parātrīśikā-laghuvṛtti (PTlv)* he presents his most concise statement on the nature of the tantric *sādhanā* or path. This important text may be grouped with four other texts in which Abhinavagupta explores and elaborates this Tantric environment. These are his encyclopedia of the Tantra entitled *Tantrāloka: Light on the Tantras* (*TĀ*); a short summary of the *Tantrāloka*, known as the *Tantrasāra: The Essence of the Tantra*; a long text, the *Parātriṃśikā-vivaraṇa* (*PTv*): *The Long Commentary on the Supreme, the Queen of the Three*, which comments on the same āgamic verses commented on in the *Parātrīśikā-laghuvṛtti* and the *Mālinīvijaya-vārtika* (*MVv*), the expository comment on the *Mālinīvijaya Tantra*. What is said below about the concept of *jīvanmukti* derives primarily from an exploration of these texts.

7. For an overall consideration of the Hindu Tantra, good sources include Teun Goudriaan and Sanjukta Gupta, *Hindu Tantric and Śākta Literature*, vol. 2; fasc. 2. of Jan Gonda's, *A History of Indian Literature* (Wiesbaden: Otto Harrassowitz, 1981) and Sanjukta Gupta, Dirk Jan Hoens, and Teun Goudriaan, *Hindu Tantrism* (Leiden: E. J. Brill, 1979).

8. See Abbreviations section for full publication details of most of the important texts herein considered. See Muller-Ortega 1989 for a longer exposition of the nature of this body of writings as well as references to the various scholars who have contributed to the "excavation" of this tradition. A dated but still useful early study is Kanti Chandra Pandey, *Abhinavagupta: An Historical and Philosophical Study*, Chowkhamba Sanskrit Studies, vol. 1 (Varanasi: Chowkhamba Sanskrit Series Office, 1963). An important and definitive study is André Padoux, *Recherches sur la Symbolique et l'Energie de la Parole*, 2d. ed., Publications de l'Institut de Civilisation Indienne, fasc. 21 (Paris: Editions E. de Boccard, 1975). One of the most prolific scholars in this field was Lilian Silburn. See, for example, her translation and study of the *Śivasūtra et Vimarśinī de Kṣemarāja*, Institut de Civilisation Indienne, fasc. 47 (Paris: Diffusion E. de Boccard, 1980), or her important study entitled *Kuṇḍalinī: the Energy of the Depths* (Albany: State University of New York Press, 1988).

9. See, for example, the discussion in *ĪPv* 4.1.1–5.

10. See, for example, Abhinavagupta's discussion of the nature of *śakti* in the opening section of his commentary on *PTv* 1.

11. For more on the Śākta lineages see Douglas R. Brooks, *Auspicious Wisdom: The Texts and Traditions of Śrīvidyā Śākta Tantrism in South India* (Albany State University of New York Press, 1992).

12. The critique found in *PHṛ* 8 is typical.

13. On the contrast in views between the Kashmiri Śaiva Siddhāntins and the Kashmiri Trika-Kaula regarding liberation, its availability only at death or before, as well as the various means for its attainment, see Sanderson 1988. See by the same author, "The Doctrine of the *Mālinīvijayottaratantra*," in *Ritual and Speculation in Early Tantrism: Studies in Honor of André Padoux*, ed. Teun Goudriaan (Albany: State University of New York Press, 1992), 286ff. See Richard H. Davis,

Ritual in an Oscillating Universe: Worshipping Śiva in Medieval India (Princeton: Princeton University Press, 1991), especially Chapter III, "Becoming a Śiva," for details of the ritual procedures in the Southern Siddhānta that effect the process of liberation.

14. See Deba Brata SenSharma, *The Philosophy of Sādhanā* (Albany: State University of New York Press, 1990), 167–173 for an approach to the topic of *jīvanmukti* that deals with another aspect of the Śaivite technicalia that surrounds this topic.

15. See Abhinavagupta's discussion in *TĀ*, ch. 13, for a discussion of the nature of the divine descent of the energy of grace (*śaktipāta*).

16. A word of caution: I have limited my exposition in this essay to the views on *jīvanmukti* of one specific, though highly influential lineage. The ideology of *jīvanmukti* here presented is drawn from a very specific, geographically confined, and temporally limited base of texts. Clearly, ideas about *jīvanmukti* in this environment may differ sharply from that which is found in earlier or later texts of different lineages and traditions. I have not explicitly approached such differences in the present essay.

On a more general note: it is clear that as tantric studies achieve a new level of maturity and sophistication, to continue to generalize about "the Tantra" in the singular is to manipulate a reified, idealized, and hypothetical construct, albeit one with a certain temporary usefulness. Additionally, while it is true that the varieties of Hindu Tantra show sharp continuities and connections with all that precedes them in orthodox "Hinduism," this statement must not be confused with the reductive claim that the varieties of Tantra had no original doctrines of their own. The somewhat disdainful wisdom which would have it that the Tantra is primarily and distinctively approachable in terms of its practices and rituals, that all that it has by way of doctrines has been borrowed or adapted from orthodox or mainstream Hinduism or Buddhism, is a distortive and simplistic falsity. It is especially as our knowledge of the pluralities of the Hindu Tantra deepens and becomes more sophisticated (and we move beyond generalizations derived primarily from the very late and even perhaps Western-influenced *Mahānirvāṇa Tantra*) that we are coming to see the originality and sophistication of the early Hindu Tantric writers and practitioners who confect novel and transgressive religious visions within the heart of orthodox Hinduism.

17. satyaṃ sphurati, sphuritam api tu tattvato na hṛdayaṇgamībhūtam. hṛdayaṇgamībhāvena ca vinā bhātam apyabhātam eva rathyāgamane tṛṇaparṇādivat. hṛdayaṇgamatāvagamanasādhyā hi tu tṛptir jīvanmuktatā, tat samāveśasādhyā hi tṛptir vibhūtirūpeti dvividhā tṛptiḥ parāmarśena vinā na bhavatīti yukta eva praśnaḥ (*PTlv* 2a commentary, pp. 2–3).

18. See Muller-Ortega 1989: 182ff.

19. See Gerald James Larson, *Classical Sāṃkhya* (Delhi: Motilal Banarsidass, 1979) for a sophisticated exploration of the Sāṃkhya position which, however, differs in crucial ways from that adopted by Abhinavagupta.

20. etat bījaṃ yo labhate sa lābhakāla eva na paśuḥ; yato'smin labdhe etat tasya hṛdayaṃ jāyate. etad hṛdayataiva bhairavatvam. atha rudrayoginīyāmalena yāvan na jātaḥ kṛtaśaktipātalakṣaṇasvarūponmīlanaḥ tāvad etad hṛdayaṃ katham asyonmīlati. asminn unmīlite sati anena hṛdayena sahayogaḥ. etad hṛdayalābhaḥ śrībhairavayāmalasamāveśalakṣaṇo jīvata eva vimokṣada iti umīlanamātre jīvanmuktatālakṣaṇā parā kaulikī siddhir anuttare saṃvinmātrarūpe yathā vidhīyate (*PTlv* 10 commentary, p. 10).

21. See Muller-Ortega 1989.

22. Compare Singh's translation and annotation of *ŚS* to that of Mark Dyczkowski, *The Aphorisms of Siva: The Sivasutra with Bhaskara's Commentary, the Vartika, ŚSD* (Albany: State University of New York Press, 1992).

23. ajarāmaratām eti so'ṇimāḍiguṇānvitaḥ
yoginīnām priyo devi sarvamelāpakādhipaḥ
jīvann api vimukto'sau kurvannapi na lipyate (*VBhTS* 141–142a, p. 131).

24. See *SpKS*. See also the very important study of this text and its related commentarial environments in Mark Dyczkowski, *The Doctrine of Vibration: An Analysis of the Doctrines and Practices of Kashmir Shaivism* (Albany: State University of New York Press, 1987).

25. On Kṣemarāja see Muller-Ortega 1989: 42–47. *SpK* 1.1 reads: tatsamāveśa eva jīvanmuktiphala iha prakaraṇa upadeśya.

26. Kṣemarāja's introductory section to comment on *SpKS* 1.23–25, p. 105 reads:

> The author now teaches that one, who is always on the alert first of all, closely observes the *spanda* energy in all these states by the technique already described, and afterwards by constant awareness of that in all the states, obtains liberation in life, which, in other words, is the realization of its permanent presence.
>
> evam etāsvavasthāsūktayuktya prathamaṃ spandaśaktiṃ pariśilya tadanu tāmevānusandadhatsarvāsvavasthasu taddārḍhyānupraveśāmayīṃ jīvanmuktatāmāharet satatodyukta ityupadiśyati.

In the commentary on *SpKS* 3.14, p. 116, Kṣemarāja says:

> When by means of the teaching imparted before, he has the unswerving knowledge that every thing is identical with Self, then he is liberated while alive.
>
> yadā tūktopadeśayuktyā sarvātmamayamevāvicilapratipattyā pratipadyate tadā jīvanmukta iti.

27. iti vā yasya saṃvittiḥ krīḍātvenākhilaṃ jagat
sa paśyan satataṃ yukto jīvanmukto na saṃśayaḥ (*SpKS* 2.5, p. 119).

28. When the bliss of *cit* is attained, one is stable in the consciousness of identity with *cit*, even while the body, etc., are being experienced. This state is called liberation while one is alive (*jīvanmukti*).

cidānanda lābhe dehādiṣu cetyamāneṣvapi.
cidaikatmya pratipatti dārḍhyaṃ jīvanmuktiḥ (*PHṛS* 16, p. 79).

29. See the complete translation of *PTv* by Jaideva Singh, *A Trident of Wisdom* (Albany: State University of New York Press, 1989). For a contrasting approach see the Italian translation of Raniero Gnoli, *La Trentina della Suprema* (Turin: Boringhieri, 1978).

30. prayojanaṃ ca sarvapramātṛṇāṃ vibhoḥ paraśaktipātānugrahaveśotpannaitāvad anuttarajñānabhājanabhāvānām itthaṃ nijasvarūpahṛdayaṇgamībhāvena nijāmodabharakrīḍābhāsitabhedasya nikhilabandhābhimatatattvavrātasya svātmacamatkārapūrṇāhantātādātmyabhairavasvarūpābhedasamāveśātmikājīvataeva muktiḥ (*PTv* 1, pp. 17–18).

31. On the notion of *ekarasa* see for example Abhinavagupta's statement in his commentary on *PTlv* 21–24, pp. 16–18, translated in Muller-Ortega 1989: 176–177.

32. See the commentary on *PTlv* 11–16, pp. 11–14, translated in Muller-Ortega 1989: 215–217.

33. On *siddhas* see the interesting treatment in S.B. Dasgupta, *Obscure Religious Cults*, 3d. ed (Calcutta: Firma KLM, 1969), 191–255.

34. See *TĀ*, ch. 29, as a classic source for a description of these concepts of transgression.

35. See Abhinavagupta's analysis of this process which is linked with the discovery of the *ekarasa* in his commentary on *PTlv* 21–24, pp. 16–19, translated in Muller-Ortega 1989: 220– 221.

36. See for example Abhinavagupta's statement on *svātantrya* in his commentary on *PTlv* 2b-3a, p. 3, translated in Muller-Ortega 1989: 207.

37. On these concepts, see Muller-Ortega 1989: 121–23.

38. On the *kaulikī-siddhi*, see the commentary on *PTlv* 10, p. 10, quoted above, and its discussion in Muller-Ortega 1989: 108.

39. Abhinavagupta discusses the notion of *mudrā* in *TĀ*, ch. 32.

40. For more on the ritual nature of the Kaulas, see Paul E. Muller-Ortega, "The Power of the Secret Ritual: Theoretical Formulations from the Tantra," *Journal of Ritual Studies* 4 (Summer 1990): 41–59. An insightful approach to the transgressive dimension is to be found in Alexis Sanderson, "Purity and Power

among the Brahmans of Kashmir," in *The Category of the Person: Anthropology, Philosophy, History*, eds. Michael Carrithers, Steven Collins, and Steven Lukes (Cambridge: Cambridge University Press, 1986), 190–216. Another very useful discussion of the Kaulas is to be found in Mark Dyczkowski, *The Canon of the Śaivāgama and the Kubjikā Tantras of the Western Kaula Tradition* (Albany: State University of New York Press, 1988).

41. On the *kula-yāga* see *TĀ*, ch. 29.

42. See Abhinavagupta's statement on the nature of purity as non-duality in the *TĀ* 4.118b–120a.

43. See Sanderson 1986.

44. An awareness of alchemy and a use of the symbolic vocabulary of transmutation seems to be pervasive in the writings of Abhinavagupta. For example commenting on *PTlv ślokas* 11–16 he says:

> But whenever a flowing form is produced by the condition of practice due to the heating of the vessel of awareness whose nature is the Heart, that flowing, by a regular absorption into the levels of body, mind, and breath, just like quicksilver penetrating into metal, negates the insentiency of body and mind.
>
> yadā tu tad eva prāṇabuddhibhūmiṣu siddharasa vidhyamānadhātunyāyena samāveśakrameṇaitad hṛdayātmakaparāmarśapātratāpādanayā prāṇabuddhyādijaḍimanyakkāriṇyā prasarad rūpam abhyāsadaśāṃ saṃpādyate.

45. See for example the classic work by Karl H. Potter, *Presuppositions of India's Philosophies* (Westport: Greenwood Press, 1976), which examines the nature of freedom and bondage in Indian Philosophy with exemplary clarity.

46. tatra jñātṛtā nāma unmeṣanimeṣalakṣaṇena saṃkocavikāsātmajñānakriyālakṣaṇena svabhāvena svaparispandanasārā. na tu pariniṣthitaparicchinnajaḍarūpaghaṭāditulyas tasya ca saṃkocavikāsayogaḥ trikoṇahṛdayaspandanādiṣu yathāyathā sphuṭībhavati tathātathā jñātṛtvam utkṛṣyate yāvad bhairavasaṃvidi. yathāyathā nyūnībhavati tathātathā tan nikṛṣyate yāvaj jaḍe pāṣāṇādau. sa cāyam saṃkocavikāsalakṣaṇo visargaḥ svātantryātmā bhagavato'nuttarasya śaktiḥ. tā etāścatasraḥ śaktayaḥ puruṣaṃ dhārayanti madhye triśaṇkuvad viśramayanti, anyathā pāṣāṇādivat jaḍabhūmim evāpatet parameśvaravad vā saṃvidgaganam evāpatet (*PTlv* 5–9a commentary, pp. 7–8).

47. The story of Triśaṅku appears in many places in the mythological literature of Hinduism including the *Viṣṇu Purāṇa*, the *Harivaṃśa*, the *Rāmāyaṇa*, and the *Devībhāgavata Purāṇa*. For excellent retellings of the myth, see Wendy Don-

iger O'Flaherty, *Dreams, Illusions and Other Realities* (Chicago: University of Chicago Press, 1984), pp. 103–109.

48. Kṣemarāja's *PHṛ* is perhaps the most accessible discussion of the nature of the transmigrating self. See the translation and exposition by Singh in *PHṛS*.

49. SenSharma (1990) presents an interesting analysis of this dilemma, especially in Chapter 4, "The Way to Ultimate Self-Realization" (See Note 14).

50. See, for example, *TĀ* 4.10, where Abhinavagupta talks about Śiva's sport of shadowing the Self. See Paul E. Muller-Ortega, "Tantric Meditation: Vocalic Beginnings," in *Ritual and Speculation in Early Tantrism: Studies in Honor of André Padoux*, ed. Teun Goudriaan (Albany: State University of New York Press, 1992) for an extended consideration of this process of self-concealment and self-revelation.

51. Once again Potter's *Presuppositions of India's Philosophies* is an excellent, initial source for these discussions.

52. See Abhinavagupta's extended discussion of this problem in *TĀ*, ch. 13.

53. The fundamental idea of the thirty-six principles is pervasive in Abhinavagupta's writings. A classic and very detailed exposition is to be found in the first half of the commentary on *PTv ślokas* 5–9a, pp. 98–160, translated in Jaideva Singh's *A Trident of Wisdom* (Albany: State University of New York Press, 1989), 87–154. A shorter, clearer rendering is in his *PTlv* commentary on the same *ślokas*, translated in Muller-Ortega 1989: 209–213. (See Note 2.)

54. The remainder of this section is based almost entirely on my understanding of *ĪPv* 3.1–2, a *locus classicus* in Abhinavagupta's writings.

55. Abhinavagupta's comment on *PTlv* 5–9a, quoted above, is very helpful as a description of the role that the *visarga-śakti* plays in the construction of this zone of contraction.

56. Abhinavagupta treats the notion of the *malas* in many places in his writings, of which perhaps the most important may be *TĀ*, chs. 9 and 13, where he directly refutes the Śaiva Siddhānta theories about the *malas*. See Sanderson (1992) for an interesting analysis of this discussion.

57. There is some variation in the number of the sheaths. See Muller-Ortega 1989: 129–131 for more detail.

58. I explore the notion of the continuous cosmogony in detail in Muller-Ortega 1992. (See Note 50.)

59. In addition to the passage already mentioned from the *ĪPv*, Abhinavagupta details the idea of the seven experiencers in his commentaries on *PTv* 1a (p. 59) and 5–8 (pp. 117–119), in *TĀ*, chs. 9 and 13, and in *TS*, ch. 9. Kṣemarāja discusses it in his comment on *PHṛ sūtra* 3.

60. See *ĪPv* 3.2.8–10.

61. See *ĪPv* 3.2.8.

62. Also called the *vijñāna-kevalas*. See *ĪPv* 3.2.7.

63. For the image of the evenly held hand-balance and more detail about this plane, see *ĪPv* 3.1.3.

64. See *ĪPv* 3.1.2.

65. See *ĪPv* 3.1.2.

66. For an extended discussion of the nature of the *AHAM*, see Abhinavagupta's commentary on *PTv* 3b-4, pp. 84–88, translated in Muller-Ortega 1989: 158–61. (See Note 2.)

67. bhagavad bhairavabhaṭṭārakarūpasamāviṣṭaḥ nijaparasaṃviccamatkāravaśanirmitabhāvakrīḍāḍambaro jīvanmukta eva prathamoktanayena bhavati ityanubhava evāyam āvartate na tvanyat kiṃciditi (*PTv* 32b commentary, pp. 269–71).

68. *ŚS* 1.12, translation my own. For alternate renderings and expanded commentary on this important *sūtra* see the translations of Singh and Dyczkowski, referred to in note 21.

69. See the analysis of the various states of bliss, including the *jagadānanda*, in *TĀ* 5.27b-53, translated in Muller-Ortega 1989: 197–98. The first verse of the very important *Mālinīvijaya Tantra* begins with praise offered to the *jagadānanda*.

70. On the *bhairavīmudrā*, a *locus classicus* is *VBhT* 77. See also the already mentioned passage in Abhinavagupta's *TĀ*, ch. 13.

71. See Abhinavagupta's comment on *PTlv ślokas* 29–32, pp. 113–139, which employs rather technical vocabulary to describe the nature of *parā-bhakti* in terms of *bhoga* or enjoyment. *Bhoga* is discussed as the offering of those things that cause a process of entry into the Heart. Abhinavagupta here mentions the enjoyment of those things that are possessed of the "blissful external power" which is useful for developing that "inner power" that allows for the entry into the Heart. See translation in Muller-Ortega 1989: 227.

72. For more on this notion of infinity moving through itself, see the ecstatic hymn of praise by Abhinavagupta in *TĀ*, ch. 26.58–65, in which he sings of the perpetual worship within the divine abode of the body of the God together with the Goddess, translated in Muller-Ortega 1989: 194.

73. See Kṣemarāja's analysis of *pratimīlana* in his commentary on *ŚS* 3.45, pp. 231–32, where he discusses the terms *nimīlana* and *unmīlana*.

74. jāgratsvapnasuṣuptabhede turyābhogasambhavaḥ (*ŚS* 1.7, p. 36).

75. See *ĪPv* 3.1.3.

76. nijāmodabharakrīḍābhāsitabhedasya (*PTv* 1 commentary, p. 17).

77. yatrāntarakhilaṃ bhāti yacca sarvatra bhāsate
sphurattāiva hi śā hyeka hṛdayaṃ paramaṃ budhāḥ
rāsabhī vaḍavā vāpi svam jagajjanmadhāma yat
samakālaṃ vikāsyaiva saṃkocya hṛdi hṛṣyati
tathobhayamahānandasauṣumnahṛdayāntare
spandamānam upāsīta hṛdayaṃ sṛṣṭilakṣaṇaṃ (*PTv* 32b commentary, pp. 270–71).

CHAPTER 8

Living Liberation in Śaiva Siddhānta

Chacko Valiaveetil, S.J.

Introduction

The *jīvanmukti* ideal is one of the significant contributions that India has made to the religious thought of the world. Though the concept of living liberation is generally associated with non-dualistic and non-devotional schools, such as Advaita Vedānta, the foregoing chapters have shown that it has played a significant role in the thought of many Hindu schools that do not fit these criteria. Śaiva Siddhānta or Tamil Śaivism, which has been extolled by G. U. Pope as "the most elaborate, influential and undoubtedly the most intrinsically valuable of all the religions of India,"[1] has the distinction of elaborating a view of *jīvanmukti* consistent with both a realistic metaphysics and devotional soteriology. At first glance the Śaiva Siddhānta concept of *jīvanmukti* may appear to lack consistency, because *jīvanmukti* and realistic metaphysics hardly seem to go together. However, the *jivanmukti* ideal of Śaiva Siddhānta is based on the living experience of Śaiva saints and mystics known as Nāyaṉārs, and the witness of their experience cannot be overlooked. These saints have given expression to their religious experience in hymns and psalms of exquisite beauty, singing the praises of the gracious Lord who saved them from the fetters of *saṃsāra*, and calling on people to take refuge under His sacred feet. The mystic knowledge and utterances of these seers became the foundation of Śaiva Siddhānta philosophy. The philosophers who systematized the Śaiva Siddhānta doctrine declare, with one voice, their indebtedness to these seers. In the opening *sūtra* of his *Śivajñāna Bodham (ŚB)*, which forms the basic text of Śaiva Siddhānta philosophy, Meykaṇṭār establishes his doctrine on the authority of the sages. Meykaṇṭār himself is traditionally acknowledged as a man who has realized the truth of what he has been writing. The term *meykaṇṭār* literally means "one who has realized the truth."[2] Those who commmented on his work were also guided in their writings by their spiritual realization. Śivāgrayogin, one of the six commentators of the *Śiva-jñāna Siddhiyār*, a commentary on *ŚB*, explicitly states that what he sets forth is "the outcome of the gracious teaching of my *guru*, my own [religious] experience, and the matter handed down in the Āgamas."[3]

In this introductory section we shall first give a historical survey of the religious and philosophical literature of Śaiva Siddhānta. The metaphysics of Śaiva Siddhānta—delineating its understanding of God, soul, and world and their non-dual relationship (*advaita*)—is given next as a background to understand the Śaiva Siddhānta ideal of *jīvanmukti*. In the second section the progress of the soul towards the goal of *jīvanmukti* is treated. There is a continuity between the stages of bondage and liberation; the grace of God is most important in the attainment of the goal. The third and fourth sections deal with the growth of the soul in the state of *jīvanmukti* through the eradication of the three bonds (*malas*) that are still present. Though he has attained the feet of Śiva, as long as the *jīvanmukta* continues his life in the world, there is the possibility of relapse against which he has to take certain precautions. The fifth and last section deals with the conduct of the *jīvanmukta*. What differentiates the life of the *jīvanmukta* from that of the non-liberated is the awareness that his life is rooted in God. It is no longer he who lives but God (Śiva) living and acting in him. This experience gives him a sense of total freedom, joy, and bliss.

Śaiva Siddhānta Literature

The canonical literature of Śaiva Siddhānta in Tamil is the collection of the Twelve Sacred Books (*Paṉṉirutirumuṟai*) containing the devotional hymns and the mystical utterances of the Śaiva saints and sages of the early centuries of the common era. These were redacted by Nampi Antar Nampi in the tenth century in ten books. The first seven books are the *Tevārams* containing the devotional hymns of Tirujñāna Sambantar, Appar (both seventh century), and Suntarar (ninth century). The eighth book contains the deep religious experience and mystical utterances of Māṇikkavācakar (ninth or possibly third century) in his *Tiruvācakam* and *Tirukkovaiyār*. The hymns called *Tiruvicaippā* and *Tiruppallāṇṭu*, by nine different saints (C.E. 900–1100) is the ninth book, and *Tirumantiram* by Tirumular (sixth century) forms the tenth book. Nampi himself added an eleventh book containing poems by Śaiva saints like Paṭṭinatār and Karaikkal Ammaiyar. The twelfth book is a later addition, *Periyapurāṇam*, by

Sekkiḻār (twelfth century), which narrates the stories of the great Śaiva saints and sages.

The fourteen philosophical treatises (*Meykaṇṭa Śāttiram*) of Śaiva Siddhānta (written in the thirteenth and fourteenth centuries) have their main inspiration in the twelve sacred books mentioned above. The other influences shaping Śaiva Siddhānta philosophy are the *Śaivāgamas*, which taught that God is personal and the efficient cause (*nimitta kāraṇa*) of the world, and the Śivādvaita of Śrīkaṇṭha (twelfth century), which is a commentary on the *Brahma Sūtra*. Śrīkaṇṭha speaks of God as both the efficient and material cause (*abhinna-nimittopādāna kāraṇa*) of the world.

The most important among the fourteen philosophical treatises is *Śivajñāna Bodham* by Meykaṇṭatevar (thirteenth century). In forty lines of closely reasoned Tamil poetry, comprising twelve *sūtras*, Meykaṇṭār sets forth the quintessence of Śaiva Siddhānta philosophy, which is considered to be the synthesis of the truth contained in the four Vedas and the twenty-eight Śaivāgamas. Meykaṇṭār's thought was elaborated by Aruṇanti, his immediate disciple, in his *Śivajñāna Siddhiyār*, which consists of two parts: *Parapakkam (ŚSP)* and *Supakkam (ŚSS)*. ŚSP refutes the teachings of other schools while ŚSS, a commentary on *ŚB*, expounds the fundamental teachings of Śaiva Siddhānta. *Śivappirakāśam*, by Umāpati Śivācāryar (fourteenth century), a pupil's pupil of Aruṇanti, is a further exposition of *ŚB* and *Siddhiyār*.[4] Śivāgrayogin (sixteenth century), who comments on the Sanskrit version of *Śivajñāna Bodham*, is more inclined toward the Śivādvaita of Śrīkaṇṭha. Śivajñānayogin (eighteenth century), the last among the great commentators, in his *Māpādiyam* (Skt. *Mahābhāṣyam*), a Tamil commentary on *ŚB*, reinterprets and tries to reconcile the different views of his predecessors. On every vital issue he follows Umāpati and criticizes Śivāgrayogin.

The Advaita of Śaiva Siddhānta and the Jīvanmukti *Ideal*

Śaiva Siddhānta philosophy claims to be the true Advaita, which upholds the absolute supremacy of God and at the same time unhesitatingly accepts the reality of the world and souls. Umapāti Śivācāryar, in his celebrated work *Śivappirakāśam*, calls this philosophy "the distilled essence of Vedānta."[5]

Śaiva Siddhānta distinguishes three eternal entities: The Lord (*pati*), the soul (*paśu*), and the world or bonds (*pāśa*). Though all three are eternal, the Lord is the only true Being, (*sat*) existing by Himself. The souls and the world are dependent on Him for their existence and activity. Compared to the reality of the Lord, who alone is really Being (*sat*), the world is non-being (*asat*), described as "writing on water, a present dream, a mirage."[6] This does not mean that the world has no reality or is illusory. The Siddhāntin here uses the term non-being, in the words of V.A. Devasenapati, "in a valuational, not ontological sense."[7] The world is real but is called unreal (*asat*), in contrast to the Lord who alone is absolutely Real (*sat*).

According to the Siddhānta philosophers, the relation between God, world, and souls cannot be confined to non-difference (*abheda*), difference (*bheda*) or difference-in-non-difference (*bhedābeda*) as in the Vedānta schools. All three relations are involved. God exists in and by Himself apart from the world (*tanēyāy*). At the same time He is one with the souls and the world (*avayēyāy*). So He is both identical with and different from them (*avayētānēyāy*) (*ŚB* 2). In the words of Aruṇanti, "God stands as the whole world, as separate from it and also along with it."[8] "The sacred scriptures do not say they are 'one' (*oṉṟu*) but 'not two' (*attuvitam*)."[9]

If the Lord is Real (*sat*), and the world unreal (*asat*), the soul is "real-unreal" (*sadasat*) participating in the nature of both the (*sat*) and the unreal (*asat*). Like a crystal that reflects its environment, the soul reflects the nature of that with which it is associated (*ŚB* 8.3.1). In its earthly condition it is conjoined to the bonds (*pāśa*) which are unreal (*asat*). Though beginningless, this is an artificial condition of the soul. Its natural condition is to be associated with the real, Śiva (*Śiva sat*). In the state of bondage the soul is in non-dual (*advaita*) relation with the root impurity (*āṇava*). Liberation consists in its realization of its true identity with God. Tāyumāṉavar, a seventeenth century mystic of Śaiva Siddhānta, expresses longing for this realization when he sings: "Oh, for the day when I shall be in non-dual (*advaita*) relation with Śiva, the source of true knowledge, as I am now in *advaita* relation with *āṇava*."[10] This *advaita* relation is understood not as mere identity, but as union where there is room for distinction. Tāyumāṉavar calls those who have realized this special relationships "adepts (*siddhar*) who have realized the equipoise of Vedānta and Siddhānta."[11]

Śaiva Siddhānta tradition considers those who have realized this *advaita* relation *jīvanmuktas*. The terms used are knowers of the truth (*meyñāni*), adepts (*siddhar*), servants (*aṭiyārs*), workers (*toṇṭar*) and, for many commentators, the term *jīvanmukta* (*cīvanmuttaṉ*) itself. Aruṇanti Śivācāryar, the immediate disciple of Meykaṇṭār, commenting on the experience of those who have the realization of oneness with Śiva, says: "Therefore, the *jīvanmuktas* continue to see only Śiva."[12] More explicitly, he claims: "In the experience of true discriminative knowledge, Śiva shines forth, and here itself one becomes a *jīvanmukta*."[13] Pāṇḍipperumāḷ, one of the early commentators on *ŚB*, commenting on *sūtras* 11 and 12, uses the term *jīvanmukti* a number of times.[14] Tāyumāṉavar explicitly speaks of

Meykaṇṭār as "the master who has experienced the sacred non-dual (*advaita*) relationship which is beyond the reach of those under delusion."[15]

Toward *Jīvanmukti*

The Odyssey of the Soul

In its earthly condition the soul is fettered by the three bonds (*malas*): *āṇava, karma*, and *māyā*. *Āṇava* is the root impurity (*mūlamala*). The soul can attain liberation only with the removal of *āṇava*. *Āṇava-mala* is compared to the cataract that affects the eye. Just as the cataract cannot be operated upon until it is mature, the root impurity cannot be extirpated until it becomes ripe and fit to be removed.

The ripening of the root impurity (*āṇava-mala*) takes place through the painful and pleasurable experiences the soul undergoes through innumerable lives. In its early state (*kevala-avasthā*), where the soul is fettered only by the root impurity, it is most helpless. It is in total darkness and cannot have any experience, since it has no instruments or objects of experience. In the next state, the Lord provides these auxiliaries of experience—the body, the senses, the world, and the objects of experience that constitute the bonds of *karma* and *māyā*. This second state (*sakala*), where the soul is fettered by all three *malas*, is an improvement on the first state, for through the soul's experiences in this state *karmas* are gradually exhausted, and the root impurity (*āṇava*) becomes ripe for removal. The Lord now appears, and through His grace frees the soul from the fetters once and for all. The freed condition is the pure (*śūddha*) state. In its arduous journey towards *mukti,* the soul is said to pass from the darkness (*iruḷ*) of the initial (*kevala*) state, where there is only the root impurity, through the confusion (*maruḷ*) and twilight of the second or fettered (*sakala*) state to the grace (*aruḷ*) and illumination of the final, pure (*śuddha*) state.

The spiritual discipline required for liberation can be undertaken only by humans. The human being is equipped with the most apt instruments for worshipping the Lord. The mind is given to contemplate Him, speech to praise Him, and the body and senses to make obeisance to Him (*ŚSS* 2.92). Those who realize the value of human birth strive to attain liberation in this life itself, before the body is laid aside. *Jīvanmukti* is their goal. Tāyumāṉavar expresses this longing for liberation when he prays: "Lord, before I put off this shirt-like body, may I be given the great initiation (*sahaca niṭṭai*) and led to seedless contemplation (*niruvikaṟ pam*)!"[16] Those blessed with this longing for liberation are detached from all desires for wealth and pleasure. They pray to the Lord: "What we beg for is neither possessions nor gold nor pleasures, but the triad of your love and grace and righteousness."[17]

*Continuity of Bondage (*Saṃsāra*) and Liberation (*Mokṣa*)*

One of the most beautiful features of the Śaiva Siddhānta view of liberation is the role divine grace plays at every stage of one's progress. "There is no treasure in the world more precious than grace."[18] Once the soul awakens to the divine grace at work in her life, she will not be satisfied with anything less than the full blossoming of this grace. The experience she undergoes is a complex one. On the one hand there is the sense of pain and misery at her helpless condition in bondage, separated from the Lord who is her final bliss and supreme blessedness. But on the other hand, she already experiences the joy that the Lord has revealed His grace to her and has given her a share in His bliss. The grace that reveals her sinfulness and misery is the same that forgives and raises her to divine union and bliss. The Lord's devotees have the experience of both bondage and liberation in their lives. The experience of bliss intensifies as they get more and more detached from creatures and draw nearer and nearer to the Lord.[19]

God's Quest for the Soul

To her pleasant surprise, the soul discovers that the Lord was present all the time, "hidden like a thief in her inmost being."[20] "Even before she was formed in the womb, He had made her His abode."[21] The love that the Lord bestows on the soul is immeasurable and incomprehensible. His love is even greater than that of "the mother who feeds her child with her own milk."[22] In order to impart saving knowledge to the soul, the formless Lord assumes human and sub-human forms. The form *par excellence* thus assumed is that of the divine *guru*.[23] Aruṇanti speaks of his *guru* Meykaṇṭār as the Lord himself appearing in human form.[24]

The condition of the soul in her association with the body and the five senses, and her subsequent liberation through the instruction of the divine *guru* is illustrated by the allegory of the prince lost among the savages (*ŚB* 8). While quite young, a prince was lost in the forest and brought up by savages. Not knowing his real status as a prince, he considered himself a savage and led a savage life. The king, hearing about the condition of his son, came to the forest, met the prince, and instructed him about his true nature and restored him to his royal status. The soul's plight is similar to that of this prince. She is by nature divine, but in her earthly condition unaware of her true nature because of her association with the body and senses. Like colors reflected in a prism, sense-impressions are reflected in the soul.[25] Deluded by these sense impressions, the soul identifies herself with the senses and lives in oblivion of her divine nature. The Lord appears to the soul in the form of a *guru*, instructs her about her real nature, and unites her to Himself.

The Spiritual Sadhāna

Of the traditional paths to release recognized in Indian spiritual tradition—knowledge (*jñāna*), action (*karma*) and devotion (*bhakti*)—the Siddhāntin rejects none. But each path is seen in light of the supremacy of the Lord who saves. Śaiva Siddhānta clearly subscribes to the teaching of the Vedas and the Āgamas that "salvation is through knowledge."[26] Saving knowledge is knowledge of the Lord (*patijñāna*), an experiential knowledge involving the total person of the seeker (*sādhaka*)—intellect, emotion, and will—and bringing about his or her total transformation. This higher knowledge (*parajñāna*) is distinguished from empirical knowledge (*pasajñāna*) and self knowledge (*pasujñāna*), which are both lower knowledge (*aparajñāna*). Knowledge obtained through study of the Vedas, Āgamas, and śāstras comes under empirical knowledge (*ŚSS* 9.2). All that the soul knows through discursive knowledge is tinged with self-love, even the knowledge "I am Brahman" (*aham brahmāsmi*), which is knowledge through self-love.[27] "True saving knowledge is permeated by the Lord's grace."[28] It not only removes the bonds (*malas*) but also "unites the soul to the Lord's feet."[29] Mere action cannot lead to release. Austerities performed without reference to the Lord and Vedic sacrifices offered to the gods are only self-centered acts (*paśupuṇya*) that cannot lead to liberation. To be fruitful, actions must be consecrated to the Lord. They are then called God-centered acts (*Śivapuṇya*), which lead to saving knowledge and liberation.

Devotion, according to Śaiva Siddhānta, is more than a means to liberation. The history of Śaiva saints speaks of many Nāyaṉārs attaining liberation through loving self-surrender to the Lord. Here devotion expressed in self-surrender is not a mere method (*sādhana*), but participation in the final liberation itself. Umāpati describes the state of liberation as "the state of love."[30] The Siddhāntin does not divide action, knowledge, and love into watertight compartments. Knowledge and love increase gradually as the seeker progresses in his spiritual realization. The love that initially is self-centered or tinged with self-love gradually gets purified till it becomes absolutely selfless and centered on God.[31]

*The Descent of Divine Grace (*Śaktinipāta*)*

The dawning of saving knowledge presupposes the descent of divine grace (*śaktinipāta*). The grace of the Lord is at work throughout the spiritual odyssey of the soul. In the early stages it remains unmanifest and allows the *karmas* to work out and the root impurity (*āṇavamala*) to ripen. The descent of grace proceeds according to the spiritual condition and needs of the seeker (*sādhaka*) as he or she advances in the divine life.

The descent of divine grace presupposes two other conditions in the soul: the balancing of *karma*s (*karmasāmya* or *iruviṉaiyoppu*) and the ripening of the *mala*s or impurities (*malaparipāka*). The first is the balancing of good and evil *karma*s, interpreted as the equanimity of the aspirant with respect to the two-fold *karma*s. Like the *karma-yogin* of the *Bhagavad Gītā* (2.47), the aspirant is detached from the fruits of his or her actions. The aspirant neither performs virtuous actions for reward nor eschews evil ones for fear of consequences. The aspirant dedicates all his actions to the Lord and considers them to belong to the Lord Himself. This attitude of enlightened indifference prevents the *mala*s from affecting the soul, constituting the process of ripening of the *malas* (*malaparipāka*). Grace that was so far unmanifest (*tirōdhānaśakti*) now becomes manifest (*anugrahaśakti*), and in torrents of grace, the aspirant becomes a *jīvanmukta*.

Growth in the State of *Jīvanmukti*

The descent of grace and the two conditions it presupposes form a gradual and progressive process full of ups and downs. Hence we cannot speak of a particular moment in the spiritual life of the aspirant (*sādhaka*) when he or she becomes a *jīvanmukta*.[32] There are ups and downs in his or her spiritual experience.

In Śaiva Siddhānta as well as in other Indian systems, liberation (*mukti*) is considered a state of freedom from the bonds that bind the soul to the cycle of birth and death (*saṃsāra*). But according to Śaiva Siddhānta, this is only the negative aspect of *mukti*; its positive aspect is the experience of union with the Lord. Both freedom from the bonds (*pāśa*) and union with the Lord take place simultaneously, like the removal of darkness in the presence of light. It is a continual process that lasts all through one's life. The *jīvanmukta*'s life continues as before, but in place of attachment to and union with the fetters (*pāśa*), now there is intense attachment to and union with Śiva. Total freedom from the bonds is possible only at liberation after death (*videhamukti*).[33]

The continuity of bondage and liberation is clear in the *Śivajñāna Bodham*. *Sūtras* 7–9 are *ex officio* concerned with the means of attaining *mukti* (*sādhanaviyal*), and *sūtras* 10–12 deal with the fruit of *mukti*. But the eighth *sūtra* in fact already speaks of "attaining the feet of the Lord."[34]

The tenth *sūtra* speaks of "the removal of the fetters (*mala māyai ta<u>n</u><u>n</u>oṭu val vi<u>n</u>ayi<u>n</u><u>r</u>e*)." Even in the final *sūtra* the *jīvanmukta* is reminded of the need to "wash away the impurities (*ammala<u>n</u>kal̲īi*) and is given the remedy against possible relapse.[35]

Meykaṇṭār compares the gradual process of the removal of the *mala*s and union with the Lord, or the destruction of *mala*s and the manifestation of the Lord, to the waxing of the moon: "Just as the moon gradually dispels the pervasive darkness, the Lord who abides in the soul through love, gradually dispels its impurity."[36] The waxing moon, day by day, dispels more and more of the darkness clouding it until finally it shines in all its brightness as the full moon. Similarly, the Lord who is ever abiding in the soul through His grace, gradually dispels the impurity in the soul until He finally shines in all His splendor.

*Freedom from the Bonds (*Pāśávīṭu*)*

Though the soul is fettered by the bonds (*pāśa*) from beginningless time, the Lord is present with it all along. It is the grace of the Lord that makes possible knowledge and action that allow removal of the bonds (*TAP* 32–33). But, blinded by the root impurity (*āṇava*), the soul considers herself the author of all her actions and knowledge. The grace of the Lord hides her Self (*tirodhānaśakti*), as it were, from the soul.

The secret for the removal of the *mala*s is the realization that the soul is one with the Lord. The state of bondage is nothing but oblivion to this fact and the illusion that makes the soul think that it is one with *mala*. Meykaṇṭār says: "When the soul becomes one [with the Lord] and abides in the service of the Lord (*i<u>r</u>ai paṇi*) the three bonds will cease to exist."[37] The gradual removal or breaking down of the bonds (*pāśakṣaya*) is the first fruit (*paya<u>n</u>*) of the spiritual journey (*sādhana*).

Removal of the Root Impurity (Āṇavamala)

Āṇavamala is not mere ignorance that will automatically be removed at the dawn of knowledge. It is not merely an epistemic reality affecting only the soul's cognition, but an ontic one infecting the soul's very core. The disease finds expression in the self-conceit that gives rise to "the delusive consciousness of the sense of 'I' and 'mine'" which is the root of all evil.[38] The rival Śivasamavādins, who argue for the equality of the soul with God, hold that knowledge is all that is required to remove the root impurity (*āṇava)*; when knowledge dawns, ignorance will automatically be removed and the soul will reach the feet of the Lord. The Siddhāntin refutes such a view. More than knowlege is required to remove the root impurity (*āṇava*), precisely because it affects the soul's whole being. The soul not only should know the Lord but must also become one with Him. Only then will the sense of "I" and "mine" (*ahaṃkāra, mamakāra*) be overcome and, consequently, *āṇava* removed.

Meykaṇṭār brings out this truth with an illustration: In those who think in terms of "I" and "He," awareness of the knowing self is prevalent; so the Lord, without manifesting His identity, appears as the soul. But as for the soul which realizes that "there is no 'I' but only 'He,'"[39] the Lord will join her with His feet and reveal His identity to her.

In discursive knowledge one distinguishes between the knower, the object of knowledge, and knowledge itself. But in the realization of oneness with the Lord this distinction is overcome. The soul realizes that apart from the Lord there is neither knower, known, nor knowledge, though none of them cease to be real.[40] This realization of oneness with the Lord, however, does not mean that the soul loses her individuality. Union is through knowledge and love, though it profoundly affects the very being of the soul. Ontologically the soul remains the same, though a tremendous transformation takes place in her because of her intimate union with the Lord.[41]

Removal of Karma *and* Māya

Meykaṇṭār expresses the second aspect of the union by which *karma* and *māyā* are removed by the phrase "abiding in the service of the Lord."[42] The cause-effect relation of service to the Lord and removal of *karma* and *māyā* assume great significance for the possibility of *jīvanmukti*. *Mukti* itself is described as the state where "the souls, leaving the bonds (*pāśa*) attain the Lord (*pati*).[43] If *jīvanmukti* is true liberation, the *jīvanmukta* must have had *pāśa* removed. But since the body itself is a product of *māyā* and *karma*, it seems contradictory to say that *māyā* and *karma* can be removed while the soul is still in the body. When the cause is removed the effect that is dependent on it should also cease to exist. The Siddhāntin agrees that "where there is the body there will also be *karma* and *māyā*"[44] and that "the *mala*s will last as long as the body lasts."[45] This means that complete cessation of *mala* is possible only at bodily liberation (*videhamukti*).

However, the Siddhāntin has no doubt that liberation is possible in bodily existence. Though *karma* and *māyā* last as long as the body lasts, they will not affect the soul of the *jīvanmukta*. Actions will affect the soul only so long as she identifies herself with the senses and their objects and considers herself agent and enjoyer. Once this false identification is removed and the soul realizes her oneness with the Lord, she also discovers that by herself she can do nothing. All that she does is through the grace of the Lord. Meykaṇṭār explains this as follows: "Because the soul cannot do anything except by the grace of the Lord, the delusion (*ajñānam*) caused by *māyā* and the various *karmas* cannot enter her."[46] This is the meaning of the statement that service of the Lord is the means for removing *karma* and *māyā*. When the *jīvanmukta* becomes a servant of the Lord (*iṟaipaṇiyār*), "in whatever body he may be, actions will not affect him."[47]

Umāpati Śivácaryar describes the cessation of the three *karma*s in the life of the *jīvanmukta*: "The accumulated *karma*s which cause endless rebirths are made ineffective like burnt seeds. The *prārabdha karma* (*paḻa viṉai*) will remain an experience of the body without affecting the soul. If new *karma*s (*tōṉṟirur viṉai*) arise, they will be burnt out in a blaze of knowledge."[48] The *jīvanmukta* lives and acts, but without attachment. The secret to the *jīvanmukta*'s life is the realization that it is not he or she who lives and acts but the Lord who lives and acts in the liberated one. Pāṇṭipperumāḷ, one of the early commentators of the *Śivajñāna Bodham*, says that the soul gets rid of the sense of agency by realizing "all my actions are Yours [the Lord's] and You from Your place act and make me act."[49]

The actions of the *jīvanmukta* can be considered service of the Lord from another perspective also; he has no self-interest and all his actions, even when they may seem wicked or foolish to others, are done for the Lord and the Lord accepts them as such. The *jīvanmukta* becomes so absorbed in his or her devotion and dedication to the Lord that the liberated one is dead to himself or herself and to the rest of the world. This state of ecstatic love, expressing itself in service to the Lord, is beautifully brought out in the story of the life of Kaṇṇappar, one of the sixty-three celebrated Śaiva saints:

> Tiṇṇaṉār was a young chieftain of the hunters. In one of his hunting expeditions he came across the image of Lord Śiva erected in Kāḷatti hill. The whole being of Tiṇṇaṉār was moved by love for the Lord (*kāḷattiyappar*) and he found it impossible to tear himself away from the image. He would spend the day in worship of the Lord and the night in keeping vigil by his side. His worship consisted in the offering of the meat of wild animals which he himself had tasted earlier and found proper. He would bring water in his mouth for bathing the image, and flowers in his matted hair for decorating it. The Brahmin Śivakocariyār, who was regularly performing worship before the image in strict accordance with the Śaivāgama rituals, was annoyed and saddened at seeing the abomination of meat offering, etc. He would remove all the impure objects from the vicinity of the image and perform the rituals in the correct way. Tiṇṇaṉār, on his return from hunting, would again make his offerings. This went on for some days. Sore at heart, the Brahmin complained to the Lord about the sacrilege. The same night, the Lord, with Umādevi at his

side, appeared to the Brahmin and said, "know that this is his (Tiṇṇaṉār's) real state: his form is the form of love towards me; all that he knows is the knowledge of me; all his actions are dear to me."

The Lord told the Brahmin that He would prove to him the love of the hunter the following day. As Tiṇṇaṉār came with his usual offerings he found the right eye of the image bleeding. He tried all the remedies he knew of to stop the bleeding, but all in vain. Suddenly he remembered the saying: the remedy for flesh is flesh" (*ūṉukkūṉ*). Without the least hesitation he scooped out one of his eyes and applied it to the bleeding eye. To his immense delight, the hemorrhage ceased. But the Lord, desiring to prove the depth of the love of his devotee, let the other eye also bleed. Tiṇṇaṉār was alarmed, but now he knew the remedy. Without a second thought he was about to pluck out his other eye, when the voice of the Lord was heard three times: "Stop, Kaṇṇappar." The bleeding stopped and the eye of Tiṇṇaṉār was made whole. The Brahmin Śivakocariyār, who was watching the whole scene from hiding, realized what it meant to love and serve the Lord. Tiṇṇaṉār, thenceforeward known as Kaṇṇappar, because of the gift of his eye (*kaṇ*) to the Lord, was found mature in his love and the Lord took him to his right side forever (*TTM* p. 143 ff.).

Attaining the Feet of the Lord

There are many views of liberation that stop with its negative aspect, removal of the *mala*s (*pāśavīṭu*) and consequent freedom from suffering. According to the Siddhāntin, the most important aspect of *mukti* is union of the soul with Śiva (*śivappeṟu*), which is manifested in the experience of God in knowledge and love (*śivānubhāva*). This is technically called "attaining the feet of the Lord."[50] The most effective way to remove the *mala*s is union with the Lord. For the soul never stands alone, but by nature is either united with the *mala*s or with the Lord. Once freed from the bonds, if not attached to the Lord's feet, she is sure to revert back to the *mala*s.

Union in Knowledge

The Lord is the life and light of the soul and is present to the soul in the form of knowledge inseparably.[51] In the state of bondage His presence is hidden from the soul because of the bonds (*mala*s). For the eye of the owl, even bright daylight is dark. Similarly for the soul, fettered by the darkness of the root impurity (*āṇava)*, the omnipresent light of the Lord remains invisible.[52] Just as the letters of the alphabet (in Tamil) cannot be pronounced unless the vowel "a" stands along with them, the soul cannot know or act unless the Lord is united with her.[53]

The knowledge that liberates is the knowledge of the Lord (*patijñāna*) that is obtained not through any human effort but through the grace of the Lord. As the soul grows in knowledge, "its human faculties are made into divine ones."[54] Even in the waking condition realization of the Lord will go on increasing and "the experience of Śiva will become self-experience."[55] As the soul is purified more and more, knowledge (*patijñāna*) blazes forth in greater intensity. And conversely, in the blaze of divine knowledge all the *mala*s are burnt to ashes. "As the crystal column casts no shadow in the noonday sun, the soul in the blaze of divine grace will have no trace of the bonds (*pāśa*).[56] As Aruṇanti says,

> Those in whom knowledge has thus fructified, go about in the world as laudable *jīvanmuktas (pukal̲ sīvan̲muttarāki)*, so intimately united with Lord Śiva that one cannot part from the other. They are above all sense of likes and dislikes such that a potsherd and a piece of gold have the same value in their sight. Everywhere they see the appearance of Śiva alone.[57]

Union in Love

God is love,[58] and He dwells in the hearts of His devotees in the form of love. As the soul grows in knowledge of the Lord and is freed from the fetters (*mālas*), God communicates His love to the soul in greater abundance till the soul is transformed into the likeness of the Lord. Conversely, "It is the realization of the Lord in love that makes the soul fit for the removal of the *malas* through the grace of the Lord."[59] It is a mutual exchange of love. The soul surrenders itself irrevocably to the Lord who accepts the self-gift of the devotee and gives Himself as a return gift. Exulting in this experience of love, Māṇikkavācakar asks the Lord: "O gracious One, you have given yourself to me and accepted me in return. Who is the cleverer of the two? I have gained infinite bliss; what is it that you have gotten from me?"[60]

The state of the final liberation itself is described as "the state of love."[61] The *jīvanmuktas* are described as the ones whose lives are "permeated with stainless love for the Lord."[62] "Having realized that God is love, they abide in God as love."[63] In the union of love the *jīvanmukta*s are transformed into Śiva Himself so that they are described as "walking Śivas."[64] The Siddhānta writers are fond of expressing this union in love in terms of mystical marriage. Śiva is the lover and the soul is the bride whose heart He has stolen by love. Sambantar, in ecstatic love, speaks of the Lord as "the thief who has stolen my heart."[65] The Siddhāntin uses an illustration to bring out the nature of this union very beautifully. The terms *tāḷ* (feet) and *talai* (head) when joined become *ṭaṭalai*, one word but in which the reality of both *tāḷ* and *talai* are present. The letters "ḷ" and "t" combine into "ṭ," in which the reality of both is preserved. In the state of ultimate union, which is represented as the devotee joining his head (*talai*) to the feet (*tāḷ*) of the Lord, the soul becomes one with the Lord without losing its individuality, so that they are neither one nor two.[66] The union is so intimate that "they cannot be considered as two; neither can it be said that they are one, because the reality of neither is lost."[67]

The soul is said to be dissolved and consumed by divine bliss.[68] This is not the loss of one's distinct personality, but "the obliteration of egoism, the sense of I and mine."[69] Though the soul is assumed by the Lord and transformed into His likeness, it remains His slave before and after the union.[70] It is the total self-gift of the *jīvanmukta* as a return gift to the Lord, who has given Himself totally to the aspirant in a divine self-gift. Māṇikkavācakar expresses this when he sings: "I'm not my own, Thy slave am I; severed from Thee, no moment can I live."[71]

Means to Persevere and Grow in God-Experience

The paradoxical state of the *jīvanmukta*, who is liberated but still living in the world, makes it imperative that he takes certain precautions to persevere in the God-experience (*śivāṇubhava*) he has gained and to guard against the possibility of relapse. There are two dangers he has to guard against: *prārabdha-karma* and *mala-vāsana*. *Mala-vāsana* are the impressions that still linger in the soul after the removal of the accumulated *(saṃcita) karma*. This is compared to the odor that still persists in a vessel even after the odorous spices it contained have been removed from it.[72] *Prārabdha-karma* is the *karma* that accounts for the continuance of the body of the liberated person. Of the threefold *karma*s, the accumulated *karma*s of the past (*saṃcita*) are burnt out in the blazing fire of knowledge. There will not be any more incoming *karma*s (*āgāmi*), as the *jīvanmukta* has no sense of agency. The *jīvanmukta* experiences the Lord living and acting in him or her. However, the *karma*s responsible for the present body (*prārabdha-karma*) are to be experienced by the *jīvanmukta*.

As long as the *jīvanmukta* continues his or her life in the body, there is the danger that the *prārabdha-karma* and the *mala-vāsana* may overpower that person and drag him or her back to slavery once again. "Like the moss on the surface of the pond" which separates for a while when a stone is hurled into it, but comes together again as the impact of the stone fades away, the *malas* may reassert themselves once the intensity of saving knowledge diminishes.[73] For the *mala*s are eternal and cannot be annihilated. What knowledge does by its illumination is to check their effect on the soul, just as "darkness vanishes in the presence of burning light."[74] The full blossoming of knowledge cannot take place unless all traces of the *malas* are destroyed.[75] The state from which there is no return is that of *videhamukti*. "Then along with the body all the *malas* disappear,"[76] and the possibility of the *karma*s arising is removed once and for all.

Is not the presence of *prārabdha-karma* a sign that the person is not liberated and has not attained saving knowledge? According to the *Bhagavad Gītā*, "the fire of knowledge burns all *karma*s to ashes."[77] It is in the face of this difficulty that philosophers like Rāmānuja deny the possibility of *jīvanmukti*. In his commentary on the *Vedānta Sūtra*, Rāmānuja tries to show that the concept of *jīvanmukti* is a contradiction like "the son of a barren woman." He says, "For what definition, we ask, can be given to this 'Release in this life?' 'Release of a soul while yet joined to a body?' You might as well say, we reply, that your mother never had any children."[78] The response of the Siddhāntin to this objection is from the experience of Śaiva saints. Though the *malas* continue to exist, the *jīvanmukta* is not fettered by them. Meykaṇṭār illustrates this through a number of analogies:

> Ascetics, even though they may lie in the fire, are not burnt by it; adepts in horsemanship ride swift horses without losing their hold; those skilled in medicinal spells are not affected by poison. Similarly, the *jīvanmuktas* (*araṉaṭi yorpavar*) who have their thoughts fixed on the Hara, even though they have the experience of the five senses, do not on that account swerve from the realization they have gained.[79]

The discipline that the *jīvanmukta* is asked to undertake in order to persevere in the state he or she has attained to guard against the possibility of relapse are: the practice of meditation called *śivo'ham bhāvana*, the recital of the five-lettered *mantra* called *mukti pañcākṣara*, and the performance of worship called *antaryāgapūja*.

Realizing that in his humble and loving service he is united with the Lord present within him, the *jīvanmukta* meditates on his oneness with Śiva saying, "I am Śiva (*sivo'ham*)." The analogy given is that of a meditation called *garuḍabhāvana*. By meditating on oneness with the eagle (*garuḍa*), saying "*garuḍo'hamasmi*," one can be freed from the effect of snake poison. Similarly, by the meditation *śivo'ham bhāvana*, one becomes free of all the *mala*s.[80]

The Siddhānta theologians draw our attention to the fact that no absolute identity of the soul with Śiva is taught here. The soul remains distinct from the Lord while contemplating her oneness with the Lord, just as in the *garuḍabhāvana* one does not become the eagle but only imagines himself or herself as such. Aruṇanti clearly says that the sayings in the Vedas like "*aham brahmāsmi*" are to be interpreted in the light of this meditation and are not to be mistaken to mean identity of being with the Absolute. He says, "It is to this meditation that the ancient religions refer when they ask us to imagine 'I have become that'."[81]

By the contemplation of the five-lettered mantra, "*Śivāya namaḥ*" ("Salutation to Śiva," called *mukti pañcākṣara* or *śrī pañcākṣara*), the Lord manifests Himself more and more within the soul as light within light. The soul realizes herself to be the servant of the Lord, surrendering herself to the Lord and being purified and transformed by Him as "iron in the fire."[82] Although the Lord transcends the world, he is present in human beings, and through the internal worship called *antaryāgapūja*, he is worshipped as seated in the "lotus heart" (*hṛd-pundarīka*).[83] As the brilliance of a mirror is made manifest when its dust-covered surface is polished, Śiva hidden in the soul because of the *mala*s is made manifest by performing internal worship (*antaryāgapūja*). Thus the three practices of meditation, recitation of the *mantra*, and worship—involving the mind, feelings, and will of the *jīvanmukta*—purify him or her more and more and prepare the aspirant for full experience of Śiva (*śivānubhava*).[84]

The Conduct of the *Jīvanmukta*

The God-realization of the *jīvanmukta* gives him or her a new vision of reality and a new scale of values. Before the liberating experience, the aspirant was attached to the senses and sense objects and was a slave to them. Henceforward all that matters for him or her is God, who leads and guides that person in all his or her actions. Just as a possessed person does nothing by himself but is led by the evil spirit that possesses him, the *jīvanmukta* does nothing by himself but is led by the Lord.[85] God is his or her supreme possession. All other possessions are "like things in the hands of a person who is asleep."[86]

Detachment from Creatures

Tāyumāṉavar brings out the detachment of the *jīvanmuktas* before created reality in the following description of their behavior:

> They wander about like an evil spirit, lie like a corpse, eat like a dog whatever alms is offered to them, roam around like a jackal, respect

women as mothers, and considering themselves the least of all, behave like a child.[87] "Even if they are offered the whole of heaven and earth, that is not going to make them elated."[88]

Life of Service of the Jīvanmukta

However, the *jīvanmuktas* are not indifferent to the true welfare of their fellow human beings; Umāpati declares that "they melt in a flood of compassion at seeing the predicament of those still under the fetters."[89] In Sekkiḻār's biography of the Śaiva saints, the *Periyapurāṇam*, we see them wandering from place to place, singing the praises of the Lord and imparting instruction to the devotees. There Sekkiḻār describes how the Lord's servants arouse devotion in the hearts of the people:

> Attired in loincloth and sacred beads, their body smeared with sacred ash, their thoughts fixed on the sacred feet of the Lord, their eyes overflowing with tears of melting love, their mouths uttering the praises of the Lord, they entered the streets.[90]

In fact, it is the Lord Himself who instructs and directs others through them. "In the guise of the *guru* the Lord acts as a decoy, alluring souls to liberation."[91] A *jīvanmukta* in Śaiva Siddhanta is known as a worker (*toṇṭar)* and servant (*aṭiyar*), signifying the aspect of service in their lives that extends to all creation. Sustained and strengthened by the Lord living and acting within them, they spend their lives serving others, guiding them to freedom. Appar sings: "It is the duty of the Lord to support me, [his] servant, while my own duty is to spend my life in service."[92] The heartfelt longing of the *jīvanmukta* is that "the bliss I have experienced become the property and possession of the whole world."[93]

Is the Jīvanmukta *Beyond Ethical Norms?*

There is some support within the Śaiva Siddhānta tradition for the view that the *jīvanmukta* has transcended the norms of *dharma*, and so judgments of good and evil can no longer be applied to his or her actions. Aruṇanti Śivācāryar, in his *Śivajñāna Siddhiyār*, describes the life of the *jīvanmuktas*:

> For those who have attained saving knowledge in this life there is neither virtue nor vice nor anything to seek. They are above all codes of conduct, life of penance or vows, duties of the different stages of life, etc. . . . Like a child, a drunkard, or a possessed person, they may go about singing and dancing according to the inspiration of the moment. . . . In impurity and

> purity, anger, love and hatred—in all that they do they never part from the feet of the Lord.[94]

Commenting on the tenth *sūtra* of *Śivajñāna Bodham*, Aruṇanti says that "the merits and demerits of the *jñāni* will accrue to those who have done good and evil respectively to him," nay more, "even the heinous crimes performed by the *jñānis* are considered by the Lord as service done to him."[95] Aruṇanti goes on to say that the knowers of Śiva (*śivajñāni*), even when they are leading the most sensual or evil lives, remain united to the feet of the Lord, whereas those without knowledge of Śiva, whatever penances they may perform, will not be freed from *saṃsāra* (*ŚSS* 10.5).

The Śaiva Siddhānta tradition has not taken these statements literally, as any sort of license for immorality. What the commentators emphasize in these passages is the need for interior detachment from everything finite and imperfect so that one can be totally attached to the Lord, the Infinite and Supreme Good. *Jñānis*, in fact, are incapable of formal evil because they have no sense of agency. It is the Lord who lives and acts in them. Virtue will be a spontaneous expression of their inner lives. Umāpati Śivācāryar says that the most heinous crimes and lascivious actions of the realized person will be taken by Śiva as His own experience (*śivānubhāva*), since the *jñāni* has no sense of agency and sees all his or her actions as the actions of Śiva himself.[96]

Love as the Ultimate Criterion

Love for the Lord is the ultimate criterion for virtue and vice. Aruṇanti says that "the sins of the devotees of the Lord are virtues whereas even the good actions performed by those without love are vices."[97] If *jīvanmuktas* transcend the conventions and laws that govern the lives of those who are still under the fetters, it is because they are guided by the light of the Lord's grace and governed by His love. Some of their actions may seem wicked to human eyes but not from the higher standpoint of God. In the lives of the Śaiva saints there are many such instances. Siruttoṇḍa Nāyaṉār kills his only son to feed a *bhairava*, a Śaiva devotee (*TTM* 665–83). Mūrkka Nāyaṉār takes to gambling to feed Śaiva devotees (*TTM* 653–56). Śatti Nāyaṉār cuts off the tongues of those who despised the *bhaktas* (*TTM*, 749–50). Caṇḍeśurar severs the feet of his father who kicked over a pail containing the milk-offering for the Lord (*TTM* 234–43). Iyarpakai Nāyaṉār gives away his wife to a Śaiva devotee and puts to the sword his relatives who tried to prevent this apparently immoral act (*TTM* 74–81).

Obviously, these actions cannot be justified when judged by normal ethical laws. But in light of the Śiva consciousness that governs the lives of *jīvanmuktas*, they become understandable. In this new consciousness they seem to become oblivious of everything else except their passionate love for the Lord and (as will be explained below) their zeal for serving the devotees.

Injunctions for the Jīvanmukta

Though the *jīvanmukta* is above all obligations and conventional laws that govern those still under the fetters, he or she still follows certain norms in daily life and action. In the twelfth and last *sūtra* of *Śivajñāna Bodham*, Meykaṇṭār lays down these norms. They are more a description of the conduct of the *jīvanmukta* than a prescription given to a liberated one, because observance of these rules comes to the *jīvanmukta* spontaneously. The Tamil verbs in the *sūtra* are in the indicative and not the imperative. Some commentators like Śivāgrayogin, more influenced by the Sanskrit tradition, say that these injunctions apply to those with a lower degree of realization. But Meykaṇṭār himself, Aruṇanti in his *Śivajñāna Siddhiyar*, and authoritative commentators like Śivajñānayogin, clearly say that they apply to *jīvanmukta*s. Meykaṇṭār uses the term *attuviti*, "you who have realized the truth of Advaita," and in *ŚSS* 12.1 clearly refers to the realized person (*meyñāni*). Aruṇandi refers here to the *śivajñānis*.[98] Among the norms that the *jīvanmukta* follow are: association with Śaiva devotees, respect for the sacred emblems, and worship of temple images.

Association with the Śiva Bhaktas

Though *jīvanmuktas* have transcended all narrow love and hatred (*uṟavum pakaiyum*), they need to be cautious of the company they keep. Proper associates are other *jīvanmukta*s who are true devotees of the Lord. The danger with others is that by their words and actions "they cause ignorance to arise."[99] Those who are not devotees of Śiva (*śīvapattar*) are, in a sense, more dangerous than the three impurities themselves; the impurities directly point to delusive knowledge, but the non-devotees, without pointing to it, lead the soul to delusion in various ways.[100] *Jīvanmuktas* must be "madly in love with the devotees"[101] who are the very embodiment of love and are truly lovers (*anpar*). These devotees will help *jīvanmuktas* to remove their forgetfulness of their *advaita* relation to God, assist them in true knowledge, free them from the pit of rebirth, and lead them to blessedness: *prārabdha karma* will not affect such *jīvanmuktas* (*ŚB* 12.2.1). The very nature of the soul, moreover, demands that the *jīvanmukta* should have the right company, for the soul by nature gets attached to that with which she is associated.

Respect for the Sacred Emblems

Jīvanmuktas not only must associate with the Śaiva devotees but also must worship their sacred forms adorned with the sacred ashes and beads as Śiva Himself. *Jīvanmuktas* who have realized the Lord see Him everywhere.[102] But of all places in the world it is in His devotees that the Lord is most manifest. In order that souls in *saṃsāra* may know Him, the Lord, who is beyond all sensory perception, manifests Himself through His devotees. He makes them shine with His sacred emblems of ashes, beads, and so forth, so that where these emblems are found one can recognize Śiva himself.[103] "The Lord's presence is manifest in those who realize Him through love, like butter in curd, whereas in those under the fetters He is unmanifest."[104] Love for the devotees of Śiva is a sure sign of one's love for God, for "those who do not love the devotees of the Lord neither love God, nor any living being, nor even themselves."[105]

Worship of God in the Temple

As the Lord is manifest in his devotees he is also manifest in the *śivaliṅga* and in the other images in the temple. The *jīvanmukta* worships these images, looking upon them as Śiva Himself.[106] Worship is an act of thanksgiving to the Lord "who has done so much to reveal Himself and make the soul one with Him. To forget such a one cannot be considered a negligible fault."[107] Worship of the Lord and service of His devotees help the soul remove the *prārabdha-karma* and to grow constantly in knowledge and love of the Lord until final union in the disembodied form (*videhamukti*) is achieved.[108]

The experience of living liberation in Śaiva Siddhānta may be best expressed with the testimony of Appar who attained the state of liberation in this life through endless trials and hardships at the hands of his enemies. The experience he has is one of tremendous power, fearlessness, and bliss:

> We are subject to none, we don't fear even the god of death; we suffered infernal torments, we have nothing to boast; we won't be deceived, we know no illness, we bow to none; we are ever full of bliss, there is no suffering.[109]

Conclusion

The real contribution of Śaiva Siddhānta towards the ideal of *jīvanmukti* is the meaning and realism it brings into the life of liberated persons, drawn from the experience of Śaiva saints. The Śaiva Siddhānta view of *jīvanmukti* may at first appear to be inconsistent. For, if the bonds (*malas*) continue to exist and if there is the possibility of relapse, can such a state be called *jīvanmukti* at all? If the body is real and the person is still subject to *karma* and suffering, how can he or she be called a liberated person?

Śaiva Siddhānta philosophy developed through interaction with other Indian schools, both heterodox and orthodox, and was especially influenced by Advaita Vedānta. One of the problems with the *jīvanmukti* ideal in Advaita Vedānta is the problem of interaction with the world. How can this interaction be possible if the world and other persons become unreal for the *jīvanmukta* in the light of his experience of Brahman as the only reality? How can such persons even impart saving knowledge, which is the reason for their continued existence, if they do not see other persons as distinct from themselves?[110] This difficulty, however, is more theoretical than practical. For the *jīvanmuktas* we know of historically, like Śaṅkara and Buddha, were men of great practical ability, noted for their efficiency in instructing others, engaging in debate, and founding monasteries. The Śaiva Siddhānta ideal of *jīvanmukti* obviates even this theoretical difficulty. Here the realization of *jīvanmukti* does not do away with the world but makes it more significant as the expression of the infinite. In awareness of oneness with Śiva, the *jīvanmukta* is freed of egoism and attachment to things and becomes God's instrument in bringing his or her salvation to the world. The apparent antinomian behavior of some of the Śaiva saints who were considered to be *jīvanmuktas*, can be seen in the light of this Śiva consciousness.

Abbreviations

- *MŚ* — *Meyakaṇṭa Śāttiram (Śaiva Sittānta Śāttiram)* Patiṉaṅku, Mūlamum Uraiyum, 2 vols. Madras: South Indian Śaiva Siddhānta Publishing Society, 1969.
- *ŚB* — *Meykaṇṭatevar, Śivajñāna Bodham. MŚ* vol 1, no. 3.
- *ŚP* — Umāpati Śivācāryar, *Śivap Pirakāśam. MŚ* vol. 2, no. 3.
- *ŚSP* — Aruṇanti Śivācāryar, *Śivajñāna Siddhiyār, Parapakkam. MŚ* vol. 1, no. 4.
- *ŚSS* — Aruṇanti Śivācāryar, *Śivajñāna Siddhiyar, Supakkam. MŚ* vol. 1, no. 5.
- *TAP* — Umāpati Śivācāryar, *Tiruvaruṭpayaṉ. MŚ* vol. 2, no. 8.
- *TM* — Tirumūla Nāyaṉār, *Tirumantiram*, with notes by A. Cidambaranār. Madras: South Indian Śaiva Siddhānta Publishing Society, 1942.

TP *Śri Tayumāṉa Śvāmikaḷ Pāṭalkaḷ*. Tirupparāytturai: Rāmakrishna Tapōvaṉam, 1980.

TTM *Tiruttoṇḍar Mākkatai*, with notes by P. Rāmanāthapiḷḷai and A. Rāmasāmippulavar. Madras: South Indian Śaiva Siddhānta Publishing Society, 1970.

TV *Tiruvācagam or Sacred Utterances of the Tamil Poet, Saint and Sage Mānikka-vācagar*, the Tamil Text of the Fifty-One Poems with English Translation, introductions and notes by G.U. Pope. Oxford: Oxford University Press, 1900.

Notes

1. Pope, in introduction to *TV*, lxxiv.

2. See note 15 below and the translation of the quote in the text.

3. Guruśaraṇararuḷ purinta vākkum eṉpār
Kū ṭumanupavantāṉum ākamattē varu poruḷum.
Śivāgrayogin, *Śivaneṟiprakāśam*.

4. The names and authors of the fourteen philosophical works in Tamil with commentaries, published under the title *Meykaṇṭa Śāttiram (MŚ)*, are as follows:
1) Tiruviyalūr Uyyavanta Tēva Nāyaṉār, *Tiruvuntiyār*, vol. 1 no.1.
2) Tirukkatavur Uyyavanta Tēva Nāyaṉār, *Tirukkaḷiṟṟuppāṭiyār*, vol. 1 no. 2.
3) Meykaṇṭatēvar, *Śivajñānabodham* (*ŚB*), with the commentary of Śivajñānamuṉivar, vol. 1 no. 3.
4) Aruṇanti Śivācāryar, *Śivajñāna Siddhiyār, Parapakkam* (*ŚSP)* with the commentary of Tattuvappirakāśar, and *Supakkam (ŚSS*) with the commentary of Śivajñānaswāmikaḷ, vol. 1 nos. 4 & 5.
5) ______ *Irupāvirupatu*, vol. 2 no. 1.
6) Maṉavācakaṅkaṭantār, *Uṇmai Viḷakkam*, vol. 2 no. 3.
7) Umāpati Śivācāryar, *Śivappirakāśam* (*ŚP*) with the commentary of Madurai Śivappirakāśar, vol. 2 no. 3.
8) ______ *Tiruvaruṭpayan* (*TAP*), vol. 2 no. 4.
9) ______ *Viṉāveṇpā*, vol. 2 no. 5.
10) ______ *Poṟṟipahroṭai*, vol. 2 no. 6.
11) ______ *Koṭikkavi*, vol. 2 no. 7.
12) ______ *Neñcuviṭu Tūtu*, vol. 2 no. 8.
13) ______ *Uṇmai Neṟi Viḷakkam*, vol. 2 no. 9.
14) ______ *Caṅkarpa Nirākaraṇam*, vol. 2 no. 10.

5. Vedāntatteḷivām śaiva siddhāntam (*ŚP* 7).

6. Nīril eḻuttum nikaḻ kaṉavum pēyttērum (*ŚB* 6.1.1).

7. *Of Human Bondage and Divine Grace* (Annamalai: Annamalai University Press, 1963), p. 47.

8. Ulakelāmaki vēṟāi uṭanumāi (*ŚSS* 2.1).

9. Arumaṟaikal onṟennāt attuvitam eṉṟaṟaiyumāṅku (*ŚB* 2.1.3).

10. Āṇavattōd attuvitamāṉapaṭi meyjñānat-
Tāṇuvinōt attuvita mākunāḷennāḷo (*TP, Ennāṭkaṇṇi* 14.28).

11. Vēdānta-siddhānta samarasa naṉṉilai peṟṟa
Vittakacittar kaṇame (*TP, Siddharkanam* 3).

12. Ātalāl śīvaṉmuttar śivamē kaṇṭiruppar (*ŚSS* 11.4).

13. Terivaṟiya meyñāṉam cērntavāṟe
Śivam pirakāśikkum inkē śīvaṉmuttaṉākum (*ŚSS* 11.3).
See also note 57 below and its translation in the text.

14. A. Duraisamipillai, *Śivañānapōta Mūlamum Ciṟṟuraiyum* (Annamalai: Annamalai University, 1968) *passim*.

15. Poykaṇṭār kāṇāp puṉitama mattuvita
Meykaṇṭa nātaṉ (*TP, Ennāṭkaṇṇi* 4).

16. Śattaiyotta ivvuṭalait taḷḷumuṉṉe nāṉ sahaja
Niṭṭai peṟṟaiya niruvikarpaṅkāṇpēno
(*TP, Kāṇpēno Eṉ Kaṇṇi* 32).

17. Yām irappavai
Poruḷum poṉṉum pōkamum alla, ninpāl
Aruḷum aṉpum aṟanum muṉṟum. (*TP, Paripāṭal*).

18. Aruḷil peritu akilattu il (*TAP* 31).

19. For a more detailed account of the anguish of the soul in bondage and her intense longing for liberation, see Chacko Valiaveetil, *Liberated Life, Ideal of Jīvanmukti in Indian Religions Specially in Śaiva Siddhānta* (Madurai: Arul Anandar College, 1980), 95–100.

20. Oḷikkuñ cōraṉaik kaṇḍanam (*TV* 3.141).

21. Urutteriyāk kalatte uḷpukuntu (*TV* 4.87).

22. Pāninaintūṭṭum tāyinum śālapparintu (*TV* 4.87).

23. For more details about the saving actions of the Lord and his revelation as *guru,* see Valiaveetil: 1980, 106–7 (Note 19).

24. See *Irupāvirupatu* 19, *MŚ* vol. 2 no. 1.

25. Panniṟam kāṭṭum paṭikam pōl (*TV* 4.87).

26. Ñāṉattāl vīṭu (*ŚSS* 8.12).

27. Kātaliṉāṉ nāṉ piramam eṉṉum ñāṉam (*ŚSS* 9.2).

28. Iṟai aruḷ ñānam (*ŚP* 84).

29. Iṟaivaṉaḍi ñāṉame ñāṉam (*ŚSS* 8.27).

30. Aṉpu nilayē atu (*TAP* 10).

31. For the progressive growth of the soul in knowledge and love through the four stages (*caryā, kriya, yoga*, and *jñāna*) and the ten acts (*daśakārya*) see Valiaveetil: 1980, 110–15 (Note 19).

32. Some Siddhānta scholars place *jīvanmukti* after the vision of the divine *guru* (*sadguru darśana*), which follows the ripening of the *malas*, and before the descent of divine grace. See J.M. Nallaswami Pillai, tr., *Śivañana Potam* (Madras, 1895), 6, 94.

33. See below, notes 45 and 46, and their explanation in the texts.

34. Araṉ kaḻal cellumē (*ŚB* 8). Aruṇanti in *ŚSS* 8.29–35 deals with the characteristics of the *jīvanmukta*.

35. To interpret the last *sūtra* as dealing not with the liberated person, but with a lower type of *sādhaka*, as some commentators do, is to go against the *Śaiva Siddānta* tradition and do violence to its spirituality.

36. Maṉṉum irulai mati turantavāṟaṉpiṉ
Maṉṉum araṉe malam turantu (*ŚB* 11.2.2).

37. Ēkanāki iṟaipaṇi nirka
Malam māyai taṉṉoṭu valviṉai iṉṟē (*ŚB* 10).

38. Yāṉ eṉatu eṉṉum śerukku (*ŚB* 10.1).

39. Nāṉ eṉa oṉṟu illeṉṟu tānē eṉum (*ŚB* 10).

40. See Umāpati Śivācāryar's *Viṉāveṇpa* 11, in *MŚ* vol. 2, no. 9.

41. See notes 69 and 70 below, with corresponding explanation in the text.

42. Iṟaipaṇi niṟṟal (*ŚB* 10.2).

43. Pāśattaip paśukkaḷ viṭṭup patiyiṉai aṭaiya mutti (*ŚSP* 295).

44. Kāyam uṇṭēl iruṅkaṉmam māyaimalam ellam uṇḍām (*ŚSS* 11.3).

45. Kāyam tiriyumaḷavum uḷatāy (*ŚSS* 11.4).

46. Avaṉaruḷāl allatu oṉṟaiyuñ ceyānākavē ajñāna kaṉmam piraveśiya ākalāṉ (*ŚB* 10.2).

47. Ettaṉuvi niṉṟu miṟaipaṇiyārkillai viṉai (*ŚB* 10.2.1).

48. Ellayil piravi nalkum iruviṉai ericēr vittiṉ
Ollayiṉ akalum ēṉṟa uṭaṟpaḻa viṉaiyatūṭṭum

Tollayil varutal pōlat tōṉṟiru viṉaiyatuṇṭēl
Alloḷi puraiyum ñāṉat taḻaluṟu aḻintupōme (*ŚP* 89).

49. Eṉṉutaiya ceyalellām uṉṉutaya ceyalē yeṉṟu ni uṉṉutaiya iṭatte niṉṟu ceyvikkiṟāy ceykiṉṟāy eṉṟu tan paṇi aṟukka. Commenting on *ŚB* 10.2.2. as quoted in A. Duraisamipillai: 1968, 318 (See Note 14.)

50. Araṉ kaḻal cellutal (*ŚB* 8, 11).

51. Āṉā aṟivay akalāṉ (*TAP* 7).

52. Ūmaṉ kaṇ pōla oḷiyum mikaviruḷēyām maṉ kānātavai (*TAP* 19).

53. Mutaleḻuttuk kellāmāy niṟkum avvuyir pōl niṉṟiḍuvaṉ (*ŚSS* 11.7).

54. Paśukaraṇaṅkaḷ śivakaraṇam āka (*ŚSS* 8.34).

55. Śivānupavam suvānupūtikamām (*ŚSS* 8.34).

56. Taṉakku niḻaliṉṟam oli kavarum tampam
Eṉakkavara nillātiruḷ (*TAP* 67).

57. Ñānam viḷaintōr . . . pūtalattir pukaḻ śīvaṉmuttarākittakka piriyāppiriyamiṉṟi ōṭṭil tapaṉiyattil samaputti paṇṇi . . . śivaṉ toṟṟam oṉṟumē kāṅpar (*ŚSS* 8.29).

58. Anpē śivam (*TM* 257).

59. Aruṭ kaṇṇal pāśattai nīkkum . . . nēśattil taṉṉuṇarntār nēr (*ŚB* 11.2.1).

60. Tantatuṉ taṉṉaik koṉṭateṉ taṉṉais Śaṅkarāyārkolo śāturar? Antamoṉṟillā ānantam peṟṟen, yātu ni peṟṟatoṉṟenpāl? (*TV* 22.10).

61. Aṉpu nilaiyē atu (*TAP* 80).

62. Mālaṟa nēyam malintavar (*ŚB* 12).

63. Anpē śivam āvatarum arinta piṉ
Aṉpe śivamāy amarntiruppāre (*TM* 257).

64. Parāvu śivar (*ŚSS* 8.35).

65. Eṉ uḷḷam kavar kaḷvaṉ. *Tevaram* 1.1 in Tēvārappatikaṅkaḷ (Aṟantirumuṟai) (Madras: Āṟumukavilāca Accukūṭam, 1898).

66. Tāṭalai pōr kūdiyavai tānikaḻā veṟṟiṉpakkūḍalai nī ēkameṉakkoḷ (*TAP* 74).

67. Onrākāmal iraṇṭākāmal, oṉṟumiraṇḍum iṉṟākāmal. Aruṇanti Śivācāryar in *Irupāvirupatu* 20, *MŚ* vol. 2 no. 1.

68. Iṉpē aruḷi eṉai urukki uyiruṇkiṉṟa emmāṉe (*TV* 44.3).

69. Yāṉ eṉatu eṉṉurai māyttu (*TV* 31.5).

70. Muṉṉavaṉē tāṉe tāṉācceytum taivam eṉṟum taivamē (*ŚB* 12.4.3).

71. Uriyēn allēn unakkaṭimai
Unnaip pirintiṅk oru poḻutum tariyēn (*TV* 44.2).

72. Iṅkuli vāṅkum kalam pōla (*ŚB* 10.2.3).

73. Nīrpāśi pōl nīṇku mala kaṉmam (*ŚB* 8.4.1).
Āśupatum malamāyai yaruṅkanmam aṉaittum
Araṉaṭiyai yuṇarumpōtakalum piṉ aṇukum (*ŚSS* 11.39).

74. Eri katiriṉ muṉ iruḷ pol (*ŚB* 10.2.5).

75. Ñānam viṉai tīriṉ aṉṟi viḷaiyā (*ŚB* 12.4.3).

76. Ellā malaṅkaḷum piṉ kāyamoṭu māyumaṉṟe (*ŚSS* 10.6).

77. Jñānāgni sarva karmāṇi bhasmasāt kurute (*Bhagavad Gītā* 4.37).

78. *The Vedānta Sūtras with the commentary by Rāmānuja*, tr. George Thibaut, *Sacred Books of the East*, vol. 48 (Delhi: Motilal Banarsidass, 1966) 186.

79. Naṇṇaṉal vēvata naṟṟavar tammiṉum
Paṇṇamara māceluttum pākariṉum—eṇṇi
Araṉaṭi yōrpava raimpulanir ceṉṟum
Avartiṟa nīṅkāratarku (*ŚB* 10.2.4).
See also *ŚSS* 10.6. For a more detailed discussion of the problem of the persistence of the body of the *jīvanmukta*, see Valiaveetil: 1980, 155–61.

80. See *ŚB* 9.2.3.

81. Paṇṭai maṟaikaḷum atu nāṉāṉēṉeṉṟu
Pavikkaccolluvatip pāvakattaik kāṇe (*ŚSS* 9.7).

82. Kaṉal cēr irumpeṉṉa (*ŚB* 9.3.2).

83. *ŚB* 9.3.3. See also *ŚSS* 9.9.

84. See K. Śivarāman, *Śaivism in Philosophical Perspective* (Varanasi: Motilal Banarsidass, 1973) 404.

85. Pēy oṉṟum taṉmai pirakkumaḷavumiṉi
Ni oṉṟum ceyyātu nil (*TAP* 77).

86. Oṇporuṭkan uṟṟārk kurupayaṉē yallātu
Kaṇpaṭuppōr kaiporuḷ pōr kāṇ (*TAP* 78).

87. Pēypōrriruntu piṇampōr kiṭant itta piccaiyellām
Nāypōlarunti naripōlulaṉṟu naṉmankaiyarait-
tāypōl niṉaintu tamar pōl aṉaivarkkun tāḻmai colli
Cēypol iruppar kaṇṭīr uṇmai ñāṉam teḷintavare (*TP*).

88. Paṭi muḻutum viṇ muḻutum tantālum kaḷiyā (*TP*).

89. Kaḷḷattalaivar tuyarkarutit taṉkaruṇai veḷḷattalaivar mika (*TAP* 100).

90. Tūya veṇṇīru tutainta poṉmēṉiyum tāḻvatamum
nāyakaṉ cēvaṭi taivaruñ cintayu nainturukip-

pāyvatu pōlaṉpu nīr poḻi kaṇṇum paṭikacceñcol
mēya cevvāyu muṭaiyar pukuntaṉar vītiyuḷḷe.
(Tirunāvukkaraśu Nāyaṉār Purāṇam 140 in *TTM* p. 268).

91. Pārvaiyeṉa mākkaḷaimun paṟṟippiḍittaṟkām
Porvaiyeṉak kāṉār puvi (*TAP* 45).

92. Taṉ kaṭaṉ aṭiyèṉaiyum tāṅkutal
Eṉ kaṭan paṇiśeytu kiṭappatē (*Tēvāram* 5.19.9. See note 65.)

93. Nān peṟṟa iṉpam peṟuka ivvaiyakam (*TM* 147).

94. Ñālamatin ñāṉanittai yuṭaiyōrukku
Naṉmaiyoṭu tīmayilai nāḍuvatoṉṟillai
Śīlamilai tavamilai viratamōṭacciramac-
Ceyalillai tiyānamilai cittamalam illai . . . .

Pālaruṭan uṉmattar piśācar kuṇam maruvip-
Pāṭalinōḍātalivai payiṉṟiḍilum payilvar . . . .

Māsataṉil tūymaiyiṉiṉ vaṟumai vāḻviṉ
Varuttatil tiruttattiṉ maituṉattiṟ śinattiṉ
Āśayiṉiṉ veṟuppiṉ ivai yallātum ellām
Aṭaintālum ñāṉikaḷtām araṉaṭiyai akalār (*ŚSS* 8.32–3).

95. Ivaṉ ulakil itamakitam ceyta ellām
Itam akitam ivaṉukkuc ceytārpāl iśaiyum . . .
Pātakattaic ceytiṭiṉum paṇiyākki viṭume (*ŚSS* 10.1).

96. See *Uṇmaineṟi Viḷakkam* 8, *MŚ* vol. 2 no. 9.

97. Araṉaṭikkaṉpar śeyyum pāvamum aramatākum
Paraṉaṭikkaṉpilātār puṇṇiyam pāvamākum (*ŚSS* 2.9).

98. Śivañāṉacceyti yuṭaiyōr (*ŚSS* 12.1).

99. Allātār aññāṉattai uṇarttuvar ākalāṉ (*ŚB* 12.2).

100. *ŚB Siṟṟurai* 12.2. For the dangers of association with non-devotees, see *TV* 42.53.

101. Pittu pattar iṉattāy (*ŚB* 12.2.1).

102. Śīvaṉmuttar śivamē kaṇṭiruppar (*ŚSS* 12.1).

103. Tiruvēṭam śivaṉuruvē yākum (*ŚSS* 12.3).

104. Taṉ uṇarum nēśattār tampāl tatineypōl nikaḻum . . . pāśattārkku iṉṟam pati (*ŚB* 12.3.1).

105. Īśanukkaṉpillār aṭiyavarkkaṉpillār
Evvuyirkkum aṉpillār tamakkum aṉpillār (*ŚSS* 12.2).

106. Ālayam tāṉum araṉ eṉat toḻumē (*ŚB* 12).

107. Taṉṉai aṟivittu taṉ tānāic ceytānaip piṉṉai maṟattal piḻaiyalatu (*ŚB* 12.4.3).

108. For a fuller treatment of the norms to be followed by the *jīvanmukta* see Valiaveetil: 1980, 143–52. See Note 19.

109. Nāmārkkum kutiyallōm namanaiyañcōm
Narakattil itarpaṭṭom naṭalaiyillōm
Ēmāppōm piṇiyaṟivōm paṇivōmallōm
Iṉpamē ennāḷum tuṉpamillai (*Tēvāram* 6.98.1).

110. For a discussion of this problem of *jīvanmukti* and social concern, see Valiaveetil: 1980, 162–72. See Note 19.

CHAPTER 9

Conclusion: Living Liberation in Comparative Perspective

Patricia Y. Mumme

Jīvanmukti: The Concept and the Term

The chapters in this book demonstrate how living liberation gradually became a recognized subject for discussion and debate both within and between Indian philosophical schools during the medieval era. The roots of the concept, of course, are found in germ form in several passages in the Upaniṣads. It is likely that the Buddhists were the first to clearly articulate that release from *karma* could be attained in a living state they called *nirvāṇa*, and this helped inspire development of a parallel concept in Hindu circles. Influence of both the Upaniṣads and Buddhism may be seen in the *Bhagavad Gītā's* discussion of the sage endowed with firm wisdom (*sthita-prajña*). The *Brahma Sūtra* contributed the notion of *karma* which has already begun manifesting (*prārabdha-karma*), and the *Sāṃkhya Kārikā* (ca. C.E. 400) proposed the seminal analogy of the potter's wheel to help explain continued embodiment among the enlightened. The Itihāsa-purāṇa explored various images of the ideal, realized sage. But the Advaita Vedānta school seems to have begun the scholastic discussion of living liberation by inaugurating use of the term *jīvanmukti* around the time of Śaṅkara and Maṇḍana Miśra. Soon other Vedānta schools, such as Viśiṣṭādvaita and Dvaita, picked up the notion of *jīvanmukti* as a point of debate. Meanwhile, the *Yogavasiṣṭha*, a syncretistic philosophical work of the eleventh century, celebrated and help to popularize the concept of *jīvanmukti*. By about the seventeenth century, it seems the term had gained sufficient currency that nearly every school of thought within the Hindu fold had something to say about *jīvanmukti*, and whether to accept it or reject it.

However, the preceding chapters also show that to classify Indian authors or schools simply by whether or not they accept or reject use of the term *jīvanmukti* is potentially misleading. There is a wide discrepancy in what the various schools and authors mean by *jīvanmukti*, whether or not they allow this term to designate the highest living soteriological stage they each recognize. As Daniel Sheridan suggests, the term *jīvanmukti* was at first so identified with Advaita Vedāntin metaphysics and soteriology that accepting or rejecting the term had much more to do with how a school viewed Advaita than with any profound similarity or difference in their respective views of liberated living. Thus we end up with a school like Śaiva Siddhānta that in its early literature (thirteenth century) employs the term *jīvanmukti* (along with other philosophical terms with Advaita connotations, including the term *advaita* itself) to describe a state that is little different from the highest state recognized by Madhva's and Rāmānuja's schools. Both of these authors recoil from using the term and argue forcefully against Advaitins regarding the legitimacy of the concept of *jīvanmukti*. By the sixteenth century, however, even a member of Madhva's school can see a parallel between its view of the post-*aparokṣa-jñāna* state of the devotee and *jīvanmukti*. During this late medieval era the growing influence of Advaita inspires authors and commentators of a syncretistic bent to try to integrate Advaita, Sāṃkhya, Yoga, and even devotional soteriologies; for such authors, *jīvanmukti* figures in this process both as a term to use and a concept to define and integrate into their own philosophical systems.

Because of the danger of equivocation, the editors and contributors to this volume find it far better to ask of Hindu authors and schools a more subtle set of questions than the yes-or-no question, "Is there such a state as *jīvanmukti*?" Rather, we explore questions such as: What is the nature of the ultimate embodied state an individual can reach? What is the conscious experience of one in such a state? What is the status of such a person's *karma*? (That is, what *karma* or karmic influences, remnants, or effects remain operative, and which have been eliminated?) What are the defining or at least dominant characteristics (psychological, ontological, behavioral, and so forth) of a person in such a state? By which, if any, of these characteristics could such an individual be recognized, and by whom? To what extent is this state clearly differentiated from the states or stages leading up to it? And to what extent does the final embodied state approximate the ultimate post-embodiment state of liberation?

Strong, Medium, and Weak Positions on Living Liberation

To get a conceptual handle on the various positions taken by the authors and schools represented in this volume, it may be helpful to classify them into three loose categories, differentiated by the strength of their views about living liberation. Those with a strong position recognize living liberation as a discrete state, clearly defined and characterized. The difference between this highest living state and previous states is emphasized by pointing to a threshold experience or event that inaugurates it: knowledge of Brahman, sudden insight into the Self, and/or the disappearance of major forms of *karma*. At the same time, the equivalence of this state with post-death liberation is also asserted by using the terms *mukti/mukta, kaivalya/kevalin* or the like to apply to both states.

In those views with a medium-strength position, the final living state is also valorized as a kind of liberation by using the term *jīvanmukti* or its equivalent, but one or more of the following "weakening" factors will be admitted. This state of living liberation may not be so clearly defined as to discretely differentiate it from prior states. The term *jīvanmukti* may be applied to a series of several higher states in the soteriological process which are variously characterized, thus diffusing the distinctiveness of living liberation. There may be no threshold experience to clearly demarcate when the *jīvanmukti* state is reached. Though use of the term *mukti* for this state (or these states) may imply continuity between the living and the post-death states, there may be a mitigating emphasis on the change in the adept's experience at the point of death. Often these schools or authors imply or insist that yogic practices, worship, or other techniques need to be practiced in this final state (or states), thus showing significant continuity between this state and the practices of the soteriological path (*sādhana)* leading up to it.

Those authors and schools holding a weak position on living liberation explicitly deny that the term liberation (*mukti)* can legitimately be applied to the highest attainable living state. This is no mere terminological quibble, for their rejection of the term follows from their doctrinal insistence that this state is discontinuous with and not at all equivalent to the post-death state of liberation. Among these schools, the final living state of the highest adept may not be defined or clearly described at all; even if it is, this state's continuity in terms of practice, consciousness, and/or karmic status with the previous states leading up to it will be emphasized far more than its discontinuity. However, these authors and schools may still admit the real or theoretical possibility that a state of assurance of freedom from future embodiment can be reached in this life. But they do not find this to be sufficient grounds to designate the highest living state as true liberation (*mukti*).

Two Hindu schools described in this volume have a strong view of *jīvanmukti* based on these criteria: Śaṅkara and some of his mainstream Advaitin followers, and the Sāṃkhya school, especially as interpreted in later Vedānta-influenced commentaries. These schools seem to have been the first to recognize living liberation as a discrete state and to clearly define and characterize it as such. The use of the term *jīvanmukti* may postdate, but fits naturally with, their descriptions of the highest living state. This state is clearly demarcated from prior states by a specific "threshold experience" of enlightening, liberating knowledge that inagurates it—knowledge of Brahman for Advaita and insight into the Self for Sāṃkhya. Use of the term *jīvanmukti* shows their emphasis on this state's difference from previous states, and its equivalence to post-death liberation. In both schools, various analogies and explanations—those of the potter's wheel, the two moons, the loosed arrow, the lingering smell of flowers or garlic, the *prārabdha-karma* theory, and so forth—are marshalled to clarify how the body can persist in liberation and/or how a liberative state of mind can exist for one who is embodied. Whatever philosophical differences there may be among the authors who employ these analogies, their chief aim is to make the existence of this state and its virtual equivalence to post-death liberation understandable and intellectually defensible within the metaphysical and logical framework of their respective schools of thought.

The Itihāsa-Purāna excerpts that Brown considers in his chapter exploring the figure of Śuka generally do not address enough of the criteria listed above to make a definitive judgment of the strength of their position on *jīvanmukti*. However, Brown thinks that the *Devī-Bhāgavata Purāṇa* would qualify as having a strong position, since it recognizes realization of the oneness (*aikyam*) of Devī and the soul (*jīva*) as a threshold event inaugurating the state of *jīvanmukti*.

Even though it is not a Hindu school by the definition used in this volume, including Jainism in this analysis yields interesting comparative insights. Christopher Chapple's treatment suggests that Jainism would also qualify as having a strong position on living liberation by the above criteria. The characteristics of the thirteenth *guṇasthāna*, the enlightened state of the *kevalin,* are explicitly defined and distinguished from previous states. Entry into this state is marked by two simultaneous events forming a kind of threshold experience: the eradication of all destructive *karmas* and the advent of omniscient knowledge. Though non-destructive *karmas* remain to keep the body alive, the crucial characteristic of liberation—omniscience—is as fully present for the adept in this stage as for the dead and finally liberated saint or *jina*. Use of the term *sayoga-kevalin,* "the *kevalin* with a body," to describe the adept in the thirteenth *guṇasthāna* makes clear that state's equivalence with the post-death liberation termed *ayoga-kevalin*. Thus the Jaina *sayoga-kevalin*, no less than the Advaitin *jīvanmukta*, is characterized as (1) having the same knowledge found in the post-death state of liberation; (2) being free from all *karma* that would necessitate subsequent rebirth and/or cloud his/her experience of supreme knowledge for the remainder of this life; and (3) possessing only the barest remnant of *karma* necessary in order to explain continued embodiment rationally.

Madhva and Rāmānuja, along with their followers in the Dvaita and Viśiṣṭādvaita traditions, clearly articulate views consistent with what I call the weak position on living liberation. Both vehemently deny the legitimacy of the term *jīvanmukti,* due in part to its connection with Advaita's understanding of Brahman's highest nature as devoid of qualities (*nirguṇa*) and its soteriology based on knowledge alone, both of which they reject. But their rejection of the term *jīvanmukti* is also symptomatic of their strong doctrinal objections to equating the highest state attainable while living with the post-death state. Unlike Sāṃkhya and Advaita, the metaphysics of both Dvaita and Viśiṣṭādvaita see karmic bondage as a real state; that is, they claim bondage effects an actual limitation on the experience of the Self which cannot be fully counteracted by knowledge alone. Both claim that embodiment, *karma* in any form, and connection with material reality (*prakṛti*) inevitably hinder one's ability to see, know, experience, and worship Viṣṇu in this world, though all such limitations will be removed at one's last death. Hence they emphasize the sharp break in the experience of the devotee which is brought about by cessation of one's final embodied state. Nevertheless, both these schools, no less than the mainstream Advaitins, do theoretically agree that there is an ultimate living state characterized by the destruction of all *karma* except that which is currently manifesting (*prārabdha-karma*). At the same time, they insist that activities of worship mandated by scripture as part of the path (*sādhana*) to liberation must continue even in this highest living state; this shows significant continuity between this state and and prior states on the path to liberation. To underscore further this continuity, neither school seems to utilize a single, convenient term to designate the individual in the highest soteriological state achievable while still embodied. However, Madhva's Dvaita school comes close to doing so, by defining *aparokṣa-jñāna* as a kind of threshold experience to a highest living state. This is further attested by Vyāsatīrtha's recognition of the similarity between one who has achieved *aparokṣa-jñāna* and the Advaita *jīvanmukta*.[1]

The remaining schools and authors represented in this volume fall into the medium-strength category in their view of living liberation. Unlike the weak-position Dvaitins and Viśiṣṭādvaitins, all use the term *jīvanmukti*; but unlike the strong-position Sāṃkhyin and Advaitin authors, they do not seem to have defined this state with such precision as to clearly distinguish the *jīvanmukta* from adepts who have not yet reached the highest possible stage on the spiritual path to liberation. Śaiva Siddhānta, with perhaps the weakest position among these, uses the terms *jīvanmukti/jīvanmukta* the most loosely, applying them to ideal devotees, worthy of emulation, who manifest more intensely the same characteristics of detachment and devotion that all seekers of liberation should and must have. No clearly identifiable characteristics or crucial "threshold experience" sets the *jīvanmukta* apart from the other devotees in Śaiva Siddhānta. As Valiaveetil presents it, the soteriological path is a seamless continuum of the practice of devotion and worship, marked by increasing detachment from the world and consciousness of Śiva, progressive infusion of Śiva's grace, and gradual eradication of the three impurities (*malas*). In fact, were it not for their use of the term *jīvanmukti,* implying some sense of equivalence between the state of the ideal devotee and post-death liberation, Śaiva Siddhānta would be placed in the weak-position category. It could be argued that their clear emphasis on the continuity between the *jīvanmukta* and the seeker (*sādhaka*) in prior states would make the Śaiva Siddhānta position perhaps even weaker than that of the Dvaita school, which at least sees *aparokṣa-jñāna* as a kind of threshold experience setting apart a final state.

The Kashmiri Śaivas are more punctilious in defining a precise series of states leading up to liberation. But according to Muller-Ortega, they freely use the term *jīvanmukta* to apply to an adept in any of the last four of the seven soteriological states (*mantra, mantreśvara, mantra-maheśvara,* and *śiva*) though apparently more emphatically to the latter. In this way they, too, end up giving comparable emphasis to both the discontinuity and continuity of the *jīvanmukti* state with the *sādhana* preceding it and the final liberation that follows.

I would argue that the Yoga school, and Yoga-influenced thinkers such as the Advaitin Vidyāraṇya, also fall short of the strong position seen in Sāṃkhya and mainstream Advaita, but for different reasons than seen in the Śaiva schools. Vyāsa's early commentary on the *Yoga Sūtras* seems to suggest that Yogic practices should continue even after the initial experience of liberating knowledge achieved in a state of meditative enstasis (*samādhi*). These must be done to eradicate the roots of manifesting *karma* and/or nullify its psychological effects which can disturb the adept's experience of detached bliss. As Lance Nelson shows, some later Advaitins echoed a similar view (Prakāśātman, Citśukha, Bhāratītīrtha). However, this may not necessarily prove influence from the Yoga school, since Śaṅkara himself seems to have at least admitted the possibility of a need for post-enlightenment yogic practices in his enigmatic comment on *Bṛhadāraṇyaka Upaniṣad* 1.4.7. A clearer and more systematic importation of yogic ideas such as this is seen in the "Yogic Advaitin," Vidyāraṇya. Though all these authors use the term *jīvanmukti,* they show reluctance to apply it to an adept who has merely passed the threshold experience of liberating knowledge, when all but currently manifesting (*prārabdha*) *karma* disappears. Some claim that the state of perfect peace and bliss rightfully called *mukti* is truly found only in a meditative state of *samādhi*, and/or suggest that this state can be disturbed by the onslaught of karmic tendencies that remain operative during the waking state. Therefore, they argue that the term *jīvanmukti* more properly applies only at some point subsequent to the arising of liberating knowledge, whereupon the machinery of manifesting *karma* (such as karmic tendencies or *vāsanās*, the impressions or remnants of ignorance) are either eradicated or their effects nullified (their "seeds fried") through further practice. Some seem to claim that even for the *jīvanmukta* who has attained full knowledge, such practices must continue throughout his or her life.

In these ways, some authors separate liberating knowledge from the state of the *jīvanmukta* and insert the need for yogic practices and disciplines in between these two states; others recommend such practices for the *jīvanmukta* to safeguard or maintain his or her status for the rest of life. Either way, these authors end up blurring the discrete character of the state of living liberation and/or its equivalence to the state achieved after disembodiment. For this reason, their views can and ought to be distinguished from those holding the strong position on living liberation.

I would submit that this way of analyzing the various views of living liberation presented in this volume renders a certain degree of conceptual clarity to the issue with minimal distortion. However, like all definitions and categorization systems, this one is contrived, and others may be illuminative in other ways. For instance, two authors considered in this volume, Vidyāraṇya of the (Yogic) Advaitin school and Vyāsatīrtha of Madhva's tradition, independently suggest a broad definition of liberation according to which virtually every school of Indian thought would qualify as teaching living liberation (*jīvanmukti*). As Andrew Fort notes, Vidyāraṇya suggests that living adepts in the highest state have in a sense already achieved disembodied liberation (*videhamukti*), since they are free from future embodiment. Sheridan notes that Vyāsatīrtha suggests that the devotees who have achieved immediate vision of the Lord (*aparokṣa-jñāna*) are in a sense *jīvanmuktas*, since their ultimate liberation is assured at the exhaustion of their currently manifesting *karma*. This definition of liberation as "assurance of freedom from future embodiment" did not catch on in the scholastic debate over *jīvanmukti*, for virtually all schools continued to make a distinction between such a state of assuredness of future liberation and liberation (*mukti*) itself. We might compare, for example, the Buddhist distinction between the non-returner, who will achieve Nirvāṇa after death on a spiritual plane without needing to take another body, and the *arhat* who has achieved Nirvāṇa in this body. The former would generally not be called "enlightened" or be deemed as having "attained Nirvāṇa."

Jīvanmukti and Scholastic Metaphysics

It is striking that the strength of a school or author's doctrine of liberation, by the criteria specified above, has little or no correlation with its ontology or metaphysics, at least not as characterized by the common classifications, such as non-dualism, dualism, and pluralism. In the strong-position camp we find Advaita's non-dualism and Sāṃkhya's dualism. In the medium-position camp we find the extreme non-dualism of Kashmir Śaivism, the Yoga school which shares Sāṃkhya's dualism, and the theistic pluralism of Śaiva Siddhānta. In the weak position we find two theistic Vedāntins, representing qualified non-dualism (Rāmānuja's Viśiṣṭādvaita) and pluralism (Madhva's misnamed Dvaita Vedānta). A particular school's view of the reality of the world, and the number of realities its contents reduce to, thus seem to have little correlation with the strength of its *jīvanmukti* doctrine.

However, as Kim Skoog suggests, a somewhat stronger correlation between metaphysics and strength of *jīvanmukti* arises by asking whether the school or author in question sees karmic bondage as apparent or real. For those who see bondage as an illusion due to ignorance, and thus correctable merely by knowledge of the true nature of the Self, it is relatively easy to admit a discrete state of *jīvanmukti* as resulting from a threshold experience in which that knowledge is attained. That, in fact, is the case in both Sāṃkhya and Advaita, the strong-position schools, though the former's dualism versus the latter's non-dualism renders their views of the content of liberating knowledge quite different. Both would nevertheless agree, as Lance Nelson puts it, that the true Self is always ontologically free; the dawn of knowledge allows that ontological reality to become an experiential one. On the other hand, there are schools that see the bondage of *karma* as real, meaning that it affects the Self in a substantive way; they tend to claim that some sort of profound self-transformation beyond dispelling of ignorance is necessary to bring about full liberation. In such schools, *mukti* may be relegated to a post-death state, when all forms of *karma* binding the Self are banished. Indeed, this is the case with the schools of Madhva and Rāmānuja, representing the two weak-position cases.

However, Jainism is a glaring anomaly for this otherwise very logical and plausible theory that realistic views of bondage correlate with weak views of *jīvanmukti*. Certainly the Jainas have an extremely realistic view of bondage, for they claim *karma* really and actually pollutes and weighs down the self or *jīva*; yet Jainism—as shown above—would qualify as having a strong position on *jīvanmukti*. This is partly explainable by noting, as Chapple does, that the type of self-knowledge parallel to Sāṃkhya and Advaita's liberating knowledge occurs in Jainism in the fourth *guṇasthāna;* such knowledge is not itself seen as liberating in Jainism. Rather, it marks the first step on the long and painful journey to actually eradicating the very real *karma* that binds and blinds the soul's omniscient freedom, which is finally accomplished only in the thirteenth and fourteenth *guṇasthānas*.

Among the medium-position schools, we find others who take karmic bondage as real. Śaiva Siddhānta, with a clearly realistic view of bondage in its theory of the three impurities or *malas,* nevertheless uses the term *jīvanmukti* to describe saints who are still subject to some extent to the *mala*s. However, Śaiva Siddhanta emphasizes the saint's psychological freedom and detachment as opposed to his still real, though attenuating, bondage. In spite of sharing the same metaphysics as Sāṃkhya, Yoga takes bondage much more seriously, admitting that even after the arising of knowledge, psychological transformation through discipline is necessary before true freedom can be continuously experienced. A Yoga-influenced author such as Vidyāraṇya, despite his non-dualistic metaphysics, takes the same stance, as do several later Advaitins, according to Lance Nelson.

The Lord and Liberation

A particular author or school's view of the Lord (Īśvara), the personal supreme deity, seems to have a slight correlation with the strength of its view of living liberation. Here, the non-theistic schools, Sāṃkhya and Jainism, both have strong positions. So does Advaita Vedānta, in whose view the personal Lord or Íṣvara, the qualified (*saguṇa*) Brahman, is less than fully real in comparison to the impersonal, unqualified (*nirguṇa*) Brahman, the sole ultimate reality. The two weak-position schools, those of Madhva and Rāmānuja, are fiercely theistic; but Kashmir Śaivism and Śaiva Siddhānta are no less theistic, though found in the medium-position category. Yoga, another medium-position school, has perhaps the most idiosyncratic view of Īśvara, acknowledging the usefulness of devoted meditation on the Lord, but denying that this Lord is the kind of supreme being described in the Vaiṣṇava, Śaiva, or even Advaita philosophies.

Those schools which do accept the existence and significance of Īśvara have a variety of ways of conceiving the Lord's role in and relation to (1) the state of ultimate liberation, (2) the state of living liberation, and (3) the path leading up to liberation. For those whose view of final liberation is an isolation *(kaivalya)* that transcends the personal Lord, meditation on and/or worship of Īśvara may be useful only in the preparatory stages of the path to salvation. This would apply to both Advaita and Yoga, where worship of and relation to the Lord is transcended and supposedly forgotten in the state of living and post-death liberation. However, in a philosophical sense, Yoga self-consciously uses Īśvara as a model for conceiving both living and post-death liberation, for the adept is trying to gain the state that Īśvara, the great Puruṣa, never lost—freedom from afflicted action. Lance Nelson suggests that Advaita Vedānta could profitably use Īśvara, and/or his incarnations such as Kṛṣṇa, as an analogical model for conceiving living liberation (but not post-death liberation), though Advaitin thinkers do not seem to have done so in any systematic way. In the Advaita system, both the *jīvanmukta* and an incarnation of Īśvara, such as Kṛṣṇa, are to some extent limited and constrained by the results of manifesting *karma*—that of others, if not their own. At least, both seem "as if" they are so limited, though their consciousness transcends or sees through this appearance.

The remaining devotional schools, Śaiva and Vaiṣṇava, all emphasize the central place of devotion to the Lord and reception of His grace in the path to salvation. Self-knowledge without devotion to the Lord, they would claim, is incomplete and ineffective. However, they have various ways of conceiving the Lord's relation to the liberated being, living or dead. For Kashmir Śaivism, liberation living and dead means a state of both ontological and psychological identity with Śiva. But for Śaiva Siddhānta, such union is only psychological or experiential, for ontologically the soul and Lord remain distinct, in a state of inexplicable "not-two-ness" and "not-one-ness." For the Vaiṣṇava schools, the soul's relationship to Viṣṇu in the state of post-death liberation (there being no true living liberation) is conceived anthropomorphically as a heaven where the freed souls, distinctly separate from the Lord in their respective non-material heavenly bodies, render loving worship and service much as in earthly temples. However, the heavenly state of service to and communion with the Lord experienced by freed souls is without the *saṃsāric* limitations of restricted knowledge and intractable physical bodies which are inevitably present to some extent in the experience of even the most adept living saint.

Karma and Conscious Experience in the Penultimate State

Nearly every school that has accepted a concept of living liberation has had to explain why the body continues to persist after the causes of *karma* and ignorance that produced it have been dispelled. Lance Nelson points out that the Buddhists speak of the *arhat's* continued embodied state as Nirvāṇa with residual conditions (*saupādisesa-nibbāna*); the Jains refer to the enlightened *jina* as a *kevalin* with a body (*sayoga-kevalin)* in whom a bare minimum of non-destructive *karma*s required to maintain the body are still operative. Among Hindu schools, the early Sāṃkhya and Yoga traditions, as well as the Advaitin Maṇḍana Miśra, seem to have developed their explanations for the *jīvanmukta*'s continued embodiment in terms of impressions (*saṃskāras*) of ignorance, rather than currently manifesting (*prārabdha*) *karma*. But later schoolmen soon integrated this explanation with the *prārabdha-karma* theory of the *Brahma Sūtra* (4.1.15–19), which henceforth became the dominant way of explaining the persistence of embodiment for the enlightened among Hindu schools. According to the *Brahma Sūtra,* full knowledge immediately eradicates *karma* collected in this or a previous birth which has not yet begun to bear fruit (*saṃcita karma*). Furthermore, such knowledge, because of the detachment it begets, will also prevent the accumulation of future *karma* (*āgāmi-karma*) (a point which is more clearly elucidated in the *Bhagavad Gītā)*. But *karma* that has already begun to bear fruit (*prārabdha-karma*) is not destroyed; rather, it is played out for the rest of the adept's life, just as an arrow loosed by an archer continues to travel its path, and the potter's wheel continues to spin after the potter has ceased action. When *prārabdha-karma* is exhausted, the individual dies his or her last death and achieves the ultimate liberation, with no more need for rebirth. The *prārabdha-karma* theory was partly based on the *Brahma Sūtra*. But it seems to have been so persuasive as a way of explaining living liberation that it found its way even into a non-Vedāntic school such as Śaiva Siddhānta and was read back into Sāṃkhya and Yoga commentaries. However, while the *Brahma Sūtra* passage compels Vedāntins to admit the possibility of achieving a state wherein only one's *prārabdha-karma* remains, the text does not demand that one call that state liberation, and thus there remained room for dispute.

The authors from the Advaita school tend to hold that the *prārabdha-karma* state after the arising of knowledge is indeed living liberation, but as Lance Nelson shows, they have had more difficulty doing so than is often recognized. Most Advaitins follow Śaṅkara in claiming that if knowledge of Brahman wiped out even *prārabdha-karma*, then no state of *jīvanmukti*, and no enlightened teachers would be possible. While admitting that liberating knowledge is thus ineffective against *prārabdha-karma*, Śaṅkara and most of his followers minimize the effect of ripening *prārabdha-karma* on the experience of the enlightened individual, emphasizing his or her supreme knowledge and detachment from the body and world. But some Advaitins have trouble fully equating a state where any *karma* and/or traces of ignorance remain with true liberation or *mukti.*

Lance Nelson shows clearly that the Advaita school is caught in a dilemma by three of its own firmly held claims: (1) that *prārabdha-karma* remains to keep the body alive after enlightened knowledge arises, (2) that *karma* is the effect or result of ignorance, and (3) that knowledge of *nirguṇa-brahman* dispels all ignorance and its effects, as light dispels darkness. Something has to be compromised or finessed here for logical consistency. If enlightening knowledge immediately removed all forms of ignorance—and hence all *karma* which is its effect—then why is not *prārabdha-karma* also removed such that the individual achieves immediate disembodied liberation (*sādyomukti*)? Śaṅkara's analogies of the potter's wheel and loosed arrow make the persistence of the body intuitively understandable, but Advaitins argued for centuries about how to describe in more precise, philosophical language exactly what remains of ignorance and/or *karma* to make for continued embodiment after enlightenment. Exactly what is this grin that remains after the 'Cheshire Cat of ignorance is dispelled? Some say it is a mere remnant *(leśa)* of ignorance itself, others an impression *(saṃskāra)* or effect *(kārya)* of ignorance that is the substratum or basis of (*prārabdha-karma*). Analogies such as the trembling that remains after fear has been removed, and the smell that lingers where garlic or flowers have rested, are marshalled to show that effects can be manifest even after causes are removed. Mainstream Advaitins (such as Vimuktātman and Sarvajñātman) are apparently willing to back off the idea that the light of knowledge removes all forms and effects of ignorance in order to save the *jīvanmukti* and *prārabdha-karma* theory. Some Advaitins seem to prefer to make the compromise elsewhere; those who hold that *prārabdha-karma* has a real basis in ignorance end up either denying that *jīvanmukti* is really or fully liberation, or else limiting the experience of its bliss to a *samādhi* state (Prakāśātman, Citśukha, Bhāratītīrtha).

The Viśiṣṭādvaita and Dvaita schools, following Rāmānuja and Madhva, also affirm the possibility of a final state where only *prārabdha-karma* remains, but without equating it with liberation. Vyāsatīrtha of the Dvaita school, as Sheridan shows, has admitted the parallel between the post-*aparokṣa-jñāna* stage of its soteriological path with the Advaitin *jīvanmukti.* It is interesting that Madhva states it may take more than one lifetime to work out *prārabdha-karma*, thus further weakening the parallel with living liberation. Kim Skoog's chapter does not fully deal with Rāmānuja's successors in the Śrīvaiṣṇava tradition, but a brief explanation of the direction they took on this point for comparison may be in order here.

Within a century of Rāmānuja's death, the Śrīvaiṣṇava sect began to admit two paths to liberation. One is the path of devotion, *Bhakti Yoga*, which Rāmānuja details in his *Brahma Sūtra* and *Bhagavad Gītā* commentaries and which is limited to twice-born males, because it uses Vedic rites and Upaniṣadic meditations (*vidyās*) as auxiliaries. The other is the simple path of surrender to the Lord, *prapatti,* which is open to all. The later Śrīvaiṣṇava tradition ends up, in effect, denying that *bhakti-yoga* can result in a state where only *prārabdha-karma* remains. This is because they claim that in order have the effect of eradicating all past *karma*, *bhakti-yoga* must be performed throughout one's life—even up to the moment of death with the "last remembrance" of the Lord (*antimasmṛti)* described in the *Bhagavad Gītā*. Omission of any part of this *bhakti-yoga* may have *karmic* results, delaying one's final liberation until the end of a subsequent lifetime, wherein the missing *bhakti-yoga* practices can be performed. However, the Śrīvaiṣṇava tradition claims that *prapatti* can in fact ensure that all past collected *karma* will be nullified at the end of this life. Thus *prapatti* becomes a threshold experience, like the Dvaitin *aparokṣa-jñāna,* which puts the individual in a state where one is "ticking off" only one's *prārabdha-karma*.[2] But in Śrīvaiṣṇavism, the *prapanna* is assured of full disembodied liberation at the end of this very lifetime (unlike the Dvaita tradition, where *prārabdha-karma* may take more than one lifetime to work out). Nevertheless, the Śrīvaiṣṇavas never equate this post-*prapatti* state with liberation (*mukti)* itself. What remains may only be *prārabdha-karma*, but for as long as it lasts, bondage to *prārabdha-karma* is experienced as bondage.

It is interesting to compare the Śrīvaiṣṇava and Śaiva Siddhānta schools—two Tamil devotional schools with comparable theologies and soteriologies—on the psychological state and karmic position of the saint in the highest living state attainable in the path to salvation. Though Śaiva Siddhānta does not come out of the Vedānta tradition, Valiaveetil shows that it has absorbed the pervasive theory of *prārabdha-karma*, which seems to be somewhat awkwardly attached to the older and more characteristically Śaiva theory of the three impurities (*malas*). Furthermore, Śaiva Siddhānta has freely utilized the term *jīvanmukti* to describe the living state of a saint and devotee who is still to some extent under the influence of *prārabdha-karma* and force of all three *malas* (*āṇava* or the root impurity of egoism, *karma,* and *māyā* or physical embodiment). The traditions of Madhva and Rāmānuja generally avoid the question of "backsliding" from the highest living state. However, Śaiva Siddhānta seems clearly to admit the real possibility that the *jīvanmukta* may slip back into ignorance and evil because of the force of traces of the impurities (*malavāsana)* and the *prārabdha-karma* that continue to operate; consequently, Śaiva Siddhānta theologians claim that continued diligence in practice is necessary. It is striking that even without clearly admitting a possibility of backsliding, the Śrīvaiṣṇava and Dvaita traditions are reluctant to call the penultimate state *jīvanmukti*; yet the Śaiva Siddhānta tradition does not hesitate to use this term. However, there is a subtle difference in emphasis in their characterizations of the saint's state that may be influential here. Valiaveetil's presentation suggests that Śaiva Siddhānta theologians emphasize the saint's extreme detachment from worldly concerns in all-absorbing devotional awareness of Śiva. The Vaiṣṇavas (at least the Śrīvaiṣṇavas) tend to emphasize the saint's disgust with this world of bondage and pained longing for Vaikuṇṭha. Thus the former are more willing than the latter to describe the saint as freed (*mukta)*, at least in a psychological sense. (I will suggest further on that there is another explanation, hinging on the *avatāra* docrine, that may account for why Śaiva schools are more eager to recognize a state of *jīvanmukti* than Vaiṣṇava schools.)

Thus, how strong the force of *prārabdha-karma* (and/or karmic *saṃskāras* and *vāsanas)* is seen to be in the conscious experience of the Brahman-knowing adept has a lot to do with whether and to what extent that state is equated with liberation (*mukti*). As Lance Nelson shows, those Advaitins who affirm *jīvanmukti* tend to minimize the importance of ripening *karma* in the experience of the *jīvanmukta,* emphasizing that his or her blissful consciousness of Brahman is not thereby diminished or clouded. Those Advaitins who deny or weaken the state of *jīvanmukti* often do so by taking the force of *prārabdha-karma* and/or karmic impressions (*vāsanas)* as a much more serious threat to the blissful peace and composure of the enlightened individual. This same train of thought is also found in the Yoga school, even though Yogic thinkers prefer to speak of remaining karmic *saṃskāras* or *vāsanas* rather than *prārabdha-karma.* Chapple shows that the *Sāṃkhya Kārikā* virtually dismisses the significance of the continuing effect of karmic impulses that arise after discriminative knowledge (analogous to the continued turning of the potter's wheel) in its emphasis on the state of enlightened freedom that ensues. The Yoga tradition, however, takes the psychological effect of remaining karmic impressions and tendencies much more seriously. Chapple shows that Yoga developed an elaborate analysis of the mechanism by which *karma* and ignorance impede the full and continual experience of bliss (the *kleśas, vāsanas,* and so forth), as well as a variety of techniques by which the psychological mechanism of bondage is to be subtilized and dismantled. We find that Yogins and Yoga-inspired Advaitins tend to emphasize the need for continued yogic practices to overcome the force of *prārabdha-karma,* karmic traces or tendencies (*vāsanas),* afflicted action (*kliṣṭa karma*) or the like on one's psychological experience even after enlightening knowledge has arisen.

In such authors, the term *jīvanmukti* may be limited to the ultimate state of one who has successfully eradicated the effects even of *prārabdha karma* and/or karmic tendencies (*vāsanas*). Alternatively, the term may be applied to a wide range of states in which one progressively overcomes remaining ignorance and karmic tendencies, deepening and stabilizing one's consciousness of knowledge or bliss. The Yoga school, at least since Vyāsa's commentary, shows the former tendency. The Kashmiri Śaiva school seems to show the latter tendency. Vidyāraṇya's *Jīvanmuktiviveka* shows both tendencies! For Vidyāraṇya, the term *jīvanmukta* does not apply to the mere knower of Brahman but to the adept in any of the four subsequent stages in which the mind and traces (*vāsanas*) of *prārabdha-karma* are gradually attenuated; better yet, Vidyāranya suggests, the true *jīvanmukta* is one who has achieved the final stage in which all "mental manifestations" cease. Neither Śaṅkara nor Īśvarakṛṣṇa would approve of this tendency to subdivide the state of liberation and to add a need for continued practices and psychological disciplines to realize fully or stabilize it, for this ends up minimizing the efficacy of the threshold experience of liberating knowledge.

Jainism, as Chapple describes it, shows how far the tendency to separate knowledge and the state of liberation can go. Here, the glimpse of true self-knowledge in the fourth *guṇasthāna* marks only the beginning of the elaborate Jaina path of physical and psychological discipline by which the various kinds of obscuring *karma* are gradually and painfully (quite literally) eradicated to reach full liberation and omniscience. Nevertheless, Jainism can be seen as promoting a strong doctrine of living liberation in its clear articulation of the thirteenth *guṇasthāna* as a discrete state with distinct psychological, ontological, and behavioral characteristics. At the same time, the elaborate Jaina soteriologial system insulates this final stage with so many interim stages and practices as to be nearly inaccessible; in fact, Jainism denies that any individual in recent history has actually attained it.

Chapple suggests a sequential relationship between Sāṃkhya and Yoga by homologizing Sāṃkhya's moment of discerning knowledge with the Jaina fourth *guṇasthāna,* where *karma* begins to be eradicated, and the Yogic *jīvanmukta* with the *sayoga-kevalin* of the Jaina thirteenth *guṇasthāna*, where *karmas* inhibiting *kaivalya*-consciousness have finally been eradicated. Though this reading of the relationship of Sāṃkhya and Yoga may be unorthodox, Chapple does well to remind us that our present reading of Sāṃkhya has probably been shaped by later Advaita-influenced commentaries which have read in the Advaitin understanding of *jīvanmukti* and ignored Yoga practice. It is quite possible that in the early centuries of Sāṃkhya and Yoga, when these two schools were more closely related and Jainism was a dominant rival, this tandem reading might have been quite natural.

Emphasis on the blissfulness and/or detachment in the experience of the adept in the highest stage seems to be a distinctive feature of those schools and authors who posit medium to strong doctrines of living liberation. In the strong-position schools of Advaita and Sāṃkhya, that detachment has an ontological basis—in reality the soul has never truly been bound. Attachment and suffering are due to error and ignorance; detachment and bliss naturally result from Self-knowledge, where one can regard the body and mind, now no longer confused with the Self, as a snake regards its cast-off skin (*Bṛhadāraṇyaka Upaniṣad* 4.4.7). But even among traditions where suffering and attachment are considered real, the final living state can still be called true liberation (*mukti* or *kaivalya*) by emphasizing the adept's blissful psychological detachment from the world and consequent continuity with post-death bliss. Absent the characteristics of blissful detachment, however, it is difficult to equate the highest living state with liberation, even if that state is seen as necessarily resulting in final liberation at death. If remaining *karma* is seen as capable of interfering with or constricting full and continual conscious experience of bliss, or if it presents a real experience of suffering and worldly involvement, then this highest living state is seen as something less than full liberation. Applicability of the term *jīvanmukti* to such a state may be denied, as in the weak-position schools. In both weak- and some medium-position schools, practices to stabilize blissfulness and prevent psychological relapse may be emphasized (even if this state is still called *jīvanmukti*). Or, the moment of death may be presented as marking such a qualitative change in the soul's experience of bliss that it overshadows any previous knowledge-experience as the "threshold experience" inaugurating full liberation.

The above line of reasoning is illustrated by the schools represented in this volume. The weak-position Vaiṣṇava schools following Madhva and Rāmānuja do claim that the devotee in the highest living state tastes the blissfulness of devotion that is to some extent continuous with the post-death bliss of *bhakti* and service. Yet they tend to place more emphasis on the discontinuity between these states. The highest bliss of devotion possible in this world, where remaining karmic impressions (*vāsanās)* still constrict one's omniscient consciousness and ability to experience the Lord, is still only a pale reflection of the supreme bliss that will be available once the physical body and remaining traces of karmic bondage and ignorance are removed. At that point, one's released soul, now with a wonderful body of pure matter (*śuddhasattva)* and full omniscient consciousness, arrives in Vaikuṇṭha to serve and experience the full presence of the Lord's supreme bodily form. In contrast, the medium-position Śaiva schools represented in this volume, partly because they do not have such an elaborately anthropomorphic view of heaven, can more easily emphasize the continuity in conscious experience of the living saint with the released saint, both of whom have their minds immersed in and/or identified with the bliss of the supreme Śiva. In the strong-position camp, the *Sāṃkhya Kārikā* and most Advaitins readily emphasize the full and complete bliss and worldly detachment that come with knowledge, and drastically minimize any suffering that is produced by remaining *karma.* But Yoga, some non-mainstream and yoga-influenced Advaitins, and Jainism all tend to delay that state of bliss by claiming that in addition to knowledge, an attack on the psychological roots of *karma* (*vāsanās*, *saṃskāras*) is needed in order to produce full and complete experience of this bliss. Nevertheless, they still claim that a fully blissful state of release—equivalent to that experienced after death—is eventually possible in this life.

The Need for Enlightened Teachers

Commenting on *Chāndogya Upaniṣad* 6.14.2, Śaṅkara states that one of the reasons a state of living liberation must be affirmed is the need for authoritative *gurus* and teachers.[3] His point is compelling: if there is no one who has attained liberation in this life, then who would be qualified to act as a *guru,* teacher, or example worthy of emulation for those who are still bound? The various traditions that aim at liberation would be reduced to the blind leading the blind.[4] Mahāvīra and the other Tīrthaṅkaras of Jainism were viewed as being *sayoga-kevalins* of the thirteenth *guṇasthāna* when they taught. Though Śaṅkara and the other Advaitins in his lineage never explicitly claimed to be *jīvanmuktas,* they were seen that way by the later tradition. So were the various sages and saints in Itihāsa-Purāṇa (such as Śuka); so were the Nāyaṉārs or Śaiva saints in the Śaiva Siddhānta tradition. In nearly every school there is a strong tendency to consider the founding theologians, authors, and saints to be fully liberated while alive. In traditions where the *guru* plays a necessary role in the path to salvation, there is pressure even to see one's own *guru* as a *jīvanmukta.* Thus *jīvanmukti* is a doctrinal concept whose practical importance is in authorizing founding teachers and *gurus*.

The central place of this function of the *jīvanmukti* doctrine can be demonstrated by noticing that all the schools that take a firm stance against full liberation in this life are Vaiṣṇava schools. Why so? That is because the Vaiṣṇava schools tend to see their founders and *gurus* not as *jīvanmuktas* but as *avatāras*, full or partial incarnations either of Viṣṇu Himself or one of the entourage of eternally-free godlings (*nityasuris)* in His retinue. Śaiva Siddhānta sees the Nāyaṉārs as *jīvanmuktas*, but the Śrīvaiṣṇava tradition sees the Āḻvars as partial *avatāras*. Śaṅkara is assumed by the later Advaita tradition to be a *jīvanmukta,* but Madhva and Rāmānuja were seen by their traditions as incarnations, respectively, of Vāyu and Anantaśeṣa. Disciples in the Yoga, Advaita, and Śaiva traditions view their *gurus* as *jīvanmuktas*; in the Śrīvaiṣṇava tradition the *guru* is claimed to be a partial incarnation of Viṣṇu himself. Thus the authority of the founders and *gurus* in the Vaiṣṇava traditions is legitimated not by the *jīvanmukti* doctrine but by the *avatāra* doctrine. This means these Vaiṣṇava schools do not have the same driving need as the other schools to recognize the highest state attainable in this life (a state where only *prārabdha-karma* remains) as true living liberation or *jīvanmukti*. Thus the *jīvanmukta* and the *avatāra* of Īśvara seem to share functional similarities on the sectarian level in addition to the philosophical and doctrinal similarities Lance Nelson points out.

Whichever way *gurus* and founders are authorized, either as *jīvanmuktas* or as *avatāras*, virtually the same practical problems arise in how to recognize them. As Mackenzie Brown shows in his study of the Itihāsa-Purāṇa stories of Śuka, the enigmas of how to recognize an authentic, and thus authoritative, liberated being predate the scholastic doctrines of *jīvanmukti* and *avatāra*. It is a recurring theme throughout the Indian tradition that the bodily form, words, and deeds of enlightened and/or liberated beings, no less than the physical forms and disguises assumed by various deities, conceal their status to some, while revealing it to others. But to whom is this status revealed, why, and how? How can those of us who are unenlightened recognize a potentially authoritative teacher by his or her words, deeds, appearance or manner? Different texts may emphasize completely opposite traits as characteristic of the divine or realized being: *saṃnyāsin* or householder status; detachment from the world or sensual profligacy; silence or eloquence; astute discrimination or obliviousness to all opposites; supreme wisdom or consummate idiocy; fastidious observance of dharmic regulations or behavior that completely ignores or even deliberately breaks all rules.

The Behavior of the Jīvanmukta: Dharma, Karma, and Freedom

The question of the highest adept's relationship to the rules of *varṇāśrama-dharma* is a particularly complicated one, due in part to inherent tensions within the *varṇāśrama-dharma* system itself. These tensions come through to some extent in Vidyāraṇya's work and particularly in Mackenzie Brown's presentation of the figure of Śuka in texts stretching over a millenium. There is a tension between the householder and *saṃnyāsin* state, the latter in some sense being freed from and not bound to the standards of purity and mandatory ritual action that are enjoined on the former. There is also tension in the question over whether the *saṃnyāsin* state can be chosen voluntarily, at a young age, or should be limited only to those who have completed the householder stage. The texts Brown studied seem to be exercises in working through these internal tensions as the *varnāśrama-dharma* system stretched its social theory to make room for the individual pursuit of liberation.

But even if we assume, as most later schools do, that *varṇāśrama-dharma* refers to the entire system, from *brahmācārya* to *saṃnyāsa,* the question of the *jīvanmukta's* relation to it is still a delicate one for schools that deem the highest state to be true living liberation. Few schools really work through the maze of logical problems entailed in fully reconciling the *jīvanmukta's* position with the rules of *varṇásrama-dharma* or even the laws of karmic cause and effect. A brief overview of the problems entailed may show why they preferred to steer clear: If the enlightened adept is truly liberated from all except *prārabdha-karma*, then does that mean he or she can no longer collect any more *karma* from any dharmic transgression committed during the rest of his or her life? If not, then living liberation is a precarious state that must be maintained by good behavior and vigilance, for there is a possibility of backsliding and collecting *karma* which may have to be experienced in a future life. Should such a state where one is likely to slip back into karmic bondage truly be called liberation? But if so, then can the *jīvanmukta* ignore all dharmic rules and break them without penalty? This could make it difficult to tell the supremely enlightened from the completely ignorant, and perhaps set a dangerous example for the unenlightened to follow. If the *jīvanmukta* does not break dharmic rules, even if he theoretically could, then why doesn't he? Is it because the self-transformation, enlightening knowledge, and/or devotion to God that come with this status makes him naturally live up to dharmic norms? Or is it that he deliberately conforms his behavior to dharmic norms in order to set a good example for the unliberated who are still bound to the results of their *karma* (the *Bhagavad Gītā*'s *loka-saṃgraha* concept). In short, is the *jīvanmukta*'s status marked by "freedom from" or "freedom to"? That is, does living liberation free him from the need to abide by dharmic standards, or free him to do so more fully and perhaps naturally?

To the extent that a school addresses the above questions at all, its answers will hinge largely on its view of dharmic rules as a whole—its philosophical evaluation and actual interpretation of "orthopraxy." There is an internal logic to this correlation. Do dharmic rules and regulations have divine sanction and does their observance play an important role in the soteriological path? Schools that answer "yes" tend to see the highest attainable living state as one of "freedom to," where the adept's liberated state enables him fully to live up to the dharmic standards appropriate to his social position (whether that be a *saṃnyāsin* or householder). Between or within such schools, however, there may be disagreement as to the adept's motives for doing so—because it comes easily and naturally to him, because he wants to set an example for the world, or because he wants to please the Lord. But there are other schools that tend to see dharmic rules as mere social convention, without divine sanction, binding only on those who lack spiritual knowledge, who are identified with the body, and/or who desire worldly rewards in this or a future life rather than liberation. These schools tend to see the *jīvanmukta*'s status as one of "freedom from": liberation frees one from any need or desire to observe dharmic constraints. The literature of many schools, however, will demonstrate both tendencies to some extent.

In the schools represented in this volume, we see a variety of positions represented on the continuum that lies between extreme "freedom from" and extreme "freedom to." Kashmiri Śaivism, which makes no room for *varṇāśrama-dharma* in its path to *mokṣa*, takes the most radical "freedom from" position in its view of the *jīvanmukta*. This tradition does not hesitate to claim that the *jīvanmukta* can flagrantly violate social norms. Śaiva Siddhānta does not go quite that far, but its antinomianism is evident in the many stories of the Nāyaṉār saints, traditionally believed to be *jīvanmukta*s, who violated ritual and social norms with impunity (one even murders his own son!) because they were inspired by zealous devotion. In Śaiva Siddhānta soteriology, temple service and *yoga*, not *varṇāśrama-dharma,* are the chief auxiliaries to the soteriological path of devotion to Śiva. Advaitins, as well as Yogins and Yogic Advaitins such as Vidyāraṇya, tend toward a more moderate position, closer to the "freedom to" side of the continuum. Observance of *varṇāśrama-dharma* is important to the soteriological path—especially observance of the last *āśrama* and its restrictions and renunciation (*saṃnyāsa*). However, they do realize that mere "by the book" *saṃnyāsa* and even moral purity do not themselves constitute or assure liberating knowledge, for such knowledge transcends all forms of action. They tend to emphasize that the *jīvanmukta* will naturally observe dharmic norms appropriate to his *āśrama,* though they may admit there is no karmic penalty for any lapse, since the adept has lost all sense of agency for his actions, the "psychological glue" that makes *karma* stick. The Dvaita and Viśiṣṭadvaita schools, since they do not accept the notion of living liberation, arguably do not belong on this continuum; but more than any others they insist that *varṇāśrama-dharma* is the Lord's will and its observance is essential to the devotional path of salvation. They imply that progress on this path and purification by the Lord's grace naturally lead to a progressive ability to please and serve the Lord, and that means not displeasing Him by transgressing His commands in *varṇāśrama-dharma*. However, I would point out that in the Śrīvaiṣṇava tradition of Rāmānuja, much as in Śaiva Siddhānta, some stories and anecdotes from the lives of the Āḻvārs suggest that the Lord may excuse violations of *varṇāśrama-dharma* if these actions are inspired out of loving devotion.

Since the Śaiva and Vaiṣṇava traditions dealt with in this volume seem to line up on opposite ends of the continuum, the former largely "freedom from" and the latter clearly "freedom to," one would expect the *Devī-Bhāgavata Purāṇa,* with its Śaiva and tantric leanings, and the *Bhāgavata Purāṇa*, a clearly Vaiṣṇava work, to reflect the same tendencies. But surprisingly enough, the visions of the ideal sage from the excerpts Brown considers suggest quite the opposite. It is the *Bhāgavata Purāṇa* that portrays Śuka, in Brown's inspired phrase, as the "enlightened idiot of dazzle and dirt." Śuka's outlandish behavior and utter inability to distinguish gold from feces (recalling the shocking behavior of the Śaiva Nāyaṉārs) calls into question the entire *varṇāśrama-dharma* system by subverting the ultimate validity of the standards of purity and pollution on which it is based. But despite its tantric connections, the *Devī-Bhāgavata* holds up King Janaka as the ideal *jīvanmukta* for Śuka to emulate—a householder who freely and easily lives up to his *dharmic* duties, and would not even think of becoming a *saṃnyāsin* before his time, much less rolling around in filth!

Conclusion: Prospects for Future Study

Clearly, scholastic explications of and arguments about living liberation in Indian thought are fraught with problems. But amid all the metaphysical hair-splitting, vague tensions, and hot disputes demonstrated in the previous pages, there are subtle patterns in lines of thought and argument. The conceptual rubric of strong, medium, and weak positions on living liberation, as formulated and presented here, helps form a kind of lens to bring into focus the range of doctrinal differences and recurring themes around the understanding of living liberation that arise in Hindu thought. Though this theory was developed on the basis of the authors and schools represented in this volume, it may prove useful in gaining comparative perspective on other authors and schools of Indian thought that address the issue of living liberation. It would be interesting to see if the strong-, medium-, and weak-position framework might be adapted to shed light on the various understandings of the living state of Nirvāṇa presented in the many schools of classical Indian Buddhism, both Hīṇayāna and Mahāyāna; that task, however, must be saved for another volume and perhaps other editors.

Modern Hindu philosophers and recent devotional movements started by contemporary *gurus* would also be fertile ground to test the extensibility of the body of theory presented here. Such a study would assuredly demonstrate that despite its difficulties, the concept of *jīvanmukti* is in no danger of dying out. It seems to have gained heightened importance under the various thinkers within the Neo-Vedānta movement, who have tried to adapt and update traditional goals of liberation and views of the ideal sage for today's educated Hindu elite. As Andrew Fort has shown elsewhere, Neo-Vedāntins uphold the ideal of a *jīvanmukta* who demonstrates his world-affirming social concern and tolerance by performing humanitarian services to increase the happiness of all.[5] Images of the Christian saint or mission worker have clearly been an influence here, which is not surprising, given the English and Christian schooling of most Neo-Vedāntins. Many contemporary gurus such as Ramana Maharshi, Muktananda, Rajneesh, and Maharishi Mahesh Yogi have been seen by their followers as examples of beings who are liberated while alive. Some of these *gurus*, such as Ananda Mayi Ma, are even women, and their recognition as *jīvanmuktas* has important implications for the future development of feminist interpretations of Hinduism. The medieval scholastic Hindu thinkers represented in this volume, unremittingly male, cannot bring themselves to clearly broach the possibility of female *jīvanmuktas*, even though the Yoga and Śaiva traditions (less tied to Vedic orthodoxy than Advaita Vedānta) have not ruled them out in principle.

Whatever direction Hindu thought and religion might take in the future, as long as *mokṣa* is recognized the ultimate goal, necessarily there will be doctrines of and arguments about living liberation, *jīvanmukti*. In over a decade of teaching Indian religious thought, I cannot remember any class where, upon presenting the concept of release from the cycle of birth and death and the liberating insight which brings it about, some student did not ask, "But what happens to such a person after that?" What indeed.

Notes

1. The state of *parama-bhakti* attained by the follower of *bhakti-yoga,* briefly referred to in some of Rāmānuja's works (particularly his *Śaraṇāgati Gadya*) may

be roughly equivalent, but Rāmānuja never sharply defined this state or clarified its karmic status. Below, I will discuss the *prapanna* who has followed the path to *mokṣa* called self-surrender (*prapatti),* as recognized by the later Śrīvaiṣṇava school following Rāmānuja. The *prapanna* is more clearly comparable to the post-*aparokṣa-jñāna bhakta* of the Madhva school and the *jīvanmukta* of the Advaita school, for all three are claimed to be in a state of living out the remainder of their fructifying (*prārabdha*) *karma*.

2. However, there is a disagreement between the Teṉkalai and Vaṭakalai factions within Śrīvaiṣṇavism as to whether this would also include future *karma,* especially deliberate sins performed after *prapatti*. See Chapter Five of my *The Śrīvaiṣṇava Theological Dispute: Maṇavāḷamāmuni and Vedānta Deśika*, Madras: New Era Publications, 1988.

3. Chapple points out this is echoed by Aniruddha's sixteenth-century commentary on the *Sāṃkhya Kārikā*.

4. Śaṅkara's Advaita tradition, unlike the Śaiva and Jaina traditions, would not be left without authoritative scripture if there were no *jīvanmukta*s, for *śruti*'s authority does not hinge on the enlightened status of teachers: it is unauthored. But Śaṅkara admits that reading *śruti* is not sufficient for liberating knowledge to arise; in practice, the Advaitin tradition came to rely on the salvific importance of the *guru*-disciple relationship and the chain of supposedly enlightened *gurus* from Śaṅkara and the authority of their writings.

5. See "Neither East nor West: A Case of Neo-Vedānta in Modern Indian Thought," *Religious Studies Review* 18 (April 1992): 95–100, and "*Jīvanmukti* and Social Service in Advaita and Neo- Vedānta," article forthcoming for volume honoring Wilhelm Halbfass, in *Poznan Studies* series, Amsterdam.

Contributors

C. Mackenzie Brown is Professor of Religion at Trinity University. He received his Ph.D. from Harvard University in 1973. His scholarship has focused on Purāṇic studies, including two books examining the historical and theological developments in two Purāṇic texts: *God as Mother: A Feminine Theology in India, An Historical and Theological Study of the Brahmavaivarta Purāṇa* (1974), and *The Triumph of the Goddess: The Canonical Models and Theological Visions of the Devī-Bhāgavata Purāṇa* (1990).

Christopher Key Chapple is Associate Professor and Chair of Theological Studies at Loyola Marymount University in Los Angeles. He received his Ph.D. from Fordham University in 1980. He has published several articles and is author of *Karma and Creativity* (1986) and *Nonviolence to Animals, Earth, and Self in Asian Traditions* (1993), cotranslator of the *Yoga Sūtras of Patañjali* (1990), and editor of *The Jesuit Tradition in Education and Missions* (1993) and *Ecological Prospects: Scientific, Religious, and Aesthetic Perspectives* (1994).

Andrew O. Fort is Associate Professor of Religion at Texas Christian University. He received his Ph.D. from the University of Pennsylvania in 1982. His articles have appeared in *Journal of Indian Philosophy, Philosophy East and West, Religious Studies Review*, and other journals. He is also the author of *The Self and Its States: A States of Consciousness Doctrine in Advaita Vedānta* (1990). He is currently working on a book about *jīvanmukti* in Advaita Vedānta.

Paul Muller-Ortega is Associate Professor and Chair of the Religious Studies Department at Michigan State University. He received his Ph.D. from the University of California at Santa Barbara in 1984. He works primarily in Indian religious traditions, with particular emphasis on Tantra.

He is the author of *The Triadic Heart of Shiva: Kaula Tantricism of Abhinavagupta in the Non-Dual Shaivism of Kashmir* (1989), and of a number of articles on various aspects of the Tantra in Kashmir Shaivism. He is the editor of the Tantric Studies Series published by the State University of New York Press.

Patricia Y. Mumme recently joined Capital University in Columbus, Ohio, as Assistant Professor of Religion, after two years with the Division of Comparative Studies in the Humanities at The Ohio State University. She received her Ph.D. in Religious Studies from the University of Pennsylvania in 1983. She has published several articles and translations on the Śrīvaiṣṇava sect of South Indian Hinduism, as well as a book, *The Śrīvaiṣṇava Theological Dispute: Maṇavāḷamāmuni and Vedānta Deśika* (1988).

Lance E. Nelson is Assistant Professor in the Department of Theological and Religious Studies at the University of San Diego. He received his Ph. D. from McMaster University in 1987. His writings on Advaita Vedānta and other aspects of South Asian religion have appeared in scholarly journals in the United States and India.

Daniel P. Sheridan is Professor of the History of Religions at Loyola University in New Orleans. He studied at St. John's and Fordham Universities in New York, receiving his Ph.D. in Theology and the History of Religions. He is the author of *The Advaitic Theism of the Bhāgavata Purāṇa* and of numerous scholarly studies in *Purāṇa, Anima, Journal of Dharma, The Thomist, The Journal of Religion*, and *Horizons*.

Kim Skoog is Associate Professor of Philosophy at the University of Guam. He received his Ph.D. from the University of Hawaii in Comparative Philosophy in 1986 and his Master's degree from the University of Washington in 1977. He has presented papers and published articles both in the United States and Asia.

Chacko Valiaveetil is a Catholic priest belonging to the Society of Jesus. He is Associate Director of Maitri Bhavan, Inter-religious Dialogue Center and Institute for the Study of Religions in Varanasi, India. He has a Licentiate in Philosophy and received his Ph.D. from Banaras Hindu University in 1973. He is the author of *Liberated Life* (1980) and various articles, and an editor of the Dialogue Series Publications.

Index